DISCOVERING
◆ *the* ◆
NEW
TESTAMENT

Contributors

Roger Hahn, Ph.D. (Duke University)
Dean of the Faculty and Professor of New Testament
Nazarene Theological Seminary
Kansas City, Missouri

David Neale, Ph.D. (Sheffield University)
Vice President for Academic Affairs, Academic Dean, and Professor of New Testament
Canadian Nazarene University College
Alberta, Canada

Jeanne Orjala Serrão, Ph.D. (Claremont Graduate University)
Dean of the School of Theology and Philosophy and Associate Professor of Religion
Mount Vernon Nazarene University
Mount Vernon, Ohio

Dan Spross, Ph.D. (Southern Baptist Theological Seminary)
Professor of Biblical Theology and Literature
Trevecca Nazarene University
Nashville, Tennessee

Jirair Tashjian, Ph.D. (Claremont Graduate University)
Professor of New Testament
Southern Nazarene University
Bethany, Oklahoma

Alex Varughese, Ph.D. (Drew University)
Professor of Religion
Mount Vernon Nazarene University
Mount Vernon, Ohio

DISCOVERING

the

NEW TESTAMENT

COMMUNITY AND *F*AITH

ALEX VARUGHESE, EDITOR

ROGER HAHN ❖ DAVID NEALE

JEANNE ORJALA SERRÃO ❖ DAN SPROSS

JIRAIR TASHJIAN

Copyright 2005
Beacon Hill Press of Kansas City

ISBN 083-412-0933

Printed in the United States of
America

Cover Design: Paul Franitza
Cover Photo: © Scala/Art Re-
source, NY. *Ecce Homo,* by Antonio
Ciseri, 1821-1891. Photographed by
Alinari. From Galleria d'arte Mod-
erna, Palazzo Pitti, Florence, Italy.
Interior Design: Sharon Page

10 9 8 7 6 5 4 3 2 1

Picture Credits
Illustrations
Gustave Doré/Planet Art: 307
Sharon Page: 306

Photographs
Todd Bolen: 44, 97, 98, 118, 143, 191 (top), 204, 211, 212, 217, 221,
225, 243, 249, 254, 257 (both), 258, 270, 271, 272, 306, 316,
317 (both), 328, 333, 339, 341, 343, 344, 345 (both)
HIP/Scala/Art Resource, NY: 28
Illustrated Bible Life/Brad Elsberg: 1, 3 (l.), 8, 11, 13, 15, 18, 42 (bot.), 61,
67, 72, 99, 107, 109, 112, 115, 121, 124, 125, 130, 132, 136
(bot.), 141, 160, 169, 173 (bot.), 184, 186, 191 (bot.), 192, 201,
202, 203, 214, 230, 231, 232, 233, 234, 248, 280, 281, 283,
287, 295, 296, 300, 311, 323, 325, 326, 330, 355
Illustrated Bible Life/Rich Houseal: 3 (ctr.), 9, 29, 66, 71, 80, 81, 85, 90,
171, 182, 297, 309, 361
Illustrated Bible Life/Greg Schneider: 3 (r.), 5-8, 16, 17, 38, 42 (top), 79,
94, 95, 104, 136 (top), 138, 139, 145, 153, 157, 166, 170, 173
(top), 187, 199, 351
Photos.com: 288
Gene Plaisted: 82, 219 (both)
Scala/Art Resource, NY: 148
Digital Stock: 19, 34, 39, 58
Alex Varughese: 161, 268, 269, 277, 338

Map List

Library of Congress Cataloging-in-Publication Data

Discovering the New Testament : community and faith / Alex Varughese, editor; Roger Hahn . . . [et al.].
    p. cm.
    Includes bibliographical references and index.
    ISBN 0-8341-2093-3 (hardcover)
    1. Bible. N.T.—Criticism, interpretation, etc. 2. Bible. N.T.—Textbooks. I. Varughese, Alex, 1945- II. Hahn,
Roger, 1950-

    BS2361.3.D57 2005
    225.6'1—dc22

                      2004021620

Contents

UNIT V
TRIALS AND TRIUMPHS OF THE NEW COVENANT COMMUNITY
295

Preface

One could argue that the New Testament is the most important collection of ancient writings ever made. Christianity, the religion with the world's largest number of adherents, draws its primary theological claims from the pages of the New Testament. The earliest written accounts of Jesus, the founder of Christianity, are found in the Gospels that form the first four books of the New Testament. The ethical teachings of Jesus are universally recognized as some of the most rigorous and influential teachings about human life. There is no disputing the influence and importance of the New Testament.

On the other hand, much of the New Testament is a closed book for the world and even in the church. A homogenized picture of Jesus has emerged combining elements from all the Gospels with little recognition of the inspiration and genius of each Gospel writer. The letters that constitute the majority of the New Testament are seldom understood in context. Rather, they are seen as disconnected tirades of old apostles trying to force their views on vibrant young churches. The final book of the New Testament, Revelation, was written to comfort and encourage a persecuted church. It is often received with fear and rejection in the Church today. Clearly the way the New Testament is understood in both the Church and the world does not match its importance and historical influence.

What is needed is an introduction to the New Testament that can bring its characters to life and make sense of its literary structures and cultural contexts. This volume, *Discovering the New Testament: Community and Faith,* can accomplish just that. It is designed as a clear, concise, easy-to-read, and pedagogically sound textbook for introductory New Testament survey courses. However, this book should also become an important resource for general readers and adult students of the New Testament. The pictures, maps, and color-coded sidebars appeal to readers who are visually oriented. Readers accustomed to computer screens will find themselves at home in the layout and design of this book.

Many introductions to the New Testament are on the market today. Some provide a detailed historical background for the New Testament. Others analyze the complex literary features of the New Testament books. Still others offer a devotional approach to the writings of the New Testament. The unique contribution of *Discovering the New Testament* is the natural and understandable way in which the perspectives of history, literature, and theological truth are all brought together in a coherent whole.

In addition to the smoothly flowing text, the historical, literary, theological, and hermeneutical sidebars offer more detailed pictures into the worlds that stand behind, within, and in front of the text of the New Testament. To simply read the sidebars is to take an easy-to-understand journey through the rich resources of a vast array of New Testament scholarship.

Students and teachers alike will find a number of helpful pedagogical aids. Each chapter begins with learning objectives, vocabulary lists, and questions to guide the reader to the most important concepts of the chapter. Each chapter concludes with summary statements, questions for further reflection and application, and resources for further study. The authors all have taught freshman level New Testament courses at Christian liberal arts colleges and universities for many years. Each author is qualified as a specialist at the doctoral level in the area of his or her writing. The students of these authors return to churches and move on to seminary with clear insights into Scripture and a lively, informed faith.

The authors wrote *Discovering the New Testament* with the assumption that the New Testament is as important today as when its individual books were first written. Through the theological and hermeneutical sidebars and throughout the text the authors' Wesleyan convictions about sin, salvation, grace, faith, holiness, and hope come through. The New Testament must be understood in its historical context, but it also must be understood as a living and vital word from God to people today. May this book be used by the Holy Spirit to help you more clearly and more joyfully hear God speaking through the pages of the New Testament.

—Roger L. Hahn
General Textbook Editor
Beacon Hill Press of Kansas City

Editor's Note to the Student

Welcome to a journey that will lead you to discover the New Testament in new and refreshing ways. As a reader and student of the New Testament scriptures, you will find this journey a challenging as well as an exciting adventure. The purpose of this book is to provide you with a clear and strategically designed road map that will make this journey an incredible learning experience.

In this journey, you will come across various major crossroads in the story and faith development of the early Christian community in the first century. The various chapters in this book are designed to help you understand the significance of these historical events and religious ideas that laid the foundation for the emergence of Christianity as a major religion in the world. You will find in this book not only descriptions of these events and religious ideas but also "markers and signposts" that will help you navigate through each chapter without much difficulty. We invite you to take some time at the outset to get acquainted with these "markers and signposts" before you embark on your adventure of discovering the New Testament.

Objectives

At the beginning of each chapter, you will find a list of objectives. These objectives explain what you should be able to do as a result of your study of each chapter. As you read and study each chapter, we suggest that you keep these objectives in mind. Underline or highlight the sections in the chapter where you find descriptions of topics that would help you accomplish the objectives.

Key Words to Understand

Each chapter contains explanations or definitions of terms and identification of key people and places. These terms are placed at the beginning of each chapter and identified in boldface type where they appear in the chapter text. Your understanding of these terms and ability to identify or describe them is essential to your successful journey through the New Testament.

Questions to Consider as You Read

At the beginning of each chapter, you will also find several questions. These questions are aimed to help you think ahead and be prepared for the historical and theological issues presented in the chapter.

Summary Statements

It is natural for every reader of a book or a chapter in a book to ask the question, "What's the main point?" We have provided you with some significant statements at the end of each chapter that summarize the main points in the chapter. Use these summary statements to review what you have learned and return to the sections you may have overlooked.

Questions for Reflection

Each chapter also ends with some questions. These questions will help you to think further about the issues, events, and religious ideas that you have learned. The goal of these questions is not only to guide you to process what you have learned but also to challenge you to apply the lessons in your own life situation.

Resources for Further Study

We do not presume that this textbook will answer all the questions you have about the New Testament. Though much work has gone into the production of this book, we also acknowledge the providence of God's grace through other scholars who contribute to our understanding of His Word. Each chapter ends with a list of Bible commentaries or resources that we hope would help you in your continued study of the New Testament.

Sidebars

Throughout each chapter we have included color-coded sidebars with brief but useful information on topics related to biblical interpretation, theology, history, and cultural and literary features found in the New Testament. The symbols and color coding of these sidebars are given below.

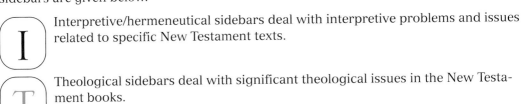

I Interpretive/hermeneutical sidebars deal with interpretive problems and issues related to specific New Testament texts.

T Theological sidebars deal with significant theological issues in the New Testament books.

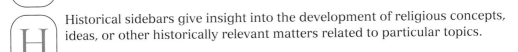

H Historical sidebars give insight into the development of religious concepts, ideas, or other historically relevant matters related to particular topics.

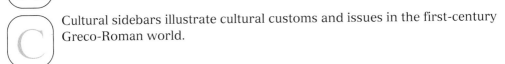

C Cultural sidebars illustrate cultural customs and issues in the first-century Greco-Roman world.

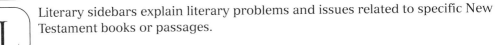

L Literary sidebars explain literary problems and issues related to specific New Testament books or passages.

Visual Aids

We have provided in this book pictures, maps, and illustrations that will be of help to you as you study this book. It is our hope that a "picture is worth a thousand words"! We also encourage you to study the maps and attempt to bridge the geographical distance between you and the actual location of the biblical events.

Finally, our prayer is that you will find these "markers and signposts" immensely useful as you begin your adventure of discovering the New Testament.

Editor's Note
to the Instructor

The primary purpose of this volume is to present a clear, concise, easy-to-read, and pedagogically sound textbook for introductory level New Testament survey courses that are an important part of the general education curriculum at Christian colleges and universities. Each chapter of the book addresses pedagogical concerns that are crucial to the mastery of the content as well as its evaluation and application. The pedagogical method includes learning objectives; vocabulary lists; questions for the students to get them oriented to the materials in each chapter; surveys of the content of the New Testament books; summary statements; questions for further reflection, evaluation, and application of lessons learned; and a list of key resources for further reading and study.

We have also included in each chapter numerous sidebars that address a variety of topics and issues. These color-coded sidebars—categorized as interpretive, theological, historical, cultural, and literary—are placed at strategic places throughout the chapter. Interpretive sidebars deal with interpretive problems and issues related to specific New Testament texts. Theological sidebars focus on in-depth analysis of key theological issues and their relevance to the modern reader of the New Testament. Historical, cultural, and literary sidebars give supplemental information that will enhance the reader's understanding of the subject matter presented in the book. It is our hope that you would find these sidebars as a valuable resource for your students' deeper understanding of God's Word.

The contributors of this book bring with them unique perspectives and specialized training in different parts of the New Testament. Chapter assignments are made on the basis of each writer's specialized area of interest and study at the doctoral level. Each chapter thus reflects the writer's scholarly interest, academic preparation, and teaching expertise. The book contains materials and methods of instruction we have tested and tried in our New Testament survey classes. Our long years of experience in teaching New Testament courses has guided us in making decisions about the structure, format, and content of this book. We present this book as a scholarly work, yet written at the level of college freshmen, in an easy-to-understand language. We have attempted to deal with critical issues with profound clarity without shortchanging scholarship with a superficial treatment of the subject matter.

Finally, we have approached this task of writing a textbook with the conviction that the New Testament does not stand alone, but in essential unity and continuity with the Old Testament. It is our conviction that the Old Testament sets the stage for the New Testament. We maintain the confident faith that Christ is the fulfillment of the Old Testament scriptures. So, wherever it is appropriate, the writers have sought to make points of contact between the story and faith of the early Christian community and that of the history and traditions of ancient Israel. Unity of the Bible, the continuity between the two testaments, and God's redemptive plan for all humanity that He accomplished through the death and resurrection of Jesus Christ are primary convictions of the writers of this volume. Old Testament passages are often used in this volume to provide the necessary background for interpreting the New Testament.

May you find this book an important tool in your hands as you teach your students God's eternal and faithful Word and minister His grace to them in the classroom!

Acknowledgments

This book is the outcome of the collaborative work of a number of scholars who have committed their lives to Christian ministry through teaching God's Word to university and seminary level students. Roger Hahn answers two key questions in chapters 1 and 2: What is the New Testament? and How should one read the New Testament? In chapter 3, Alex Varughese paints the portrait of the world of the New Testament. Jirair Tashjian introduces the reader to the Gospels, life and teachings of Jesus, the Gospels of Matthew, Mark, and John in chapters 4, 5, 6, 7, and 9. David Neale is the author of the chapters on the Gospel of Luke and the Book of Acts (chapters 8, 10, and 11). The Pauline materials take up chapters 12—17. These chapters contain materials contributed by Roger Hahn, Dan Spross, and Alex Varughese. Jeanne Serrão is the author of the chapters that cover the General Epistles and the Book of Revelation (chapters 18—21). I am profoundly grateful to these writers who have devoted their valuable time and energy to the successful completion of this significant project.

Roger Hahn, the Centennial Initiative general editor for the Church of the Nazarene, and Bonnie Perry, managing editor of Beacon Hill Press of Kansas City, have been faithful supporters of this project. This volume reflects the strong commitment of Beacon Hill Press to provide quality academic resources to Christian colleges and universities as well as to pastors and laity. I also express my gratitude to Judi King, editor of *Illustrated Bible Life,* for her help in securing the photographs, and Sharon Page for her skillful design and layout of this book. Richard Buckner, project coordinator at Beacon Hill Press, gave special oversight to the publication of this volume.

This volume is dedicated to the glory of God who grants wisdom generously to all who earnestly seek it from Him (James 1:5), and for His service in His kingdom.

Alex Varughese, Editor

UNIT I

INTRODUCTION

Your study of this unit will help you to:

- Discuss the literary structure and the major literary forms of the New Testament.
- Describe the process by which New Testament books were transmitted and established as canon of the Christian Church.
- Identify the three worlds of New Testament interpretation.
- Discuss the historical, political, and religious setting of the New Testament.

■ What Is the New Testament?

■ How Should One Read the New Testament?

■ The World of the New Testament

1 | What Is the New Testament?

Objectives:

Your study of this chapter should help you to:
- Describe the literary structure of the New Testament.
- Identify the major literary genres used in the New Testament.
- Discuss the process by which the New Testament canon emerged.
- Discuss the concept of the covenant community as the context and creation of the New Testament.

Key Words to Understand

Narrative
Gospels
Prophecy
Aramaic
Koine
Papyrus
Parchment
Textual criticism
Variants
Manuscript
Canon

Questions to consider as you read:

1. How is the New Testament organized?
2. What is the significance of the genres used in the New Testament?
3. How does the Church come to agreement on what books belong in the New Testament?
4. What is the significance for us that the New Testament arose from and created a covenant community?

The New Testament may be the most influential book in the history of humanity. The New Testament and the Old Testament form the Christian Scriptures, which have provided inspiration and identity to the Christian faith for almost 2,000 years. For many centuries the Christian faith has had the largest number of followers of any of the world religions. The New Testament has been translated into more languages and read by more people than any other book ever written. It is the primary source of the teachings of Jesus of Nazareth, who has been one of the most influential persons in the history of humankind. It is hard to overestimate the influence the New Testament has had on the world through its influence on Christianity.

Beyond the influence on Christians, the New Testament has provided some of the most famous and significant literature in the history of the world. The "love chapter" found in 1 Corinthians 13 and the "faith chapter" in Hebrews 11 are moving examples of literary composition. The Beatitudes in Matthew 5:3-12 and the Sermon on the Mount in Matthew 5—7 have been widely studied in ethics classes and as religious resources for comparative religious studies. The Lord's Prayer (found in different forms in Matthew 6:9-13 and Luke 11:2-4) is a model prayer studied and repeated by both Christians and non-Christians alike.

The Structure of the New Testament

Because the New Testament is so influential in both world and Christian history, it is important to understand how it is put together. Twenty-seven different pieces of ancient Christian literature form the New Testament. Like the Old Testament, the New Testament is a collection of those writings, organized according to their respective literary types. The arrangement of the New Testament shows some striking similarities to that of the Old Testament. Like the Old Testament, the New Testament begins with a narrative collection. These narratives describe the life, ministry, and message of Jesus, as well as that story of selected individuals in the earliest Church. This narrative section is followed by a collection of occasional writings written within that narrated history. The New Testament, like the Old, concludes with a prophetic view to the future.

■ The Narratives of the New Testament

The opening narrative collection of the New Testament consists of four books describing the life, ministry, and message of Jesus, and a book that provides highlights of significant individuals and events in the first 30 years of the history of the earliest Christian Church. The four books describing the life and message of Jesus are the Gospel of Matthew, the Gospel of Mark, the Gospel of Luke, and the Gospel of John. The book of Church history is called Acts or the Acts of the Apostles. These narratives possess the basic characteristics of story or **narrative** literature. In each there is a plot or story line. The descriptions of the actions of key characters and their dialogues and monologues carry the plot line forward. In each there is rising conflict and a resolution of that conflict.

For the past two centuries certain scholars have debated whether these narratives were historically accurate or the literary inventions of their authors. There is little substantial reason to doubt the essential historical accuracy of the Gospels and the Book of Acts. On the other hand, it is also important to realize that these books were not written for the purpose of simply providing historical data. They were written to proclaim the truth of the Christian message about Jesus Christ. They possess a certain sermonic character in the best sense of the word "sermonic."

The Gospels

The Books of Matthew, Mark, Luke, and John are called **Gospels** and are named after the person traditionally thought to have written or collected the material in them. Though some events and words of Jesus are common to two or three or even all four of the Gospels, each Gospel writer created a unique portrait of the life and the meaning of Jesus. The Gospel of Matthew is especially suited to be the first Gospel and to function as the transition book from the Old Testament to the New. It is written with a Jewish perspective in mind and gives special attention to the way Jesus fulfilled various prophecies (and the Law) of the Old Testament. Matthew also contains large blocks of teachings of Jesus. Jesus is portrayed as a teacher or rabbi and as the Son of God. This first Gospel is one of two Gospels that provide a narrative and interpretation of Jesus' birth.

The Gospel of Mark is the shortest of the Gospels and was most likely the first of the four Gospels to be written. Mark is characterized by the energetic activity of Jesus. Mark's descriptions are actually more detailed than Matthew's, but Mark contains very few sections of the teachings of Jesus. Teaching is accomplished through the dialogues, parables, and interpreted actions of Jesus. The kingdom of God, Jesus as the Messiah, Jesus as the Son of God, and Jesus as the Son of Man are common themes treated in Mark. There is also a significant portion of the Gospel devoted to the meaning of Jesus' death.

The Gospel of Luke is the longest of the Gospels. It is also the only Gospel with a sequel (the Book of Acts). Luke gives special attention to the poor, to the sick, to the inclusion of Gentiles in God's plan of salvation, and to the participation of women in the work and ministry of Jesus. This third Gospel is noteworthy for its literary artistry and its powerful use of the parables of Jesus. The picture of Jesus begins by portraying Him as the Messiah and Prophet of Nazareth, then develops a picture of Jesus as the servant of God and finally presents an understanding of Jesus as Lord.

The Gospel of John is often characterized as the most "theological" of the four Gospels. There is a strong emphasis on Jesus as Messiah and as Son of God, with a special focus on the unique Father-Son relationship of Jesus and God. John's Gospel is characterized by long teaching passages in which Jesus reveals the significance of His person and ministry. The parables disappear, and the miracles are described as "signs" pointing to the meaning of Jesus in the work of God in the world. There is an almost philosophical use of abstract terms like "light," "life," "truth," "word," and "one."

Each of the Gospels devotes almost a third of its content to the final week, death, and resurrection of Jesus. This focus on Jesus' final days and the varied ways in which the meaning of Jesus is taught by the four Gospels raises the question of what kind of literature the Gospels represent. This question of the literary genre can be expressed by raising an imaginative question. If the chief librarian of the great ancient library of Alexandria, Egypt, had received a copy of the Gospels, with what other literature of the ancient world would the Gospels have been shelved? For much of the 20th century the Gospels were thought to represent a unique kind of literature. The Gospels do not fit very well in any of the genres of either the ancient or modern world. There has been a tendency in recent decades to characterize the Gospels as ancient biographies, but that does not really account for the focus on the death and Resurrection that plays such an important theological role in each Gospel. The same problem undermines attempts to understand the Gospels as collections of miracle stories or collections of virtuous teachings or simply as ancient history. The Gospels are clearly narratives, but they are a unique kind of narrative.

The New Testament History Book

The fifth narrative book is the Book of Acts, which is clearly a second volume by the author of the Gospel of Luke. The prologues of both Luke and Acts make it clear that Luke intended these two volumes to be understood as part of the ancient genre of history. That fact should not lead to the conclusion that these books were written with the modern understandings of history in mind. Luke clearly selects and interprets the historical material he includes to persuade the reader of the truth of the Christian mes-

sage. Part of the purpose of Acts is to portray the expanding mission of the Church as the fulfillment of Jesus' words that when the earliest believers received the Holy Spirit they would be empowered to witness to Christ in Jerusalem, Judea, and Samaria, "and to the ends of the earth" (Acts 1:8). Thus the themes of witness, power, the Holy Spirit, and the expansion of Christianity play a major role in Acts. The other major purpose of Acts is to show the success of the missionary outreach to Gentiles. The narrative of Acts portrays this success by shifting from describing the ministry of Peter to describing the ministry of Paul as the two major characters of the book.

■ The Letters of the New Testament

Following the Gospels and Acts, the New Testament contains two collections of early Christian letters. The first collection contains letters written by the apostle Paul to various churches or individuals. The second collection of letters is often called the General or Catholic Letters. The term "Catholic" comes from the fact that many (though not all) of these letters were written to churches rather than to individuals. All the letters address specific concerns—usually problems or potential problems—which the author was trying to correct by the letter. Most of the letters follow the standardized letter form used in the Greco-Roman world of the first centuries B.C. and A.D. They begin with the author's name, followed by the recipients' name(s) and a greeting. A thanksgiving to God usually forms the next section of the letters, before the author begins the body of the letter. The body of the letter varies in length a great deal, with some of the longer New Testament letters (such as Romans and 1 and 2 Corinthians) having very lengthy bodies compared to the typical letters of that time.

Letter writing was a developing art form during the first century, as travel became safer and international trade expanded to include shipping across the expanses of the Mediterranean Sea. Manuals or handbooks on how to write various kinds of letters were published. These letter handbooks make it clear that ancient letters had three primary purposes. First, letters served as a substitute for the physical presence of the author. This meant the New Testament letters were understood by their recipients as a way in which the author could be present with them even while absent. This contributed to the second purpose of the ancient letter, to establish or improve friendly relationships between the author and the recipients. Even the letters of the New Testament that seem most harsh to us were designed to promote a sense of unity and fellowship between the author and those who first read the letter. The third purpose of an ancient letter was to continue a conversation between the author and the recipient(s). In some cases the letter actually began the conversation. Perhaps as in some other cases it ended the conversation, but an important purpose of ancient letters was to promote conversation and dialogue between the author and the readers. These purposes are clearly at work in the New Testament letters.

The Letters of Paul

The letters of Paul are arranged in order from the longest, Romans, to the shortest, Philemon. Nine of the letters attributed to Paul in the New Testament are addressed to churches or congregations. Four are addressed to individuals. Most of the Pauline letters address a particular issue or problem in a church or group of churches. In Romans Paul seeks to overcome a division between Jewish believers and Gentile believers so the Roman church can provide a strong base for Paul's proposed missionary journey to Spain. First Corinthians is written to deal with a series of problems at Corinth: disunity in the church, sexual immorality in the church, worship problems, and a loss of belief in the resurrection of either Jesus or believers. Second Corinthians attempts to repair a relationship between Paul and the Corinthian church that has been damaged by misunderstanding and to defend Paul's ministry at the church in Corinth. Galatians is written to a group of churches that has fallen into the error of thinking believers had to become Jewish before they could become Christian. These first four letters of Paul are sometimes called the doctrinal letters or the head letters.

The next Pauline letters are called the Christological letters. Ephesians may have originally been a circular letter written to several churches in western modern Turkey. It deals with the nature of the church. Philippians was written to the church at Philippi in modern Greece. This church may have been one of Paul's favorite churches. It had provided financial support for his missionary work, and part of the purpose of Philippians is to thank the church for their support and to give a report of what Paul hoped would be a continuing partnership in ministry. Philippians is noteworthy for a powerful poem about Christ found in Philippians 2:6-11. This is thought to be one of the first great hymns of the Christian Church. Colossians was written to correct erroneous teachings about the nature of Christ in the area of Colossae in western modern Turkey. As is often the case, these faulty teachings about Christ were leading to un-Christlike behaviors in the church.

First and Second Thessalonians are often called the eschatological letters. They were written to the church in Thessalonica (in northern Greece) to address misunderstandings about the second coming of Christ. Once again, faulty theology was contributing to patterns of life that fell short of the purity and devotion expected in the Early Church.

The final four letters attributed to Paul are addressed to individuals. First and Second Timothy and Titus are often called the Pastoral Letters. They focus on issues of pastoral or church leadership in the area of Ephesus and on the island of Crete. The letter to Philemon asks the owner of a runaway slave, Onesimus, to accept him back as a brother in Christ, since Onesimus had become a believer through Paul's ministry.

The General or Catholic Letters

Like the Pauline letters, the general letters address specific problems in some local church or a group of churches. Also like the Pauline letters, the general letters are arranged in order from the longest, Hebrews, to the shortest, Jude, with the exception that all letters ascribed to the same author (Peter and then John) are kept together regardless of their length. These letters also address specific problems in the life of local churches.

Hebrews is unusual in that the genre of much of the book is similar to the other New Testament letters, but no author, audience, or greeting are mentioned. The book appears to be written to Jewish believers being persecuted or about to be persecuted for their faith in Christ. Their temptation was to return to the protective umbrella of Judaism, which had legal standing in the Roman Empire. The author warns against abandoning their faith in Christ by arguing the superiority of Christ to the great persons and institutions of the Old Testament.

James is the closest piece of New Testament writing to the Old Testament genre of wisdom. This letter contains many of the echoes of Jesus' teachings about justice and mercy to the poor and guarding one's tongue. First Peter, like Hebrews, addresses a group of believers who are either being persecuted or fearful of a soon-approaching persecution. In contrast to Hebrews, 1 Peter seems to address Gentile believers located in the northwestern section of modern-day Turkey.

Second Peter and Jude are similar in content. Both warn against false teachers creating turmoil and confusion in the church. Both address the question of a coming day of judgment and warn their readers to live with the high moral and doctrinal standards that will keep them prepared for the time of judgment. Jude is unique among New Testament books in quoting from the Jewish pseudepigraphal book of Enoch.

The Books of 1, 2, and 3 John appear to respond to a church undergoing a painful division over the correct understanding of Christ. First John, like Hebrews, lacks any mention of an author, audience, or greetings and so is often considered a sermon rather than a true letter. It emphasizes the love of God but clearly rejects those who do not believe that Jesus was truly incarnate in the flesh and truly the Son of God. Second and Third John are very brief letters (about the length of the typical Greco-Roman letter) addressed to individuals involved in the difficult divisions in the church.

The New Testament Book of Prophecy

The final book of the New Testament is Revelation. Though the interpretation of Revelation is debated more than the interpretation of any other book of the New Testament, it was written with a prophetic purpose. Like the Old Testament, the New Testament concludes with a word of hope for the future. Part of the difficulty in understanding Revelation is that it combines elements from three different genres: apocalyptic, prophecy, and letter. Apocalyptic literature uses visions, symbols, otherworldly creatures, and a devastating picture of final judgment to speak of the coming judgment of God when the present, evil age will be destroyed and God's new and final era for His obedient children comes on the scene. New Testament **prophecy** calls for God's people to turn from their sinful and vacillating

ways to lives of complete obedience to God, even if it costs them their lives. Revelation moves back and forth between the genre of apocalyptic and the genre of prophecy, with letters and occasional letterlike structures woven in also.

■ The Literary Nature of the New Testament

It is clear that the New Testament makes use of several different literary genres. Narrative, letter, and prophecy are the primary literary structures used by New Testament authors. Within each genre a variety of literary forms are used. These forms include: admonitions, benedictions or blessings, call narratives, chronicles or historical accounts of events, farewell speeches, brief letters, miracles, parables, prayers, sermons, and many others. The New Testament authors were talented communicators who made use of a wide variety of literary forms to communicate their message.

The Language of the New Testament

With one or two probable exceptions, all the authors of the New Testament books were Jewish in both nationality and religion. The Jewish people were widely scattered across the Roman Empire during the first Christian century. They spoke a variety of languages and dialects and participated in a variety of cultures. However, it is almost certain that each of the books of the New Testament was written in the common Greek dialect that was used throughout the eastern half of the Roman Empire at that time.

Aramaic Echoes in the New Testament

A number of Aramaic words appear in the New Testament and are preserved in the traditional translations.

Talitha cum—Little girl, get up (Mark 5:41)

Ephphatha—Be opened (Mark 7:34)

Eloi, Eloi, lama sabachthanai—My God, My God, why have you forsaken me? (Mark 15:34) (Matthew 27:46 uses Hebrew rather than Aramaic.)

The following words are Aramaic but also are used in Mishnaic Hebrew:

Raka—fool (Matthew 5:22)

Corban—an offering for God (Mark 7:11)

Abba—father (Mark 14:36)

The common language of the Jews who lived in Palestine at Jesus' time was Aramaic. **Aramaic** is a Northwest Semitic language, as is Hebrew. The people of Judah who were taken captive to Babylon in 587/586 B.C. learned Aramaic in captivity, and when they returned, it became the common language of the area of historic Israel instead of Hebrew. Hebrew was still read in the Scripture lessons of the worship services of the synagogue during Jesus' time, but an oral translation into Aramaic was made so the people could understand the Scripture. Because Aramaic was the language of Judea, it would have been the primary language of Jesus.

The last half century of New Testament scholarship has increasingly recognized, however, that Palestine was a multilingual society. The publication of the charge on Jesus' cross in Aramaic, Latin, and Greek reflects the variety of languages that were commonly spoken and understood in Jerusalem during Jesus' time. It is quite possible that Jesus spoke both Aramaic and Greek. A few scholars have suggested that some of the words of Jesus were first written in Aramaic and then translated into Greek when the Gospel writers began to compose their Gospels. However, it is clear that the Gospels themselves were first written in Greek, not in Aramaic or Hebrew.

The New Testament was written in a form of Greek that developed in the three centuries prior to Christ. Classical Greek is the form of the language used by the philosophers Plato and Aristotle, the historian Thucydides, and the authors of the Greek tragedies. A new form of Greek began to emerge about three centuries before Christ as a result of the conquests of Alexander the Great. Alexander attempted to impose the Greek language (classical Greek) on all the peoples he conquered. However, in the process the language was changed. Old grammatical usages and terminology disappeared, and new usages and words developed. This new form of Greek was called **Koine** (Greek for "common"), and it became the common language of first the Greek and then the Roman Empires. It is the language of the New Testament, and it was the form of Greek that remained in use for several centuries following the completion of the New Testament.

Koine Greek was not the language of the classical authors but the language of business and international relations during the time of Jesus. Evidence of its use (and thus help in understanding nuances and wordplays of the New Testament authors) comes from a variety of letters, contracts, official notices, and other documents preserved on papyrus primarily in Egypt. Clearly the New Testament was written in a living, energetic language. Part of the rapid expansion of Christianity in its earliest centuries is due to the Christian use of Koine Greek, since it was the lingua franca used throughout the Roman Empire. Though Latin was used by the Romans for military and governmental documents, the empire created a widespread network of those who spoke, understood, wrote, and read in Greek.

The Transmission of the New Testament

The books of the New Testament were written between A.D. 50 and A.D. 100. At that point they existed only as separate documents. As far as we know, only a single copy of each book existed and that copy was at the church to which or for which the book had been written. Second-century documents suggest that these writings were read aloud in the church along with the Old Testament readings. It is clear even from the letters of Paul that many early Christians traveled a great deal and visited churches other than the church in their home city. In the course of visiting other churches, these traveling believers would have heard the book/books written to the church they were visiting. They would have asked for a copy, and the process of copying the New Testament began.

Minuscules and Uncials

Some of the early manuscripts from the 3rd to 6th centuries are in formal letters, similar to capital letters. These manuscripts are called uncials. The cursive style of writing that connects one letter to another became the dominant method of copying at a later period. Manuscripts in cursive style follow a smaller script known as "minuscule." Since minuscule manuscripts were easier and more economical to produce, we have thousands of manuscripts in the minuscule form. However, scholars regard uncials as the earliest and the most reliable sources of the New Testament.

The following are the key uncials, all on leather parchments in codex form:

Codex Sinaiticus, dated to the 4th century, contains all the 27 books. During his search for biblical manuscripts at St. Catherine's Monastery on Mount Sinai, Constantin von Tischendorf discovered Codex Sinaiticus in 1859. He copied it, and it was first published in 1862. Today it is in the British Library in London.

Codex Vaticanus, also dated to the 4th century, is missing the section after Hebrews 9:13. This manuscript received its name from its association with the Vatican library. Though the manuscript has been known since 1475, it was first published in 1867 by Tischendorf.

Codex Alexandrinus, dated to the 5th century, is missing the Gospel of Matthew. This codex, also kept in the British Museum, was a gift from Cyril Lucar, patriarch of Constantinople, to King James I. It is believed that Lucar, once patriarch of Alexandria, brought this manuscript to Constantinople from Alexandria. It was brought to England in 1627 after the death of King James.

A page from
Codex Sinaiticus.

gue that it is impossible to determine what the New Testament authors originally wrote since all that remains are copies and probably copies of copies with the resulting variety of copying errors. However, the picture is not nearly as bleak as skeptics often portray it. Fortunately, most copying errors are predictable. If the copying is a visual process, the errors will most frequently consist of letters, words, or lines either omitted or repeated. If the copying is oral (one reads the text aloud and the other[s] writes), most of the errors will be misspellings, confusion of similar-sounding words, or words or short phrases omitted.

Because these kinds of copying errors are so predictable, if one has multiple copies made in different places at different times, it is quite possible to "reconstruct" the copying errors and thus determine the original text. There is a whole field of New Testament scholarship devoted to just that task. The field is usually called New Testament **textual criticism.** It involves comparing copies of ancient manuscripts, analyzing the errors (called **variants** since no original **manuscript** is known to survive), and reconstructing the original words of the New Testament authors. A manuscript refers to a handwritten copy of all or part of the New Testament.

The oldest known copy of a New Testament book is a small piece of papyrus found in Egypt and containing a few verses from John 18. Specialists believe it was written about A.D. 125, within a single generation of the time the fourth Gospel was first written. Several partial papyrus copies of the Gospels, Acts, and Paul's letters, which were copied between

The earliest surviving copies of books of the New Testament are written on **papyrus,** which was the ancient form of paper created by gluing together strips of the reedlike papyrus stalks. By the first century the Old Testament was copied on **parchment,** which is made of durable leather specially prepared for writing. While it is possible that some books of the New Testament were written on parchment (such as Luke and Acts, which may have been prepared for general publication), it is most likely that the majority of the New Testament was first written and then copied on papyrus.

The process of copying the books of the New Testament inevitably produced errors in copying. Though most believers in the present do not think about this, it is extremely difficult to copy hundreds of pages by hand without some errors creeping in. Some skeptics who are aware of this ar-

A.D. 180 and 220, have been found in the last century. Complete copies of the New Testament written on parchment around A.D. 325 have also been found in the past two centuries. New Testament textual critics now have more than 5,000 whole or partial manuscripts (handwritten copies) of the Greek New Testament, most of them discovered in the past 200 years.

Analyzing these manuscripts with the methods developed by textual criticism has enabled the textual critics to "reconstruct" the original text of the New Testament with more than 98 percent certainty. Textual uncertainty about the original reading only exists for a couple of paragraphs (the ending of Mark's Gospel and the story of the woman taken in adultery found in John 7:53—8:11) and a small number of single words. These have been clearly marked in virtually all modern translations of the New Testament. Given the huge number of handwritten copies of the books of the New Testament that were

made prior to the invention of the printing press in 1452 and the many variants that occurred during the copying process, this high degree of accuracy and confidence is almost miraculous.

The New Testament Canon

The New Testament books were first written and copied individually. The process of how they came to be collected into the 27 books we now know as the New Testament is the story of the development of the New Testament **canon.** The word "canon" comes from a Semitic root word meaning a "reed" or "stalk." The word came to be used especially for what we might call a measuring stick, a reed or stalk with a standardized length. The word was adapted into Greek, and the meaning of "rule" or "standard" developed. It eventually came to be used to describe a set of books that establish the rule of faith and practice of a religious community. The canon of the New Testament

The earliest copies of the New Testament manuscripts were written on papyrus made from the reedlike stalks of papyrus plants.

History of the Printed New Testament

Erasmus of Rotterdam is the first scholar to publish a copy of the New Testament in Greek (1516). He first published this edition with a Latin translation of the Greek text. Later he published four more editions (1519, 1522, 1527, 1535) of this New Testament, the fourth edition in three columns—Greek text, Latin Vulgate translation, and his own Latin translation.

Robert Stephanus, a printer and publisher, published four editions of the New Testament in Greek (1546, 1549, 1550, 1551). Theodore Beza published nine editions of the Greek New Testament between 1565 and 1604. The Elzevir brothers, two Dutch printers, published the New Testament with the claim that their edition provided the "received text," *textus receptus,* to the readers.

All of these above editions of the New Testament (Erasmus, Stephanus, Beza, Elzevir brothers) were based on a 4th-century manuscript, often called Lucianic, because of its association with Lucian of Antioch, who died in A.D. 312. This text is also known as Byzantine, Antiochian, Syrian, Ecclesiastical, Koine, or Common text. This text tradition remained as the standard text of the New Testament in Greek until the end of the 19th century. For over 400 years since Erasmus first published it in 1516, Christians seldom challenged its authority.

Following the publications of Codex Sinaiticus and Vaticanus in the mid-19th century, B. F. Westcott and F. J. A. Hort published a critical edition of the Greek New Testament in 1881. Their study of thousands of manuscripts and New Testament quotations in the writings of the Church Fathers led them to conclude that Codex Sinaiticus and Codex Vaticanus contain the most reliable text of the New Testament. The Greek New Testament published by the United Bible Societies in 1966 is based on the work of Westcott and Hort. This critical edition gives us an "eclectic" text based on the best witness of New Testament passages found in ancient manuscripts and early Christian writings. The United Bible Society edition has become an important source for modern English translations.

consists of 27 books, but it took several hundred years before the picture was completely clear.

The beginning of the canonization process probably began with a couple of churches exchanging copies of letters they had received from the apostle Paul. It is likely that the first collection of books was a collection of the Pauline letters. Some have suggested that this collection was done as early as the A.D. 80s or 90s. Most believe it was accomplished in the first 25 years of the second century. Sometime between A.D. 100 and 150 the four Gospels were collected and bound together for publication. The earliest surviving copies of the New Testament books, other than the fragment of John's Gospel mentioned above, are parts of collections of either Pauline letters or the four Gospels.

The first list of books regarded as canonical appears to have been developed by Marcion. Marcion was fascinated by the teachings of Paul but eventually interpreted them in such an unbalanced way that he was condemned as a heretic. He began a rival church that competed with the early Christian Church for several decades. Marcion strongly opposed the Law of the Old Testament and eventually the Old Testament in general. He taught that the God of the Old Testament was not the Father of Jesus Christ and was an evil deity. When he formed his list of books, he naturally omitted the New Testament books most reliant on Judaism and the Old Testament.

Marcion's list consisted of the Gospel of Luke (with the first two chapters edited out) and 10 of the letters of Paul (all but 1 and 2 Timothy and Titus). It is not clear that the Christian Church developed its New Testament canon as a reaction against Marcion, but such a proposal makes sense. The first "lists" of canonical books of the New Testament begin to appear about a generation later than Marcion.

Irenaeus grew up in Asia Minor (modern-day western Turkey), studied in Rome, and became a bishop in France. About A.D. 180 he wrote a major work, *Against Heresies,* in which he attacked the teachings of gnosticism. He argued forcefully for the canonical status of the four Gospels. He was reacting against both a move in Syria to reduce the four Gospels to a single composite Gospel and the widespread springing up of other Gospels written by representatives of several heretical movements in Christianity. It is clear from Irenaeus that he also regarded Acts, 1 Peter, 1 John, and all the letters of Paul except Philemon as canonical. He described the books of Revelation and the *Shepherd of Hermas* as scriptural.

The oldest list of New Testament books responding to Marcion is found in a document usually called the Muratorian fragment. This document appears to have been written between A.D. 180 and 200. The beginning of the list has been destroyed, but the surviving text begins with a reference to the third Gospel, that according to Luke. This clearly implies that Matthew and Mark were mentioned in the portion of the text that was destroyed. The Muratorian fragment then lists John's Gospel, Acts, the 13 letters of Paul, the letter of Jude, two letters of John, the Wisdom of Solomon, the Revelation of John,

and the Revelation of Peter. It indicates debate in the church about the Revelation of Peter and the *Shepherd of Hermas* and then lists several heretics whose writings are not acceptable for reading in the church.

A generation later, Origen, a priest who served in both Alexandria, Egypt, and Caesarea on the coast of Palestine, compiled a list of New Testament books. He further developed the concept of categories of books that appeared in the Muratorian fragment. Origen listed the books accepted by all the Church as the four Gospels, Acts, the 13 letters of Paul, 1 Peter, 1 John, and the Revelation of John. Another group of books was described as disputed by some local churches. These books included Hebrews, 2 Peter, 2 and 3 John, James, Jude, the Letter of Barnabas, the *Shepherd of Hermas,* the *Didache,* and the gospel according to the Hebrews. He then listed a large group of false or spurious writings that were not accepted by orthodox churches at all.

Thus, by A.D. 200 or shortly after, 21 of the 27 books of the New Testament were clearly recognized as having the authority of Scripture by churches throughout the Roman Empire. About 10 other books were accepted in many churches but rejected in others. Of those, 6 would eventually be recognized by virtually all the churches and 4 would be rejected by all. What is not often understood by modern believers is that there were dozens and dozens of other religious books claimed by a few to be equally authoritative. The Early Church was well aware of these writings and recognized that they contained teachings that would be harmful to the Church and its mission. A number of these books were "rediscovered" in the late 20th century and promoted as "lost" gospels or other "lost" books of the Bible. The implication was that these "lost" books should be returned to their rightful place as canonical Scripture. However, they were not "lost"; they were rejected as harmful books that were subversive to the Christian faith.

The Early Church did not rush to resolve the disagreements over the canon of the New Testament. Contrary to popular modern opinions, there was not a church council that arbitrarily determined which books should be included in the canon of the New Testament. The decision came about through the life, worship, and teaching processes of the Church through time. The Church lived with the three categories of Origen (accepted, disputed, rejected books) for over a century. It is not until the end of the fourth century that the Church began to arrive at an agreement about the exact 27 books now found in the New Testament.

The first time we find these 27 books, no fewer and no more, listed as the New Testament is in A.D. 367. Each Easter Athanasius, bishop of Alexandria, Egypt, wrote a letter to his churches. The subject of the A.D. 367 letter was the books of Scripture that were authoritative or canonical and thus should be read in the worship of the Church. After listing the 27 books now known as the New Testament, Athanasius also mentioned that the *Didache* and the *Shepherd of Hermas* were not part of the canon but provided useful devotional material. He also declared

that no place was to be given to "the apocryphal works," which he described as the "invention of heretics." The writings of Augustine, the great theologian, and Jerome, the great Bible scholar, whose lives span the end of the fourth and the beginning of the fifth centuries, both indicated the canonical status of the 27 books now known as the New Testament.

The closing decade of the fourth century was the first time a council of the Church made an official statement regarding the canon of Scripture. It appears that the Synod of Hippo in North Africa officially recognized the 27 books of the New Testament as canonical Scripture in A.D. 393. Unfortunately, the written documents of this council have been lost in the course of history. However, the actions of that council were read again and accepted by the Synod of Carthage in A.D. 397. The notes from this council clearly identified the 27 books we know as the New Testament as canonical Scripture. A few local churches continued to debate books such as Hebrews, Revelation, and 2 Peter for several more centuries, but in effect the question of the canon was finally decided by the end of the fourth century.

It should be recognized that the process of the canonization of the New Testament was neither hasty nor arbitrary. It appears that several criteria of canonization were used to determine which books were to be recognized as the Word of God and which were not to be so accepted. However, these criteria were not applied in a mechanical or rigid way. The most important criterion was that of the use of the Church in general.

When churches in the East and in the West of the Roman Empire used books in worship alongside the Old Testament and considered them as part of the Word of God, then those books were understood to be canonical. When there was disagreement about whether to use some books in the worship and teaching of the Church, then the Church simply waited. Final agreement did not come until the end of the fourth century, but it came without pressure or administrative initiative. It came as a result of the people of God thinking, praying, worshiping, and evangelizing together.

At some points the question of whether an apostle wrote or did not write a book was part of the debate. However, this criterion was not a simple one and does not appear to have been applied consistently through the process of canonization. For example, the Gospels of Mark and Luke were not written by apostles, but they were recognized as canonical very early in the process. Later writers tried to explain this by noting that Mark had been influenced by Peter, and Luke was associated with Paul. On the other

Is the New Testament Canon Closed?

Recent decades have witnessed an increased interest in the canon of the New Testament. One of the questions that is always in the background is whether the New Testament canon is closed. That is, is it possible to change the canon by removing or especially by adding some books? What if we were to discover another letter of the apostle Paul? Should it not be added to the canon of Scripture? Should not the various gospels not included in the New Testament now be added to the canon?

In theory the canon is always open. Since it was the recognition of the Church that established the canon, the Church can theoretically change the canon at any point in history. However, in reality the matter is much more difficult. The Church took almost 400 years to come to an agreement on the existing canon. The Church today is much larger and far more diverse in backgrounds and theological opinions. It would be very difficult to conceive of a consensus of all Christians today agreeing to add a book to the canon of the New Testament.

Further, the fact that the New Testament contains 27 books is not for lack of other candidates. In fact, an awareness of the historical development of the canon makes it clear that the Church purposefully rejected a number of books either because they taught concepts considered heretical and dangerous to the Church life or simply because not everyone in the Church agreed that those books spoke an authoritative word from God. There is no reason for the Church to add books to the canon that have already been rejected because of their false teachings.

Some of the books rejected were considered written by apostles. So even if we should discover another genuine letter of Paul, that does not automatically mean it should be included in the canon of the New Testament. Such books were more likely to have been known in the first four centuries than they are now. Christians today can trust the decision-making process that led to the New Testament canon. So, although in theory the canon is open, in practical terms it is closed. The need of the Church is not to find more books to put in the New Testament but to live up to the standard of holiness and love taught in the books already there.

hand, the Revelation of Peter was accepted in some churches for a while but did not end up being recognized as part of the canon. In fact, many of the apocryphal books claimed to be written by apostles, so the Church had to sort through the issues of claims of apostolic authorship and authentic apostolic teaching.

The criterion that the Early Church most often claimed to determine the canonical books was what they called the rule of faith or the canon of truth. This criterion dealt with whether the book taught apostolic truth. The Early Church developed a strong sense of continuity with the teachings of the original apostles. They often described this as that which was taught everywhere by everyone from the beginning. (In contrast, the heresies began as localized movements.) This consensus of orthodox faith is what they called the rule of faith or the canon of truth, and it was the ultimate court of appeal for keeping books out of the canon. No book

containing teaching contrary to the rule of faith was considered canonical. However, there were books that were completely orthodox that did not make it into the canon. So the rule of faith was not an adequate criterion in itself. It functioned in conjunction with apostolic authorship and universal use and acceptance in the churches.

The Covenant Community

It is a serious mistake to assume that one can understand the New Testament simply by studying its literary characteristics and its historical background. The New Testament was not written to inform people; it was written to transform people. Though it is full of fascinating historical, literary, and even theological details that are worthy of study, the New Testament itself intends to form people into a community of fully devoted followers of Jesus Christ. Its influence throughout the past 2,000 years has not come from its

The Bible is the rule of faith for the Christian Church.

literary qualities or from its historical context. Its influence is the result of the theological truths it proclaims and the vision of transformed lives that it seeks.

The process of canonization makes it clear that the New Testament is a Church book. It is the product of a community of faith. Not only did the Church discern as a community which books belonged in the New Testament and which books would not be included, but the books themselves were written for and to the Church. In only a few cases are New Testament letters addressed to individuals, and even then the content of those letters deals with how the individuals in question provide leadership for the Church. Every book of the New Testament portrays in some way what the Church of Jesus Christ should look like. What the Church believes, how the Church lives its life in community, and how the Church witnesses to its faith in the world all comprise the purpose of the New Testament.

The faith, life in community, and prophetic witness in the world of the Church is neither generic nor formless. It is a specific, intentional, and structured community. Specifically the Church that gave form to the New Testament and was formed by the New Testament understood itself to be in continuity with the Old Testament people of God, the covenant community of Israel. The authors of the New Testament believed that God's saving activity in the Old Testament was part of the story and preparation for God's saving activity in Christ. The covenant that God made with Israel was not rejected or laid aside with the com-

ing of Christ. It was renewed and through the Holy Spirit internalized into human hearts. Thus the community of faith that forms in and through the New Testament does not regard itself as a completely new thing. Rather, it is the logical outcome of what God had been doing through salvation history in response to both human rejection and acceptance of His grace.

Old Testament Israel understood herself to be bound to God by the covenant of Mount Sinai. That covenant came into being because of God's saving works for Israel. The covenant envisioned a people whose life together and whose lives individually would reflect the holiness of the God to whom they were bound. This vision created expectations for the people of God, and the covenant laid out the consequences of living up to those expectations or failing to accomplish them.

In a similar fashion the Church of the New Testament understood that believers were part of a covenant community in continuity with Israel. The renewal of that covenant came into being because of God's saving work for them in Christ. The New Testament envisions a people whose life together and whose lives individually reflect the holiness and the love of the God who revealed himself in Christ. That vision creates expectations for the covenant community, and the New Testament, especially the letters and Revelation, describes the consequences of the Church's living up to or failing to live up to God's vision for them.

Central to this concept of covenant is the community of faith. The

Church of the New Testament never envisioned faith as a purely private matter. Though an individual's relationship with God was intensely personal, it was always lived out in community. Individual believers understood their life together in worship, instruction, and ministry as the context for their personal relationship with God. There are many places in the New Testament where the word "Christ" refers to Jesus as a historical individual who was crucified and raised from the dead. There are many other places where the word "Christ" means the Church, the Body of Christ, the community expression of Christ.

The New Testament was written by the community of faith for the community of faith. The New Testament also calls the community of faith into being, nurturing and challenging it to become fully like Christ. The New Testament invites its readers into that covenant community.

Summary Statements

- The New Testament has been highly influential in both the Church and the world.
- The New Testament is structured into narrative material, letters, and prophecy.
- The four Gospels represent a unique narrative form focusing on the story of Jesus' ministry, death, and resurrection.
- The letters of Paul and the general letters address specific problem areas in the life of the Church representing the author's effort to solve the problem at a distance.
- Though Jesus spoke Aramaic, the New Testament was written in Koine Greek.
- The Greek New Testament is only available to us in copies and copies of copies.
- Textual criticism allows us to reconstruct the original reading of the Greek Testament with confidence.
- By the late second century the Church had quickly developed a consensus regarding over three-fourths of the books that would eventually be part of the canon of the New Testament.
- The criteria of consensus and use in the Church were the main qualifications for a book's being included in the New Testament canon.
- The New Testament was written to form a covenant community of those who followed Jesus Christ.

Questions for Reflection

1. How does the structure of the New Testament reflect its "real-to-life" character and its applicability?
2. To what degree do you see the direction of God in the process of canonization? What conclusions does that lead you to?
3. In what ways have you experienced life in a covenant community like that which produced and was produced by the New Testament? In what ways has your life in the Church lacked elements of a covenant community?

Resources for Further Study

Bailey, James L., and Lyle D. Vander Broek. *Literary Forms in the New Testament: A Handbook*. Louisville, Ky.: Westminster/John Knox Press, 1992.

Comfort, Philip Wesley. *The Quest for the Original Text of the New Testament*. Grand Rapids: Baker, 1992.

Metzger, Bruce M. *The Canon of the New Testament: Its Origin, Development, and Significance*. Oxford: Clarendon, 1987.

Patzia, Arthur G. *The Making of the New Testament: Origin, Collection, Text and Canon*. Downers Grove, Ill.: InterVarsity Press, 1995.

Wegner, Paul D. *The Journey from Texts to Translations: The Origin and Development of the Bible*. Grand Rapids: Baker, 1999.

Willimon, William H. *Shaped by the Bible*. Nashville: Abingdon, 1990.

2 How Should One Read the New Testament?

bjectives:

Your study of this chapter should help you to:

- Identify the three worlds of New Testament interpretation.
- Identify aspects of the historical and cultural context of the New Testament that are important for interpretation.
- Describe the ways in which the literary study of the New Testament provides keys for understanding.
- Describe the role of the reader in understanding New Testament texts.

ey Words to Understand

Hermeneutics
Exegesis
Herod the Great
Pax Romana
Honor-shame culture
Genre
Form
Apocalyptic
Proverbs or wisdom
  sayings
Legal sayings
Prophetic sayings
Pronouncement stories
Parable
Similitude
Parable proper
Example story
Allegory
List
Household codes
Word chains
Diatribe
Hymns
Interpretive framework

Questions to consider as you read:

1. How does knowledge of the historical context of the New Testament enable a reader to see the New Testament as more "real"?

2. How do the literary features of the text, such as genre and form, influence understanding of the text?

3. How does one arrive at appropriate theological understanding from the text of the New Testament?

People often assume that it is easy to read and understand the New Testament. While this may seem to be true, often we find a variety of interpretations when people read the New Testament. It is not unusual for two people to read the New Testament and come to different conclusions about its meaning for the Christian life today.

The process of canonization described in chapter 1 assumed a role or an authority for the New Testament as the Word of God. While Christians may differ on how God made the New Testament a Divine Word, almost all Christians agree that the New Testament has such scriptural authority. This means that the New Testament is attempting to communicate a message from God. Since we discover that not everyone reads and understands the same message, we must give attention to how to read the New Testament.

The study of how to read and interpret the New Testament is called **hermeneutics.** It includes patterns to study how a text was understood when it was first written and how it can be applied to Christian life today. The study of a text to determine its meaning either in its historical context (when it was first written and read) or in its literary context (as the text now stands) is often called **exegesis.** Much of the work of people usually described as "Bible scholars" is devoted to the work of exegesis.

Recent decades have witnessed a wide variety of opinions about the best methods of exegesis and hermeneutics. Some of the strongest debates in theological colleges and seminaries, as well as in denominations, are debates about exegesis and hermeneutics.

This chapter will present one widely accepted approach to reading and interpreting the New Testament. It is not the only approach that is influential in circles of Christian biblical scholarship today, but it incorporates many of the current ideas about how to organize the study and interpretation of the New Testament.

This approach recognizes three major perspectives from which a reader may gain useful understanding of the New Testament. These three perspectives "create a world" in which the New Testament is studied. The perspective of the world behind the text studies the historical and cultural background of the New Testament documents. This perspective attempts to re-create the political, economic, social, and religious world in which the New Testament documents came into being. This is the world in which the author and the original audience lived. By understanding this world one can better understand the New Testament.

The perspective of the world within the text studies the language and literary characteristics found in the New Testament. This perspective creates the literary world of the text and focuses on the means by which communication of biblical materials takes place. By understanding how the New Testament communicates its ideas one can better understand the New Testament. The perspective of the world in front of the text studies how we read the New Testament today and how we apply it both to our own lives and to the life of the Christian Church. This perspective attempts to understand the world in which the New Testament is read, studied, and preached as the Word of God to people of Christian faith. This is the world of the contemporary reader. By understanding how the New Testament speaks to the life and faith issues of today one can better understand the New Testament.

Clearly the three worlds of New Testament interpretation are not completely isolated from each other. The history of the way people from the New Testament period used and understood literature clearly impacts both the world behind the text and the world within the text. The theological insights of the New Testament authors may well be of interest for those studying the world behind the text, the world within the text, and the world in front of the text. In practice the three worlds of the text often intersect (or collide) with each other. However, for the purpose of study it is helpful to consider the three worlds separately.

The World Behind the Text

Chapter 3 will describe some of the basic characteristics of the world behind the text, the historical and cultural backgrounds of the New Testament. The purpose of this section of this chapter is to show how the historical and cultural backgrounds of the New Testament provide help in understanding and interpreting the New Testament.

■ The Historical Background of the New Testament

For several centuries now, Bible scholars have considered the historical background an essential part of the study of the New Testament. The importance of the historical background can be understood by an analogy between understanding another person and understanding the Bible. We believe we understand other persons better when we know something of their life story. We try to discover where they come from, the major events of their lives, and the various influences that seemed to shape them. In a similar fashion, Bible scholars believe we can understand the New Testament better if we know where it came from, what the significant events in the New Testament are, and what the various influences that shaped the New Testament were.

The World from Which the New Testament Came

The New Testament entered history at a period that was extremely formative for Western civilization. The events leading up to the establishment of the Roman Empire and the first century of that empire provide the historical context for the New Testament. The events described at the beginning of the New Testament took place during the reign of Caesar Augustus, who founded the empire and gave initial direction to it. However, the New Testament did not arise at center stage in the Roman Empire. It came into being on the margins of the empire—always interacting with it but always in dialogue with the story of Judaism. The history of Israel as revealed in the Old Testament lies behind the New Testament. The history between the conclusion of the Old Testament (variously dated between 400 and 200 B.C.) and the reign of Herod the Great in Jerusalem from 37 to 4 B.C. pro-

Caesarea Maritima. Herod built this coastal town in honor of Caesar Augustus.

the Maccabees and other Jewish partisans pushed the issues of Sabbath observance, circumcision, dietary laws, and the study of the Old Testament Torah to the front of Jewish concerns for identity. Those concerns would play a major role in the New Testament. The series of controversies between Jesus and Jewish scribes over Sabbath observance was directly related to the events of the second century B.C. The struggles between Paul and the so-called Judaizers regarding the role of circumcision and other "works of the Law" were the direct result of the Jewish identity struggles in the second century B.C.

vides the background of the New Testament. (See this historical context in the next chapter.)

The most pivotal event in Jewish history between the Testaments was the attempt of Antiochus IV (Epiphanes) to destroy Judaism in the first third of the second century B.C. The Maccabean Revolt that began in 167 B.C. was both a battle to preserve Jewish identity and to set Israel free from the ongoing power struggles of the remaining factions of Alexander the Great's Hellenistic Empire. The actions of Antiochus IV and the response of

The issues at stake in the Jews' struggle to maintain their religious and national identity were intertwined with the great political movements in the Greco-Roman world. These events include the short-lived independence of the Jewish nation under the Hasmonean rulers, the incorporation of Judea as a part of the Roman Empire, struggle for power within the Roman Empire and the rise of Caesar Augustus as high priest

Roman theater at Caesarea Maritima. This theater provided entertainment for Herod's guests.

(pontifex maximus) and father of the fatherland (pater patriae), and the ascension of Herod as king of Judea.

The New Testament authors who narrate Jesus' birth set that birth in the context of both the Roman Empire at center stage and Herod the Great on the margin. Matthew identifies Jesus' birth as occurring in the days of Herod the king. Luke notes that Jesus was born when Augustus Caesar was the emperor.

The Significant Events of the New Testament Era

The birth of Jesus was the most significant event marking the beginning of the New Testament pe-

riod. On the margin the death of **Herod the Great** most significantly shaped the opening years of the New Testament era. After more than 30 years of stable but cruel rule, Herod's death began a period of gradual destabilization in Judea and Galilee, with the kingdom now divided among his three sons, Archelaus, Antipas, and Philip. This period of instability continued for more than half a century. The Herodian family reigned with no regard for the people of Judea and Galilee, as they lined their own pockets to bribe the emperor into supporting them. Eventually Rome placed Judea and Galilee under the Roman procurators who ruled with

Significant Historical Events in the New Testament Era

63 B.C.	Rome captures Jerusalem
37 B.C.	Herod becomes king of the Jews
27 B.C.	Octavian proclaimed as "Caesar Augustus"
6-5 B.C.?	Birth of Jesus
4 B.C.	Death of Herod the Great
A.D. 14	Tiberius becomes Roman emperor
A.D. 27	Ministry of John the Baptist
A.D. 28-30	Ministry of Jesus
A.D. 30	Death of Jesus
A.D. 41	Claudius becomes Roman emperor
A.D. 44	Death of (Herod) Agrippa I
A.D. 47-48	Paul's first missionary journey
A.D. 48 or 49	Apostolic Council in Jerusalem
A.D. 49	Claudius expels the Jews from Rome
A.D. 49-52	Paul's second missionary journey
A.D. 50-51	Paul in Corinth
A.D. 51-52	Gallio's proconsulship in Corinth
A.D. 52-56	Paul's third missionary journey
A.D. 54	Nero becomes Roman emperor
A.D. 62	Death of James the brother of Jesus
A.D. 66	Jewish war of independence begins
A.D. 68	Death of Nero
A.D. 70	Destruction of Jerusalem
A.D. 95-100	Final books of the New Testament are written

cruelty and decreasing regard for Jewish religious sensitivities. Taxes and oppression increased. It is not surprising that Jewish unrest increased and came to a head in the latter part of 60s, fueled by Roman oppression, Jewish apocalyptic expectations, and the rising antagonism of the Zealots against foreign domination. The outcome was the tragic destruction of Jerusalem by the Roman army in A.D. 70.

As a result of Roman victory, the Jewish sects of the Sadducees, the Essenes, and the party of the Zealots were destroyed. Only the Pharisees and the Jewish followers of Jesus remained. In the following decades the Pharisees attempted to reestablish Jewish identity and pride by emphasis on observance of the Law with continued attention to circumcision, Sabbath observance, and dietary laws. Since the followers of Jesus were increasingly engaged in a mission to Gentiles, this had the effect of defining the followers of Jesus out of the new form of Judaism. Most New Testament scholars believe Matthew's

Gospel was written to urge Jewish believers in Jesus to remain true to both their Jewish heritage and the Gentile mission.

Because the destruction of the Temple and Jerusalem in A.D. 70 was such a traumatic experience for Jews, scholars seek to understand how a number of New Testament books—including all four Gospels, Hebrews, and James—fit into the chronology of Jewish history leading up to and following that destruction.

Other Historical Influences on the New Testament

The death of Jesus had been ordered by Pontius Pilate, the Roman procurator stationed in Judea. The date of the Crucifixion is most likely A.D. 30. Following the resurrection of Christ the Book of Acts indicates that the first believers in Jerusalem began evangelizing Greek-speaking Jews from throughout the Mediterranean world who had come to the Holy City. These believers (called Hellenistic Jewish Christians) provided the connections and the persons who would begin evangelizing across the Roman Empire.

The gospel was first preached to friends and family in the various Mediterranean cities from which they had come. This took place from Antioch in northwestern Syria to Rome itself. Acts indicates that the church that had been established at Antioch began preaching the gospel to Gentiles in that city. Soon the church at Antioch commissioned Saul and Barnabas for a preaching mission westward.

As the journey unfolded, a pattern emerged in which the Jewish synagogue became the starting

Antioch in Northern Syria became a leading center of the Christian faith in the first century.

point for the preachers. After some time the preaching of Jesus created division in the synagogue. Paul and Barnabas would take those Jews who believed in Jesus with them and form a rival synagogue. From that base they began to preach the gospel to the Gentiles of the city. Within 20 years of the crucifixion of Jesus the gospel had spread throughout the major cities of modern-day Turkey and the church was being established in Greece. Similar expansion of the gospel took place into Northern Africa and east into Mesopotamia and on toward India.

The rapid expansion of the Christian faith was facilitated by a widespread network of Hellenistic Jewish synagogues that already existed, the common use of Koine Greek throughout the Roman Empire and beyond the eastern boundaries of the empire, and by the increased safety for travel throughout the empire made possible by the Roman peace **(Pax Romana)**. Both the system of Roman roads and the increased safety of the shipping routes under Roman rule made travel easier and more secure than it had ever been before in human history. Wherever the earliest Christian preachers traveled they were able to communicate the gospel because Greek was spoken and understood everywhere in the empire. Wherever the earliest preachers traveled they found Hellenistic Jewish synagogues providing a ready base from which to begin their work.

The rapid and secure travel meant that the Christian faith was not the only religious influence spreading throughout the empire. Various mystery and fertility religions spread throughout the empire from the eastern Mediterranean, and several philosophical systems spread from centers in Greece and Rome. In every city and village where the gospel was preached, Judaism, the mystery religions, the fertility religions, and several Greek or Roman philosophies were also proclaimed. The many competing religious voices made confusion among Christian converts a likely result. A number of New Testament books—including Romans; 1 and 2 Corinthians; Galatians; Colossians; 1 and 2 Thessalonians; 1 and 2 Timothy; Titus; James; 1, 2, and 3 John; 2 Peter; and Jude—were written to clear up theological confusion that arose in churches where the earliest believers listened to many religious voices seeking to persuade them of the truth.

The religious confusion was a problem also for the empire, and some local civic leaders thought it harmful to social order and security. In a number of locations either the empire or local officials or both began trying to reduce the religious confusion by limiting or eliminating the spread of religions from the eastern part of the empire. These religions included the mystery religions, the fertility religions, and early Christianity. Several New Testament books—including Hebrews, 1 Peter, and Revelation—were written to encourage early believers to remain faithful to Christ in the face of actual or threatened persecution that was attempting to reduce the religious confusion of the time.

The New Testament in Its Historical Context

It is clear that an understanding

of the historical context of the New Testament books is very helpful in providing a perspective from which to understand the message of those books. For this reason the careful study of the historical context of New Testament books has been an important part of New Testament studies for more than two centuries. Scholars seek to determine the date of each of the New Testament books, the audience(s) to which each was written, and the purpose each book hoped to accomplish. Discovery of the author of each book and the place from which the author wrote the book has also been the object of study. With such information scholars attempt to place each book in the historical context described above and thus to understand the way that historical context shapes a proper understanding of the book.

■ The Cultural Context of the New Testament

In addition to the historical context, the study of the world behind the text investigates the social and cultural context of the New Testament. The outcome of the study of the historical context tends to focus on how books of the New Testament fit into the history of the first century. The outcome of study of the social and cultural context tends to focus on understanding specific passages within the books. The study of the social and cultural context includes a study of social structures of the Mediterranean world, of cultural assumptions of that world, and of religious patterns of that world.

The study of social structures in the Mediterranean world gives attention to the social organization

of the earliest Church and to the social strata from which the earliest Christians came. While the Jewish synagogue provided the primary model of social organization for the earliest Church, the Hellenistic world also influenced the Church's organization. In the first century A.D. trade guilds and interest groups developed in a number of the major cities of the empire. The meeting of the trade guilds provided the first social structures in which people of diverse ethnic and religious backgrounds met and socialized together in peaceful and constructive ways. These meetings provided a model by which the earliest Church could reach beyond Jewish believers and invite Gentiles from a variety of ethnic and religious backgrounds to participate in corporate worship, discipleship, and service. These trade guilds and interest groups provided a model for the Church to understand itself as transcending traditional ethnic, religious, and gender divisions of the ancient Mediterranean world.

It is not surprising that Christianity spread most rapidly among the poor and socially disadvantaged of the ancient world. These included slaves and women. The social strata that divided masters and slaves, husbands and wives, parents and children were governed by specific expectations for how the persons in each stratum were to play their role. The passages of the New Testament in Ephesians 5:22—6:9; Colossians 3:18—4:1; and 1 Peter 2:18—3:7 clearly attempt to help early believers receive the liberating power of the gospel in their lives and social relationships without completely violating the rules governing the social strata of their world. Paul's letter to Philemon is best understood in light of the complex rules of slaves and masters of the Mediterranean world. Paul believed the gospel created a new relationship between the Christian slave master, Philemon, and his newly converted slave, Onesimus. However, Philemon would not naturally understand the meaning of the gospel on his master-slave relationships and thus Paul writes the letter to gently point out the implications of Onesimus's conversion.

The cultural assumptions of the New Testament world also impact our understanding of various New Testament passages. The Mediterranean world was an honor-shame culture. This meant the circumstances of a person's social strata, economic resources, education, and standing in the community created an established level of honor for that person. Much of life in the Mediterranean world involved attempts to gain further honor and to avoid loss of honor through actions and reactions that would bring shame upon a person. Many of the teachings of Jesus are best understood in light of the **honor-shame culture** of that time. Where one sat at a banquet, how one was greeted in public, and the invitations one received from neighbors all impacted one's honor or shame.

The cultural assumptions of betrothal and marriage in the Mediterranean world are reflected in the accounts of Mary and Joseph leading up to the birth of Jesus. The assumptions of death and funerals can be seen in both the accounts of funerals in the Gospels and in Jesus' challenge of the would-be disciple of Luke 9:59 who wanted to bury his father before following Jesus. Since death was almost immediately followed by preparation of the body and burial, it is likely the would-be disciple's father had not yet died. Rather, this would-be disciple wanted to postpone the decision to follow Jesus until some future day when his father had died and all the issues of inheritance had been settled.

The cultural assumption of the Mediterranean world that considered the group rather than the individual to be the primary unit of society also impacts understanding of the New Testament. In Romans 5:12-21 Paul seems to move easily back and forth between viewing Adam as the first human and as the whole of the human race. Likewise he moves back and forth between viewing Christ as the individual, Jesus, and as the corporate group, the Church, the Body of Christ. Such corporate understandings of both humanity and the Church reflect the cultural assumptions of Paul's world.

The religious patterns of the Mediterranean world also provide an important perspective for understanding the New Testament, especially when contrasted with modern understandings of religion. Most ancient religions used a sacrificial system to express worship to the deity of that religion. As a result the language of sacrifice, offering, and blood plays a more significant role in the New Testament expressions of appropriate response to God than is typically found in modern, Western religions that place a high premium on ethics. The New Testament also values ethical liv-

Biblical "Criticism"

For some people the use of the word "criticism" to describe methods of studying the Bible seems inappropriate. The use of that word arose from the German term "Kritik" used to describe various methods of analyzing documents and texts. Thus the various biblical criticisms are methods of analyzing aspects of the Bible and its background. Following are some of the more common forms of biblical criticism:

Historical criticism—the analysis of the historical background and historical accuracy of the Bible.

Textual criticism—the analysis of manuscripts of either the Old or New Testaments to determine the most likely reading of the original.

Source criticism—the analysis of biblical books seeking to determine possible sources used by the biblical author.

Form criticism—the analysis of the literary forms of individual paragraphs of the biblical text. Form criticism was severely criticized (in the normal sense of the word) when it tried to establish historical authenticity on the basis of literary forms.

Redaction criticism—the analysis of the way biblical authors edited (redacted) the sources available to them in the writing of the biblical books.

Tradition criticism—the analysis of the way Old Testament authors made use of historical "traditions" from an earlier period of the Old Testament.

Composition criticism—the analysis of the way biblical authors composed their books by studying the beginning, the structure and flow of materials, and conclusion of the book.

Social-scientific criticism—the analysis of the biblical world and biblical text from the perspective of the social sciences, especially sociology and cultural anthropology.

Rhetorical criticism—the analysis of the rhetorical strategies used by the biblical authors.

Canonical criticism—the analysis of the way the various parts of the biblical canon are to be related to each other or the analysis of the forces that led to the particular shape of the biblical canon that now exists.

Narrative criticism—the analysis of the way narrative texts are shaped and the way they shape readers.

Reader-response criticism—the analysis of the way readers participate with a text in creating meaning for that text.

ing but intertwines the explanation of holiness with sacrificial terminology that is rarely understood by modern readers.

The social and cultural world of the New Testament is an arena of study that has been especially emphasized in recent decades. It is clear that further study in this area will be fruitful in understanding the world behind the text of the New Testament.

The World Within the Text of the New Testament

The study of the world within the text is the study of the literary character of the New Testament. Of particular interest is the way in which the literary art of the text creates a world into which the reader or listener can enter. Further, the literary character of the text may enable the reader or listener to discover new insights and truths by entering that world created by the text. Certainly from an evangelical perspective one would hope the reader or listener would be empowered by the new truths and insights to bring them into the so-called real world.

It is clear that different kinds of literature have different ways and different abilities to create a world into which a reader or listener can enter. For that reason the study of the literary genres of the New Testament is extremely important. From the genres of New Testament books to the literary forms of individual paragraphs in the New Testament is a small step.

■ The Major Literary Genres of the New Testament

The New Testament makes use of three or perhaps four major literary genres. In this chapter the word **genre** will be used for the kinds of literature of the various books of the New Testament. The word **form** will be used for the kinds of literature found in individual paragraphs in the New Testament. Obviously there are important relationships between the genre(s) of a book and the forms that are used in that book. If we think of three genres in the New Testament, they would be narrative, letter, and apocalyptic. Some persons prefer to separate the Gospels from the general genre of narrative and so propose four genres: gospel, history, letter, and apocalyptic.

A skilled author (and the authors of the New Testament were all skilled authors) will select the genre in which he or she writes to accomplish certain purposes. Thus the author's choice of genre is one of the first clues to the reader of what should be understood in the text and how it should be understood. The very structure of a genre creates certain "rules" regarding the kind of communication that can be accomplished and how the genre should be understood. New Testament authors followed these rules (or conventions), and we must also abide by them if we are to understand New Testament texts.

A letter is part of a dialogue and should be understood as part of the process of communication. It presumes either a prior relationship between author and readers or intends to develop a relationship that will continue. New Testament letters responded to communication that the authors of those letters had received from the churches to which the letters were being sent. The communication is directly addressed to the church and expects the dialogue to continue.

On the other hand, narrative is much more indirect in its method of communication. It is not usually addressed directly to a person or a church but to an implied reader or listener. The actual reader or listener is implicitly invited to listen in on the narrative. The narrator expects the listener to enter into the narrative and to participate in various ways in the story. But the narrator does not begin a dialogue and does not expect a dialogue to develop from the story. The very genre of a New Testament book implicitly suggests to the reader or listener the appropriate strategy for reading or listening to that book to correctly understand it.

However, the rules (or conventions) of genres are not hard-and-fast rules. Authors may play with the rules a bit or bend them. There is latitude within the rules of a genre to adapt it in ways that also communicate. The rules of narrative require characters, setting, and plot. However, those rules do not specify how the narrative begins, how it ends, nor how conflicts develop and are resolved. The author's choice of how to begin the narrative very much shapes the message it will communicate.

The significance of the choice of a beginning of a narrative can be seen the way each Gospel writer begins. Matthew's Gospel begins with a genealogy that connects Jesus to two of the major figures of Israel's history, Abraham and David. The opening paragraphs following the genealogy emphasize the ways in which Jesus' conception, birth, and earliest years fulfilled Old Testament prophecy. This beginning signals Matthew's interest in the ways Jesus could be connected to the Old Testament. It is not surprising that Matthew will especially emphasize Jesus' Jewishness in this Gospel.

On the other hand, Mark begins the story of Jesus quite abruptly. The ministry of John the Baptist, the baptism of Jesus, and the temptation of Jesus are all narrated in less than 13 verses. The sense of urgency in Mark's quick-paced Gospel is not surprising in light of its beginning. Luke tips off the reader to his interest in Gentiles and the universal appeal of the gospel by a prologue styled after the prologues of the well-known ancient books of history. John begins his Gospel by setting the ministry of Jesus in the eternal character of God.

Narrative authors can also adapt the composition of their story to accomplish their literary purposes. Matthew alternates large blocks of story line and teaching materials. For every major section of Jesus' teaching he matches selections from Jesus' life and ministry. This material from Jesus' life and ministry actually illustrates what Jesus taught. Mark arranges the events in the opening eight chapters of his Gospel to constantly raise the question of who Jesus is. Then in Mark 8:27 Jesus asks that very question of His disciples. The remainder of Mark then describes Jesus in terms of His identity as Servant and Suffering Savior. In a very different way Luke arranges his Gospel to highlight Jesus' final journey to Jerusalem (beginning in Luke 9:51). Thus the different Gospel writers use the freedom available within narrative to create the points of emphasis they want to make.

Letter writers also have a certain flexibility that they can use within the constraints or conventions of letters. Unlike narratives, letters do not have freedom to change the basic structure of the beginning of each letter. The New Testament letters all follow the basic conventions of the typical Greco-Roman letter: Salutation, consisting of author's name, recipient's name(s), and greeting; thanksgiving, body of the letter, closing conventions. However, within that basic structure letter writers were free to adapt the letter to their purpose. One can see in Romans 1:1-7 a much longer salutation than was typical of Paul's letters. (Compare that with the salutation of 1 Thessalonians 1:1-2.) The primary expansion occurs in the author's

The Structure of Pauline Letters

	Romans	1 Cor.	2 Cor.	Gal.	Phil.
Salutation					
a. author	1:1	1:1	1:1	1:1-2	1:1
b. addressee	1:7	1:2	1:1	1:2	1:1
c. greeting	1:7*b*	1:3	1:2	1:3	1:2
Thanksgiving	1:8-17	1:4-9	1:3-7	none	1:3-11
Body	1:18—11:36	1:10—4:21	1:8—13:10	1:6—4:31	1:12—4:1
Ethical Instructions	12:1—15:13	5:1—16:12	13:11	5:1—6:10	4:2-6
Closing					
a. greetings	16:3-16	16:19-21	13:12	none	4:21-22
b. doxology	16:25-27	none	none	none	4:20
c. benediction	16:20	16:23	13:13	6:18	4:22

name. Rather than simply naming himself, Paul describes himself with a brief summary of the gospel. This fits very well with the crucial role played by the gospel in the Book of Romans.

We can see perhaps the greatest freedom in adapting the basic structure of a genre in the Book of Revelation. Most scholars believe the basic genre of Revelation is **apocalyptic.** Apocalyptic literature made use of visions, symbols, and journeys through heaven to paint a picture of either God's coming judgment on the enemies of God's people or of God's coming salvation of His people. Some apocalyptic literature portrays both judgment and salvation. It is easy to observe the characteristics of Revelation that suggest its genre is apocalyptic.

However, the author of Revelation also describes the book as prophecy and has constructed it so that it has many of the structures of a letter. Thus the author of Revelation has freely adapted three different genres in con-

structing the book. Though most scholars believe apocalyptic is the primary genre, some simply conclude Revelation is a mixed genre book. In terms of understanding Revelation, we need to keep all three genres in mind and note the ways in which the author both follows and departs from the basic structures of each genre.

Representative Literary Forms in the New Testament

The literary forms of individual paragraphs of the New Testament are usually genre specific. That is, certain forms are used in a particular genre while others are used in different genre. Thus it is best to describe the forms in reference to the genre in which they are used.

Literary Forms Commonly Used in the Gospels

A variety of literary forms are used in the Gospels. Some are quite brief and can be classified together simply as sayings. Others are actually brief narratives in their own right.

Sayings

A number of sayings of Jesus appear in the Gospels. These sayings are short, usually one-line statements that can stand alone or could be spoken in several different contexts. The **proverbs or wisdom sayings** are open-ended. They require the listener to think through the fact that they can be applied in either a universal way or in many ways. Jesus' statements, "Many who are first will be last, and many who are last will be first," found in Matthew 19:30, and "Those who want to save their life will lose it," found in Mark 8:35, are examples of wisdom sayings.

Legal sayings are sayings that pronounce the law of the kingdom or describe ministry principles. Examples of legal sayings are: "Laborers deserve their food" (Matthew 10:10); "If anyone will not welcome you or listen to your words, shake off the dust from your feet as you leave that house or town" (v. 14); and "Truly I tell you, whatever you bind on earth will be bound in heaven, and whatever you loose on earth will be loosed in heaven" (18:18).

Prophetic sayings are sayings that announce the coming of either salvation or judgment. A double example is found in Matthew 24:40-41, "Two will be in the field; one will be taken and one will be left. Two women will be grinding meal together; one will be taken and one will be left."

Some of the sayings of Jesus are so embedded in stories about Jesus that the story is necessary to get the point of the saying. These stories are often called **pronouncement stories.** The saying usually comes at or near the end of the story. To correctly interpret the story one must focus on the saying rather than on the details of the story. Those details are only told in the Gospel to make sure the closing saying has the impact it needs. An example of a pronouncement story is the account found in Mark 2:23-28 of Jesus' disciples plucking grain in the field on the Sabbath and eating it, only to be challenged by the Pharisees. The point of this pronouncement story is the saying of Jesus that concludes it, "The Sabbath was made for man, not man for the Sabbath. So the Son of Man is Lord even of the Sabbath" (v. 28, NIV).

Parables

Many of the teachings of Jesus found in the Gospels are found in one of the **parable** forms. Jesus' parables are expansions of a central figure of speech, usually either a simile or a metaphor. They make use of common truths or ordinary circumstances of life that are easily understood, though some parables work by catching the listener off guard. Scholars usually describe Jesus' parables using four categories.

The **similitude** is an extended simile. Most of the similitudes were Kingdom parables and began, "The kingdom of God is like . . ." They appeal to a common truth, and once the listener is willing to consider the comparison, the teaching point has been successfully made. A good example is the similitude of the mustard seed. The form found in Mark 4:30 begins with a question, "With what can we compare the kingdom of God, or what parable will we use for it? It is like a mustard seed, which, when sown upon the ground, is the smallest of all the seeds on earth; yet when it is sown it grows up and becomes the greatest of all shrubs." The commonly known truth was that the mustard seed was the smallest seed in general use in Palestine in Jesus' time. However, in contrast to its small beginning the mustard seed produced one of the largest bushes commonly found in Palestinian gardens. The point of comparison is the small beginning—great result. If one will admit that the kingdom of God is like a mustard seed, then it is clear that the kingdom of God will begin in a small and inconspicuous way. However, its final outcome will be great and worthy of notice.

A second type of parable is often called a **parable proper.** It usually begins with a phrase like, "A certain person . . ." Similitudes appeal to general truth—every mustard seed is small. A parable proper gives a specific person for a point of comparison and tells a story. Often the parable proper begins in a very real-to-life way, but just as the listener has entered into the story and identified with the main character, Jesus introduces a very unusual twist to the story. This would drive home the point He was trying to teach. The parable of the workers in the vineyard found in Matthew 20:1-15 is a parable proper. It describes a landowner coming to the village square at various hours of the day to hire workers for his vineyard. He negotiates a wage for the first group that was the common day's wage of that era. He tells the second group he will pay them what is fair and no further mention is made of the wages until the parable reaches its conclusion at the end of the day. The owner tells his

manager to pay everyone the same full day's wage but to begin by paying those who only worked one hour.

Naturally when those who worked all day saw the owner's generosity to those who worked only one hour, they expected a huge bonus but also received a full day's pay. When they complained, the owner responded that they had received what they agreed upon and that it was the fair wage for a day's work. He also pointed out that since it was his money he was free to be generous to some who had worked less. This parable is often disturbing to those who think they can earn the favor of God, but it effectively teaches that God is gracious in surprising ways that may have nothing to do with what we have done.

An **example story** is a parable that clearly focuses on an expected response from the listener. The best known example story is the parable of the Good Samaritan found in Luke 10:29-37. The parable begins in a very typical, real-to-life way by describing a traveler between Jerusalem and Jericho who was attacked by thieves, robbed, beaten, and left for dead. Though a priest and Levite passed by without helping, a traveling Samaritan had mercy on the injured man and went to great risk and expense to help him. Though Jesus' Jewish listeners generally hated Samaritans because of their religious and ethnic differences from the Jews, the parable forced those listeners to admit that the Samaritan of the parable was the one whose behavior they should emulate.

A fourth type of parable is the **allegory.** Allegories are extended metaphors with several points of comparison. An allegory is a message in code about another subject, usually a theological truth. The parable of the sower found in Mark 4:1-9 is presented by Mark as an allegory. The seed, the sower, and each type of soil is compared to a spiritual or theological matter. The seed is the word of God, the sower is Jesus (or some other preacher), the seed falling on the path and picked up by birds stands for people who hear the word of God but Satan snatches the truth away before it can take root in them, and so on. Allegories have been used very effectively for centuries to teach basic moral and doctrinal truths.

The parables illustrate the power of the world within the text. Parables appeal to the listener's imagination and enable the listener to enter a world created by the parable. There the listener is able to see truths and to make responses that he or she might not make if left to simply consider the matter from the standpoint of logic or argument. The world within the text is a place that allows the reader or listener to participate in the story without understanding or even thinking about the world behind the text, the historical background.

Literary Forms Commonly Used in Letters

Because letters are direct communication and dialogical rather than indirect like narratives, letters often will use forms different from those found in narratives. In some instances, however, letters will use a similar form in a very different way.

One of the common forms found in letters is a **list**. Some

lists are of virtues or vices. Colossians 3:12-14 contains a list of virtues, while Colossians 3:5-8 contains a list of vices. Characteristically, the reader is urged to put on the virtues and to put off the vices. The lists of virtues and vices was a common form for moral and ethical teaching in the Greco-Roman world. The apostle Paul also used a list of circumstances in several passages in 2 Corinthians 11 and 12. Another particular form is sometimes called a list of rules for behavior. These lists are also called **household codes.** Examples can be found in Ephesians 5:21—6:9; Colossians 3:18—4:1; 1 Peter 2:13—3:7; and 1 Timothy 2:1-15. These codes describe the expected behaviors of husbands and wives, parents and children, and masters and slaves. Such household codes were also common teaching tools in the Greco-Roman world.

In some ways **word chains** are similar to lists. However, word chains are a list of concepts linked together in order to produce a movement toward a climax. These word chains are created for rhetorical effect to persuade the reader or listener. An example can be found in Romans 5:3-5, which links suffering, endurance, character, and hope together to a climactic conclusion that hope does not disappoint. A similar word chain appears in 2 Peter 1:5-7.

The **diatribe** is a common form used in Paul's letters. Diatribes are rhetorical questions that anticipate objections of the reader or listener and give voice to those objections. This enables the author to answer the objection. The diatribe draws the reader or listener into the argument but shapes the argument in ways the author wishes to have it shaped. The diatribe creates a world within the text into which the reader or listener enters to have his or her questions answered.

Hymns are a literary form found in both letters and narratives of the New Testament. The opening two chapters of Luke are the primary location in the Gospel narratives where hymns are used. There they appear on the lips of key characters, and the story narrates the characters singing the hymn. In this way the characters articulate truths about God the author wishes to communicate.

In the letters hymns are simply quoted by the author, and it may be difficult to recognize the hymn as a distinct composition from the rest of the letter. It is only the formal characteristics of poetry and unusual style that reveals the hymns. The author of the letter seems to expect the readers or listeners to recognize the hymn. Thus the hymn is a message already shared by both author and audience. In this way the author of the letter invites the readers or listeners into a shared world within the text, the world created by a hymn already known and loved.

The World in Front of the Text

The study of the world in front of the text is the study of the way readers create meaning from the text. It deals with the ways in which the message of the text is recognized and appropriated by contemporary readers. Thus the world in front of the text focuses on the role of the reader and on the theological and practical applications that contemporary readers draw from the text.

■ The Role of the Reader

The process of hermeneutics has long recognized the role of the author in creating the meaning he or she intended to invest in a text. The role of the text as the vehicle by which meaning is carried and communicated has also long been recognized. The role of the reader has not received equal attention in hermeneutics, though that lack has been somewhat remedied in recent decades. Authors may produce texts. But the text produced by authors never communicates without readers or listeners. An author may send a message through a text, but unless a reader or listener receives the message from the text, no communication takes place. The world of the author and the world of the reader meet in the text to produce meaning.

This does not mean that the reader can create any meaning he or she desires from the text. The way in which the author shapes the text clearly rejects many meanings a reader might like to impose on a text. However, a wise author recognizes that the process of communication will not be complete until the reader or listener has encountered the text and taken meaning from it. The wise author writes in such a way as to influence the meaning the reader will encounter in and take from the text.

One of the realities of communication is that the sender (author or speaker) can never completely control the meaning that the receiver (reader or listener) will receive. Language itself and texts in particular will always have certain "gaps" in meaning. For example, when Paul writes of "the love of God" being poured into our hearts in Romans 5:5, are we to understand the "love of God" to mean the love we have for God or the love God has for us? This is an example of a *grammatical gap*. English does not (nor does Greek) answer the question of which way we are to understand "the love of God." But a reader will fill in that gap by determining which way to understand the phrase. That action of the reader may happen instinctively, or it may require conscious thought. The author may try to control the result by the context or may instinctively trust the reader to arrive at the correct understanding.

Grammatical gaps are usually easily resolved. *Literary or poetic gaps* may be more difficult for the reader or listener to resolve. James 1:13 states, "For God cannot be tempted by evil and he himself tempts no one." Should the reader add the words "with evil" to the final phrase? This is a poetic or literary gap. The author may have purposely created this gap to engage the reader in thinking about the role of God and temptation. The use of literary devices such as simile, hyperbole, and metaphor create literary gaps. The reader must determine the point of comparison for the communication to be successful. When Matthew quotes Jesus' saying, "You are the salt of the earth, . . . you are the light of the world" (Matthew 5:13-14), he requires the reader to determine the significance of the metaphors salt and light.

It should be clear that the closer the world of the author and the world of the reader are to each other, the more likely the reader will be to successfully close the gaps in the text. Likewise, it should be clear that the reader's presuppositions will play an important role in determining the way in which he or she closes the gaps in the text. The presuppositions or assumptions that a reader brings to a text become filters that allow some meanings to pass through the text into the understanding of the reader and causes other meanings to be filtered out. It is possible for a reader to become aware of at least some of his or her presuppositions. When this takes place the reader may then examine, reflect upon, and perhaps modify those presuppositions.

The reader's presuppositions are often held subconsciously. In contrast, one's beliefs are usually conscious. Those beliefs will also function as filters of meaning when reading a text. A person's presuppositions, beliefs, and attitudes constitute an **interpretive framework** that shapes the way a person reads the New Testament.

Part of what the reader brings to the text of the New Testament are theological presuppositions. These theological presuppositions may include a commitment to certain theological conclusions that the reader will find in a text. However, the theological presuppositions of a reader most often function to shape what the reader believes the New Testament to be. Thus when readers believe the New Testament to be the inspired word of God revealing the will of God for all things necessary to salvation, they will read given texts in the New Testament differently from the readers who do not share that presupposition.

Though some academic teachers of the New Testament believe such theological presuppositions about the New Testament should be removed when studying the New Testament academically, it is better to simply seek to recognize one's presuppositions. An academic reading of the New Testament should cause the reader to reflect on his or her theological presuppositions about the text rather than to reject those presuppositions. Reflection on one's theological presuppositions offers the opportunity for new insights that may lead one to modify those theological presuppositions and beliefs. Obviously such modification might reject the presuppositions and beliefs previously held, or it might affirm and strengthen the beliefs and presuppositions with deeper understanding.

■ Theological and Practical Applications of the Text

The reader who presupposes that the New Testament is the Word of God that reveals God's will for salvation will read the New Testament differently from a person who believes the New Testament is simply a collection of religious writings from antiquity. The person who believes the New Testament is the Word of God will interpret the New Testament in ways that are theological and practical for Christian living. How is this world in front of the text created?

First, if one believes that the

Terms Expressing Faith in the Bible as the Word of God

The following terms are often used to express theological presuppositions about the Bible as Word of God:

Revelation—This is the activity of God in making himself known to human beings. It is often discussed under two headings: general revelation (meaning all that God reveals of himself through nature) and special revelation (the specific act of God making himself known through the Bible).

Inspiration—This is the way God accomplished revelation through the Bible. Inspiration describes the activity of God in making the Bible the vehicle of revelation. Inspiration is often discussed in the following terms:

A *dictation view* of inspiration—This is the view that God completely controlled the process of the writing of the Bible by "dictating" every word in it to a human author who functioned as a recording secretary.

A *plenary view* of inspiration—This view affirms that God fully inspired all the Bible but does not describe how that took place.

A *dynamic view* of inspiration—This view affirms that God used the human creativity and natural abilities of the biblical authors to accurately communicate the message He wished to communicate through the Bible.

Inerrancy—This is the view that no errors of any fact or expression occurred in the autographs (first written form) of the biblical books.

Infallibility—This is the view of inspiration that God successfully revealed everything necessary to faith and Christian life through the Bible.

The authority of the Bible—This expresses the confidence that Scripture speaks for God in communicating His will for people.

A prayerful attitude is important when we read the Bible.

theological truth that should be understood from the text. If the text is a hymn of praise to Christ, the reader who believes the New Testament is the Word of God will take the message of that hymn to be the theological truth that is to be understood from the text.

In some instances the text will make direct theological affirmations. First John 4:16 declares that God is love. Leviticus 19 and Isaiah 6 (as well as many other passages) declare that God is holy. Certain texts declare that Jesus is the Messiah, the Son of God, and Lord. Other texts state that the Church is chosen by God to be holy. Once a reader presupposes that the New Testament is an inspired word from God, it is not difficult to derive theological truth from such direct affirmations.

In other instances, particularly in narrative sections, the text creates a world into which the reader imaginatively enters. The understanding that emerges from that encounter with the text will be regarded as theological truth for a reader who believes the New Testament to be the Word of God. For example, Jesus' statement that the kingdom of God is like a mustard seed does not make a direct affirmation about the Kingdom (other than the affirmation that it is like a mustard seed). However, once the reader grasps the point of the similitude that the kingdom of God may have a small beginning and a great conclusion, that insight grasped by imagination is taken as theological truth. Narrative sections of Scripture yield theological understanding by such imaginative acts of reading much more often than by direct affirmation.

In some instances a text will

New Testament is the Word of God, that reader will usually conclude that the theological message communicated by the text is true. Thus theological meaning will be sought through both the world behind the text and the world within the text. Particularly, the literary strategies used by the author of the text are seen as sources of theological understanding. The fact that the author chose the genre of gospel will be taken by the reader who believes the New Testament is the Word of God to mean that the message of that text is good news from God. If the text is a proclamation story, the reader will conclude that the particular saying that is the point of that proclamation story is the

give instructions to the original readers in a way that seems clearly bound by the culture of the author and audience. For example, in 1 Corinthians 11:2-16 Paul carefully argues that a woman should have a veil over her head when she prays and prophesies publicly in the church. Likewise a man should not cover his head when speaking in church. Though a few Christian groups understand this to be a direct affirmation of appropriate dress for men and women in church today, most understand Paul's words to be conditioned by cultural assumptions of his time that are not shared by many modern cultures. In such cases a person who believes the New Testament to be the Word of God does not simply disregard the teaching of this passage. Rather, such a reader seeks to understand an underlying theological principle that led Paul to give the instructions he gave. Rather than regarding the literal instructions of Paul as that which expresses truth for today, the reader will take that underlying principle as the theological truth that applies today and will seek to apply it in the reader's own cultural context.

■ Humility and Grace in Reading the Text

It is often easy for a reader who believes the New Testament to be the inspired Word of God revealing God's will for people's salvation to assume that his or her theological reading of the text is as authoritative as the Scripture itself. The act of discovering theological truth in the text arises from theological presuppositions and beliefs that the reader brings to the text. In many texts it requires an imaginative act of interpretation of literary devices. Such theological interpretation should be done with humility and grace toward those who may not see the same truths in the text. If God is truly revealing himself and His will through the text, then one may trust God to accomplish that through the work of the Holy Spirit and the reading of each reader. God does not need one reader to coerce another reader to reveal truth to that second reader.

Conclusion

If one believes the New Testament to be the Word of God or even a significant religious message, then the reader of the New Testament needs to enter all three worlds discussed in this chapter. The world in front of the text is where meaning ultimately connects to the reader; it cannot be ignored. The world within the text provides the vehicle by which the meaning of the text can be discovered. The world behind the text offers insight into the real-life circumstances in which the text first came into being. There its energy and power was first known.

The serious reader of the New Testament cannot allow himself or herself to live in only one or two of those worlds. One may become skilled enough at reading the New Testament to work at the intersections of those worlds, for they often overlap. However, understanding each and developing skill in working in each is essential to reading the New Testament.

Summary Statements

- The diverse understandings at which people arrive when reading the New Testament means we need a method by which we can read the New Testament and agree on its meaning.
- The world behind the text, which deals with the historical and cultural backgrounds of the New Testament, provides an important framework in which to understand the New Testament.
- The world behind the text helps us understand the New Testament as a real-to-life book.
- The world within the text of the literary characteristics of the New Testament helps us understand the communication strategies used in the New Testament books.
- Readers of the New Testament are important partners with the author and text to allow meaning to emerge from the text.
- The theological presuppositions of the reader shape the ways in which he or she finds theological truth in the New Testament.

Questions for Reflection

1. How have questions you have had about the meaning of the New Testament helped you understand the importance of a method of interpretation?
2. Do you think of the biblical world as a make-believe world or as the real world? How does study of the historical and cultural background help you see the real-world nature of the biblical world?
3. What are some literary forms of the present world that you are familiar with? How does understanding them help you understand the way biblical authors used literary forms?
4. What are your theological presuppositions about the nature of the Bible? How have those presuppositions influenced the way you have understood the Bible?

Resources for Further Study

Bailey, James L., and Lyle D. Vander Broek. *Literary Forms in the New Testament: A Handbook.* Louisville, Ky.: Westminster/John Knox Press, 1992.

Dyck, Elmer, ed. *The Act of Bible Reading: A Multi-disciplinary Approach to Biblical Interpretation.* Downers Grove, Ill.: InterVarsity Press, 1996.

Fee, Gordon D., and Douglas Stuart. *How to Read the Bible for All Its Worth.* 2nd ed. Grand Rapids: Zondervan Publishing House, 1993.

Green, Joel B., ed. *Hearing the New Testament: Strategies for Interpretation.* Grand Rapids: William B. Eerdmans Publishing Company, 1995.

Hauer, Christian E., and William A. Young. *An Introduction to the Bible: A Journey into Three Worlds.* 3rd ed. Englewood Cliffs, N.J.: Prentice-Hall, 1993.

Tate, W. Randolph. *Biblical Interpretation: An Integrated Approach.* Rev. ed. Peabody, Mass.: Hendrickson Publishers, 1996.

Tuckett, Christopher. *Reading the New Testament: Methods of Interpretation.* Philadelphia: Fortress Press, 1987.

3 The World of the New Testament

Objectives:

Your study of this chapter should help you to:

- Describe the political events that culminated in the takeover of Judea by the Roman Empire and the destruction of the Temple in Jerusalem.
- Describe the significance of the Torah, the Temple, the Synagogue, and the Sanhedrin.
- Discuss the theological perspectives of the Sadducees, the Pharisees, and the Essenes.

Questions to consider as you read:

1. What significant political events prepared the way for the advent of Jesus Christ into the world?

2. What are the cultural elements that shaped the Jewish life in the first century A.D.?

3. What are the various theological perspectives that emerged within Judaism during the intertestamental period?

Key Words to Understand

Intertestamental period	Titus
	Domitian
Alexander the Great	Mystery religions
	Torah
Ptolemaic dynasty	Scribes
	Synagogue
Seleucid dynasty	Temple
Septuagint	Priests
Diaspora Jews	Sanhedrin
Hellenization	Sadducees
Hasidim	Pharisees
Mattathias	Shammai
Judas	Hillel
Maccabean war	Oral Law
Hanukkah	Dead Sea Scrolls
Hasmonean dynasty	Essenes
Antipater	Zealots
Herod the Great	Herodians
Herodium	The people of the land
Masada	Samaritans
Vespasian	

Historical Context of the New Testament

The New Testament is the story of the fulfillment of God's redemptive plan through His Son Jesus Christ, and the establishment of a new community of faith that responded to the mission and ministry of Jesus. Paul sums up this perspective most clearly in Galatians 4:4-5: "But when the fullness of time had come, God sent his Son, born of a woman, born under the law, in order to redeem those who were under the law, so that we might receive adoption as children." According to Paul, the coming of Jesus into the world took place at the "fullness of time." Paul seems to think that the time was ripe for the advent of Jesus Christ; God's redemptive plan intersected with world events at the most critical time in the history of humanity. To this critical moment in history, we will now turn.

Toward the end of the fifth century B.C., the history of Israel transitioned to what is traditionally called the **intertestamental period**, the period between the Old Testament and the New Testament. The nation once known as Israel, made up of the 12 tribes of Jacob, no longer existed as a political entity. The Assyrians destroyed the Northern Kingdom in the last part of the eighth century, and the Babylonians exiled the population of the Southern Kingdom to Babylon in the early part of the sixth century. The decline of the Babylonian Empire and its eventual conquest by the Persians opened the door for the exiled Judeans to return home around 538 B.C. and rebuild their Temple and reestablish their worship. What was left of the nation Israel was the remnant of the tribe of Judah. Under the leadership of Ezra and Nehemiah, this community reorganized their life and took on a religious identity as Jews who were committed to a way of life in strict adherence to the Law of Moses. The Law regulated every aspect of their community and religious life. Judaism thus emerged as the religion of Israel in the intertestamental period.

■ Jews Under the Greek Rule

In the second half of the fourth century, Persian strength declined and soon became the target of the young Macedonian king Alexander, who was on his way to conquer the world and establish a world empire. Judah remained a province under the Persian rule until it was incorporated into the Greek Empire by **Alexander the Great** in 333 B.C. Alexander granted freedom to the Jews to continue their religious faith and practice.

The death of Alexander the Great in 323 B.C. changed the fate of the Jews once again. The empire was inherited by Alexander's successors, of which two are important to the history of the Jews in Palestine. Egypt was taken over by general Ptolemy; rulers from the **Ptolemaic dynasty** controlled Egypt for about 300 years. The last of the rulers of this dynasty was Cleopatra, who died in 30 B.C. Syria was annexed to the kingdom of Seleucus, which extended from Mesopotamia to India. Rulers of the **Seleucid dynasty** wanted to control Palestine also, but Ptolemy had already annexed this region to his kingdom. The Seleucid rulers of Syria made several attempts to take over Palestine; their final victory came under the powerful military campaigns of Antiochus III, who defeated the Egyptians in 198 B.C. and made Palestine a part of the Seleucid kingdom.

During the Ptolemaic rule, large numbers of Jews made Egypt their home, and a substantial number settled down in Alexandria and adopted the Greek culture and language. This eventually led to the translation of the Hebrew Scriptures into Greek (the **Septuagint**). Several cities in these Greek kingdoms received Greek names. Greek language and culture rapidly spread throughout these Greek kingdoms, and this region remained under the Hellenistic (Greek) influence for several centuries that followed. The **Diaspora Jews** (those who lived outside of Palestine) who lived in these kingdoms absorbed the Greek culture and language. The Jews in Palestine were also not immune from the Hellenistic influence. Obviously there were some Jews in Palestine who more readily supported the Hellenistic culture than those who were more traditional and conservative in their thinking; the traditionalists wanted to protect their faith and culture from any foreign influence.[1]

Hellenization

The Seleucid rule of Palestine at the beginning proved to be a period of good fortune for the Jews. Antiochus III granted special privileges to them, including a 3-year tax rebate, the right to worship, and assistance to repair damages to the Temple. However, within 23 years, steps were taken by his son Antiochus IV Epiphanes (175-163) to foster Hellenistic culture and religion **(Hellenization)** throughout the kingdom, which brought hardship and persecution upon the Jewish population in Palestine. This program included the worship of Zeus and other Greek gods, and of the emperor himself as the visible manifestation of Zeus. Rivalry and struggle for power among religious leaders, particularly the office of the high priest, only worsened the already deteriorating condition of the Jews. When the Seleucids gained control over Palestine, the ruling high priest was Onias III; however, his brother Jason bribed Antiochus IV and succeeded in gaining control of the high-priestly office. Jason, who was an active supporter of Hellenization, was soon replaced with Menelaus, who offered more money to the king. With the support of Menelaus, Antiochus IV looted the Temple treasury and later sent troops, which massacred many innocent people and built a citadel called Acra and a military garrison within Jerusalem. Jerusalem and the Temple in turn became part of this citadel, a Greek city with total control over Jerusalem and the Jewish Temple. The resistance of the faithful Jews only brought more serious measures from the Greek ruler to suppress any religious freedom to the Jews. He banned the practice of the Jewish religion, including festivals, Sabbath, and circumcision, and an altar to Zeus was set up in the Temple in December 167.

The Maccabean War

Not all Jews responded to Hellenization in the same way. Some were eager to adopt the Hellenistic culture and religion; others unwillingly complied with the royal decree. Still a few passively resisted any compliance with the program of Hellenization, which resulted in cruel acts of reprisal from the Greek soldiers, including the murder of many Jews.

This last group, comprised of loyal and pious Jews **(Hasidim)**, strived to maintain their traditional faith in the midst of growing and intense persecution. The first act of open rebellion against Antiochus's decree took place at Modein, a village located 20 miles northwest of Jerusalem. When the Greek soldiers came to the village and demanded **Mattathias,** a local priest, to officiate a pagan sacrifice, he refused. When another Jew agreed to carry out the ritual, Mattathias cut down both the apostate Jew and the soldier who brought the royal decree. He and his sons (John, Simon, Judas, Eleazer, and Jonathan) fled to the nearby hills where other loyal Jews joined the freedom fighters. The group carried out guerrilla war against the Greek army and took actions to preserve the Jewish law and customs as they marched against the enemy. A year later, Mattathias died and **Judas,** also known by a nickname (Maccabeus, meaning "the hammer"), assumed the leadership of the movement. The struggle for freedom came to be known as the **Maccabean war,** after its prominent leader. Judas and his soldiers successfully defeated various Greek army contingents that tried to stop them as they marched toward Jerusalem. He and his supporters finally arrived at the citadel town of Acra and removed all the pagan objects from the Temple area, cleansed the Temple, and erected a new altar and rededicated the Temple in December 164. The Jewish festival **Hanukkah** commemorates the Maccabean victory over the Greek army and the Temple dedication.

■ Hasmonean Dynasty

The Maccabean war was also a war against the pro-Hellenists, those Jews who were supporters and promoters of Hellenization. The war continued even after the recapture of Jerusalem in 164 to drive out the Greek army from the surrounding areas of Jerusalem and to destroy the pro-Hellenistic Jews. In the continuing battle, Eleazer and Judas were killed. John was killed by a marauding tribe on the way to Nabatea. Jonathan, who became high priest and governor (161-143), was killed by the Greek army while he was on a mission of diplomacy. Thus, in the end, of the five sons of Mattathias, only Simon survived. He was able to unify the nation and secure complete freedom for the Jews from the Greek power (142-134). This marks the beginning of the **Hasmonean dynasty** (named after Hasmon, the great-grandfather of Mattathias), the independent Jewish kingdom that ruled Judah from 142 to 63 B.C. Simon became the high priest, commander in chief, and governor of the Jews. He entered into a treaty with Rome, which brought the Jewish state under the protection of Rome.

The story of the Hasmonean dynasty is filled with internal rivalry and struggle for power among its members. The political ambitions and power struggle in the ruling family brought discontentment among the loyal and pious Jews, who separated themselves into the Pharisaic movement as guardians and promoters of the Mosaic Law. Other devout Jews left the Jerusalem area to establish for themselves a strict religious community in the wilderness (Essenes). The priestly group who supported the Hasmoneans became the Sadducees. We will discuss more in detail the significance of these and other religious groups within Judaism later in this chapter.

Simon's son-in-law murdered him in an attempt to seize power; however, the throne went to John Hyrcanus, Simon's son (134-104 B.C.). Hyrcanus was a powerful ruler who annexed Samaria and Edom into the kingdom; he also forced the Edomites to accept the Jewish religion. After Hyrcanus's death, his son Aristobulus succeeded him; he ruled only for one year (104-103 B.C.). Though he designated his wife Salome Alexandra to succeed him, she married her husband's brother Alexander Jannaeus, who in turn became ruler and high priest (103-76 B.C.). During his reign, he ordered the death of a large number of his political opponents, including many Pharisees. Following his death, Alexandra ruled the kingdom for about nine years (76-67 B.C.). Her son John Hyrcanus II, who became high priest, followed a path of reconciliation and religious reformation. However, after her death, civil war broke out between the supporters of her sons Aristobulus II and Hyrcanus II, each group vying for power. Aristobulus II, who was commander of the military, finally gained power, and Hyrcanus II escaped to Petra where he allied himself with the king of Petra and **Antipater**, governor of Idumea (Edomite territory). Both brothers sought the support of Rome, which was establishing its firm control over the Syria-Palestine region. Though Rome initially supported Aristobulus II, later when Pompey took control of Judea, he placed Hyrcanus II in power and appointed him as high priest and ethnarch of Judea, subject to the authority of the Roman governor of Syria (63-40 B.C.). The independent Jewish state thus came to an end, with Judah being made a part of the expanding Roman Empire in 63 B.C.

■ Jews Under the Roman/ Herodian Rule

As a part of the Roman province of Syria, Judea lost control over Samaria and other neighboring areas annexed to the Jewish kingdom by the Hasmonean rulers. Though Hyrcanus was the appointed ruler of the Jews, the real power behind the throne was Antipater, the governor of Idumea. Both Hyrcanus II and Antipater submitted to the authority of Julius Caesar when he defeated Pompey. In return, Caesar appointed Antipater as procurator of Judea. Caesar was assassinated in 44 B.C. and a year later Antipater was poisoned. At Philippi, the forces of Octavian and Antony defeated the anti-Caesar forces led by Brutus and Cassius in 42 B.C. Antony, who came to have control over the eastern part of the empire, appointed Antipater's sons Phasael and Herod as joint rulers of Judea. Two years later, the Parthians gained control of Judea and placed Antigonus, the son of the Hasmonean king Aristobulus II, as priest king over the Jews. Phasael was killed and Herod escaped to Rome, where he was confirmed as king of Judea by the Roman senate in 37 B.C. With the help of Antony's army, Herod recaptured Judea in 37 B.C. His loyalty to Antony quickly changed when Octavian (Caesar Augustus) defeated

Remains of Herod's palace at Caesarea.

cho. The family of the boy knew well who was responsible for this accident. Later, he killed his wife Mariamne on charges of infidelity. Alexandra, who brought charges of crime against Herod, was the next one to be killed. He ordered the execution of his two sons by Mariamne, on suspicion of plotting against him. His victims included even some of his closest friends, whom he suspected of disloyalty.

Herod's legacy as a master builder can be seen even today in Israel. Early in his reign, he rebuilt the Hasmonean fortress northwest of the Jerusalem Temple and renamed it Antonia in honor of Antony, his friend and patron. Other well-known Herodian fortresses include **Herodium** in Bethlehem and **Masada** in the far south of the land. Herodium was built to be his burial place, but no one knows today where he was actually buried. Masada, the impenetrable fortress, was built as a place of escape in case of a treacherous plot against his life. He rebuilt Samaria and renamed it Sebaste in honor of Augustus. He undertook the building of numerous cities, the most important of which is the city of Caesarea on the Mediterranean coast, the later Roman capital of the Roman Palestine. His palaces include a summer palace at Jericho and his royal residence in Jerusalem. His most calculated attempt to win the favor of the Jews was the restoration of the Temple, which he began in 19 B.C. It took 10 years to complete the initial work of reconstruction. The restoration work continued until A.D. 64, long after the death of Herod. Six years later, in A.D. 70, the Romans destroyed this magnificent structure.

Antony at the battle of Actium in 31 B.C. At a meeting called by Augustus, Herod gave assurance of his loyalty to the emperor and remained loyal to him throughout his reign. In return for his assurance of loyalty, Herod received from the emperor not only the kingdom but also a number of cities on the Mediterranean coastal area and on both sides of the Jordan River.

■ Herod the Great

Herod the Great was a skillful and cunning diplomat, a military strategist, and a ruthless and murderous ruler. He was an Idumean (Edomite) by birth but Jewish in religious identity. He was Greek in culture but thoroughly loyal to Rome in politics. His actions were calculated to win the support of loyalty from his subjects, but he did not hesitate to kill anyone who stood in his way of securing his power. He married Mariamne, the daughter of Alexandra and the granddaughter of Hyrcanus II. Though he appointed Mariamne's brother, the 17-year-old Aristobulus III, as high priest at the insistence of Alexandra, a few months later the boy priest was drowned in Herod's swimming pool at Jeri-

Masada. Herod built this fortress and his palace as a place of escape.

For a while, it seemed that Antipater, Herod's son by Doris, his first wife whom he divorced to marry Mariamne, was going to inherit the throne after his father's death. However, Herod became jealous of Antipater and named Antipas, his youngest son by a Samaritan woman, to be heir to the throne. A few days before his death in March 4 B.C., he ordered the execution of Antipater and named as his successors Antipas and Archelaus, sons by his Samaritan wife, and Philip, son by another woman from Jerusalem. Antipas (4 B.C. to A.D. 39) received the region of Galilee and Perea; Archelaus (4 B.C. to A.D. 6) received the region of Judea and Samaria; and Philip (4 B.C. to A.D. 34) received the territory east and northeast of the sea of Galilee. Philip rebuilt Paneas and renamed it Caesarea Philippi, in honor of himself and Caesar. He also rebuilt Bethsaida on the northeast part of the Sea of Galilee and named it Julias in honor of Augustus's daughter. A few years after his death, Caligula gave his territory to Herod Agrippa I, grandson of Herod the Great (A.D. 37).

Herodian Kingdom.

Roman Emperors Connected to the New Testament History

Augustus (27 B.C.—A.D. 14)—the birth of Jesus
Tiberius (A.D. 14-37)—the ministry of Jesus
Caligula (A.D. 37-41)—demanded emperor worship
Claudius (A.D. 41-54)—expelled Jews from Rome
Nero (A.D. 54-68)—persecution of Christians; martyrdom of Peter and Paul
Vespasian (A.D. 69-79)—Jewish revolt and the destruction of Jerusalem, which was carried
        out by his son Titus
Domitian (A.D. 81-96)—persecution of Christians; John the apostle exiled to Patmos

Rome removed Archelaus after 10 years because of his ruthless activities and placed Idumea, Judea, and Samaria under the administration of governors/procurators who were responsible for keeping peace and order and collecting taxes. Three such officials are important to the New Testament story: Pilate (A.D. 26-36); Felix (A.D. 52-60); Festus (A.D. 60-62). Rome banished Antipas because of his insubordination and placed the region of Galilee under the rule of Herod Agrippa I in A.D. 39. Later, in A.D. 41, the region of Judea and Samaria was added to his territory, which he governed until A.D. 44. Agrippa I thus had control over the whole region that was once ruled by Herod the Great. Agrippa I ordered the death of James the son of Zebedee, one of the 12 apostles. He also put Peter in prison, to show his positive attitude toward the Jews (see Acts 12:1-4). After his death in A.D. 44 (see Acts 12:21-23), his young son Herod Agrippa II was named the ruler of his father's territory. Paul appeared before this king while he was in Roman custody in Caesarea (Acts 25:13—26:32).

Roman Governors of Judea (A.D. 6-66)

A.D. 6-9	Coponius
A.D. 9-12	Marcus Ambibulus
A.D. 12-15	Annius Rufus
A.D. 15-26	Valerius Gratus
A.D. 26-36	Pontius Pilate
A.D. 36-37	Marcellus
A.D. 37-41	Marullus

(Judea and Samaria under the kingship of Herod Agrippa I from A.D. 41 to 44)

A.D. 44-46	Cuspius Fadus
A.D. 46-48	Tiberius Alexander
A.D. 48-52	Ventidius Cumanus
A.D. 52-60	Felix
A.D. 60-62	Festus
A.D. 62-64	Albinus
A.D. 64-66	Florus

The Jewish Revolt

Judea was under the rule of 14 governors between A.D. 6 and 66. By and large, these governors were inept administrators who ruled Judea with a heavy hand and were cruel to anyone who opposed their rule. The Jewish population became more and more resentful of the corruption of the governors. Meanwhile, a nationalistic spirit flared up in the land under the leadership of a revolutionary leader named Judas the Galilean. The group he led, known as the Zealots, aimed to establish peace in the land by overthrowing Roman domination. Felix, before whom Paul stood trial, responded to the Zealots with harsh measures, which added more fuel to the anti-Roman sentiment in the land. Albinus was recalled by Rome because of his mistreatment of innocent people. A riot broke out in Jerusalem when governor Florus robbed the Temple and imprisoned a Jewish delegation that went to plead with him. The riot intensified in Jerusalem, and rebellion spread throughout the land. Nero sent **Vespasian** to restore order in Judea. Vespasian sent his son Titus to bring reinforcement from Egypt. The attack against the Zealots in Galilee resulted in the mass suicide of Galileans in the fortress city of Gamla. Vespasian moved to Jerusalem and besieged the city. Within the city itself there was fierce fighting between the extremely fanatical and violent groups of Sicarii and Zealots and the moderate groups who wanted to make peace with Rome. Meanwhile, Vespasian became emperor and he assigned the military campaign against Jerusalem to **Titus.** The army entered the city in A.D. 70, and in the battle that followed, mass destruction and death occurred, including the destruction of the Temple, the renovation of which was completed in A.D. 64. Several thousand Jews were killed during this battle with Rome. Romans continued their campaign against the Zealots and followed them to Masada, the fortress built by Herod the Great, where the Zealots took refuge

from the enemy. After a three-year siege, the Roman army finally broke the walls of the fortress (A.D. 73), only to find dead bodies of the freedom fighters, who took their own lives rather than surrendering or being killed by the enemy.[2] Jewish leadership relocated to the Mediterranean coastal town of Jamnia, which became an important center of Jewish learning and literary activity. Another major outbreak of violence took place when Emperor Hadrian built a temple to Jupiter at the site where the Jewish Temple once stood (A.D. 132-135). Bar Kochba, a self-proclaimed messianic leader, led this rebellion. The Roman army crushed this rebellion by killing thousands of Jews and rebuilding Jerusalem as a Roman colony with the name Aelia Capitolina (A.D. 135). Rome prohibited Jews from entering this newly established city, which became mostly a camp for the Roman army.

Religious Context

■ Pagan Religious World

Christianity was born in the Greco-Roman religious world, and more specifically in the context of first-century Judaism. The influence of Greek culture and religion contributed to an assimilation of the Roman gods and goddesses into the Greek pantheon.[3] Subsequently, for every Roman god/goddess, there was a Greek counterpart. Throughout the Roman Empire, there were temples built to the worship of the Greco-Roman deities. By the time of Christ, there was less interest in worshiping these deities largely because they were not held in equal importance throughout the empire. Rather, they had become objects of local cults in cities in which they were worshiped as patron gods/goddesses. Along with the growth of the Roman Empire, the idea the emperors possessed divine powers also emerged, which in turn led to their deification and the imperial cult. The Roman Senate ascribed divinity to the emperors after their death since the time of Augustus. Some of them (Caligula, Nero, and Domitian) claimed divine status while they were alive. Caligula demanded that his statue be erected in the Jewish Temple in Jerusalem, though this order was not carried out. **Domitian** was the first to enforce emperor worship, an act that was unacceptable to the monotheistic faith of both Jews and Christians. The claims of the emperor made sense to the Greco-Roman culture in which the idea of many gods was a commonly held religious view, and the Roman citizens counted it as their religious duty to worship the emperor as a sign of their loyalty to the state. For Christians, this show of patriotism to the state was a direct violation of their allegiance to Christ, who alone is Lord and Savior of the world.

The Greco-Roman culture also had its share of popular Greek, Egyptian, and Oriental **mystery religions**. This included the cult of Cybele, the Great Mother (Asia), the cult of Isis and Osiris (Egypt), the cult of Mithra (Persia), and many other local cults. These cults offered purification and immortality of the soul to its adherents. Each cult centered on the myth of a god/goddess who died and was later resuscitated. Rituals included secret initiations, ceremonial washing, blood sprinkling, sacramental meals, intoxication, and ritualistic union of worshipers with the deity. These religions offered equal status to people of all levels of society, which attracted both rich and poor to these cults.

Magic and other forms of superstitious practices were also common in the Greco-Roman culture. People consulted horoscopes and used other omens to predict the future. Such practices go back to the ancient Mesopotamians, who had developed an elaborate collection of omen-related literature. Exorcism by the use of magical formulas was a trade practiced by professionals who were skilled in casting out demons. Both Jews and non-Jews were attracted to these practices. Some think that Jews were more attracted to these magical rites than their pagan neighbors. Astrology was also popular in the first-century Roman Empire. Astrologers kept a careful record of the movement of the planets, which they consulted to ascertain the time of birth and destiny of people.

■ Jewish Religious Context

Judaism was a popular religion in the Greco-Roman world. Though always associated with Palestine, the place of its origin, Jewish religion infiltrated the Greco-Roman world through Jews who, for some reason or other, settled down outside of their homeland. These Diaspora Jews were primarily responsible for the growth of Judaism beyond the borders of Palestine.

By the middle of the second century, various theological perspectives emerged in Judaism, though the Law of Moses guided

Ruins of a fourth-century A.D. synagogue at Capernaum.

the everyday life of the Jews. The Law (the **Torah**) here is much more than the five books of Moses; rather, it is the whole will of God, the content of God's revelation that required Jews to live in submission to the commandments of God. The Torah provided the necessary guidelines for Jewish life and conduct. This significant place of the Law in the lives of the Jews accounts for the origin of the **scribes** *(Sopherim),* Jewish scholars who were the authoritative interpreters of the Law. In the early part of the intertestamental period, the priests carried out this task. Later, however, laypeople also became trained as scholars, who not only interpreted the Law but also had the task of copying and preserving the sacred Scriptures.

The center of the study and teaching of the Torah was the **synagogue.** It is likely that the custom of people meeting together to read and study the Torah originated in Babylon during the exilic period. During the intertes-tamental period, the synagogue became an established religious institution in Palestine. The synagogue (meaning "assembly") became the center of Jewish life throughout the Greco-Roman world; this institution served not only as a center for religious education but also a place of prayer and worship. A typical synagogue service included the recital of the Shema (Deuteronomy 6:4-9; 11:13-21; Numbers 15:37-41), prayer, singing of psalms, reading from the Law and the Prophets, a sermon, and a benediction. The synagogue consisted of a rectangular auditorium with a raised platform for speakers. The portable shrine containing the scrolls was located behind the platform. The ruler of the synagogue presided over the service and introduced visitors. The synagogue attendant was in charge of the scrolls, lamps, trumpets, and announcements. In addition to its religious function, the synagogue was also the center of the Jewish social, educational, and political life.

The Temple united all the various sectarian movements in Judaism.

The **Temple** remained the center for sacrificial worship in first-century Palestine until the Romans destroyed it in A.D. 70. The first-century Jewish Temple was a magnificent structure, surrounded by courts and colonnades. The Court of Gentiles was a clearly marked area with specific instructions for worshipers not to cross over into the Inner Court. The Inner Court included separate areas for the Israelites proper (men) and women. Within the Inner Court was the Court of the Priests, at the center of which stood the Temple. The altar of burnt offering was located just outside of the Temple. The Temple included the outer room (the holy place with its furnishings) and the holy of holies, the innermost and the most sacred sanctuary. A veil separated the holy place from the holy of holies. Private and public offerings and sacrifices were made at the Temple daily, weekly, and on special days such as the Day of Atonement. Songs by the Levitical choir accompanied by musical instruments, priestly prayers and benedictions, and the blowing of trumpets were regular parts of the ceremonies at the Temple.

Multitudes of **priests** from several priestly families took turns officiating in the Temple rituals. By law, they all had to be descendants of Aaron. At the head of the priests was the high priest, who exercised very high authority over the Jewish people. He was the representative of the nation with whom political powers negotiated and made their treaties. It is likely that in the first century, the high priest also presided over the Sanhedrin, the highest judicial court of the Jews. High priests came from wealthy and aristocratic families. In the Greek period and during the Hasmonean period, this office was the most coveted office in the land due to the power that was vested in the high priest. The influence of the high priest continued until the destruction of the Temple in A.D. 70.

The **Sanhedrin,** the Jewish supreme court, handled all religious violations and breaking of the rules of the Torah. Since the Torah was the rule for both religious and civil life, there was no distinction made between civil and religious crimes. The Sanhedrin thus controlled every aspect of Jewish life. The Roman government recognized the authority of the Sanhedrin over the affairs of the Jewish people, and it intervened to exercise the Roman law only on matters of capital offenses, such as violation of the Roman law and treason against the empire.

■ Jewish Religious Groups

We have noted earlier that in the Greek period, Judaism ceased to exist as a homogenous religious group. Within Judaism, there were those who were pro-Hellenists who were not only politically subservient to foreign

Jewish Religious Festivals

In addition to daily and weekly services, various religious feasts and festivals also played a significant role in the religious life of the Jews. The following is a summary of the key religious festivals, some prescribed by the Law of Moses and some established by later Judaism. These festivals also followed the religious calendar of Judaism. Pilgrims from throughout Palestine and from the Diaspora lands came to Jerusalem to participate in the three major festivals: Passover, Pentecost, and Tabernacles.

Passover and Unleavened Bread (observed during the month of Nisan/March-April) commemorated Israel's deliverance from Egypt. This festival also marked the beginning of wheat harvest. Seven weeks after the Passover came Pentecost or the Feast of Weeks, celebrated in commemoration of the giving of the Law at Sinai. This "50th day" event also marked the end of the wheat harvest (month of Sivan/May-June). The Jewish New Year or the Feast of Trumpets (Rosh Hashanah) was on Tishri 1 and 2 (September-October), which marked the beginning of the civil year and the end of the fruit harvest season. Eight days after the New Year came the Day of Atonement or Yom Kippur, the national day of repentance and fasting. The Feast of Tabernacles or Booths also was celebrated during the month of Tishri, in commemoration of Israel's tent dwelling days during their wilderness journey. To these religious days prescribed by the Law, Jews also added the festival of Hanukkah or Lights to commemorate the cleansing and rededication of the Temple at the end of the Maccabean war (25th of Kislev/December), and Purim to celebrate the deliverance of Jews from the plot of Haman during the Persian period (14th and 15th of Adar/February-March).

rule but also willing to accommodate their religious faith to show their loyalty to those who dominated them. The Hebraic Jews, on the other hand, strove to remain religiously conservative and loyal to the traditions of their faith. Hellenistic culture perhaps changed the religious perspectives of the Diaspora Jews more significantly than those of the pro-Hellenistic group within Palestine. However, we find divergent theological developments and the rise of various sectarian movements within Palestine itself, which served as the theological context in which Christianity was born in the first century. We shall now briefly survey the key religious groups that dominated the religious scene of first-century Palestine.

Sadducees

The **Sadducees** were considered to be the priestly aristocracy in Jerusalem, made up of families that controlled much wealth and power in the land of Palestine. Though no one clearly knows the origin of this name, one view is that the name originated from the Zadokites, the priestly group that claimed to be the legitimate successor of Zadok, the high priest of Solomon, and the Aaronic priesthood in Israel. Not much is known about the Sadducees because we have no literature available to us from them. Some trace their origin to the second century B.C. during the period of John Hyrcanus, the Hasmonean ruler (135-104 B.C.). According to Josephus, Hyrcanus favored the Sadducees, who taught that the people should observe only those rules that are in the written word and reject those practices that derived from the traditions of the ancestors.[4] Since the Torah and the rules and regulations that governed the Temple shaped their theological perspective, they considered only the Books of Moses (the Pentateuch) as their central authority. They interpreted the Law literally and considered the Temple and the sacrificial system as the fulfillment of God's faithful promises to Israel. They maintained the view that Israel's destiny in the world as God's chosen people is fulfilled through the Temple and its rituals. Though they did not reject the Prophets and the Writings (the rest of the Hebrew Scriptures), they did not regard them as authoritative. They rejected religious ideas not found in the Law, which include concepts such as resurrection, angels, demons, future reward, and apocalyptic thought that emerged in the pre-Christian period. Since their power and prestige was centered on the Temple, with the destruction of the Temple in A.D. 70 by the Romans, they disappeared from the scene without leaving any trace of their influence in the shaping of later Judaism.

Pharisees

Our knowledge of the **Pharisees** is also limited, since we do not know of any literature that comes directly from this group. Josephus, the New Testament, and the Mishna provide us what little we know about this religious movement, which came into existence in the mid-second century B.C. It is commonly believed that this group descended from the Hasidim, the loyal and pious Jews who were staunch allies and supporters of the Maccabean family. The name Pharisee is associated with the idea of separation; thus the common meaning "separated ones" may be either a self-designation or a derogatory label given to them by their opponents.[5] Josephus remarks that the Pharisees have taught the people a great many observances that are not in the Law, and that there were disputes and differences between the Sadducees and the Pharisees. He also points out that though the Sadducees had only the rich on their side, Pharisees had the general population ("multitude") on theirs.[6] This group was a "well organized political movement" during the Hasmonean period and continued to exert political power during the days of Herod the Great. While Herod had a friendly relationship with them during the early part of his reign, he later considered them his enemies, and executed several leaders of the movement.[7]

The Pharisees originated within the laity in Judaism and established themselves as teachers and scholars whose teachings laid the foundation of the vast collection of Jewish religious literature known as the Mishna and the Palestinian and Babylonian Talmuds. The synagogue was the center of their activity. Though they considered the Torah as central to the Jewish religious life, the Pharisees also respected the authority of the rest of the Hebrew Scriptures. It was at a Pharisaic council that met at Jamnia around A.D. 95 that the canon of the Old Testament was established.

In the first century A.D., two prominent schools of the Pharisaic movement existed in Palestine.

The School of **Shammai** was a conservative movement, whereas the School of **Hillel** was more liberal and popular, with its emphasis on the significance of the Law to everyday life. Some scholars think that the School of Shammai controlled Nazareth, where Jesus was treated with hostility at the synagogue. Capernaum, where Jesus made His home, was most likely under the influence of the School of Hillel.

As promoters of the Law, the Pharisees emphasized both the written Law and the **oral Law**, the latter of which is the interpretation of the Law handed down by the previous generations of great rabbis. Since the Law was central to the life of Jews in their thinking, Pharisees observed and taught strict obedience to both the written Law and the oral Law. They also promoted concepts such as the kingdom of God, the coming of the Messiah, resurrection of the dead, and the future that God would usher in by destroying sin and evil in the world. Though they did not involve themselves in local politics or anti-Roman movements, they supported the national interests during the Roman invasion of Jerusalem in A.D. 70. They receive the credit for the recovery and survival of Judaism after that tragic date.

Essenes

The **Dead Sea Scrolls**, the discovery of which began in 1947, and Josephus provide us with our knowledge of this third religious group in Judaism. Scholars think that this group came out of the Hasidim during the Maccabean period. Koester thinks that they belonged to the priestly circles of the Hasidim, who joined the Maccabean war in opposition to the appointment of Menelaus, a non-Zadokite person, as high priest by Antiochus IV.[8] When the Hasmonean ruler Simon appointed himself as high priest, they made the break with the ruling family, since this was an outright defiance of the Zadokite right to hold the high priestly office. Some think that the "Wicked Priest" in the Qumran texts may be an indirect reference to Simon, who ruled the nation with violence and cruelty.[9]

The **Essenes** established themselves as a self-exiled religious community at Qumran, near the northwestern shore of the Dead Sea. They made a complete break from the social, political, and religious life of Jerusalem and made Qumran their home perhaps around the middle of the second century B.C., during the early part of the Hasmonean rule. The remains of Qumran show a central complex with several rooms including a scriptorium, assembly hall, meeting hall, and common rooms, and many other surrounding buildings that were used for storage and as workshops. Cisterns and reservoirs of water and a bath for ritual cleansing *(mikveh)* were also found at Qumran. The nearby caves yielded a large number of manuscripts, which include copies of the Hebrew Scriptures and the literature produced by this community. The literature from this community includes writings such as the *Damascus Document, Commentary on Habakkuk, Manual of Discipline* (or *Rule of the Community*), and *War of the Children of Light Against the Children of Darkness*.

The Essenes lived a strict life,

organizing themselves into groups of priests, Levites, and laypeople. Entrance into the community required a two-year period of initiation. A characteristic of this group was their community life, which centered on prayer, worship, common meal, and various trades to meet the needs of the community.

The Qumran society saw themselves as members of the new covenant and as the true remnant of Israel. They also saw themselves as the poor who will one day inherit the earth. They regarded themselves as the Children of Light, who were oppressed by the Children of Darkness. Those who were the Children of Darkness included the Roman Empire and the Jews who were apostate and unfaithful to the Law. They also believed that in the end, with the help of the heavenly hosts of God, the Children of Light would prevail against the Children of Darkness in the final battle, which would bring an end to all evil forces. The community lived with strong messianic expectations, in which their leader, the Teacher of Righteousness, seems to have played a key role. The community ceased to exist beyond A.D. 70. Some scholars believe that the Roman army destroyed the sect during the siege of Jerusalem in A.D. 68. Anticipating the Roman invasion, the community took the measure of protecting and preserving their writings by hiding them in jars in nearby caves. The remarkable discovery of the Dead Sea Scrolls preserves for us their legacy, and more than that, a glimpse of the cultural, social, political, and religious conditions of the pre-Christian times.

Zealots

Zealots were not a religious movement but a fanatical and political movement that opposed the foreign rule of Judea by the Romans. This revolutionary movement was intent on overthrowing Roman power. They showed their resistance to Rome by refusing to pay taxes and causing uprisings against the Roman army. This group is responsible for the Jewish revolt that led to the destruction of Jerusalem in A.D. 70 and the later revolt that led to the establishment of Jerusalem as a Roman colony in A.D. 135. Sicarii, who carried concealed daggers, were perhaps a more violent branch within this movement.

Other Groups

Herodians were likely a political party rather than a religious movement. They seemed to have exercised their influence in the Galilean area, where Antipas ruled. They were supporters of the Herodian dynasty. The Gospels mention them, along with the Pharisees, as opponents of Jesus (Mark 3:6; 12:13; Matthew 22:16). The masses of Jewish people, who were ignorant of the Law and who were indifferent to the customs of the Pharisees, are called **"the people of the land."** They did not have any political or religious power, though they constituted the majority of people in the land. Pharisees despised them because of their lack of knowledge of the Law and their association with Jesus. The **Samaritans,** who lived in Samaria, the area between Judea and Galilee, were a people despised by the Jews. The history of the Samaritans goes back to the Assyrian occupation of the Northern Kingdom (Israel) in 722 B.C. They were descendants of the Assyrian colonists and the Israelite population that was left in the land. The Jews viewed them as a mixed and defiled people who did not belong to the Jewish nation. The Samaritans considered themselves the true keepers of the Law and worshipers of Yahweh, the God of Israel. They had their own version of the Pentateuch (the Samaritan Pentateuch), and their own temple, located at Mount Gerizim. The Jews avoided any contact with this group, and both groups held hostility toward each other, which often resulted in violence and murder. The Jews traveled around the Samaritan region, because they considered even the land as unclean. The Samaritans were not hospitable to the Jews who wanted to travel through their region (Luke 9:51-56). Jesus' travel to Samaria (John 4:1-42) and His conversation with a Samaritan woman display the revolutionary and life-transforming power of His gospel.

Another particular religious thinking and perspective that emerged during the intertestamental period deserves our attention. During the period of intense religious persecution, despair, and disillusionment, Jewish visionaries began to promote the view that God would come suddenly to destroy all evil and set up His ideal kingdom. This perspective, known as apocalyptic thinking, may have its origin in the Old Testament visionary thinking found

in Ezekiel 38—48 and Isaiah 56—66. Some scholars maintain the view that the Book of Daniel, the only apocalyptic book in the Old Testament, originated in the context of Hellenization in the early part of the second century. Some of the popular Jewish apocalyptic writings include Enoch, the Assumption of Moses, 2 Esdras, also called 4 Ezra, the Apocalypse of Baruch, the Sibylline Oracles, the Testament of the Twelve Patriarchs, and the Apocalypse of Moses. The apocalyptic writings portray its content as "revelations" about the future. Dualistic thinking, symbolic language, use of numbers, and the final triumph of God over evil are some of the characteristic features of this type of religious thinking.

We conclude this chapter with this note. Jesus came into a world that was fractured by religious, social, political, and cultural tensions. Religious and political corruption, social oppression, and misguided theological perspectives were all characteristics of this period. Judaism itself was plagued by divergent political ideologies and religious perspectives. We had to limit our survey to some key events and people that identify for us what Paul perhaps meant by the phrase "when the time had fully come." Indeed the world was ripe for the coming of God's Son.

We will now turn to the story of Jesus' advent and the fulfillment of His mission as found in the Gospels.

Summary Statements

- In the early part of the second century, Palestine became a part of the Seleucid kingdom.
- The Seleucid ruler Antiochus IV Epiphanes instituted the program of Hellenization, which threatened to destroy the Jewish religion and culture.
- Under the leadership of the Maccabeans, the Jews were able to drive out the Greek rulers and establish an independent Jewish state.
- Struggle within the Hasmonean family led to the takeover of Judea by the Roman Empire.
- The Torah was central to the Jewish life in the first century.
- Various religious groups within Judaism attempted to guide the destiny of the Jews with their particular theological perspectives.
- The Sadducees promoted the Temple and the sacrifices as necessary to the existence of Judaism.
- The Pharisees required strict adherence to both the written Law and the oral Law.
- The Pharisees receive the credit for the recovery of Judaism after the destruction of the Jerusalem Temple in A.D. 70.
- The Essenes established a sectarian community at Qumran and identified themselves as the true Israel.
- The Dead Sea Scrolls come to us from the Essenes.

Questions for Reflection

1. What parallels do you find between the theological and cultural conditions of Judaism in the 1st century A.D. and that of the Christian Church in the 21st century?
2. In spite of division and fragmented theological perspectives within Judaism, what are the forces that contributed to the unity of this religion in the first century? What does that say to the Church today?

Resources for Further Study

Bright, John. *A History of Israel,* 4th ed. Louisville, Ky.: Westminster/John Knox Press, 2000.
Bruce, F. F. *New Testament History.* New York: Doubleday, 1972.
Kee, Howard C., Franklin W. Young, Karlfried Froehlich. *Understanding the New Testament.* Englewood Cliffs, N.J.: Prentice-Hall, 1965.
Koester, Helmut. *Introduction to the New Testament: History, Culture and Religion of the Hellenistic Age.* Vol. 1. New York: Walter de Gruyter, 1982.
Tenney, Merrill C. *New Testament Survey.* Grand Rapids: Eerdmans, 1961.

UNIT II

JESUS ACCORDING TO THE GOSPELS

Your study of this unit will help you to:

- Describe the nature and characteristics of the Gospels as a unique literary genre.
- Discuss the setting and purpose of the four Gospels.
- Compare and contrast the portrait of Jesus found in the four Gospels.
- Describe the unique themes and characteristics of the four Gospels.

■ What Is a Gospel?

■ Who Was Jesus?

■ The Gospel According to Matthew

■ The Gospel According to Mark

■ The Gospel According to Luke

■ The Gospel According to John

4 What Is a Gospel?

O bjectives:

Your study of this chapter should help you to:

- Describe the origin and nature of "gospel" as a literary genre.
- Understand the importance of genre for interpreting the four Gospels.
- Understand the significance of oral tradition.
- Evaluate the relationships among the Synoptic Gospels and the uniqueness of the Gospel of John.
- Understand diverse types of material in the Gospels.
- Describe the narrative world of the Gospels.
- Discuss the setting, audience, and purpose of the four Gospels.

K ey Words to Understand

Euangelion
Literary genre
Salvation history
Oral tradition
Synoptic Gospels
Synoptic problem
Two-source hypothesis
Form criticism
Redaction criticism
Narrative criticism

Q uestions to consider as you read:

1. How did the Gospel writers get their information about Jesus?

2. Why are there so many similarities, as well as differences, between one Gospel and another?

3. Was the purpose of the Gospels to address people outside the Church or to instruct those within the Church?

4. Is there a preferable method of studying the Gospels, or is it best to use a variety of methods?

Roman inscription showing Pilate's name found in Caesarea.

First, then, what type of writing is a Gospel? In other words, what is its **literary genre**? A proper interpretation of a literary piece requires that some attention be given to its genre. A reader can readily see that the Gospels were written primarily in narrative form. They told a story. Why is it that the Good News was proclaimed in story form?

The four Gospels also call for some explanation as to why there are so many similarities as well as differences between one Gospel and another. How were they composed? Is there any evidence that the writers made use of earlier sources? Did one Gospel writer have access to one or more of the other Gospels? What was the purpose of the Gospels? What did the writers hope to accomplish?

Even a casual reader of the Bible will note that the first four books of the New Testament are similar. All four have the word "Gospel" in their titles.[1] Furthermore, the contents of these four writings are similar and even identical in many places. Yet a closer examination will reveal that the four Gospels are in fact significantly different from one another.

L Origin of the Word "Gospel"

"Gospel" is the simplified form of the Old English *godspell* that translates the Greek *euangelion,* meaning "good news." How is it that such a title was given to these four writings of the New Testament? Mark uses the word in the first line of his Gospel, "The beginning of the *euangelion* of Jesus Christ," and again in summarizing the message of Jesus as *euangelion* (1:14). It is possible that the Early Church was familiar with this word from two possible sources. First, the Greek translation of the Old Testament (the Septuagint), the Bible of early Christians, uses a form of *euangelion* to signify the good news that God was about to end the Exile and restore Jerusalem. The prophet in Isaiah 52:7 says, "How beautiful upon the mountains are the feet of the messenger who announces peace, who brings good news, who announces salvation, who says to Zion, 'Your God reigns.'" In the same vein, the Early Church and the Gospel writers saw the story of Jesus as the announcement of the good news of salvation.

A second possibility is that the Gospel writers were familiar with Roman inscriptions that heralded the good news of peace brought by Roman emperors. One such inscription celebrates Caesar Augustus as a "savior," "the birthday of the god," "the beginning of the gospel" (Greek *euangelion*).[2] The Gospels and the Early Church were saying that the real good news was not Caesar Augustus but Jesus Christ. In time, Christians would be persecuted and even put to death because their faith in Jesus was interpreted as treason against the Roman Empire.

The Origin and Nature of the Gospel Genre

The authors of the four Gospels would most likely have been familiar with a genre of writing known as popular biography produced by Greek, Roman, and Jewish authors to entertain and instruct readers and hearers. While there may be some resemblance between the Gospels and Greco-Roman and Jewish biographies, New Testament scholars today agree that the Gospels were the unique product of early Christianity.[3] What then are the unique characteristics of a Gospel that set it apart from a biography, whether ancient or modern? For one thing, many of the details of a hero's life that would normally be part of a biography are simply absent from the Gospels. The birth of Jesus is told only in Matthew and Luke, but not in Mark or John. The Gospels tell us virtually nothing about Jesus' childhood, adolescence, and early adulthood, except for the single story of Him at age 12 at the Temple (Luke 2:41-51). Instead, the focus of the Gospels is on His teaching and healing ministry and His death and resurrection. The Gospels proclaim the good news of the kingdom of God inaugurated through Jesus' words, deeds, death, and resurrection. The Gospels do not entertain, inform, or educate the reader with all the details of Jesus' life. They instead tell in narrative form what God has done in Jesus to save the world. The Gospels are a theological narrative, meaning that their purpose was to tell the story of God's action in the world through the life, death, and resurrection of Jesus. We will return to this theme later in this chapter.

It is important that we have a proper understanding of the literary genre of Gospel so that we can avoid misconceptions and false expectations. The Gospels are not a precise, chronological account of the life of Jesus. While they give us many historical facts from the life of Jesus, they do not allow us to write a sequential, orderly, chronological account of His life. The Gospels often place the same event or saying of Jesus in two or three different settings. Without a proper understanding of the Gospel genre, one may incorrectly conclude that the Gospels contradict each other. We must firmly keep in mind that a Gospel is primarily a theological statement rather than a historical biography.

On the other hand, the Gospels are not legends or imaginative stories about Jesus. The good news that they announce is what happened in the life of a particular historical person, Jesus of Nazareth, and in a specific culture and social world. The Gospels were written not as abstract, timeless truths but for the specific purpose of communicating a message to people in the real world of the first century A.D.

While the Gospels say much about the person of Jesus, they do not allow us to sketch His psychological profile. The Gospels do not develop the personal qualities of Jesus as such. Was He jovial or somber, extroverted or introverted? As much as we might like to, we cannot give assured answers to such questions. Rather, they answer the theological question as to what God did in history through Jesus.

A noteworthy characteristic of the Gospels is the extent to which they echo and indeed quote the Old Testament. The Gospel writers place the story of Jesus within the vast panorama of **salvation history.** Even though the Gospels portray the Christ event as a new thing that God has done in history, they nevertheless see continuity between what God had done in the past and what God did through the life, death, and resurrection of Jesus. The story of Jesus does not displace the Old Testament; it moves the story of God forward; it fulfills God's promises given in past ages (Matthew 5:17; Luke 24:44; John 5:39).[4]

The Significance of Oral Tradition

It is necessary now to explore an even more basic question. How did the Gospel writers get their information about Jesus? We must at once dismiss the notion that the disciples took down notes as Jesus taught, preached, and did His work. Nowhere does Jesus tell His disciples to write something down. Instead, we often hear Him say, "Listen" or "Hear" (Mark 4:9; Matthew 7:24). Just like other prophets, teachers, and rabbis, Jesus communicated orally rather than in writing.[5] Those who heard Jesus teach or preach and saw the events in His life passed on their stories of Jesus to others by word of mouth. This is what scholars call **oral tradition.**

Now, it may be that one or more of the Gospel writers themselves were personal eyewitnesses of Jesus during His earthly ministry. On the other hand, it is certain that at least the author of the Gospel of Luke was not a disciple during the lifetime of Jesus.[6] He says so in so many words in his preface to his Gospel (Luke 1:1-4). Luke informs the reader that the details of the story of Jesus have come to him through other people who personally saw

Analysis of Luke 1:1-4 (NRSV)

A closer look at Luke's preface would give us a clue as to how this Gospel and possibly all the Gospels were composed:

> Since many have undertaken to set down an orderly account of the events that have been fulfilled among us, just as they were handed on to us by those who from the beginning were eyewitnesses and servants of the word, I too decided, after investigating everything carefully from the very first, to write an orderly account for you, most excellent Theophilus, so that you may know the truth concerning the things about which you have been instructed.

Luke acknowledges that others had written earlier accounts of Jesus (v. 1). He apparently had access to these accounts, since he tells us that he knew of them and had investigated everything carefully from the very first (v. 3). He also tells us that he received oral traditions about Jesus from "those who from the beginning were eyewitnesses and servants of the word" (v. 2). The verb that he uses, "were handed on," is a technical term for passing on oral tradition.[7] Luke identifies the source of these oral traditions as those who "from the beginning" were eyewitnesses, meaning the beginning of the ministry of Jesus. It is clear that Luke himself was not such an eyewitness.

and heard Jesus during His life-time. Luke was dependent on oral tradition and some earlier written accounts.

There is evidence from Paul's letters that he received and passed on oral traditions of the life and ministry of Jesus (1 Corinthians 11:23; 15:3). Even his statement in Galatians 1:11-12, that his gospel was not of human origin but came through divine revelation, is not a denial of the role of oral tradition but an affirmation that the ultimate source of the gospel tradition is Jesus Christ himself.

Oral tradition seems rather suspect to modern people who have greater confidence in printed documents. This is not so in ancient cultures, or even tribal cultures in some parts of the world today. We must remember that relatively few people in biblical times knew how to read or write. The vast majority of people were illiterate and thus depended on oral tradition. Widespread literacy did not take place until after the invention of the printing press in the modern period. Thus the contents of the four Gospels as well as many books of the Old Testament were passed on orally before being written down.[8]

Oral tradition alone, however, cannot explain the extensive similarities between the Gospels, particularly the first three Gospels. Scholarship has been puzzled by this high degree of similarity and has attempted to explain it.

The Synoptic Gospels and the Gospel of John

The **Synoptic Gospels** are Matthew, Mark, and Luke. The word "synoptic" means "to see to-

The Synoptic Gospels connect much of Jesus' ministry with the region of Galilee.

gether" or "alongside one another." When scholars placed these three Gospels side by side in order to compare them, they discovered that the wording of one Gospel in many cases was identical to the other two. In other cases the wording varied from one Gospel to another. They concluded that there must be some sort of connection between one Gospel and another. But what exactly is this connection? This question is what has come to be known as the **Synoptic problem.**

One can easily see from the sidebar on the next page how similar the three accounts are, particularly the identical wording of Jesus' question to the disciples, "But who do you say that I am?" Oral tradition alone cannot adequately account for such identical wording in the Greek text of the three Gospels, since originally the stories would have been told in Aramaic, the language of Jesus and the disciples. The fact that the Greek text of the three Gospels shows identical wording has led scholars to conclude that there must have been some sort of relationship between the *written* texts of the three Gospels.

Further study has convinced a

An Illustration of Synoptic Parallels

The following account of Peter's confession of Jesus as Messiah illustrates the high degree of similarity between the three Gospels:

Matthew 16:13-17, 20

Now when Jesus came into the district of Caesarea Philippi, he asked his disciples, "Who do people say that the Son of Man is?" And they said, "Some say John the Baptist, but others Elijah, and still others Jeremiah or one of the prophets." He said to them, "But who do you say that I am?" Simon Peter answered, "You are the Messiah, the Son of the living God." And Jesus answered him, "Blessed are you, Simon son of Jonah! For flesh and blood has not revealed this to you, but my Father in heaven." . . . Then he sternly ordered the disciples not to tell anyone that he was the Messiah.

Mark 8:27-30

Jesus went on with his disciples to the villages of Caesarea Philippi; and on the way he asked his disciples, "Who do people say that I am?" And they answered him, "John the Baptist; and others, Elijah; and still others, one of the prophets." He asked them, "But who do you say that I am?" Peter answered him, "You are the Messiah." And he sternly ordered them not to tell anyone about him.

Luke 9:18-21

Once when Jesus was praying alone, with only the disciples near him, he asked them, "Who do the crowds say that I am?" They answered, "John the Baptist; but others, Elijah; and still others, that one of the ancient prophets has arisen." He said to them, "But who do you say that I am?" Peter answered, "The Messiah of God." He sternly ordered and commanded them not to tell anyone.

---

majority of scholars that Mark was the first Gospel to be written and that Matthew and Luke depended on Mark but wrote independently of each other.[9] A small group of scholars contests this hypothesis. They contend that Matthew was written first, then Luke, and then Mark, and that Luke was dependent on Matthew's text and Mark was dependent on the text of both Matthew and Luke.[10] In Mark, for example, Peter confesses, "You are the Messiah." In Matthew Peter says, "You are the Messiah, the Son of the living God." Which is more likely, schol-

ars asked, that Matthew added the words "Son of the living God" to the text he found in Mark, or that Mark deleted those words that he found in Matthew's text? If Mark were dependent on Matthew, there would be no adequate explanation as to why Mark would expunge "Son of the living God" from Peter's confession. Mark very clearly declares in other places that Jesus is indeed the Son of God (Mark 1:1; 15:39). It makes much more sense that Mark was the earliest Gospel and that when Matthew made use of Mark's text he added those words to give voice to the Church's confession of Jesus as Son of God through the mouth of the great apostle Peter.

However, there is still a further issue to contend with. The three Gospels are not only similar but also considerably different from one another. Even in the story of Peter's confession one can see that the three accounts are not exactly the same. Moreover, in Matthew and Luke there are many sayings of Jesus in similar and even identical Greek wording that are absent from Mark. How can this be explained? One could theorize that either Matthew depended on Luke or that Luke depended on Matthew. However, after careful analysis of these texts for more than a hundred years, scholars formulated the hypothesis that Matthew and Luke were not dependent on one another but on another source that they both had access to independently of each other. Since no such document has ever been found, this remains only a hypothesis. The German scholars who first formulated this hypothesis named this source "Q," which stands for the German word *Quelle,* which simply means "source." By definition, then, a "Q" saying is one that is found only in Matthew and Luke but not in Mark. Most of the material identified in Matthew and Luke as "Q" consists of the sayings of Jesus, and therefore "Q" is often referred to as the sayings source.

To conclude, the dominant scholarly hypothesis today is that Mark was the first Gospel to be written and that Matthew and Luke were dependent on the texts of Mark and "Q" as sources. This explanation has come to be known as the **two-source hypothesis** of

> ## L · An Illustration of a "Q" Saying
>
> **Matthew 6:22-23**
> The eye is the lamp of the body. So, if your eye is healthy, your whole body will be full of light; but if your eye is unhealthy, your whole body will be full of darkness. If then the light in you is darkness, how great is the darkness!
>
> **Luke 11:34-35**
> Your eye is the lamp of your body. If your eye is healthy, your whole body is full of light; but if it is not healthy, your body is full of darkness. Therefore consider whether the light in you is not darkness.

the Synoptic Gospels, meaning that Mark and "Q" were the two sources for Matthew and Luke. It may be diagramed as follows:

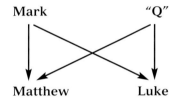

There is still one more thing to consider. In addition to materials from Mark and "Q," each of the two Gospels Matthew and Luke has material unique to itself, which indicates that Matthew and Luke each had access to other sources not available to the other Gospels. The label "M" has been given to passages that are only in Matthew and "L" to passages that are only in Luke. "M" and "L" are considered traditions rather than well-defined documents. They are shorthand for passages that are only in Matthew or Luke respectively. An example of "M" would be the story of the wise men found only in Matthew 2:1-12. An example of "L" would be the parable of the Good Samaritan found only in Luke 10:29-37.

What About Inspiration of Scripture?

The purpose of discussing these issues about the Gospels, their sources, their relationships to each other, and their unique or shared characteristics is to clarify the nature of the Bible. The Gospels were produced through a lengthy process. Followers of Jesus passed on stories and sayings from Jesus by word of mouth. They told stories about Jesus, His ministry, His life, and His death and resurrection. Oral traditions were formed and were eventually written down, collected, and copied. Gospel writers made use of traditions and sources to produce a connected story of Jesus.

If this is how the Gospels came into existence, what about the belief that Scripture is the inspired Word of God?

One does not need to decide between two alternatives, either belief in inspiration of Scripture or scholarly hypotheses concerning the formation of biblical books. The Holy Spirit has inspired, illuminated, and guided the whole process of divine revelation, including the formation of oral traditions, collection of materials, composition of books, the process of canonization, and the interpretation of Scripture by the Church in subsequent times. Both human and divine factors are at work in the formation and appropriation of Scripture. In this view, the inspiration of Scripture is much broader and more dynamic than the narrower meaning attached to it by those who restrict inspiration to God's dictation of exact words to a biblical author.[11]

In contrast to the Synoptic Gospels, the Gospel of John stands alone. Although a later chapter will be devoted to John, here we must simply note its uniqueness. Whereas the texts of the Synoptic Gospels are clearly related to one another, as shown on page 86, the Gospel of John stands alone in its wording, structure, and general characteristics. Its vocabulary is unique. The words of Jesus in John are considerably different from His words in the Synoptics. Although John seems familiar with the Synoptic tradition, there is no evidence that this Gospel was dependent on the written text of Matthew, Mark, or Luke.[12]

Other Approaches to the Gospels

■ Diversity of Materials in the Gospels

Another approach to the Gospels, besides making observations about sources, is to note the different types of material used within individual units in a Gospel. This approach, known as **form criticism**, notes that in the Gospels we find such diverse materials as parables, proverbs, miracle stories, controversy stories, beatitudes, woes, eschatological discourse, passion narrative, and so on. Form critics have analyzed and classified each of these types of material. They have asked such questions as: What are the typical features of a parable? What are the components of a miracle story? What constitutes an eschatological discourse? What social setting in the life of the Early Church has called for the passing on of such stories?

The hypothesis of form critics has been that different situations in the life of the Early Church gave rise to the formation of particular types of stories or sayings from Jesus. Some of the more radical form critics have gone so far as to say that the Early Church that came into existence after the death and resurrection of Jesus created much of this material. More moderate form critics have argued that while the social setting in the Early Church was the context within which traditions about Jesus were formed, the Church itself did not create this material. Sayings of Jesus and stories about Him were recalled and kept alive because they were needed for particular functions in the life of the Church, such as instruction of new believers, worship, evangelism, debate with opponents, and so on. The life of the Early Church and its convictions about Jesus gave rise to the formation of Jesus traditions. The Gospels and their earlier sources were not literary masterpieces produced for their own sake or for the purpose of impressing, entertaining, and delighting hearers or readers. They are rather the product of the Church's proclamation of God's act in Jesus. They are primarily theological rather than biographical.[13]

■ The Gospel Writers as Editors

One of the shortcomings of form criticism has been that it focused on individual units within a Gospel rather than taking into view the entire Gospel. Scholars around the middle of the 20th century began to point out that the Gospels were not an arbitrary collection of independent units of tradition haphazardly stitched together. Although the Gospel writers did use older traditions and sources, they did not thoughtlessly throw these together. They carefully composed their Gospels to create a particular design, to paint a specific portrait of Jesus, to make an intentional theological point. The Gospel writers were not merely collectors of traditions; they were authors who edited, adapted, and arranged older

materials to fit their theological purposes. Such an approach to the Gospels came to be known as **redaction criticism**.[14] Redaction criticism has most effectively been applied to the manner in which Matthew and Luke edited, adapted, and incorporated Mark's text into their Gospels. A good example of redaction is Peter's confession discussed earlier. Matthew and Luke expanded Peter's words given in Mark; they did not blindly copy from Mark.

Matthew and Luke quite often reword and simplify statements from Mark to smooth out what they perceive to be stylistic or theological awkwardness. Here is an example (author's translation):

Matthew 13:57*b*-58	Mark 6:4-6*a*	Luke 4:24
But Jesus said to them, "Prophets are not without honor except in their own country and in their own house." And he did not do many deeds of power there, because of their unbelief.	Then Jesus said to them, "Prophets are not without honor, except in their hometown, and among their own kin, and in their own house." And he could do no deed of power there, except that he laid his hands on a few sick people and cured them. And he was amazed at their unbelief.	But he said, "Truly I tell you, no prophet is accepted in the prophet's hometown."

Note first that Matthew simplified Mark's text by cutting out several statements. More significantly, he changed Mark's "he could do no deed of power" to "he did not do many deeds of power" in order to forestall possible misunderstanding that Jesus was powerless. Luke has omitted much of Mark's statement except for the first sentence, which he has changed to read "no prophet is accepted in the prophet's hometown."

■ The Narrative World of the Gospels

In more recent years scholars have taken a still further step to understand the Gospels. Their argument has been that it is not enough to know what sources and traditions lie behind the present form of the Gospels or how the Gospel writers redacted, adapted, and changed earlier materials. It is not even enough to know the similarities and differences between one Gospel and another. We must rather give full attention to the narrative plot of a particular Gospel in and of itself. We must understand its story line, characters, symbols, and everything else that will enable us to enter fully into the narrative world of that Gospel. This method of study is called **narrative criticism**.[15] It is not surprising that words such as "story" or "narrative" have appeared regularly in the titles of recent publications on the four Gospels.[16] In

later chapters, the narrative plot of each of the four Gospels will be explored. It may be useful at this point, however, to elucidate some of the basic principles of narrative criticism and its application to the Gospels.

Scholars who have applied narrative criticism to the Gospels have done so at least partly because they have become dissatisfied with the other approaches that have dominated Gospel studies since the Enlightenment. The dominant approach, including source, form, and redaction criticism, has been preoccupied with historical sorts of questions, such as: What did Jesus really say or do? What is the oldest version of this or that story? What are the earlier sources behind the present form of the Gospels? How has Matthew or Luke redacted, adapted, and incorporated materials from Mark and "Q" into their Gospels? These sorts of questions are largely historical in nature, making a tacit assumption that the best way to study the Gospels is through the lens of the historian. While recognizing the contribution that these approaches have made, narrative critics have challenged the assumptions of the historical method and have proposed that we must now raise a different set of questions. Their proposal is that we must ask literary questions.

A word of explanation may be necessary here. Secular literary critics have asked these sorts of questions to study novels, that is, fictional literature. The application of narrative criticism to the Gospels may be problematic for some people of faith. It may communicate the notion that narrative criticism regards the Gospels

The Gospels record the area around the Sea of Galilee as a place of Jesus' ministry.

as pure fiction. Therefore, before proceeding any further, it would be well to clarify what narrative criticism really does or does not do, particularly in contrast to the historical method.[17]

First, narrative criticism focuses on the finished form of the text of a Gospel rather than the process through which the Gospel has come into existence. Narrative criticism is not so much concerned with the earlier stages of development, such as oral traditions and written sources, but with the text as it is now.

Second, narrative criticism emphasizes the unity of the text as a whole. The Gospels are viewed as coherent wholes rather than loosely connected units of tradition, as form criticism tended to do. The individual units are interpreted in relationship to the story as a whole.

Third, narrative criticism views the text as an end in itself. Much like music or art appreciation, narrative criticism focuses on a literary piece for its own sake rather than as a means to something else. Historical criticism, on the other hand, views the text as a means to an end, as a window through which one must go to find something else. In the case of the Gospels, this "something else" may be a so-called authentic life and message of Jesus. In narrative criticism, by contrast, the text is more like a mirror. Narrative criticism attempts to understand the text's impact and power and to analyze the interaction and encounter between text and reader.

At the risk of oversimplification, the difference between a narrative approach and a historical approach to the Gospels may be diagrammed as follows:

Narrative Criticism	Historical Criticism
Gospel ◄► Reader	Historical Event (Jesus)
	↓
	Oral Tradition
	↓
	Early Written Sources
	↓
	Author of Gospel
	↓
	Gospel

This does not mean that narrative critics naively accept the historical factuality of everything in the Gospels. Nor does it mean, on the other hand, that they consign everything in them to the realm of fiction. What they do is to bracket out historical questions and focus on literary characteristics of the Gospels.

Value of Variety in Methods

One can see from this brief discussion that scholars have used a variety of methods to study the Gospels. There are still other methods that were not mentioned. These can be explored by consulting the resources at the end of this chapter. The best approach to the Gospels, or any book of the Bible for that matter, is to use several methods. Our insight into the Gospels will be enriched by the variety of questions that we bring to the task. If, for example, we grasp the fact that traditions about Jesus circulated orally in the Early Church before the written Gospels, it enables us to appreciate the church setting within which stories about Jesus were circulating. This means that the primary reason behind the composition of the Gospels was not idle curiosity about Jesus but communal identity and social formation.[18] Stories about Jesus were cherished and preserved precisely because they gave meaning and identity to the emerging community of faith, the Church. What the Gospels say about Jesus is a commentary on what the people of Jesus understood themselves to be.

It is clear from the materials in the Gospels that their target audience is people in the Church rather than outsiders. Certain passages do of course concern people outside the Church, but a Gospel as a whole was written in the context of the Church and for the Church. Mark's opening words, "The beginning of the good news of Jesus Christ, the Son of God," are straightforward and give no explanations, presupposing that Mark's readers know the identity of Jesus Christ. The same is true about Matthew's opening words, "An account of the genealogy of Jesus the Messiah, the son of David, the son of Abraham." Matthew concludes his Gospel with the Great Commission, which is addressed specifically to the followers of Jesus who are instructed to make disciples of all nations (28:19). Luke addresses his Gospel to Theophilus, who had already been instructed about the story of Jesus (1:4). John starts out his Gospel with the words, "In the beginning was the Word, and the Word was with God, and the Word was God." Since no explanation is given as to who the Word is, it is assumed that the hearers would know that the reference is to Jesus Christ. The Gospels in their present form as well as the oral traditions standing behind them demonstrate that their target audience was the Church. Study of oral tradition by form critics has provided support for such an understanding of the Gospels.

Source criticism, another method of study, has provided an understanding of the similarities and differences between one Gospel and another. Placing the Gospels in parallel columns and noting how the wording of one Gospel differs from the others makes it possible for us to understand the unique theology of each Gospel. Furthermore, assuming the correctness of the two-source hypothesis, we can gain insight into the theology of Matthew or Luke by noting the way that they adapted and used Mark's text.

On the other hand, the value of narrative criticism is that it focuses on the present form of the text rather than earlier stages of development. It is this text that the Church has canonized as Scripture and has affirmed in liturgy and sermon as the Word of God. While the other methods have value in the task of exegesis and interpretation, there is no substitute for giving attention to the voice of Scripture as we now have it.

Summary Statements

- A Gospel is a literary genre unique to Christianity in that it is a theological narrative about God's acts in the world through Jesus Christ.
- Prior to the writing of the Gospels, the early followers of Jesus passed on His words and deeds by word of mouth, thus forming oral tradition.
- The Synoptic Gospels are Matthew, Mark, and Luke and are literarily related to one another, whereas the Gospel of John stands alone.
- According to the two-source hypothesis, Matthew and Luke were dependent on Mark and "Q."
- Form criticism is a study of individual units of tradition in a Gospel.
- Redaction criticism is a study of a Gospel as a whole and its author's editorial activity and theological perspective.
- Narrative criticism is a literary rather than a historical approach to the Gospels, focusing on the narrative plot or story line of a Gospel in its present form.
- There is value in utilizing a variety of methods in the study of the Gospels.

Questions for Reflection

1. In what way can a Gospel become for you good news from God?
2. What difference would it make in your life if you read a Gospel as an address to Christians rather than as a biography of Jesus?
3. How would you respond to the objections of a person who sees the Gospels as inconsistent and mutually contradictory?

Resources for Further Study

Allen, O. Wesley. *Reading the Synoptic Gospels: Basic Methods for Interpreting Matthew, Mark, and Luke.* St. Louis: Chalice, 2000.

Bauckham, Richard. *The Gospels for All Christians: Rethinking the Gospel Audiences.* Grand Rapids: Eerdmans, 1998.

Burridge, Richard A. *Four Gospels, One Jesus? A Symbolic Reading.* Grand Rapids: Eerdmans, 1994.

Cosby, Michael R. *Portraits of Jesus: An Inductive Approach to the Gospels.* Louisville, Ky.: Westminster/John Knox, 1999.

Hengel, Martin. *The Four Gospels and the One Gospel of Jesus Christ: An Investigation of the Collection and Origin of the Canonical Gospels.* Harrisburg, Pa.: Trinity Press International, 2000.

Kelber, Werner H. *The Oral and the Written Gospel.* Philadelphia: Fortress, 1983.

Kingsbury, Jack Dean, ed. *Gospel Interpretation: Narrative-Critical and Social-Scientific Approaches.* Harrisburg, Pa.: Trinity Press International, 1997.

Nickle, Keith Fullerton. *The Synoptic Gospels: An Introduction.* Louisville, Ky.: Westminster/John Knox, 2001.

O'Grady, John F. *The Four Gospels and the Jesus Tradition.* New York: Paulist, 1989.

Powell, Mark Allan. *Fortress Introduction to the Gospels.* Minneapolis: Fortress, 1998.

Senior, Donald. *Invitation to the Gospels.* New York: Paulist, 2002.

Stuhlmacher, Peter, ed. *The Gospel and the Gospels.* Grand Rapids: Eerdmans, 1991.

5 Who Was Jesus?

Objectives:

Your study of this chapter should help you to:

- Appreciate the importance of historical knowledge about Jesus.
- Identify the major events in the life of Jesus.
- Recognize the significance of the kingdom of God in the parables of Jesus.
- Understand historical and theological issues relative to the crucifixion and resurrection of Jesus.

Questions to consider as you read:

1. How do the temptations of Jesus relate to His mission?
2. Why did Jesus perform miracles?
3. In what sense are the parables of Jesus subversive?
4. Why did Jesus go to Jerusalem and what factors led to His crucifixion?
5. In what sense is the resurrection of Jesus eschatological?

Key Words to Understand

Historical-critical method
Quest of the historical
  Jesus
Virgin Birth
Herod the Great
Bethlehem
Nazareth
Archelaus
Christology
Docetists
Herod Antipas
Pontius Pilate
Sanhedrin
Eschatological

Virtually everyone agrees that Jesus was a historical figure who lived in the first century A.D. and was crucified. However, scholars disagree about the details of His life and message. The reason is that the Gospels are primarily proclamations of salvation in Christ rather than historical biographies of Jesus. Since details of the life of Jesus vary from one Gospel to another, biblical scholars have used the **historical-critical method** to establish historical facts about Jesus, also referred to as the **quest of the historical Jesus.**[1]

Importance of Historical Knowledge About Jesus

One reason we must be concerned about Jesus as a figure of history is His enormous impact. Understanding our history entails knowing something about the significance of Jesus. Since the Christian claim is that God acted in history in the person of Jesus, historical knowledge about Jesus is particularly crucial for Christians.

How can we gain such historical knowledge? Scholars have used the following tests to determine historical facts about Jesus.

Multiple Attestation

A statement about Jesus is more likely to be authentic if it occurs in several independent sources than if it is only in one.

The Test of Dissimilarity

Since Jesus often challenged the Judaism of His time, material about Him that stands in contrast to Judaism is likely to be authentic. Similarly, material about Jesus that is different from the theology and practice of the Early Church is also authentic. This test, however, must not be overdone. Jesus, after all, had much in common with the Judaism of His time, and the Early Church was greatly impacted by Him.

The Linguistic and Cultural Test

Jesus spoke Aramaic whereas the Gospels were written in Greek. If a saying of Jesus can be shown to have Aramaic flavor, it is likely to be authentically from Jesus.

Coherence

Material about Jesus is authentic if it resembles material already established as authentic by the other tests.

Today more than ever, there is intense interest in Jesus as a historical figure. Although many details are still debatable, we can be certain of the major outline of His life and message.

Major Events in the Life of Jesus

■ Birth

The birth of Jesus is told in Matthew 1—2 and Luke 1—2. Though not the same, the two narratives agree theologically that Jesus was conceived by the Holy Spirit and born of the Virgin Mary. In Mark, which does not have the birth story, people refer to Jesus as "the son of Mary" (6:3) instead of son of Joseph. On the other hand, John 6:42 reports that people were saying, "Is not this Jesus, the son of Joseph, whose father and mother we know?" In Galatians 4:4 Paul declares that Jesus was "of a woman." This unusual phrase may imply that Paul was familiar with the **Virgin Birth** tradition. The Gospels and Paul agree that Jesus had a human birth but was also the Son of God (Romans 1:3-4; Luke 1:31-32; John 1:1, 14).

Paul also says in Galatians 4:4 that Jesus was "born under the law," without explaining what he means. Paul's meaning may be clarified if we keep in mind Luke's story of the circumcision of Jesus (2:21) and other ceremonial acts performed shortly after His birth. It is significant that Luke repeatedly says that these acts were done according to the Law of Moses (2:22, 23, 24, 27, 39), which agrees with and elaborates Paul's statement that Jesus was born under the Law.

Jesus was born during the reign of **Herod the Great** (Matthew 2:1), who was king over Palestine in 37-4 B.C. Because of his paranoia, Herod decreed the death of the children of Bethlehem who were two years old or under, in an attempt to get rid of Jesus whom the magi identified as king of the Jews (v. 16). Shortly thereafter, Herod died. Jesus must have been under two years old at the time of Herod's death. This puts the birth date of Jesus around 6-4 B.C.

Matthew and Luke concur that Jesus was born in **Bethlehem.** Matthew finds this to be theologically significant in that Jesus fulfills the prophecy of Micah 5:2 that the Messiah will come from Bethlehem.

The details of the story in Matthew and Luke are not the same. Matthew 2:11 mentions a house where Joseph and Mary and the infant Jesus lived, implying that they were residents of Bethlehem but later moved to **Nazareth** of Galilee because of the political threat in Judea from **Archelaus,** a son of Herod the

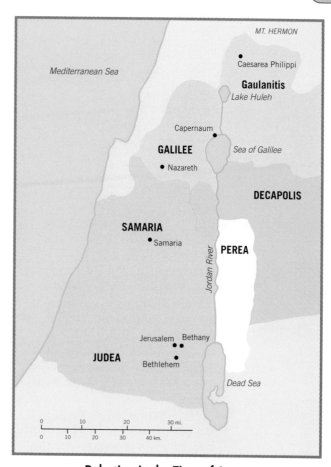

Palestine in the Time of Jesus.

Bethlehem, the traditional birthplace of Jesus, is a large town with many houses and shops today.

Modern Nazareth has a population of about 50,000, half Muslim and half Christian.

■ Baptism and Temptation

Baptism

The Gospels narrate the ministry of John the Baptist before getting into the public ministry of Jesus. It is certain that John baptized Jesus. The Early Church could not have made up such a story. In fact, Jesus' baptism posed a theological difficulty. Why would Jesus, the sinless Son of God, come to John for a baptism of repentance (Matthew 3:13)? The Gospel of John omits Jesus' baptism altogether, even though it tells about the ministry of John the Baptist (1:19-34; 3:22-30).

Why did Jesus come to John for baptism? Jesus believed that John was a true prophet sent by God to prepare Israel for the final coming of the kingdom of God. Jesus intended to be part of John's movement. Later in His ministry, Jesus had high praise for John (Matthew 11:7-11; Luke 7:24-28).

The Gospel of John implies that Jesus may have been a disciple of John the Baptist at one time. John's disciples tell him that the One who was with him (i.e., Jesus), to whom he testified, was baptizing and everyone was going to Him (John 3:26). Perceiving

Great. Conversely, Luke indicates that Joseph and Mary lived in Nazareth and were temporarily in Bethlehem for taxation when Jesus was born (2:4-7). All four Gospels agree that Nazareth was Jesus' hometown (Matthew 2:23; Mark 1:9; Luke 2:51; 4:16; John 1:45).

The Gospels say virtually nothing about the childhood and adolescent years of Jesus, with the single exception of Luke's story of Jesus at the Temple at the age of 12 (Luke 2:42-52). Jesus had brothers and sisters (Matthew 13:55-56; Mark 6:3) who were not particularly sympathetic to His message during His lifetime (John 7:3-7; Mark 3:21, 31-35).

Ritual of Baptism in Judaism

The readers of the Gospels often wonder how it was that John's ministry included the ritual of baptism. John was not the only one who practiced a water ritual. A sect known by the name Essenes at a place called Qumran near the Dead Sea practiced a ritual immersion in water to symbolize purification.[2] Other groups practiced ceremonial washing of the hands as a symbolic act of cleansing (Mark 7:3-4). Some of these ritual washings and immersions may go back to Old Testament regulations for priests (Leviticus 16:4, 24). John the Baptist insisted, however, that a mere ceremonial cleansing was far from sufficient. Repentance and a genuine change of lifestyle were necessary in preparation for the imminent coming of the final judgment (Mark 1:4; Matthew 3:7-12).

a jealousy, John assures them that it was meant to be this way. "He must increase, but I must decrease" (v. 30). This implies that at one point John's relationship to Jesus was that of master and disciple.

Temptation

Immediately after His baptism, Jesus withdrew to the desert for a period of solitude. Satan lured Him with the following strategies to accomplish His mission (Matthew 4:1-11; Mark 1:12-13; Luke 4:1-13):

- Perform miracles to serve His own needs by turning stones to bread.
- Jump from the pinnacle of the Temple, trusting God to protect Him, and thereby convince onlookers that He is the Messiah in accord with the prophecy of Malachi 4:1.
- He can have all the kingdoms of the world if He would fall down and worship Satan.

Jesus rebuffed the tempter with

an uncompromising, "Away with you, Satan!" (Matthew 4:10). He refused to compromise His faithfulness to God even if it meant a hard road ahead.

These temptations dogged Jesus throughout His ministry. On one occasion, when asked for a miracle from heaven, He replied, "Why does this generation ask for a sign? Truly I tell you, no sign will be given to this generation" (Mark 8:11-12).

After the miraculous feeding of

The traditional site of Jesus' temptation near Jericho.

Jesus, Temptation, and the Christian

Christology has to do with the question of who Jesus is. Since He is the sinless and powerful Son of God, how can He be tempted? Some early Christians known as **Docetists** believed that Jesus merely appeared to be human but in reality He was not. Christianity rejected the docetic view and affirmed that Jesus was truly human and was tempted as all of us. Jesus struggled in the desert in prayer and fasting over the issue of His ministry. To be tempted means that the possibility of yielding to it was available to Him, but He determined to remain faithful to God regardless of the cost. He "in every respect has been tested as we are, yet without sin" (Hebrews 4:15).

Just as Christ was tempted, yet without sin, so also a Spirit-filled follower of Christ may still face temptations without yielding to them. Just as Christ faced temptations and resolutely rejected the lure of the tempter, so also a Christian is empowered by God to say no to the enticement of sin. Unlike the story of the Garden of Eden in Genesis 3, where the man and the woman yielded to temptation and sinned, Jesus remained faithful and obedient to the purposes of God. God offers all of us the possibility of a victorious life and empowers us to remain faithful under the most trying circumstances.

the 5,000, the crowd was about to take Jesus by force and make Him king. Jesus would have nothing to do with that sort of Messiahship. He immediately withdrew to the mountain by himself (John 6:14-15).

The supreme test came when Jesus was on the Cross. The spectators and religious leaders taunted Him and said, "Let the Messiah, the King of Israel, come down from the cross now, so that we may see and believe" (Mark 15:32). Jesus refused to compromise the integrity of His vision and His commitment to the divine purpose to the point of death.

■ Ministry of Healing and Exorcisms

In spite of the philosophical bias of modern science against miracles, the historical-critical study of the Gospels strongly suggests that Jesus devoted a significant part of His ministry to healing and exorcisms. Even His

opponents acknowledged that Jesus performed miracles, even though they attributed them to Satan's power (Mark 3:22).

A more important question is why Jesus performed miracles. His purpose was not to prove His divinity. Jesus himself put it this way: "But if it is by the finger of God that I cast out the demons, then the kingdom of God has come to you" (Luke 11:20). His miracles demonstrated that the kingdom of God had come.

Many in the first century viewed illness as God's judgment on sin, as illustrated in the question of the disciples to Jesus about a man born blind. "Rabbi," they asked, "who sinned, this man or his parents, that he was born blind?" (John 9:2). Jesus replied that the blindness was not because of sin but that it provided the occasion for God to work in the man's life.

When Jesus was criticized for healing a crippled woman on the Sabbath, He said, "Ought not this woman, a daughter of Abraham whom Satan bound for eighteen long years, be set free from this bondage on the sabbath day?" (Luke 13:16).

Quoting the words of Isaiah, Jesus described His ministry of healing as a demonstration of God's liberating power for the poor and oppressed (Luke 4:18-19). Sick people, the blind, and lepers were no longer social outcasts. To stress this point, He healed lepers by touching them, which the Law had forbidden (Leviticus 13). The kingdom of God had come, and it included them.

■ "Nature" Miracles

Scholars have been much more skeptical about the historicity of

H

Demon Possession and Exorcism in the First Century

Belief in evil spirits was widespread in the first century among Jews as well as Gentiles.[3] Because people feared these evil, destructive forces that infested the universe, there was a high demand for the services of exorcists. Epileptic seizures, mental and emotional abnormalities, and certain chronic illnesses were thought to be caused by demon possession. In addition to such terms as "demon" and "evil spirit," the New Testament also refers to these spiritual forces as rulers, authorities, "cosmic powers of this present darkness, . . . spiritual forces of evil in the heavenly places" (Ephesians 6:12). Various methods of exorcism were thought to be effective against demons, such as the holy character of the exorcist, or certain objects, actions, words, or names.

the so-called nature miracles, including the feeding of the 5,000 (Mark 6:32-44; John 6:1-15), the walking on the water (Mark 6:45-52; John 6:16-21), the stilling of the storm (Mark 4:35-41), the miraculous catch of fish (Luke 5:1-11; John 21:1-11), and the turning of water to wine (John 2:1-11).

Rather than starting with the philosophical bias of modernity against miracles, one can apply several tests of historicity to these accounts. Three of these miracles occur both in the Synoptic Gospels and in John, providing us with multiple attestation.

The test of dissimilarity applies here also. The Early Church was not noted for these types of miracles and therefore not likely to create them to make Jesus look larger than life.

The linguistic and cultural test shows that the details of these stories fit well in the Galilean setting of Jesus, such as crowds in the countryside without food, fishing and a storm on the Sea of Galilee, or a wedding in the Galilean village of Cana running out of wine. There would be no reason for the Early Church to invent such local coloration.

Though using the same stories, the Gospel writers often adapt them for their own theological purposes. The feeding of the 5,000 in Mark shows the compassion of Jesus for the hungry multitudes (6:34), whereas in John it stresses the spiritual meaning of eating the body of Christ and drinking His blood symbolized in Holy Communion (6:53-56).

■ Disciples

Just as ancient Israel consisted of 12 tribes, Jesus chose 12 disciples to be the nucleus of a new Is-rael. After Israel had experienced the judgment of God in the Exile, Judaism hoped that some day God would restore Israel and establish His kingdom in a decisive way. Jesus believed that that time had come. His own ministry inaugurated the kingdom of God, and the 12 disciples were to be part of that inauguration. Jesus said to the Twelve, "I confer on you, just as my Father has conferred on me, a kingdom, so that you may eat and drink at my table in my kingdom, and you will sit on thrones judging the twelve tribes of Israel" (Luke 22:29-30; cf. Matthew 19:28).

The disciples often misunderstood the nature of the reign of God or the meaning of discipleship. They expected a triumphant, royal messiah and a glorious kingdom, which was not what Jesus had in mind. Halfway through Mark, when Jesus told them that suffering and death awaited Him in Jerusalem, Peter rebuked Jesus (8:31-32). Jesus said that if they wanted to be His disciples, they must deny themselves, take up their cross, and follow Him (v. 34). "Whoever comes to me and does not hate father and mother, wife and children, brothers and sisters, yes, and even life itself, cannot be my disciple" (Luke 14:26). Some of His most radical statements about discipleship are in the parables that He told.

Parables of the Kingdom of God

Not only did Jesus act out the presence of the reign of God by associating with outcasts and offering them healing, but He also told subversive parables to issue a radical message to the hearers. Although the details of His para-

I   Types of Parables That Jesus Told

There is not a single method of classifying the parables of Jesus. Some scholars classify them by making a distinction between parables that have a lengthy narrative plot, such as the prodigal son (Luke 15:11-32), and parables that are one-liners, without much of a plot, such as the mustard seed (Mark 4:31). Some scholars classify them by using the part of the social world from which Jesus drew the elements of His parables. On this basis, one scholar has classified the parables under three categories: (1) family, village, city, and beyond, (2) masters and servants, and (3) home and farm.[4] Still others have classified them on the basis of the theological points that the parables make. A good example of such a method is that of Arland Hultgren who places the parables under seven headings: (1) revelation of God, (2) exemplary behavior, (3) wisdom, (4) life before God, (5) final judgment, (6) allegorical parables, (7) parables of the kingdom.[5] Regardless of the method, scholars agree that the parables of Jesus must be studied in the historical context of the life of Jesus without reading into them elaborate allegorical meanings derived from the later theology of the Christian Church.[6]

bles came from everyday, familiar occurrences, Jesus invariably introduced a twist that puzzled the hearers. The parables of Jesus were not harmless illustrations of the status quo. They presented an alternate reality that stood at odds with the familiar.

The kingdom of God is like a mustard seed, very small, but when it has grown it becomes a great shrub (Matthew 13:32). Mustard is a nasty weed that spreads rapidly and takes over a garden. The Kingdom is also like yeast that leavens a large quantity of flour (v. 33). Yeast was not always a positive symbol. The kingdom of God is revolutionary. It

can be unobtrusive and subtle and yet so powerful and captivating that a laborer might sell all of his possessions to buy a field because he happened to find a treasure in it. It is like a merchant who sold everything he had to buy a single pearl of exquisite quality (vv. 44-45).

The parables of Jesus often made people uncomfortable and even angry, as in the case of the parable of the vineyard and tenants (Mark 12:12).

The parable of the Good Samaritan (Luke 10:29-37) is particularly poignant. To test Jesus, a Jewish theologian asked Him what he must do to inherit eternal life. Jesus asked him what the Scriptures said. The theologian pointed out the two great commandments of loving God and loving one's neighbor. Jesus told him to do this and he would have eternal life. Embarrassed that the test was too easy, the theologian asked, "And who is my neighbor?" Jesus told him the story of the Good Samaritan and ended it by asking the theologian which of the three—the priest, the Levite, the Samaritan—proved to be a neighbor to the one victimized by robbers. The theologian could not even use the word "Samaritan." Instead, he said, "The one who showed him mercy." Jesus said to him, "Go and do likewise."

Modern readers do not often grasp the offensiveness of that last statement. Jews despised Samaritans and did not associate with them. For Jesus to hold up a Samaritan as a model of virtue would be an ultimate insult to a Jewish theologian. To grasp the finer points of the parables, one needs to understand the social world of Jesus.

Journey to Jerusalem

Halfway through the Gospels Jesus turns His face toward Jerusalem to carry His message to the very center of the religious and political establishment.

Jewish pilgrims came to Jerusalem for Passover to celebrate ancient Israel's liberation from Egypt. Roman authorities knew that pilgrims, resentful of Roman occupation, could explode in their nationalistic feelings and start an uprising. Roman soldiers had standing orders to strike hard at the least sign of disturbance. Jewish leaders felt responsible to keep pilgrims calm. One cannot imagine how dangerous it was at a time like this for Jesus to speak to crowds in Jerusalem about another kingdom within earshot of Jewish and Roman authorities. Yet speak He must. Jesus was so compelled by His vision of the kingdom of God that not even the elite in Jerusalem were exempt from being confronted by it.

The Gospels say that Jesus predicted three times that He would suffer and die in Jerusalem (Mark 8:31; 9:31; 10:33-34). Roman crucifixions of Jews were common during Jesus' lifetime. He was certainly aware that **Herod Antipas,** the son of Herod the Great, executed John the Baptist (Mark 6) and was threatening to kill Him also (Luke 13:31). The Herodian family and the Romans were suspicious of anyone who spoke of another kingdom.

■ Conflict in Jerusalem

Entry into Jerusalem

Jesus entered Jerusalem riding on a donkey as a deliberate act of messianic demonstration. The re-

Messianic Expectation in First-Century Judaism

There is no doubt that the Jewish people in the first century fervently expected the Messiah, the Anointed One. Several messianic movements besides the Jesus movement got underway, but they were all crushed violently by the Romans. But what type of messiah did people expect? Passages in the Gospels and Acts, the writings of the Essenes at Qumran, as well as the writings of the first-century Jewish historian Josephus, attest to the fact that Judaism longed for deliverance from bondage to Roman domination and the dawning of a golden age. The Dead Sea Scrolls, the library of the Essenes at Qumran, indicate that this Jewish sect seems to have expected a royal Messiah as well as a priestly Messiah.[7] Even the followers of Jesus hoped for a messiah who would bring political victory to Israel. After the feeding of the 5,000, the crowd wanted to take Jesus by force and make Him king (John 6:15). James and John asked Jesus that they sit on His right and left in His kingdom (Mark 10:37). After the resurrection of Jesus, the disciples asked Him, "Lord, is this the time when you will restore the kingdom to Israel?" (Acts 1:6).

ligious leaders and the crowd of Jewish pilgrims perfectly understood the symbolism from the messianic prophecy of Zechariah 9:9: "Rejoice greatly, O daughter Zion! Shout aloud, O daughter Jerusalem! Lo, your king comes to you; triumphant and victorious is he, humble and riding on a donkey, on a colt, the foal of a donkey."

The crowd shouted a psalm (118:25-26) that celebrated victory over Israel's enemies: "Hosanna! Blessed is the one who comes in the name of the Lord! Blessed is the coming kingdom of our ancestor David! Hosanna in the highest heaven!" (Mark 11:9-10).

Why did Jesus deliberately stage such a messianic demonstration, given the fact that in His Galilean ministry He avoided it? He intended to proclaim the arrival of the kingdom of God into the tightly controlled precincts of Jerusalem and the Temple. This staged drama did get the attention of the religious authorities (Matthew 21:10). They said to Jesus, "Teacher, order your disciples to stop" (Luke 19:39). They feared that this much public demonstration might lead to a major crackdown by nervous Roman authorities (John 11:47-48). The kingdom of God threatened their vested interests and political power structures.

Some Christians identify Golgotha with this stone with skull-like features, outside of the wall of the Old City of Jerusalem.

Disturbance at the Temple

Jesus went to the Temple, drove out the buyers and sellers, and overturned the tables of the money changers (Mark 11:15-17), quoting to them Isaiah 56:7 and Jeremiah 7:11, "Is it not written, 'My house shall be called a house of prayer for all the nations'? But you have made it a den of robbers." Jesus became angry at the chaotic merchandising going on in the Outer Court of the Temple, the only part where Gentiles could enter. The Temple had become a noisy bazaar, far from a house of prayer for all nations.

The Temple authorities justified all of this buying and selling because it had to do with animals for sacrifices. The money changers exchanged Roman currency for sacred money appropriate for Temple offerings. Jesus, though, accused them of turning the Temple into a den of robbers, implying that devout pilgrims were charged exorbitant prices. The Temple had become an oppressive institution of injustice that benefited the priestly aristocracy.

The Temple leaders confronted Jesus and asked Him by what authority He was doing this. They began to look for a way to take Him into custody (Mark 11:18, 28).

The Last Supper and Gethsemane

While Jesus engaged in public activity and debate, He also met with His disciples privately. The Last Supper and the subsequent prayer in Gethsemane are particularly intriguing because they give us a glimpse into Jesus' understanding of His own death.

The different accounts of the Last Supper (Mark 14:22-25; Matthew 26:26-29; Luke 22:17-20;

1 Corinthians 11:24-25), agree on several points. First, the death of Jesus, symbolized by the bread and wine, would be a renewal of the Old Testament covenant celebrated at Passover. Second, His death was to be for others. Third, His death would not be the end but part of the kingdom of God with a future dimension.

The Gethsemane episode shows the utter horror with which Jesus faced the prospect of His own death. He was distressed, horrified, and agitated (Mark 14:33-34). He prayed that this hour pass from Him, that God remove this cup from Him. The final line of His prayer, however, was, "Not what I want, but what you want" (v. 36). He would be faithful to God regardless of the consequences.

Crucifixion and Resurrection

■ The Crucifixion of Jesus

Since crucifixion was a Roman form of execution, **Pontius Pilate,** the Roman governor, who was cruel, arrogant, and utterly contemptuous of Jews, was responsible for crucifying Jesus. Yet the Gospels portray Pilate as reluctant to condemn Jesus but forced to do so under pressure from the Jewish elite (Matthew 27:24-25; Mark 15:9-11; Luke 23:4-5; John 19:12). The historical fact is that Pilate, with the collaboration of the **Sanhedrin,** the highest Jewish council in Jerusalem, condemned Jesus to death.

The Sanhedrin charged Jesus with blasphemy because He claimed divine prerogatives by identifying himself as the Son of Man of Daniel 7:13 seated at the

> **H** **Crucifixion in the Roman World**
>
> Since the Romans used crucifixion as a deterrence, it was always carried out in a public place. It was generally reserved for non-Romans, revolutionaries, the lowest classes, and the most dangerous criminals. Prior to crucifixion, the convict was stripped and brutally flogged with the Roman flagellum, which was a whip with sharp bones or metal pieces attached to it, calculated to tear the flesh. The convict was then led to the place of crucifixion and was attached to the horizontal and vertical beams of the cross with ropes or nails. Death often came slowly, only after several days of sheer agony. The victim died of asphyxiation when the legs and arms could no longer provide the needed support to fill the lungs with air.[8]

right hand of God and coming on the clouds of heaven (Mark 14:61-64). The Sanhedrin invoked the law in Leviticus 24:16 that imposed the death sentence on anyone who "blasphemes the name of the Lord."

Only the Roman governor, not the Sanhedrin, could impose the death penalty (John 18:31). However, since Jewish scruples against blasphemy would not carry much weight with the Romans, the religious leaders brought the more political charge that Jesus was aspiring to be king (Luke 23:2; John 18:33-35). All four Gospels agree that the inscription on the cross of Jesus included the words "King of the Jews."

In the first century, there was no clear demarcation between religion, politics, and economics. The Jewish leaders saw themselves as the duly authorized representatives of God. The Romans equated allegiance to the gods with loyalty to the empire. Jesus' death resulted from collaboration between the

T   Son of Man

In the Gospels Jesus often refers to himself as the "Son of Man." The phrase most likely comes from Daniel 7:13 where Daniel says that he saw in a vision someone "like a son of man, coming with the clouds of heaven" (Daniel 7:13, NIV). Jesus apparently used this title as a self-reference possibly because it had only vague messianic connotations. He avoided the title Messiah because most people expected a powerful messiah who would bring political liberation from Roman domination.

Many scholarly studies and debates have been carried on the Son of Man sayings of Jesus. Scholars have noted that these sayings generally fall under three categories: (1) those that refer to the earthly ministry of Jesus and His identification with humanity; (2) those that predict His humiliation, suffering, and death for others; and (3) those that speak of His future coming in glory.

The designation Son of Man certainly affirms the humanity of Jesus, His identification with all of humankind, and His self-sacrifice for others. However, the statement in Daniel 7:13 and its adaptation by Jesus in Mark 14:62, that the Son of Man will be seated at the right hand of the Power and coming with the clouds of heaven, surely implies something more than the humanity of Jesus. The language of exaltation to the right hand of God implies that Jesus in some significant way shares in divine status and glory.

religious elite of Judaism and the political power of Rome.

■ The Resurrection of Jesus

The crucifixion of Jesus could not put a stop to the kingdom of God. After His death, the followers of Jesus have testified that He appeared to them. In spite of diversity in details, the Synoptic Gospels, John and Paul attest to the resurrection of Jesus. The differences in details actually strengthen the evidence. If all the witnesses said the same thing, we

would suspect that they harmonized their stories.

Paul mentions the appearances of the resurrected Jesus to Cephas (Peter), the Twelve, 500 people, James (Jesus' brother), all the apostles, and last of all Paul himself (1 Corinthians 15:3-8). The Gospels and Acts provide parallels to some of these appearances, but not all. According to the Gospels, Jesus appeared to Peter (Luke 24:34) and the other disciples (Matthew 28:16-17; Luke 24:33, 36). Acts 9:4-5 recounts Jesus' appearance to Paul. The Gospels and Acts do not mention the appearances to the 500 or to James.

Paul wrote 1 Corinthians around A.D. 55-60. He says that he had passed on to them the story of Jesus' death and resurrection (15:3), which he had heard from eyewitnesses. Here we have a very early tradition to attest to the resurrection of Jesus.

Paul does not mention the appearance of Jesus to Mary Magdalene, as Matthew and John do (Matthew 28:1, 9; John 20:14-18). Given the low status of women in the first century, it is unlikely that these Gospels invented a Resurrection appearance to a woman. If they wanted to create stories, noteworthy apostles such as Peter, James, and John would have been better candidates for Resurrection appearances.

A more theological question has to do with the nature of the Resurrection itself. The Gospels affirm that the body of Jesus was resurrected, thus leaving the tomb empty. Other writings, such as 1 Corinthians 15:3-8, speak of Resurrection appearances without the mention of an empty tomb. Does "appear" mean a bodily resurrection?

Some Christians regard this tomb located in the setting of a garden, outside the wall of the Old City of Jerusalem, as a possible site of Jesus' burial.

The New Testament answer is yes. Christ's bodily resurrection means that God intends to redeem all of creation, including the material part. Resurrection is much more than the survival of a bodiless soul.

The resurrection of Jesus, however, was much more than resuscitation of a dead corpse. God did something utterly new. It was an **eschatological** event, meaning that the final age of history has already begun. The resurrection of Jesus inaugurated a new reality in history. Just as Jesus was raised, so also will those who are in Christ. Believers in Christ have already been raised spiritually to a new way of life, but they will also be raised bodily in the final resurrection (Romans 6:8-9; 1 Corinthians 15:20-23).

Summary Statements

- Historical knowledge about Jesus is crucial because the Christian faith affirms that God acted in history through Jesus.
- The Gospels affirm that Jesus was born as a human being but also that He was the Son of God.
- The birth of Jesus in Bethlehem, the city of David, has implications of royal Messiahship for Jesus.
- The baptism and temptation of Jesus are signs of His identification with humanity.
- The miracles of Jesus were a demonstration that the kingdom of God had come.
- Jesus chose 12 disciples to be the nucleus of a new Israel.
- The parables of Jesus often shocked people and called them to repentance in response to the kingdom of God inaugurated through His life and ministry.
- Jesus deliberately went to Jerusalem to challenge the religious leaders with the reality of the kingdom of God.
- Jewish and Roman authorities collaborated to bring about the death of Jesus.
- Jesus died with the conviction that through His death and resurrection the kingdom of God would ultimately prevail against injustice and sin.
- The resurrection of Jesus is an eschatological event in the sense that the final age has already begun and a new reality of divine victory has been inaugurated in history.

Questions for Reflection

1. If Jesus were alive today, in what circles would we most likely find Him?
2. What does it mean to make the kingdom of God the central focus of your life?
3. Do people today mix religion and politics in the same way that people in Jerusalem did and ended up crucifying Jesus?

Resources for Further Study

Borg, Marcus J., and N. T. Wright. *The Meaning of Jesus: Two Visions.* San Francisco: HarperSanFrancisco, 1998.
Crossan, John Dominic, and Richard G. Watts. *Who Is Jesus?* Louisville, Ky.: Westminster/John Knox, 1996.
Nolan, Albert. *Jesus Before Christianity.* New York: Orbis, 1992.
Sanders, E. P. *The Historical Figure of Jesus.* London: Penguin, 1993.
Strobel, Lee. *The Case for Christ.* Grand Rapids: Zondervan, 1998.
Theissen, Gerd. *The Shadow of the Galilean.* Philadelphia: Fortress, 1987.

6

The Gospel According to Matthew

O bjectives:

Your study of this chapter should help you to:
- Describe Matthew's purpose for writing.
- Identify the literary characteristics of Matthew.
- Summarize the prominent themes in Matthew.
- Discuss Matthew's portrait of Jesus.

Q uestions to consider as you read:

1. Why is Jesus as a kingly Messiah and Teacher important for Matthew?
2. How does Matthew relate the story of Jesus to the Old Testament?
3. In what way does Matthew urge the Church of his time to remain faithful to the past teachings of Jesus?

K ey Words to Understand

Q
Redaction criticism
Genealogy
Royal Messiah
Sermon on the Mount
Torah
Ekklēsia
Ecclesiology
Great Commission
Narrative
Discourse
Beatitudes
Antitheses
Anti-Semitic
Eschatology
Olivet Discourse
Delay of the Parousia

Since Mark was the first Gospel to be written, as discussed in chapter 4, why did the other Gospel writers feel the need to write their own accounts? And how is it that Matthew ended up in first position in the order of New Testament books?

By comparing and contrasting the different Gospels, scholars have discovered that Matthew used at least 80 percent of the material in Mark.[1] However, Matthew has at least 50 percent more material than Mark. This additional material in Matthew happens to be in Luke also and consists mostly of the sayings of Jesus. Most scholars today accept the hypothesis that Matthew and Luke used Mark and an additional source that contained the sayings of Jesus. Scholars have called this additional source **Q**, which stands for the first letter of the German word *Quelle,* which means "source." In addition to Mark and Q, Matthew may have had access to other traditions that are part of his Gospel but not in Mark or Luke. Matthew sensed the need to add these materials to Mark's story of Jesus.

The Purpose of Matthew

Matthew carefully designed his Gospel. He introduced certain changes into the material from Mark. He condensed Mark's stories, improved awkward sentences, lessened references to the feelings of Jesus, and avoided or altered some of Mark's favorite expressions.[2] In spite of these editorial changes, Matthew incorporated much of the public ministry and suffering and death of Jesus that he found in Mark into his own narrative. In addition to the sayings of Jesus that Matthew used to supplement what he found in Mark, Matthew also added the birth story of Jesus at the beginning and the Resurrection appearances of Jesus at the end, both of which are absent in

Mark. **Redaction criticism,** a scholarly approach to the study of the biblical books, helps us to understand how a biblical author has arranged, adapted, and edited earlier materials to achieve a particular theological purpose.

What, then, was Matthew's purpose? Like Mark, Matthew does not state why he wrote his Gospel. We must discover his purpose by examining the text. Since much of Mark is in Matthew, what was said about Mark's purpose can also be said about Matthew's.

A good clue for understanding Matthew's purpose is the opening statement of the Gospel: "An account of the **genealogy** of Jesus the Messiah, the son of David, the son of Abraham" (1:1). Following this opening statement, Matthew lists the ancestors of Jesus in a more detailed genealogy. The fact that Matthew shows Jesus to be a descendant of David, Israel's most venerated king, and of Abraham, Israel's primal ancestor, alerts the reader to the fact that Jesus is a **royal Messiah** whose ancestry is firmly rooted in Jewish history. As the royal Messiah, Jesus fulfills all the hopes and messianic expectations of the Old Testament.[3] This connection of Jesus to the Old Testament is one reason why the Gospel of Matthew ended up as the first book of the New Testament canon.

A second purpose, which is related to the above, is that Matthew as a Jewish-Christian writer wrote his Gospel to show that the Christian movement arising from Jesus was not a departure from Judaism but its ultimate fulfillment. More than any other New Testament writer, Matthew shows

how the life and teachings of Jesus fulfill prophecies of the Hebrew Bible. The statement of Papias about Matthew is consistent
with the scholarly view that
Matthew is the most Jewish of the
four Gospels (see sidebar).

Third, by adding the sayings of
Jesus to Mark's Gospel, Matthew
intended to highlight the teachings of Jesus. Matthew's focus on
Jesus as Teacher is evident from
other features of the Gospel, such
as large blocks of teaching material and explicit references to the
teaching ministry of Jesus. In the
Sermon on the Mount in Matthew 5—7, Jesus is presented as
One who has authority to give a
definitive interpretation of the
Torah, the Hebrew Scriptures.
Yet Matthew is careful to say that
Jesus has come not to abolish but
to fulfill the Law and the Prophets
(5:17).

Matthew's purpose, however,
goes even beyond that. Not only
does the authority of Jesus sur-
pass that of Moses and the
prophets from the past, but it also
extends to the future life of the
Church. Of the four Gospels,
Matthew is the only one where
we find the term *ekklēsia,* the
Greek word for church. After Peter's confession of Jesus as the
Christ, Jesus says to Peter,
"Blessed are you, Simon son of
Jonah! . . . And I tell you, you are
Peter, and on this rock I will build
my church" (16:17-18). Chapter
18, which is one of the major discourses of Jesus in Matthew, is
devoted to issues related to life in
the Church. People in the Church
must be like little children. They
must not despise "one of these little ones." They must make every
effort to forgive and be recon-
ciled to one another. If someone

L The Statement of Papias

We have certain statements from Early
Church fathers concerning the four Gospels. Eusebius, a church historian of the fourth century,
quotes the second-century church father Papias
who had received and passed on traditions about
the writing of some of the Gospels, including the
Gospel of Matthew.

Papias reports that "Matthew put together
the oracles [of the Lord] in the Hebrew language,
and each one interpreted them as best he could."[4]
However, this statement has several ambiguities.
It is uncertain whether "the oracles of the Lord"
refers to the Gospel of Matthew as we have it now.
The Gospel of Matthew is much more than the oracles or sayings of Jesus. Furthermore, this Gospel
was most likely composed in Greek rather than
Hebrew or Aramaic. It may be that Papias refers to
an earlier writing coming from Matthew, written in
Aramaic and containing sayings of Jesus, something similar to what we call Q.[5]

sins against another member of
the Church, certain steps are to
be taken to bring about a resolution. If efforts by individuals and
small groups fail, the whole
Church must take action. "If the
offender refuses to listen even to
the church," Jesus says, "let such
a one be to you as a Gentile and a
tax collector" (18:17). Jesus gives
the Church extraordinary authority and responsibility when He
says, "Whatever you bind on
earth will be bound in heaven,
and whatever you loose on earth
will be loosed in heaven" (v. 18).

However, the Church does not
have a privileged position independent of Christ. Matthew's **ecclesiology,** the nature of the
Church, is that the Church must
live its life under the authority of
Jesus and receive its identity in
relation to Christ.[6] It must main-

tain its faithfulness to Jesus by living a righteous life, serving others, and bearing witness to the gospel. Otherwise, it might find itself under judgment on the final day (7:21-25; 25:12). Matthew concludes his Gospel with what has come to be known as the **Great Commission.** In this final word, the resurrected Christ meets with His disciples and commissions them, and by doing so, He addresses the future Church:

> All authority in heaven and on earth has been given to me. Go therefore and make disciples of all nations, baptizing them in the name of the Father and of the Son and of the Holy Spirit, and teaching them to obey everything that I have commanded you. And remember, I am with you always, to the end of the age (28:18-20).

This word of Jesus underscores several concerns that Matthew has for the Church. The Church must live under the authority of Jesus, which is not of human origin but part of a Trinity of Father, Son, and Holy Spirit. The Church must bear witness to Jesus by making disciples of all nations. Whereas earlier Jesus sent His disciples to the house of Israel (10:5-6), now He sends them out to all the nations of the world. The gospel is not exclusively for Israel. Finally, as the Church engages in mission, Jesus promises that His presence in the Church will continue to the end of time.

Literary Characteristics

One of the prominent characteristics of the Gospel of Matthew is its structure. Even a cursory reading of Matthew will reveal that the contents alternate between **narrative** and **discourse.** In the narrative sections, Matthew uses stories about Jesus that come from Mark. However, Matthew often condenses Mark's narrative material by omitting vivid details from the stories. A good example is Mark's lengthy story of Jairus's daughter and the hemorrhaging woman, compared with Matthew's greatly abbreviated version (Mark 5:21-43; Matthew 9:18-26). This may be because Matthew intends to place greater emphasis on the teachings of Jesus.

In the discourse sections, Matthew presents the teachings of Jesus. The most widely recognized feature of the Gospel of Matthew is the alternation between five

A special characteristic of Orthodox Jews is their concern for the strict observance of the Torah.

Literary Structure of Matthew

The alternation between narrative and discourse material is one of the ways that scholars have understood Matthew's literary scheme, as follows:

Narrative (chaps. 1—4):	Birth, baptism, temptation of Jesus and inauguration of His ministry
Discourse (chaps. 5—7):	Sermon on the Mount
Narrative (chaps. 8—9):	Miracles of Jesus
Discourse (chap. 10):	Mission instructions to the Twelve
Narrative (chaps. 11—12):	Opposition to Jesus and controversies
Discourse (chap. 13):	Parables of the kingdom of God
Narrative (chaps. 14—17):	Various types of stories including death of John the Baptist, miracles, controversies, Peter's confession, Passion predictions, and transfiguration of Jesus
Discourse (chap. 18):	Instructions concerning Christian community
Narrative (chaps. 19—23):	Journey of Jesus toward Jerusalem, leading to controversies with scribes and Pharisees
Discourse (chaps. 24—25):	The eschatological discourse
Narrative (chaps. 26—28):	Passion and Resurrection narratives[7]

major discourses and six narrative sections, as illustrated in the sidebar. Matthew may have wanted to pattern his Gospel after the five books of the Torah (Genesis through Deuteronomy), thus portraying Jesus as One who is greater than Moses.

Other scholars have suggested that this popular way of understanding Matthew's structure does not do justice to all the material in Matthew, particularly Matthew's use of Mark. Consequently, they have proposed another way of understanding the structure of Matthew. They have taken their cue from an identical statement at two significant junctures in the Gospel: "From that time Jesus began to . . ." (4:17; see 16:21). Accordingly, they divide the Gospel into the following three sections, arguing that such a structure does greater justice to Matthew's use of Mark's narrative material:

Introduction to the person of Jesus (1:1—4:16)

The public ministry of Jesus (4:17—16:20)

The journey of Jesus to Jerusalem and His suffering, death, and resurrection (16:21—28:20)

Still others have proposed various combinations of the above methods.[8] Be that as it may, it is clear that Matthew has supplemented Mark's narrative with sayings of Jesus that He collected from other sources and organized them into five major discourses, intending to pattern his Gospel after the five books of the Torah to provide his Christian community with "the messianic equivalent" to the Law of Moses.[9]

Matthew tends to place similar materials in groups of three, as in the following examples: threefold division of the genealogy of Jesus (1:17); three illustrations of righteousness (6:1-5); and three eschatological parables (chap. 25). Matthew may have been influenced by the Law of Moses that requires two or three witnesses as evidence of authenticity, another instance of Matthew's Jewish tendencies (Deuteronomy 19:15; cf. Matthew 18:16).[10]

Finally, Matthew's use of the Old Testament is another significant characteristic of this Gospel.[11] There are over 60 quotations from the Old Testament in Matthew, not counting a great many allusions. Understanding Matthew's use of these quotations is a challenge. Although Matthew frequently uses the word "fulfill" to indicate the relationship between Jesus and an Old Testament text, our popular notions of prediction and fulfillment are inadequate to explain what Matthew has done. Some of the quoted texts are not even predictions of future events. For example, after Matthew describes Herod's massacre of children in Bethlehem, he goes on to say, "Then was fulfilled what had been spoken through the prophet

Jeremiah: 'A voice was heard in Ramah, wailing and loud lamentation, Rachel weeping for her children; she refused to be consoled, because they are no more'" (2:17-18). Two things are worth noting. First, the town mentioned in Jeremiah is not Bethlehem but Ramah. Second, the statement in Jeremiah is not about future events but about past events. This is not to suggest that Matthew was careless in his quotations, but simply to illustrate the inadequacy of our popular notions of prediction and fulfillment to explain Matthew's use of the Old Testament.

Another example of prophecy and fulfillment in Matthew is found in 8:17, where the writer quotes Isaiah 53:4: "This was to fulfill what had been spoken through the prophet Isaiah, 'He took our infirmities and bore our diseases.'" Matthew quotes this prophetic word in the context of Jesus' healing ministry and identifies Jesus as the Suffering Servant. However, the verb in Isaiah's statement is past tense, referring to events that had already taken place, rather than making future predictions. Many scholars believe that the Suffering Servant in Isaiah 53 is the nation of Israel that had gone through the agony of the Babylonian exile.

Prominent Themes in Matthew

■ The Law and the Prophets

No other Gospel uses the phrase "the law and the prophets," or a variant of it, as extensively as Matthew does, an indication of Matthew's Jewish roots

---

T

Prophecy and Fulfillment

How should we understand Matthew's use of Old Testament prophecies? Perhaps the most important point to observe is that Matthew begins with Jesus and then looks back to the Old Testament to show the continuity. In Matthew's mind, "fulfill" means that the life, message, death, and resurrection of Jesus bring fuller meaning to the Old Testament scriptures. The meaning of Old Testament texts becomes complete as we come to grips with God's self-disclosure in Jesus. It is not a matter of God predestining future events and revealing these to prophets in advance. Rather, it is a matter of being able to understand the deeper meaning of the Old Testament in light of what we see in Jesus.[12]

This hillside northwest of the Sea of Galilee may have been the site of the Sermon on the Mount.

and his intention to show that Jesus and the Old Testament scriptures are a single, continuous story of revelatory events. Jesus has not come to abolish the Law or the Prophets but to fulfill them (5:17). In a similar vein, Jesus encapsulates all the commandments of the OT in the two great commandments of loving God with all the heart, soul and mind, and loving one's neighbor as oneself. "On these two commandments hang all the law and the prophets" (22:40).

Nevertheless, something new and decisive has taken place in Jesus, starting with John the Baptist. This is the final epoch in the history of God's saving acts; "all the prophets and the law prophesied until John came" (11:13). Jesus is much more than another Moses or another prophet. We will return to this theme later.

■ Righteousness

Correlated with Matthew's emphasis on the Law and the Prophets is the theme of righteousness,

particularly in the Sermon on the Mount (chaps. 5—7). The **beatitudes,** the nine statements that begin with "Blessed," are the opening words of the Sermon on the Mount. In one beatitude Jesus says, "Blessed are those who hunger and thirst for righteousness, for they will be filled" (5:6). In another beatitude he says, "Blessed are those who are persecuted for righteousness' sake" (v. 10). In verse 20, another key passage in the Sermon on the Mount, Jesus states, "Unless your righteousness exceeds that of the scribes and Pharisees, you will never enter the kingdom of heaven." The rest of the Sermon on the Mount is in effect an elaboration of the theme of righteousness.

The next major section of the Sermon on the Mount consists of six **antitheses** (5:21-48). All six are constructed the same way, contrasting what was said earlier in the Hebrew Scriptures and what Jesus was saying now: "You have heard that it was said . . . But I say to you . . ." Each antithe-

"Christian Perfection" in Matthew

Far from being less demanding, Jesus reminds His disciples of the true meaning of the Old Testament commandments. Obedience to God is a matter of one's heart rather than merely a matter of external conduct.

The antitheses in Matthew 5 conclude with the highest possible standard of life when Jesus says, "Be perfect, therefore, as your heavenly Father is perfect" (v. 48). The context makes it clear that this perfection of the Christian is that of perfect love that refuses to return evil for evil. Perfect love is forgiving and charitable to both friends and enemies. The pattern of Christian perfection is God, who "makes his sun rise on the evil and on the good, and sends rain on the righteous and on the unrighteous" (v. 45).

sis is an illustration of the principle stated in verse 20 that the righteousness of the disciples must exceed that of the Pharisees. For example, it is not enough to refrain from murder; one must not even be angry.

The theme of righteousness continues in 6:1-18, where Jesus warns against practicing one's piety (literally, "righteousness") before others to be seen by them. Almsgiving, prayer, and fasting are to be done secretly and without fanfare, to be seen by God rather than by people.

Instead of worrying over food and clothing, one must "strive first for the kingdom of God and his righteousness, and all these things will be given to you as well" (6:33). A true disciple acts

Matthew and Anti-Semitism

After the destruction of Jerusalem by the Romans in A.D. 70, the Pharisees and the Christian movement were the two surviving sects that vied with each other for the future of Judaism. The two groups eventually became two world religions, Judaism and Christianity. The beginnings of the debate between these two communities can be seen in Matthew. Matthew 23 is a strong polemic against the Pharisees. Other passages in Matthew have been taken to be anti-Jewish, particularly 27:25, where the crowd at the trial of Jesus shouts, "His blood be on us and on our children!" Because of such statements, many Jewish as well as Christian interpreters of the Gospel of Matthew have noted a strong anti-Jewish and even **anti-Semitic** tone in this Gospel. Others have asked, How can the most Jewish of the four Gospels be charged with anti-Semitism?[13]

Unfortunately, the future history of Christendom, which became overwhelmingly Gentile, was checkered with prejudice and persecution against all Jewish people, who were labeled as "Christ killers." That kind of polemic ultimately led to the most radical form of anti-Semitism, namely, the genocide of 6 million Jews in Nazi Germany during World War II. Such sinful acts against the Jewish people no doubt found biblical support, however illegitimately, in Matthew and other New Testament writings, in much the same manner as Christian slave owners used the Bible to support slavery in America.

One must remember that in the first century A.D. there were several Jewish groups that debated passionately with one another about what it meant to be Jewish. Matthew's Jewish Christian community and a Jewish synagogue led by Pharisees saw themselves as two rival Jewish sects rather than two different religions. For Matthew, faith in Christ did not mean accepting a religion different from Judaism. Consequently, the charge of anti-Semitism, which is really racial rather than religious, does not fit the historical context of Matthew.

on the words of Jesus and lives a fruitful life (7:15-29).

The theme of righteousness continues beyond the Sermon on the Mount. In a scathing denunciation of the Pharisees in chapter 23, Jesus likens them to "whitewashed tombs, which on the outside look beautiful, but inside they are full of the bones of the dead and of all kinds of filth. So you also on the outside look righteous to others, but inside you are full of hypocrisy and lawlessness" (vv. 27-28).

Matthew directs the charge of hypocrisy not only toward outsiders but also to members of his own Christian community, to those who may have made a confession of faith in Jesus but whose lifestyle and ethic did not show it.

In the eschatological discourse of chapters 24—25, where Jesus speaks of "the end-times," several parables target not those who were outside the Christian community but those who were inside.[14] In the parable in 25:1-13, all 10 bridesmaids were waiting for the return of Christ, the Bridegroom. But 5 of them did not have enough oil for their torches. While they were gone to purchase oil, the Bridegroom came and shut the door. When they returned, they found themselves left out of the wedding party. These bridesmaids represent those who profess the name of Christ but do not live the life of righteousness demanded by Christ. In the end they will find themselves under judgment. Earlier, in the Sermon on the Mount, Jesus says, "Not everyone who says to me, 'Lord, Lord,' will enter the kingdom of heaven, but only the one who does the will of my Father in heaven" (7:21).

The last parable in Matthew 25 is a scene of the final judgment when the Son of Man makes a distinction between the righteous and the unrighteous as a shepherd separates the sheep from the goats (vv. 31-46). In this parable, it is the Gentile nations that are being judged (v. 32). Those who welcome and care for "the least of these" will be invited to "inherit the kingdom prepared for you from the foundation of the world" (v. 34). Christ the Judge identifies the least of these as "members of my family," literally, "my brothers" (v. 40), that is, the missionaries whom Christ will send out to all nations (28:19). Those Gentiles who have ministered to the needs of the hungry, thirsty, estranged, naked, sick, and imprisoned messengers of Christ have unwittingly rendered service to Christ. On the other hand, the unrighteous are those who have failed to serve Christ by neglecting the needs of "the least of these." They will hear this word of judgment: "Just as you did not do it to one of the least of these, you did not do it to me" (v. 45).

To summarize, Matthew's indictment of unrighteousness targets not only the Jewish community and his own Christian community but also the whole Gentile world. Matthew issues a serious call to everyone to heed the demands of righteousness proclaimed and lived out by Christ.

■ Weeping and Gnashing of Teeth

Matthew uses another favorite phrase, "weeping and gnashing of teeth," as a threat of final judgment for so-called Christians who do not live a life of faithful service to Christ. The parable of the wedding banquet (22:1-14) is particularly significant in this regard. The guests originally invited to the banquet refused to come, and some of them even killed the messengers. Then the king invited people off the street. Among those who came off the street and entered the banquet hall was a man without a wedding robe. The king was indignant when he saw him. "Bind him hand and foot," he ordered the attendants, "and throw him into the outer darkness, where there will be weeping and gnashing of teeth" (v. 13). This man clearly represents those in Matthew's Christian group who may have accepted the call of Christ but failed to put on the "robe of righteousness" demanded by Christ. In the end they will be liable to judgment.

■ The End of the Age

A final theme in Matthew is **eschatology,** the theology of the end of the age, particularly the issue of

Christ's return. All three Synoptic Gospels contain the **Olivet Discourse,** so named after the Mount of Olives where Jesus spoke these words (24:3; Mark 13:3).[15]

The setting in which Jesus gives the discourse is found in Matthew 23:38—24:3. A sequence of events precedes this discourse. The events begin with Jesus' lament over Jerusalem: "See, your house is left to you, desolate" (23:38). Later, when the disciples point out to Jesus the buildings of the Temple, Jesus says, "You see all these, do you not? Truly I tell you, not one stone will be left here upon another; all will be thrown down" (24:2). The disciples then ask Him while they were with Him on the Mount of Olives, "Tell us, when will this be, and what *will* be the sign of your coming and of the end of the age?" (v. 3, emphasis added). Their question was about the time of (1) the destruction of the Temple, (2) the coming of Christ, and

The Temple Mount on the last Friday of Ramadan, a holy month in the Islamic calendar.

(3) the end of the age. The discourse of Jesus weaves together these three matters.

In the first part of the discourse, Jesus warns against anxious speculations about the end time. If Matthew wrote his Gospel in the mid-80s of the first century, he and his readers would have been familiar with the Jewish-Roman war that ended with the destruction of Jerusalem and the Temple in A.D. 70. Speculations about the end of the world would have been very much up in the air. It is in a context like that that Matthew reminds his readers what Jesus taught about such matters. Jesus said to His disciples: "You will hear of wars and rumors of wars; see that you are not alarmed; for this must take place, but the end is not yet" (v. 6). Wars, famines, earthquakes, and other cataclysmic events are not the signs of the coming of Christ and the end of the age.

Second, no one knows the time of Christ's coming except God (v. 36). Therefore, it would be futile to look for signs of its nearness. It will happen suddenly and without warning (vv. 36-44).

Third, there are indications in the Olivet Discourse that the coming of Christ may be later than what was thought at first. Scholars refer to this as the **delay of the Parousia** ("parousia" in Greek means "coming"). In the parable in 24:45-51, the slave whose master has gone away acts wickedly because he thinks to himself, "My master is delayed" (v. 48). In the parable of the 10 bridesmaids, the bridegroom arrives later than anticipated (25:5).

However, Jesus makes this puzzling statement in the middle of the discourse: "So also, when you see all these things, you know that he is near, at the very gates. Truly I tell you, this generation will not pass away until all these things have taken place" (24:33-34). What are "all these things"?

Prior to this statement, conditions related to the Jewish-Roman war and the fall of Jerusalem are alluded to in 24:4-26. Certainly, these events were part of "these things" that took place before the passing away of "this generation" to whom Jesus spoke. However, Jesus goes on to speak of the sun, the moon, and the stars being darkened and shaken and the Son of Man coming on the clouds of heaven and gathering His elect from the four corners of the earth (vv. 29-31). Following that, He makes the statement about this generation not passing away before all these things have taken place. Did Jesus mean that His coming would occur within the lifetime of those who were listening to Him? If so, does that mean that Jesus was mistaken?

Rather than looking at it that way, Matthew and the rest of the New Testament give us a unique understanding of time, namely, that the present time is already the end-time. God has already invaded the present age in the person of Jesus Christ. The Church is the proof that the end-time gathering of God's elect from the "four winds" (v. 31) has begun. Thus from Matthew's perspective, "this generation" is beginning to see the gathering of people from all nations in fulfillment of what the prophets of the Old Testament envisioned as the eschatological, messianic age. Long ago Isaiah said, "And on that day a great trumpet will be blown, and those who were lost in the land of As-

Already, and Not Yet

The phrase "already, and not yet" describes the New Testament understanding of the present time between the first and second coming of Christ. Christians live in the new age of Christ but also in a world dominated by the old age. The present time is the overlap of two ages, illustrated this way:

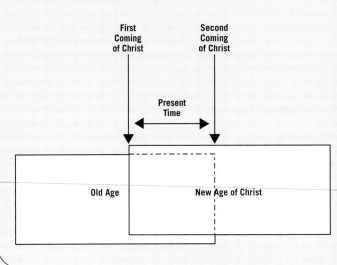

The Christian life is radically different from the norm of the old age. At the same time, there is the hope that at Christ's return the Christian will be perfected to a degree unimaginable now. Matthew describes this by using a rare Greek word *(palingenesia)* translated "the renewal of all things" (19:28). To that end, we continue to pray in the words of the Lord's Prayer, "Your kingdom come. Your will be done, on earth as it is in heaven" (6:9).

syria and those who were driven out to the land of Egypt will come and worship the LORD on the holy mountain at Jerusalem" (Isaiah 27:13). In the Great Commission, Jesus sends His messengers to make disciples of all nations and promises that He will be with them to "the end of the age" (Matthew 28:18-20).

Matthew's Portrait of Jesus

We will focus in this section on titles that have unique significance for Matthew.

■ Royal Messiah

As noted earlier, Matthew's opening statement, "Jesus the Messiah, the son of David, the son of Abraham" (1:1), is a clear indication that Matthew intends to portray Jesus as the fulfillment of Jewish messianic expectations. As a descendant of David, He is a royal Messiah, an anointed king. The name "Christ" comes from the Greek translation of the Hebrew word *mashiach,* meaning "the anointed one." Matthew's account of Jesus' birth is full of references to His royal status. When the wise men come to King Herod's palace looking for the infant Jesus, they ask, "Where is the child who has been born king of the Jews?" (2:2).

Alarmed to learn of the birth of a rival king, Herod assembles the religious leaders to inquire of them where the Messiah was to be born. They quote to him Micah 5:2 that speaks of Bethlehem, the city of David, as the town from where "shall come forth for me one who is to rule in Israel." Of the three Gospels, Matthew by far has the most occurrences of "Son of David" as a title used by people to address Jesus, another indication of Matthew's interest in portraying Jesus as a royal descendant of David and therefore Messiah, or Christ.

In the Passion narrative, Matthew repeatedly emphasizes the royal status of Jesus by adding materials to his Markan source. In the Triumphal Entry, Matthew comments that the entry of Jesus into Jerusalem riding on a donkey fulfilled Zechariah's words: "Look, your king is coming to you, humble, and mounted on a donkey" (21:5; see Zechariah 9:9).

In the parable of the great banquet (22:1-14), it is a king who has prepared a marriage feast for his son. The son in this parable is Jesus. In the parallel story in Luke 14:16-24, it is simply "a man" who has prepared a feast, not a royal wedding banquet.

Matthew heightens the soldiers' mockery of Jesus as a king during His trial by adding other elements not found in Mark. In Matthew's account the soldiers put a reed in His right hand, as a mockery of a royal scepter, and kneel before Him to scoff at Him as king (27:29).

■ A Teacher Greater than Moses

In Matthew Jesus is much more than a Davidic messiah. As noted earlier, He is also portrayed as the Teacher who has a greater authority than even Moses. Just as Moses received and then delivered the Ten Commandments from Mount Sinai, so now Jesus also delivers the Sermon on the Mount with an authority that surpasses that of Moses. Jesus

Herod built this fortress about seven miles south of Jerusalem as a desert retreat for him and his family.

speaks as the supreme Teacher whose word has greater authority than the Law of Moses (see the antitheses in Matthew 5).

Matthew repeatedly portrays Jesus as Teacher, as the five teaching blocks in Matthew make clear. During His ministry, Jesus sends the disciples out to preach but not to teach. The teaching role is reserved for Jesus. In a saying that is only in Matthew, Jesus says to His disciples, "You are not to be called rabbi, for you have one teacher, and you are all students. . . . Nor are you to be called instructors, for you have one instructor, the Messiah" (23:8, 10).

Only after the resurrection of Jesus, when He sends out His disciples to all nations, are the disciples commissioned to teach. But even then, they are to teach not their own precepts but the commandments of Jesus (28:20).

■ Son of God

In Matthew, Jesus is not only a Jewish Messiah and a Teacher greater than Moses, but, above all, the Son of God. Although all four Gospels make this affirmation, Matthew does it in a unique way. Matthew connects the divine Sonship of Jesus to the Hebrew Scriptures and to Israel.

The announcement of the angel

to Joseph concerning the conception of Jesus clearly focuses on the theme of Jesus as the Son of God. The child conceived in Mary is "from the Holy Spirit. She will bear a son, and you are to name him Jesus, for he will save his people from their sins" (1:20-21). The name Jesus, which means "God saves," is the same name as the Old Testament Joshua. Matthew adds, "All this took place to fulfill what had been spoken by the Lord through the prophet: 'Look, the virgin shall conceive and bear a son, and they shall name him Emmanuel,' which means, 'God is with us'" (v. 23; see Isaiah 7:14). Thus Jesus is conceived by the Holy Spirit, His name means "Savior," and His birth signifies that God is with us. Old Testament echoes are unmistakable in affirming that Jesus issues from the very being of God, and thus He is Son of God.

In the birth narrative, Matthew tells the story of the flight of Joseph and Mary and the infant Jesus to Egypt because of the threat of Herod the Great who was plotting to kill Jesus. When Herod dies and Joseph brings his family out of Egypt, Matthew sees a parallel between Jesus and Israel's exodus from Egypt. He quotes Hosea to explain this parallel: "Out of Egypt I have called my son" (2:15; see Hosea 11:1). Just like Israel, Jesus himself as Son of God experiences an exodus out of Egypt.

When Jesus walks on the water to the disciples in the boat and calms the storm, their response to Jesus is significantly different in Matthew from that in Mark. Whereas in Mark they are astounded, they do not understand, and their hearts are hardened (Mark 6:51-52), in Matthew they fall down and worship Jesus and say, "Truly you are the Son of God" (14:33). The confession of Peter in Matthew 16:16 has the additional affirmation that Jesus is "the Son of the living God," which is lacking in Mark 8:29.

Matthew is the only Gospel to report that when Jesus was on the Cross, the jeering crowd taunted Him to come down from the Cross by shouting, "If you are the Son of God . . ." (27:40). The Roman centurion and the soldiers who watched the Crucifixion exclaimed, "Truly this man was God's Son!" (v. 54).

Finally, the two most significant statements in Matthew about the intimate relationship between Jesus and God as Son and Father happen to be on the mouth of Jesus himself. Jesus says, "All things have been handed over to me by my Father; and no one knows the Son except the Father, and no one knows the Father except the Son and anyone to whom the Son chooses to reveal him" (11:27). The same statement is also in Luke 10:22, which would suggest that it was in the source Q. This would also suggest that although Matthew endeavored to portray Jesus as Son of God, he did not invent that portrait. Matthew was convinced that that portrait went back to Jesus himself.

Matthew's portrait of Jesus as Son of God does not go so far as to make Jesus equal to God. Jesus is always subservient to God and never usurps the role of God. This is evident in Jesus' assertion that no one knows the day or the hour of the Second Coming, not even the Son, but only the Father (24:36).

The second statement about the relationship between the Father and the Son is in the Great Commission, which is found only in Matthew. The resurrected Jesus commands the disciples to baptize "in the name of the Father and of the Son and of the Holy Spirit" (28:19). Although the doctrine of the Trinity emerged later, the foundations of it are found here in Matthew as well as in several other places in the New Testament.

Summary Statements

- Matthew shows that Jesus as a descendant of David is a royal Messiah and the fulfillment of the Hebrew Scriptures.
- Matthew emphasizes the teachings of Jesus and presents Jesus as a Teacher whose authority surpasses that of Moses, especially in the Sermon on the Mount.
- Jesus teaches that righteousness must come from within and be a quality of the heart.
- The Gospel of Matthew indicts hypocrisy not only among outsiders but also among those in the Church.
- One must not be overly concerned about the time of Christ's return but always be alert and faithful in service.
- Matthew portrays Jesus not only as a royal Messiah and as an authoritative Teacher but above all as Son of God.
- In the Great Commission, the resurrected Jesus sends out His disciples to make disciples of all nations.

Questions for Reflection

1. How important is it to affirm that Jesus was a Jew and His story had its roots in the Hebrew Scriptures?
2. How can one be sure that one's righteousness is truly from the heart and not hypocritical?
3. What are the implications of our faith affirmation that Jesus is the Son of God?

Resources for Further Study

Garland, David E. *Reading Matthew.* New York: Crossroad, 1993.
Hare, Douglas R. A. *Matthew* in *Interpretation: A Bible Commentary for Preaching and Teaching.* Louisville, Ky.: John Knox, 1993.
Harrington, Daniel J. *The Gospel of Matthew* in *Sacra Pagina.* Collegeville, Md.: Liturgical Press, 1991.
Kingsbury, Jack Dean. *Matthew* in *Proclamation Commentaries.* Philadelphia: Fortress, 1977.
Senior, Donald. *The Gospel of Matthew.* Nashville: Abingdon, 1997.

7 The Gospel According to Mark

O bjectives:

Your study of this chapter should help you to:
- Describe the authorship and purpose of the Gospel of Mark.
- Give an outline of Mark's description of Jesus' ministry.
- Discuss Mark's portrait of Jesus.
- Make conclusions about the meaning of discipleship in Mark.

K ey Words to Understand

The Synoptic problem
Two-source hypothesis
Olivet Discourse
Passion narrative
Messianic secret
Caesarea Philippi
Passion predictions
Disciples
Apostles
Followers

Q uestions to consider as you read:

1. How does the structure of the Gospel of Mark give us a clue as to its purpose?

2. Why does Mark describe Jesus as the powerful miracle worker only to shift gears at midpoint to focus on the suffering and death of Jesus?

3. In what contexts in Mark is Jesus called Son of God? Is there any significance to this pattern?

4. How does Mark portray the disciples? What is the significance of such a portrayal?

Most scholars believe that Mark was the first Gospel to be written.[1] Scholars have noted similarities and differences between Matthew, Mark, and Luke in their general outline, contents, and vocabulary. The puzzle of such similarities and differences has been labeled the **Synoptic problem.** To explain this puzzle, scholars have formulated the widely recognized **two-source hypothesis,** which proposes that Matthew and Luke used two sources to write their Gospels. One of these was the Gospel of Mark. The other was a hypothetical source often referred to as Q (from *Quelle,* meaning "source"), which contained many of the sayings of Jesus but is no longer in existence.

Authorship

All four Gospels are anonymous. Their titles were added in the second century to distinguish one from another. The form of these titles, "The Gospel According to . . . ," implies that the names Matthew, Mark, Luke, and John are not simply indications of authorship in the strictest sense but a reference to earlier traditions that arose from circles associated with these four names.

Papias, the second-century church father, says that Mark interpreted what Peter preached and later he wrote down what he remembered, but not in exact order (see sidebar). Mark and the other Gospels originated from earlier oral proclamations of the story of Jesus. They collected and edited earlier traditions about Jesus for different purposes such as to instruct believers, defend the faith, and safeguard the theological heritage of the emerging Church.

Several New Testament passages mention a person by the name Mark. According to Acts 12:12, a young man by the name John Mark was the son of a prominent woman in Jerusalem in whose house the church met. This Mark traveled with Paul and Barnabas on their first missionary journey but deserted them and returned to Jerusalem (13:13). Later, Paul refused to take him on a second journey and had a sharp disagreement with Barnabas so that the two parted company (15:36-40). Apparently, Barnabas wanted to give Mark another chance, partly because the two were cousins (Colossians 4:10). Eventually Mark turned out to be a faithful coworker both of Paul and of Peter (2 Timothy 4:11; Philemon 24; 1 Peter 5:13).

The Statement of Papias

In the same passage where Eusebius reports what Papias had said about Matthew (see the previous chapter), he also reports the statement of Papias about Mark:

"Mark having become the interpreter of Peter, wrote down accurately whatsoever he remembered. It was not, however, in exact order that he related the sayings or deeds of Christ. For he neither heard the Lord nor accompanied Him. But afterwards, as I said, he accompanied Peter, who accommodated his instructions to the necessities [of his hearers], but with no intention of giving a regular narrative of the Lord's sayings. Wherefore Mark made no mistake in thus writing some things as he remembered them. For of one thing he took especial care, not to omit anything he had heard, and not to put anything fictitious into the statements."[2]

Although some scholars question whether Papias's Mark is the same as the New Testament Mark,[3] other scholars find the statement of Papias consistent with the New Testament picture about John Mark, his associations with Christians in Jerusalem, his Jewish descent, and his close relationship with Peter and Paul.

Date and Setting

More important than the issue of authorship for our understanding of the purpose of Mark is the question of when and where it was written. There is considerable agreement that it was written in Rome in the late 60s of the first century, during or shortly after Nero's persecution of Christians and a year or two before the destruction of Jerusalem by the Romans in A.D. 70.[4]

Purpose

Since Mark does not state the purpose for his Gospel, we must deduce this through careful reading of the Gospel. The clearest indication of Mark's purpose is perhaps his opening words: "The beginning of the gospel of Jesus Christ, the Son of God" (1:1, NASB). We are accustomed to think of a Gospel as a type of writing. However, this was not Mark's meaning. The Greek word translated "gospel" means "good news." Mark's purpose was to tell the good news of Jesus.

Mark's further designation of Jesus as Christ and Son of God is significant for our understanding of the nature of this good news. Jesus is the Christ, the Anointed One of God. He is the Son of God. The good news is that Jesus has come to inaugurate "God's sovereign rule, the Kingdom, through his words and deeds."[5]

Content

Although Mark designates his story of Jesus as good news, it is a story of conflict, opposition, and death. Exactly how it is good news will not be clear until we have read the Gospel and have noted its main features.

Mark's story of Jesus is a "Drama in Three Acts."[6] In the first act (1:1—8:21), Jesus prepares for and begins His ministry in Galilee, proclaiming the inauguration of the kingdom of God, healing the sick and casting out evil spirits. Yet almost from the start, Jesus meets with controversy and opposition. This section may be outlined more specifically as follows:

1:1	Title: Good news
1:2-8	Ministry of John the Baptist as one who prepares the way for Jesus
1:9-13	The baptism and temptation of Jesus
1:14-15	The theme of Jesus' preaching: the kingdom of God
1:16-20	The calling of four disciples
1:21-45	Ministry of healing and preaching
2:1—3:35	Controversies over the ministry and message of Jesus
4:1-34	Jesus' use of parables to explain the paradoxical nature of the kingdom of God
4:35—5:43	The authority of Jesus over storm, demoniac, disease, and death

6:1-6	The rejection of Jesus at Nazareth
6:7-13	The mission of the 12 disciples
6:14-29	The death of John the Baptist
6:30-56	Miracles around the Sea of Galilee that heighten the mystery of Jesus: Feeding the 5,000, walking on water, and healing the sick
7:1-23	Jesus' rejection of the tradition of the elders concerning ritual purity
7:24—8:10	Mission of Jesus in Gentile territories

In the second act (8:22—10:52), Jesus is on a journey with His disciples on the way to Jerusalem. This segment is also fraught with conflict and tension. Jesus teaches His disciples about the way of the Cross and impending suffering and death, but they resist His teaching.

In the third act (11:1—16:8), Jesus comes to Jerusalem, where He is arrested, tried, and crucified. The following is a more detailed outline of this section:

11:1-11	Jesus enters Jerusalem riding on a donkey in a messianic demonstration.
11:12-25	Jesus curses the unfruitful fig tree, which withers, and drives out the merchants and money changers from the Temple (note: v. 26 is not in all ancient manuscripts).
11:27—12:44	Jesus has confrontations with the religious authorities of Jerusalem.
13:1-36	In His **Olivet Discourse,** Jesus foretells the destruction of the Temple, wars and persecutions, and His coming on the clouds of heaven.
14:1-11	The religious leaders plot to kill Jesus, and Judas agrees to betray Him, while a woman anoints Jesus with expensive perfume.
14:12-31	Jesus institutes the Lord's Supper during the Passover meal with His disciples.
14:32-42	Jesus prays in Gethsemane.
14:43—15:15	Jesus is arrested, tried, and condemned by the Sanhedrin and by Pilate.
15:16-47	Jesus is mocked, crucified, and buried.
16:1-8	Three women discover the empty tomb and are told by a young man that Jesus has been raised.

In this last section of Mark, known as the **Passion narrative** among scholars, Jesus dies in utter humiliation. All of His follow-

The Ending of Mark

Almost all English translations of the Bible place the ending of Mark (16:9-20) either in brackets or in a footnote. The reason is that these verses are later additions to Mark, possibly from the second century. Even though these verses are present in many manuscripts of the Gospel of Mark, they are absent from Codex Sinaiticus and Codex Vaticanus, two important fourth-century manuscripts, which happen to be among the oldest of New Testament manuscripts. Some manuscripts of Mark have a shorter ending and others have the longer ending of verses 9-20, most of which consists of the Resurrection appearances of Jesus from the other Gospels. Early copyists apparently tried in various ways to provide a better closure to the story of Jesus.

Scholars have proposed various theories about the Gospel of Mark. Some have suggested that Mark's original ending was somehow lost. Others have suggested that for some reason Mark was not able to finish his Gospel. Still others have proposed that Mark intentionally ended his Gospel at 16:8.[7]

ers desert Him. How can this be good news when it seems nothing but a story of failure? Jesus is buried, but when three women come to the tomb after the Sabbath they find it empty. A young man in a white robe tells them that Jesus has been raised and that they ought to go and tell His disciples. The story ends abruptly in 16:8; verses 9-20 are a later addition. The Gospel ends with the women fleeing from the tomb in utter terror and saying nothing to anyone. The reader is left perplexed as to how it is that a story that was supposed to be good news comes to such an anticlimactic and terrifying end.

If Mark intended to end his Gospel at 16:8, what was his purpose? The opening words of the Gospel, "The beginning of the good news," and the open-ended conclusion in 16:8 may give us a clue. Jesus in His lifetime was the embodiment of the reign of God in the world. But He was opposed, ridiculed, abandoned, and executed. His disciples ran away. Even the women were terrified and told no one that Jesus was resurrected.

Yet Mark has written his Gospel to address a community of Christians four decades after the events of the life and death of Jesus. The story of Jesus *had* been told after all. The Gospel of Mark was most likely written in Rome to encourage a community of Christians persecuted by Roman authorities (Mark 10:30). The persecuted believers whom Mark addressed with his Gospel were proof that the story of Jesus did not end at Mark 16:8. What Mark wrote in his Gospel was just "the beginning."

Mark's Portrait of Jesus

There are already hints in the above paragraphs as to how Mark portrays Jesus, but now we will more explicitly spell out that portrayal. Simply put, Mark presents Jesus as the powerful Son of God whose mission leads to suffering and death. But how can this be? How can the Son of God end up on a Roman cross?

A century ago William Wrede argued that Mark created the **messianic secret.** According to his hypothesis, Jesus never claimed to be the Messiah. It was early Christians who after the death and resurrection of Jesus made this claim. Wrede argued that in various ways Mark's narrative creates the impression that Jesus kept His Messiahship a secret, which explains why people did not recognize Him as Messiah in His lifetime. Wrede proposed that messianic secrecy was Mark's own creation. Although many scholars today question Wrede's hypothesis, the concept of messsianic secrecy is still useful in understanding Mark's portrait of Jesus.[8]

Mark begins his Gospel with his Christian affirmation that Jesus is the Son of God (1:1). The voice of God confirms this at the baptism and transfiguration of Jesus (1:11; 9:7). Even demons recognize Jesus as Son of God, but Jesus silences them (1:24-25; 5:7). Jesus often instructs people whom He heals not to tell anyone about Him, but they do it anyway. It is historically credible why Jesus would not want excessive publicity, particularly because most people expected a political messiah who would establish God's kingdom by vanquishing the Romans by force.

We must note, however, that in Mark no human being confesses Jesus as Son of God during His ministry. Even Peter's confession of Jesus as the Messiah in Mark 8:29 says nothing about Him being the Son of God.

In spite of His mighty works of healing and exorcisms, people respond to Jesus with doubt, anger, and murderous plots (2:6-7; 3:6, 22; 6:2-6). Even the disciples are often perplexed and flounder. After Jesus walks on the sea and calms the storm, the disciples are "utterly astounded, for they did not understand about the loaves, but their hearts were hardened" (6:51-52; cf. 8:17-21).

The incident at **Caesarea Philippi,** where Peter confesses Jesus to be the Messiah or Christ, is a turning point in the Gospel.

Remains of Peter's house in Capernaum, the center of Jesus' Galilean ministry.

In spite of his great confession, Peter and his fellow disciples are about to face a crisis. Peter rebukes Jesus when he learns that Jesus must undergo great suffering, be rejected and killed, and be raised after three days (8:29-33). Three times Jesus makes such **passion predictions,** and each time the disciples demonstrate utter lack of comprehension (8:32; 9:32; 10:32-45).

This sort of misunderstanding and opposition to Jesus reaches a crescendo when the Sanhedrin in Jerusalem asks Jesus if He is "the Messiah, the Son of the Blessed One" (14:61). When Jesus answers, "I am," they determine that He has committed blasphemy and condemn Him as deserving death. The Roman governor Pilate imposes the death sentence and crucifies Him.

The closing scene in Mark is the discovery of the empty tomb by the three women and the declaration of the heavenly messenger that Jesus has been raised (16:6-7). This is the final divine confirmation that Jesus is indeed the Son of God.

Discipleship in Mark

Next to Jesus, the most significant characters in the Gospel of Mark are the **disciples.** Mark weaves into the story of Jesus their attitudes, responses, and conduct.

Mark's portrayal of the 12 disciples seems ambivalent at best. The disciples have both positive and negative attributes. On the positive side, when Jesus calls the disciples, they immediately leave everything and follow Him (Mark 1:18, 20; 2:14). Jesus calls them to have a part in His own mission, that they might "be with him, and to be sent out to proclaim the message, and to have authority to cast out demons" (3:14-15; cf. 6:12-13). The call comes from Jesus; they are not volunteers as such.

When Jesus' own family come to take custody of Him because they think He has gone mad (3:21), He says in exasperation, "Who are my mother and my brothers?" (v. 33). Looking at His disciples and others around Him, He says, "Here are my mother and my brothers! Whoever does the will of God is my brother and

T A Crucified Son of God

The only human recognition in Mark that Jesus is the Son of God comes from a most unlikely source and in a most unlikely context. As Jesus dies in utter agony and humiliation, the Roman centurion who most likely had a role in the execution exclaims, "Truly this man was God's Son!" (15:39). Mark's point is clear. Rather than refuting the divine Sonship of Jesus, His death evokes a Roman soldier's confession that He is the Son of God.

For 2,000 years, Christians have recited the creeds that affirm Jesus as the Son of God and have almost taken it for granted. Not so with Mark. What Mark did was nothing short of a subversive act. Only the Roman emperor, the symbol of ultimate power, could be called the son of a god. Yet Mark and other Christians dared to proclaim that the One who was crucified by Roman authorities was the true Son of God. In effect, Roman authorities could take Mark's writing as an act of disloyalty to the empire.[9]

I Follower, Disciple, Apostle

Mark uses the term "disciples" most often to refer to the 12 **apostles** whom Jesus called to be particularly close to Him and to send them out on a mission (Mark 3:13-14). The Greek word for "apostle" means "someone who is sent out," and the word for "disciple" means "someone who is taught or instructed by a master." Mark also understands that the circle of **followers** around Jesus was larger than the 12 apostles or disciples. Even before Jesus chose and appointed the Twelve (v. 14), Mark describes those who were in the company of Jesus as disciples (2:15-18).

Mark seems to make a distinction between apostle, disciple, follower, and crowd, as seen in 8:34: "He called the *crowd* with his *disciples*, and said to them, 'If any want to become my *followers*, let them deny themselves and take up their cross and follow me'" (emphasis added).

were hardened (6:52; 8:17-18). In the end, one of His disciples, Judas, will betray Him. Peter, the leader of the Twelve, will deny Jesus three times. The other disciples will abandon Him and run away.

The picture is even more disheartening in the second major section of Mark (8:22—10:52), when Jesus begins to instruct His disciples concerning upcoming events in Jerusalem.

The section begins with the healing of a blind man (8:22-26). At first, his healing is partial. He can see people but "they look like trees walking around" (v. 24, NIV). When Jesus touches him again, his sight is fully restored.

At the end of the section there is a second story of a blind man, that of Bartimaeus (10:46-52). Mark's concluding comment that Bartimaeus "regained his sight and followed him [Jesus] on the way" clearly implies that he became a disciple.

These two stories of blind men function as brackets that enclose

sister and mother" (vv. 34-35).

In spite of this positive portrait of the disciples, Mark repeatedly points out their shortcomings and failures. He says that their hearts

Some of Jesus' early disciples were fishermen. This is a model of a fishing boat from the first century A.D.

the whole section of Mark 8:22—10:52 on the theme of discipleship. Mark has structured this section with great literary skill. The first story of the blind man, whose sight is restored in two stages, functions as a paradigm that describes the condition of the disciples. In fact, right before that story, Jesus rebukes His disciples with the question, "Do you have eyes, and fail to see?" (8:18). The disciples, like the blind man, are beginning to see, but their sight is not clear. They do not understand Jesus and His mission. Jesus continues to instruct them so that they may see clearly.

After the healing of the first blind man, Mark weaves various materials together on the subject of discipleship. The backbone of this section consists of three Passion predictions, all of which follow the same pattern. The section concludes with the healing of blind Bartimaeus.

■ First Passion Prediction (8:27—9:29)

Jesus and His disciples leave Galilee and come to Caesarea Philippi where Peter makes his great declaration about Jesus, "You are the Messiah." However, Jesus sternly orders them not to tell anyone because their vision is still blurred.

Following Peter's confession, Jesus makes His first Passion prediction (8:31). Peter rebukes Jesus, which then earns him a harsh rebuke back from Jesus, "Get behind me, Satan! For you are setting your mind not on divine things but on human things" (v. 33).

Now Jesus instructs the disciples on the meaning of discipleship (8:34—9:1) to lead them to a second stage of complete sight. Discipleship means denying oneself, taking up one's cross, and following Jesus. Those who lose their life for Jesus' sake will save it.

The story of the Transfiguration (9:2-13) and the healing of the epileptic child (vv. 14-29) come next, both of which have a bearing on the meaning of discipleship.

In the Transfiguration story, Peter, James, and John, the inner circle of disciples closest to Jesus, are on the mountain with Jesus. When Peter sees Jesus gloriously transfigured, he suggests that they stay on the mountain and build three dwellings for Jesus, Moses, and Elijah. A voice from the cloud says, "This is my Son, the Beloved; listen to him!" (v. 7). This is God's corrective to Peter and the others who continue to resist listening to Jesus speak of suffering and death (vv. 9-13).

As they descend from the mountain, a desperate situation awaits Jesus (vv. 14-29). A distraught father had brought his epileptic son for healing, but the disciples were unable to do anything. Argumentative scribes and a large crowd made matters worse. In the absence of Jesus, the disciples were powerless and pitiful. The father wants to believe that Jesus can do the healing, but doubts linger. He cries out to Jesus, "I believe; help my unbelief!" (v. 24). After Jesus casts out the evil spirit, the disciples ask Jesus why they could not do it. Jesus says, "This kind can come out only through prayer" (v. 29). Could Mark be saying to his church in Rome some 40 years later that without prayer and trust in Christ the church would be helpless like the disciples at the foot of the mountain?

■ Second Passion Prediction (9:30—10:31)

Now Jesus and His disciples are back in Capernaum (9:33). We find the same narrative structure here: Jesus makes a Passion prediction (v. 31); the disciples still do not understand and are afraid to ask (v. 32); and they argue who among them is the greatest (vv. 33-34). They are still half-blind and need further instruction. Jesus reminds them that whoever wants to be first must be a servant to all, even to a child (vv. 35-37).

The disciples try to stop an unknown exorcist from using the name of Jesus because he was not following them. Jesus tells them not to stop him because "whoever is not against us is for us" (v. 40). There is to be no exclusivity or elitism in the kingdom of God.

Jesus warns of judgment on anyone who puts an obstacle before the "little ones" who believe in Him (vv. 42-50).

The question of marriage and divorce in 10:1-12 may seem irrelevant for discipleship. Jesus announces here that the Mosaic ruling that made allowances for divorce was a concession to the "hardness of heart" (v. 5), whereas the disciples must live by God's original purpose in creation. Husband and wife are to be one flesh throughout their life (v. 9).

The disciples reprimand parents for bringing their children to Jesus, presuming that He would have no time for such trivial matters (vv. 13-16). Jesus is indignant at the disciples and tells them that the kingdom of God belongs precisely to children. One must receive the kingdom of God as a child. Discipleship to Jesus means radical reevaluation of previous social hierarchies. Children, the weakest members of society, matter to God and they must matter to disciples.

Discipleship also means radical reevaluation of wealth. A rich man asks Jesus what he must do to inherit eternal life (vv. 17-22), assuming that he can obtain eternal life by *doing* things. The end of the story will undermine such an assumption.

The story has some puzzling elements. Jesus tells the man to keep the commandments, but interestingly Jesus cites the second half of the Ten Commandments, which have to do with social relationships. Jesus also adds one that is not in the Ten Commandments: "You shall not defraud" (v. 19). Perhaps Jesus implies that the man had become wealthy by defrauding poor peasants by charging them interest on loans in violation of the Law. Yet the rich man says that he has kept the commandments since his youth.

Jesus does not mention the first four of the Ten Commandments that have to do with one's relationship with God. The final word of Jesus and the man's response bring the story to a soul-searching climax. Jesus says, "You lack one thing; go, sell what you own, and give the money to the poor, and you will have treasure in heaven; then come, follow me" (v. 21). Jesus puts His finger on the central issue. The man leaves grieving because he had many possessions. The man thought that he had kept all the commandments when in fact he had not settled the issue of the first and most important of the Ten Commandments: "You shall have no other gods before me" (Exod. 20:3). His wealth had taken the place of God.

Following this encounter, Jesus uses a bit of humor to make a point to the disciples: "It is easier for a camel to go through the eye of a needle than for someone who is rich to enter the kingdom of God" (v. 25). This makes the disciples wonder whether anyone can be saved. Jesus says that for God all things are possible, meaning that God's saving power can free a person from the tyranny of wealth.

With a touch of spiritual superiority, Peter declares that he and his fellow disciples have left everything and have followed Je-

Garden of Gethsemane where Jesus prayed before He was arrested.

The interior view of a tomb in Jerusalem. Some Christians claim that this was the place where Jesus was buried.

sus; they are not like the rich man. Jesus responds with the promise that in this life they will receive back houses, fields, and families a hundredfold, meaning that in the community of the kingdom of God their material and social needs will be cared for (cf. 6:8). However, there is a twist: the hundredfold return will come "with persecutions" (v. 30)! Another twist is that they will receive eternal life in the age to come, which is a throwback to the original question of the rich man to Jesus. Negotiating with God for bargains is laughable.

■ Third Passion Prediction (10:32-45)

As the disciples follow Jesus on the way to Jerusalem, they are "in a daze, and . . . apprehensive" (10:32, NJB). Jesus tells them again what will happen to Him in Jeru-

salem. This is the longest and most detailed of the three predictions (vv. 33-35). Yet, ironically, and oblivious of what Jesus has repeatedly said, James and John request that they sit on His right and left in His glory. When the other 10 disciples hear this, they are angry. For the last time, Jesus teaches them what discipleship means (vv. 42-45). They are not to be like the rulers of the Gentiles who lord it over them as tyrants. If they wish to become great, they must become a slave to all, for even Jesus himself came "not to be served but to serve, and to give his life a ransom for many" (v. 45)

Mark's purpose in this section is to show how blind and uncomprehending the disciples were during the lifetime of Jesus. However, Mark also knows that in spite of their failures, Jesus never gives up on them.

After the crucifixion and burial of Jesus, the final word of the heavenly messenger to the women at the empty tomb is for them to go and tell the disciples and Peter that Jesus has been raised and is going ahead of them to Galilee; there they will see Him (16:7). The good news that Mark has told is that in the end Jesus will still meet with His faltering disciples and they will finally see clearly who Jesus is and what it means to be His disciples.

Summary Statements

- Mark was probably the first of the four Gospels to be written and was used by Matthew and Luke.
- Mark's purpose was to announce the good news of Jesus Christ, even though it involved conflict, misunderstanding, opposition, suffering, and death for Jesus.
- The disciples reach a crisis point following Peter's confession at Caesarea Philippi when they hear about suffering and death for Jesus and for them.
- The only human affirmation in Mark's story that Jesus is the Son of God comes from a Roman centurion at the time of Jesus' death on the Cross.
- The Gospel of Mark originally ended at 16:8, with the women running from the empty tomb in fear and trembling.
- The remaining verses of Mark (16:9-20) are later additions to make up for the lack of the Resurrection appearances of Jesus.

Questions for Reflection

1. From what you read in Mark, what does it mean for you to make the confession that Jesus is the Son of God?
2. In what sense is the Caesarea Philippi incident a turning point in the life of the disciples? In your journey with God, have you experienced such a turning point?
3. Do you find Mark's portrait of the disciples encouraging or discouraging?

Resources for Further Study

Achtemeier, Paul J. *Mark* in *Proclamation Commentaries*. Philadelphia: Fortress, 1975.
Best, Ernest. *Following Jesus: Discipleship in the Gospel of Mark*. Sheffield: JSOT, 1981.
Collin, Adela Yarbro. *The Beginning of the Gospel*. Minneapolis: Fortress, 1992.
Flanagan, Patrick J. *The Gospel of Mark Made Easy*. New York: Paulist, 1997.
Heil, John Paul. *The Gospel of Mark as Model for Action*. New York: Paulist, 1992.
Juel, Donald. *The Gospel of Mark*. Nashville: Abingdon, 1999.

8 The Gospel According to Luke

O bjectives:

Your study of this chapter should help you to:
- Describe the authorship of the Gospel of Luke.
- Discuss the content and message of the Gospel of Luke.
- Make assessment of Luke's distinctive concerns in reporting the Jesus story—especially his empathy for women, the poor, and sinners.
- Describe the complexity of Jesus' social and religious world as reported by Luke.
- Explore the importance of hospitality and table fellowship in the ministry of Jesus.

Q uestions to consider as you read:

1. How does Luke's Gospel differ from the other Gospels in terms of his historical method?

2. What did Jesus experience in His relationship with fellow Jews at home in Nazareth, and as He traveled about Galilee and Judea?

3. In what ways does Luke's Gospel express Jesus' concern for the underprivileged and oppressed?

K ey Words to Understand

"We" sections
Quelle
L-material
New Testament
  Apocrypha
John the Baptist
Redaction
Bat kol
Galilee
Sepphoris
Capernaum
Pharisees
Sect
Haburah
Prayer of Manasseh

Author

Early Christian tradition ascribes the Gospel to Luke, an early companion of Paul, and evidently a physician (Colossians 4:14). This author combines two significant strands of early Christian history in a way that makes him a unique biblical writer. As a historical researcher, Luke documents the life of Jesus in light of earlier sources (1:1-4). He then goes on to tell the story of the early Christian movement in the Book of Acts, something no other author's extant work does. This two-volume work comprises almost a quarter of the New Testament and makes Luke one of the most significant authors in the Bible.

Though we do not know much about the identity of the author, we think he was a Gentile and a traveling companion of Paul. Scholars often cite the **"We" sections** in Acts (16:10-17; 20:5-15; 21:1-18; 27:1-29; 28:11-16) as evidence in support of Luke's authorship of the Gospel and Acts. The writer of Acts changes the third-person narrative to first-person plural in these sections. It is possible that Luke may have joined Paul's traveling team at Troas during his second missionary journey. The Book of Acts also begins with an address to Theophilus, and the author of Acts presents his work as a continuation of his "first book" (Acts 1:1). This "first book" is in all likelihood the Gospel of Luke.

Date of Writing

It is difficult to assign a precise date for the writing of Luke's Gospel. Some scholars assign this book to the early 60s. They also think that Luke would have completed his second volume (Acts) before Nero's persecution of Christians in A.D. 64. Some others place the Gospel in the second century. We believe that Luke utilized materials found in Mark's Gospel, which was composed in the late 60s. This would put the writing of Luke in the 70s or later. We assign this book to the late 70s or early 80s.

Purpose and Method

Luke's purpose and method is described in the prologue to his Gospel. Writing to Theophilus, or "lover of God," Luke states his purpose: "to write an orderly account of the events that have been fulfilled among us . . . so that you may know the truth concerning the things about which you have been instructed" (1:1, 4). He indicates that he has scoured existing sources for information on Jesus' life. The careful recording of the political context of Jesus' life and the events of the Early Church is also characteristic of his writings (see Luke 1:5; 3:1; Acts 18:12). Of the numerous sources that were already in circulation in Luke's day, we can assume that the Gospel of Mark was in his possession since he seems to rely heavily on its contents. His other sources may have included one source he shared with Matthew (the "source" or **Quelle** document, often called Q). He also had his own special material, a source that no other Gospel writer had. As we will see, this special material, or **L-material**, contains many of the themes and parables found only in the Gospel of Luke.

Content

■ **Jesus' Birth and Early Life (1:1—2:52)**

The information on the birth

and early life of Jesus is an interesting feature of Luke's Gospel. By the time Luke writes his Gospel in the late 70s or early 80s, a great deal of interest in Jesus' early life had arisen. This was a topic Mark, Matthew, and John did not address. This L-material is not only very warm and human but also full of personal detail that must have been carefully preserved by the first Christians and then collected by Luke. If Luke had not passed it along to us, it would have been lost for all time.

The story of Zechariah and Elizabeth (1:5-80), parents of John the Baptist, is a good example of this kind of personal detail about the events surrounding Jesus' early life. It also demonstrates the importance of women to the gospel history, a theme that will prove to be of particular concern to Luke. Elizabeth and Mary share a special relationship with one another as the mothers of John and Jesus (see 1:39-58). In Luke, Mary declares that God has "lifted up the lowly" (1:52), show-

Shepherd's Cave in Bethlehem.

ing the disadvantaged position of women in Jesus' culture. Time and again in Luke's writings women will emerge as important to the spread of the Good News.

Luke not only gives us more information about Jesus' birth than any other evangelist but also preserves the only information we have about His childhood. The account of the boy Jesus in the Temple at age 12 (2:39-52) describes how He amazed the elders and teachers with His wisdom. Jesus shows a sense of destiny with regard to the Temple that will be

The New Testament Apocrypha

If early biblical sources were reticent to describe the early life of Jesus, the so-called **New Testament Apocrypha**, or "hidden" documents, were not so reserved. Some have argued that a few of these sources, such as the Gospel of Thomas, are as old as the Gospels themselves. Apocryphal New Testament documents contain gospels, letters, apocalypses, acts of the apostles, and liturgy. One recent source listed 75 such extant works. It is easy to see why the Church chose not to include such material in the Bible. For example, the Infancy Gospel of Thomas, written about A.D. 150, tells the story of Jesus being criticized as a five-year-old for making clay pigeons on the Sabbath. He clapped His hands and said "Off with you," and the clay pigeons came to life and flew away! In another story, Jesus is playing in the second story of a home with another child. When the child accidentally falls to his death, his parents accuse the young Jesus of pushing him out the window. Jesus raises the child from the dead to prove His innocence! These exuberant stories were the pulp fiction of ancient Christian literature. Students of the New Testament can read these and other stories in collections of the New Testament Apocrypha.[1]

seen through the remainder of the narrative. After being left behind in Jerusalem on a family pilgrimage trip, He asks His parents, "Did you not know that I must be in my Father's house?" (v. 49). For Luke, from birth (vv. 28-32) to death (19:45-48), Jesus was filled with passion for Jerusalem and the Temple.

■ Beginning of the Ministry of John the Baptist and Jesus (3:1 – 4:44)

Among men, **John the Baptist** is second in importance only to Jesus in Luke (7:28). Luke's inclusion of additional information on the birth and early ministry of John reinforces this status. In Luke, the births of both men are miraculously announced by an angel (1:11, 26); the two mothers have a poignant meeting while pregnant (vv. 39-45), and hymns of praise are raised for each (vv. 46-55, 68-79). Elizabeth is the relative of Mary and thus, the two men are related, perhaps cousins. For a time, Jesus and John conduct contemporary ministries in which they preach, baptize, call disciples, and inhabit the desert. The differences are also important. John is an ascetic and firebrand, who preaches more about the imminent judgment of God than His love. He is a transitional figure who heralds the One who is to come. The Gospel focuses more on the ministry of Jesus in chapter 4, and we see into His struggle and ministry (4:1-14). Whereas John is the fiery prophet who precedes, Jesus is God's Son (3:22). Jesus later announces that the Law and the Prophets ceased to be in effect when John came to usher in the new age of the kingdom of God (16:16).

The narrative shifts its emphasis from John to Jesus at the so-called **bat kol** ("daughter of a voice"), or heavenly voice in Luke 3:21-22. Jews of the first century A.D. came to believe that prophe-

---

I

Luke and History

Although Luke writes with the inspiration of the Holy Spirit, he also is a human historian who must collect oral and narrative material and then select and arrange the presentation of that material. How can we discern between raw historical data, or *facts*, in a Gospel and an author's interpretation of this data? Consider the engagement of the human writer with both his material *and* the presence of the Holy Spirit. Luke's personality, perspective, and community shape his telling of the gospel story, yet the Spirit inspires the process. In all historical narrative there is interplay between the events, their perception, their preservation in a community, and the author's final **redaction,** or reworking of sources. While these factors have led some to conclude that the Gospel history cannot possibly be reliable, others have argued that the Gospel writers did a defensible job of getting the basic history correct. Remember, the Gospels are neither sterile histories nor simply personal memoirs; they are the stories of Jesus preserved and interpreted by an individual for a community of faith. Luke's Gospel shows the work of an insightful author, one who records and interprets history perceptively. Sensitive readers will find Luke's distinctive themes and motifs reward careful study. There will always be those whose primary goal is to prove or disprove the historical veracity of the Gospel records, but a world of truth awaits those who enter into an intimate and trusting relationship with Luke the author.

The Galilee and Nazareth

The **Galilee** ("The District") was a largely rural and agrarian area of northern Israel. It was divided into two regions, upper and lower, and was known for its olives, figs, grapes, grains, and fishing. Many of the Galilee's slopes and terraces would have been marked out in small, cultivated plots of land. Galilee was not an impoverished area, but absentee landowners made peasant life difficult. As with all land tenants in the ancient world, the people were often only one failed crop from starvation. The Galilee was also situated on an important trade route, which explains the presence of troublesome toll collectors. There were several substantial towns there—Capernaum and Tiberius among them. Though not mentioned in the Bible, the most prominent city was the Roman administrative center **Sepphoris**, a city of 30,000 just four miles north of Nazareth. Jesus may well have worked on building projects there as a tradesman. Nazareth, however, was so small that it is never mentioned in the Old Testament or any existing extrabiblical source, including *Josephus*, who catalogues 54 towns in the Galilee. The famous Sea of Galilee is actually only a lake, and known as Kinneret, or harp, in the Gospels because of its shape. The Galilee area is known for its mild climate and fertile land with flowering plants and trees.

cy ended in the postexilic times, and they anticipated God to speak to humankind with a voice from heaven. Thus, it is significant that Jesus is proclaimed God's Son by such a voice: the new age of communication has come! Following His temptation (4:1-13), Jesus begins His public ministry. Again, it is Luke who gives us greater detail of Jesus' first days of ministry. After a stay at Capernaum where He begins to teach, reports of Jesus begin to spread around Galilee (v. 14).

Jesus returns from His travels to His hometown Nazareth to visit the synagogue. What happens on this occasion is important for the whole of Luke and Acts. While Jesus rarely ministers to Gentiles himself, His mission of salvation will eventually extend to all people, as prophesied by Simeon, "For my eyes have seen your salvation, which you have prepared in the sight of all peoples, a light for revelation to the Gentiles and for glory to your

people Israel" (2:30-32). Initially, His fellow villagers respond positively to Jesus (4:22). When the people plea for healing, Jesus refuses, saying that God sometimes healed only foreigners rather than Jews. He cites by way of example the healing of the widow of Zarephath in Sidon by Elijah (1 Kings 17:8-24) and the healing of the Syrian Naaman, whom Elisha sent to bathe in the Jordan seven times (2 Kings 5:1-14). These examples foreshadow the ultimate concern of the Book of

Aerial view of Sepphoris.

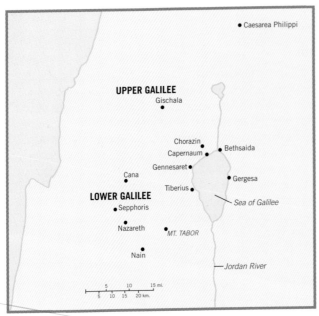

Upper and Lower Galilee.

(Luke 4:28-30), and it is not surprising that later Jesus often referred to the Book of Jonah, a text that chides Israel for just such an attitude. Galilee was famous for its zealotry and later became an important center of opposition to Roman occupation in the Great Revolt of A.D. 65 to 70. It is poignant to observe that, as far as is known, Jesus never returned to His home, and He remained an outcast to the end of His ministry.

Following this incident, Jesus returns to **Capernaum** approximately 10 miles away, to the house of Peter where He was often a guest. Capernaum means "the village of Nahum," an unknown individual.

■ Luke's Portrait of Jesus and His Ministry (5:1—19:48)

Chapters 5 to 19 form the middle portion of Luke's Gospel. These chapters are preceded by the birth narratives and early ministry on one side and followed by His arrival in Jerusalem on the other. The compression of time in this central section is so great that these few chapters represent al-

Acts, which is the story of Paul carrying the gospel to the heart of the pagan empire in Rome.

In a tragic turn of events, Jesus' friends and neighbors drive Him out of town to throw Him off a cliff, the prelude to stoning for apostasy. Intense parochial support for Jewish nationalism and ethnicity led them into a rage

Capernaum, Jesus' Home Base for Ministry

Capernaum is one of the most interesting archaeological sites in the Galilee. The Franciscans excavated the almost completely undisturbed site in the first years of the 20th century. The ruins of an impressive 4th-century A.D. synagogue made of limestone were uncovered. Beneath that was a basalt foundation wall and flooring believed to be from the 1st-century synagogue of Jesus' ministry. It is also the site of the events of John 6:25-59, where Jesus describes himself as the Bread of Life. John tells us specifically, "He said these things while he was teaching in the synagogue at Capernaum" (John 6:59). His comments there stirred such controversy that He was eventually expelled from Capernaum (Luke 10:15-16). Thirty meters from the synagogue is Peter's House, a hexagonal church built in the 4th century. This site is believed to have been the place of Christian worship since the late 1st century. Tradition associates this site with Peter's house, also the location of Jesus' home during His Galilean ministry. A modern hexagonal-shaped Catholic church now stands over the site, preserving the original remains.

most three years of events and teaching. As a result, Luke carefully selects his material to show his concerns in retelling the Gospel story. As we have noted, he also brings a source to his writing that the other Gospel authors did not have. Much of what we will discuss now comes from that distinctive material. The following themes represent Luke's perspective on Jesus and His story.

Jesus in His Jewish Environment

We have already noticed in the preceding sections, Luke's presentation of Jesus' birth and His early life in His Jewish environment. His ministry began in the synagogues of lower Galilee, where it was His habit to attend weekly (4:15-16). The events of Luke's narrative frequently take place in the synagogue, especially the many incidents of conflict with fellow Jews. On two occasions, Jesus heals in the synagogue on the Sabbath to demonstrate that compassion for the sick comes before considerations of law and religious propriety (6:6-11; 13:10-17). Yet, His faith is complex; He loves Judaism, yet wants to renew and reform it. Ironically, as we have already seen, He was expelled from His home synagogue, which could not tolerate His radical views on the Law.

Jesus' Jewishness is also highlighted by His loyalty to the Temple in Jerusalem. Luke tells us He encouraged those who were healed to make the appropriate offerings to local priests (5:14; 17:14). In the feeding of the 5,000, the 12 baskets of pieces of bread were likely the tithe that had been separated for the priestly portion

Old Synagogue in Nazareth.

by the crowd (9:17). If that were the case, the baskets would have been delivered to the local priests. However, Jesus was convinced of the need to reform the Temple practices. His disruption of Temple trade was perhaps the primary cause of the hostility He met in Jerusalem (19:45).

Luke also presents Jesus' debate with His fellow Jews on a wide range of issues, such as work on the Sabbath, ritual washing, tithing practices, the source of His authority, fasting and prayer, and the issue of fellowship with known sinners. His perspectives on these matters show His intense concern for proper understanding and practice of the Torah. He affirms the Jewish way of life, but He believes the practice has been corrupted, especially by some of the Pharisees.

The Pharisees, lawyers, and scribes are His most frequent opponents. The Pharisees in Luke receive very rough treatment from Jesus. They are "fools" and "unmarked graves, and people walk over them without realizing it" (11:40, 44). He says to the lawyers, "You have taken away the key of knowledge; you did not enter yourselves, and you hindered those who were entering" (v. 52). The greatest source of conflict was Jesus' association with "sinners," those whom some Jews deemed unworthy of God's grace. As we shall see later in the chapter, this conflict gives rise to the central theme of Luke's Gospel: even sinners can repent and find salvation in the kingdom of God. The parable of the Good Samaritan, found only in Luke, is a good illustration of this theme (10:29-37). Some scholars consider this parable to be the heart of Luke's Gospel. Luke's Jesus had a highly inclusive view of who could be saved!

H Pharisaism in Jesus' Day

The **Pharisees** were a small but influential **sect** or denomination in Judaism that emerged in the Maccabean period, about 150 B.C. While they were only about 1 percent of the population (about 6,000 members), they were highly regarded for their devout piety. Pharisees had two central concerns: eating food that is declared clean by the Law of Moses, and scrupulous tithing of *all* income, a practice only required of farmers and ranchers in the Bible (Luke 11:42). Pharisees joined voluntary associations called *haburah* where they encouraged one another in these voluntary observances. Men, women, rich or poor could join, and this inclusiveness was part of the attraction of this populist movement. One could choose to observe only parts of these practices or go to great extremes to be fully observant, a path taken only by the few.

Before leaving the subject of the Jewish environment in the life of Jesus, a word must be said about the place of Jerusalem in Jesus' life. The Temple in Jerusalem had been greatly expanded by Herod the Great and was one of the architectural wonders of the world. Normally, Jerusalem had a population of about 25,000, but in the time of a major festival it could swell with 180,000 pilgrims to the Temple. It is clear from the Gospel accounts that Jesus loved this city. However, we find in Luke's Gospel the portrait of Jerusalem as the city of destiny for Jesus. This is made clear in Luke 9:51: "When the days drew near for him to be taken up, he set his face to go to Jerusalem." This consuming passion drove Jesus ever closer to the sacred city (13:22), and He declares: "Yet today, tomorrow, and the next day I must be on my way, because it is impossible for a prophet to be killed outside of Jerusalem" (v. 33). Other references detail His focus on the city (17:11; 18:31 ff.; 19:28), and Jesus foresaw the destruction of Jerusalem, still 40 years away in A.D. 70 (19:41-44; 21:5-6, 20 ff.).

Women in Luke

Women play a prominent role in Luke and are a significant part of Jesus' entourage (8:1-2). Two passages in Luke particularly highlight Jesus' concern for women. First, Luke gives us a personal glimpse of the lives of two women, Martha and Mary from Bethany (10:38-42). Martha is "distracted by her many tasks" during Jesus' visit to her home and even implores Him to make Mary, who is sitting at His feet, join in the chores. Jesus' response is an example of His extraordinary view of women, given that day's patriarchal culture. "But the Lord answered her, 'Martha, Martha, you are worried and distracted by many things; there is need of only one thing. Mary has chosen the better part, which will not be taken away from her'" (vv. 41-42). To welcome a female student was a radical departure for a rabbi; this story shows Jesus' egalitarian concern for women.

Second, in one of the most emotional scenes in the New Testament, Jesus extends kindness and forgiveness to a woman known to be a sinner, possibly a prostitute (7:36-50). While Jesus is eating in the home of a Pharisee, the woman enters and weeps at Jesus' feet, anoints Him with ointment and tears, and then dries His feet with her hair. It is a poignant scene of penance from a broken woman and is characteristic of the way Luke highlights compassion for women. The Pharisee's heart is hardened, and so he inwardly chides Jesus for allowing her to touch Him. Jesus responds with a parable about indebtedness and points out to the Pharisee that the greater the debt forgiven, the greater the gratitude. Jesus tells the woman, "Your sins are forgiven" (v. 48). Luke certainly shows us the side of Jesus that was tender and compassionate to the plight of women.

Social Dislocation and Civic Expulsion

It would be a mistake to assume that Jesus lived a happy life, filled with miracles and adoring crowds. While He did heal, teach, and enjoy some popular support, He lived a life of intense personal and social dislocation. We have already seen how His own neighbors drove Him out of His hometown because of His teaching about Gentiles (4:14-30). He assumed an itinerant life of ministry in which there was no room for a secure homelife. He reassures His disciples that whoever has "left house or wife or brothers or parents or children, for the sake of the kingdom of God" will be rewarded in the age to come (18:29). In other passages He describes himself as homeless (9:58) and encourages would-be followers not to be distracted by their social and family obligations (vv. 60-62).

It is also certain that Jesus experienced family problems when His ministry called Him away as the eldest son of a widowed mother with at least seven children (Mark 6:3). It cannot be disputed that Jesus put His work for the Kingdom before His earthly ties to family. When He was told that His mother and brothers were waiting to see Him, He responded: "My mother and my brothers are those who hear the word of God and do it" (8:21). He promised not peace but division within the household to those who chose to follow Him (12:49-53; 14:25-26). While this aspect of His life may trouble us, it helps us to understand Jesus' experience as a human being who was compelled to make difficult choices for the sake of God's kingdom.

There is also evidence that Jesus was expelled from numerous towns and cities for His controversial stance on the Law and other issues. Nazareth is one example, but He was also expelled from Chorazin, Bethsaida, and even His base of operations in

Capernaum (10:13-16). Not only families but also whole towns were divided on how to respond to Jesus! Such expulsions may well have been based on Deuteronomy 13, where one who leads a town astray is to be shown no mercy (vv. 1-11). Significantly, the false prophet in Deuteronomy 13 is not one whose prophecies *fail* to come true but the one whose omens and portents *do* take place, yet is considered a heretic. This text seems to have a particular relevance to the ministry of Jesus as a wonderworker and a radical. It also had implications for His disciples, for whom the decision to follow Jesus meant a life of hardship and ostracism.

Rembrandt's *The Return of the Prodigal Son.*

Jesus' Message: Sinners Find Repentance

The central message of the Gospel of Luke is repentance, and the central section (chaps. 5—19) tells the stories of five sinners. The first story is about Levi the tax collector who gives a banquet for all of his friends in Jesus' honor (5:29-32). When the Pharisees complain about this unseemly gathering of tax collectors and sinners, Jesus answers with a key phrase for Luke's Gospel: "Those who are well have no need of a physician, but those who are sick; I have come to call not the righteous but sinners to repentance" (vv. 31-32).

The second sinner is the woman who anoints Jesus' feet (7:36-50), whom we have already considered. The third passage is the whole of chapter 15, the so-called heart of the third Gospel. This moving chapter, once again, places its message in the context of the Pharisees' complaint that Jesus eats with sinners (15:1-2; cf. 5:27). There are three parables in chapter 15. In the parable of the lost sheep (vv. 3-7), one lost animal is the main concern of the shepherd. The second is the parable of the lost coin, where a woman searches the whole house having lost one of her 10 coins (vv. 8-10). The third is the famous parable of the prodigal son, who is welcomed back by his father (vv. 11-32). It is significant that only Luke chains these three parables together, demonstrating his particular concern for forgiveness for sinners.

The poignant and almost comical story of the Pharisee and the tax collector presents the fourth sinner in the central section of Luke (18:9-14). This character is

T The Prayer of Manasseh

Judaism was a religion with a strong theology of repentance and forgiveness. The **Prayer of Manasseh,** considered deuterocanonical by the Eastern Orthodox community and included as part of the Apocrypha, is a moving example of this theme. The prayer is significant for its profound theology of God's mercy to sinners. King Manasseh was considered the most evil king in the history of Judah, and his wicked deeds led directly to her downfall (2 Kings 21:1-18). However, he repented late in life, was forgiven by God, and returned to his throne. The prayer implies that if God could forgive the worst sinner in Jewish history, then His mercy must be boundless and extends to all. The prayer predates Jesus' life and He may well have been influenced by its message and language. The following is an excerpt from this prayer:[2]

For you are the Lord Most High, of great compassion, long suffering, and very merciful, and you relent at human suffering. O Lord, according to your great goodness you have promised repentance and forgiveness to those who have sinned against you, and in the multitude of your mercies you have appointed repentance for sinners, so that they may be saved. Therefore you, O Lord, God of the righteous, have not appointed repentance for the righteous, for Abraham and Isaac and Jacob, who did not sin against you, but you have appointed repentance for me, who am a sinner. For the sins I have committed are more in number than the sand of the sea; my transgressions are multiplied, O Lord, they are multiplied! I am not worthy to look up and see the height of heaven because of the multitude of my iniquities . . . And now I bend the knee of my heart, imploring you for your kindness. I have sinned, O Lord, I have sinned, and I acknowledge my transgressions. I earnestly implore you, forgive me, O Lord, forgive me *(vv. 7-13a).*

typical of all Luke's sinners who always respond rightly to God, in contrast to the religious people who cannot see the truth. In this reversal of expectation, the sinners become the heroes of the gospel story and the religious the antiheroes!

The theme of repentance finds its ultimate fulfillment in Luke's delightful story of Zacchaeus (19:1-10). When Jesus approaches Jericho, His ministry outside of Jerusalem is fittingly crowned by the repentance of this tax collector. The diminutive Zacchaeus cannot see over the crowd, so he climbs a tree to catch a glimpse of Jesus. When Jesus invites himself to stay at Zacchaeus's house, the people who see it grumble that

Jesus had "gone to be the guest of one who is a sinner" (v. 7). Zacchaeus repents, and Jesus proclaims, "Today salvation has come to this house, because he too is a son of Abraham. For the Son of Man came to seek out and to save the lost" (vv. 9-10). Here is the same message we found in chapter 5 (see vv. 31-32) noted above. These two statements of Jesus bracket the beginning and end of this central section. The message of repentance and salvation for sinners has been proclaimed from Levi to Zacchaeus and met with great success.

The effect of this theme on the reader of Luke should not be overlooked. It was perhaps Luke's plan to structure his Gospel to convince the reader that if these sinners could be saved, then so could the reader.

The Poor First, the Rich Last

Many students of Luke have noticed his concern for the poor and disdain for the rich. A good example is Luke's presentation of the beatitude "Blessed are you who are poor," as compared to Matthew's "Blessed are the poor in spirit" (Luke 6:20; Matthew 5:3). Matthew records a blessing on the persecuted (Matthew 5:11-12), but Luke's text adds bad news for the rich: "But woe to you who are rich, for you have received your consolation. Woe to you who are full now, for you will be hungry" (Luke 6:24-25).

While warnings to the rich are common in all three Synoptic Gospels, Luke has extra material: the rich man who fills his barns dies unexpectedly and must give an accounting for his life (12:13-21); the exhortation to "sell your possessions" (v. 33); the description of Pharisees as "lovers of money" (16:14); and the rich man and Lazarus (vv. 19-31). While wealth is not viewed as wrong, these sayings and stories clearly contain a warning that wealth can displace the Kingdom in one's affections. It may be that economic suffering in Luke's community gave rise to the prominence of this theme in his Gospel.

■ The Final Days in Jerusalem (19:28—24:53)

While the Gospel of John records three visits to Jerusalem in Jesus' ministry, the Synoptic Gospels record only the last visit. The Gospel of Luke focuses on Jesus' journey toward Jerusalem in chapters 9—19 (see 9:51; 19:28).

It is apparent from the moment Jesus enters the city that His visit will lead to violence. Mark's Gospel reflects the sense of fear among His disciples who followed Him to Jerusalem (Mark 10:32). Peter expresses his willingness to go to prison or even die for Jesus in Jerusalem (Luke 22:33). It was also necessary for Jesus to limit His travels within the southern part of the country (Judea) because of the dangers to His life (John 7:1). Luke states specifically that there were plots to kill Jesus (Luke 19:47-48; 22:2-6). Why was Jesus in such mortal danger from those who opposed Him? A brief look at the account of the Triumphal Entry will give us a sense of the dangerous situation surrounding Jesus' presence in Jerusalem.

The Triumphal Entry (19:29-48)

An enthusiastic celebration greets Jesus as He enters the city. Although it was short-lived, the Triumphal Entry was the crowning moment of His long journey from Galilee to Jerusalem. That a rabbi would allow himself to be hailed as a "King" was shocking to local leaders, so they implored Him to silence the crowd. Perhaps they were afraid that the crowd would seize this opportunity to start an uprising against Rome. The Roman authorities would not have tolerated any anti-Roman activities in the city. In fact, Roman troops were stationed at the northern end of the Temple Mount to deal swiftly with insurrection. Compounding this dangerous beginning, Jesus entered the Temple and began to disrupt normal festival commerce, driving out those who were selling animals for sacrifice and changing money. Both the Temple leaders and Roman authorities alike would have viewed this action with extreme disapproval. It would likely have appeared as an act of political protest, even though we now understand Jesus' motive as a concern for the sanctity of the Temple precincts. His fate may have been sealed after having been in the city only a few hours.

Luke's Vision of Salvation for All

Luke records the last days of Jesus' life in a manner very similar to Mark. However, one part of the Passion story special to Luke seems to capture once again the theme of repentance for sinners. At the Last Supper Jesus said,

"You are those who have stood by me in my trials; and I confer on you, just as my Father has conferred on me, a kingdom, so that you may eat and drink at my table in my kingdom, and you will sit on thrones judging the twelve tribes of Israel" (22:28-30).

As we have seen, Jesus welcomed all at table to eat and drink and share fellowship with the Son of Man—the tax collector Levi and his friends, the sinful woman who cried at His feet as He dined, the banquet set for the prodigal son, the feast of Zacchaeus as he joyfully welcomed Jesus into his home. The universal scope of Jesus' message is clear: "Then people will come from east and west, from north and south, and will eat in the kingdom of God" (13:29).

Summary Statements

- Luke's Gospel is the first volume of a two-volume work composed by Luke, the second volume being the Book of Acts.
- The Gospel of Luke contains a substantial amount of materials not found in other Gospels.
- Infancy narratives that contain stories about Jesus' birth and early life are a special feature of the Gospel of Luke.
- Luke presents the early life and ministry of Jesus in the setting of the Jewish life and culture of the first century.
- Women play a prominent role in the Gospel of Luke.
- Luke presents Jesus as a person who was rejected and ostracized by His community because of His teachings about God's kingdom.
- The central message of the Gospel of Luke is the salvation of sinners who respond to God through repentance.
- Luke presents Jesus as committed to His journey to Jerusalem, though He was certain that this journey would lead Him to His violent death.

Questions for Reflection

1. Jesus' life contained a tension between being a faithful Jew and the desire to bring reform and renewal to Judaism. Does your own faith journey sometimes present you with conflicting agendas and tensions? How do you work to reconcile them?
2. In what ways does Jesus' concern for the marginalized challenge you in your life of faith? Are there ways you can act to follow His example?
3. Many accept the historical accuracy of the Gospel records, but others challenge their reliability as historical sources. How do you feel on this issue and what, in your view, are the implications of this issue for the life of a modern Christian?

Resources for Further Study

Corely, Kathleen E. *Private Women, Public Meals: Social Conflict in the Synoptic Tradition.* Peabody, Mass.: Hendrickson Publishers, Inc., 1993.

Fitzmyer, Joseph A. *The Gospel According to Luke* in *The Anchor Bible,* 2 Vols. New York: Doubleday and Co., Inc., 1985.

Freyne, Sean. *Galilee, Jesus and the Gospels: Literary Approaches and Historical Investigations.* Philadelphia: Fortress Press, 1988.

Green, Joel B. *The Gospel of Luke* in *The New International Commentary on the New Testament.* Grand Rapids: Wm. B. Eerdmans, 1997.

Johnson, Luke T. *The Writings of the New Testament: An Interpretation.* Philadelphia: Fortress Press, 1988.

Neale, David A. *None but the Sinners: Religious Categories in the Gospel of Luke.* Journal for the Study of the New Testament Supplement Series, 58. Sheffield: JSOT Press, 1991.

Wright, Tom. *Luke for Everyone.* London: SPCK, 2001.

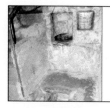

9 The Gospel According to John

O bjectives:

Your study of this chapter should help you to:
- Describe the unique features of the Gospel of John.
- Explore the major themes in John.
- Gain insight into John's portrait of Jesus.
- Discuss the purpose of this Gospel.

Q uestions to consider as you read:

1. Why is the language of Jesus in John so different from the Synoptics?
2. Who is the beloved disciple?
3. What is the significance of the prologue in John?
4. Why are the miracles of Jesus in John called signs?
5. What perspectives does John bring to the sacraments of baptism and the Lord's Supper?
6. How does John portray the person of Jesus?

K ey Words to Understand

Johannine literature
The beloved disciple
Johannine community
Prologue
Epilogue
Logos
Incarnation
Docetism
Christological
Farewell discourse
Sacraments
Eucharist
Paraclete
"I am" sayings

The Gospel of John, often referred to as the fourth Gospel by New Testament scholars, is part of **Johannine literature**, which also includes the three letters of John. The Book of Revelation, though included in this group by some, is most likely separate from it because of its language and literary genre.

Even though the Gospel of John does not identify its author, it became associated with the apostle John from the time of Irenaeus in the late second century. The question of authorship of the fourth Gospel is intertwined with the identity of **the beloved disciple,** who appears in the second half of the Gospel as "the disciple whom Jesus loved." Although Christian tradition has linked him with John the apostle, many modern scholars have disputed the accuracy of this linkage.[1]

More important than determining the identity of this disciple is what we can infer about the composition of the Gospel. References to the beloved disciple in the third person seem to indicate that someone else may be making the statements about him. This also suggests the likelihood that the Gospel of John may have emerged in several stages. Scholars think that in the earliest period, the beloved disciple had played a significant role in forming a group of Christians that they refer to as the **Johannine community.** Since the Gospel of John shows familiarity with Palestinian conditions, particularly in and around Jerusalem, it is likely that the beloved disciple was a native of Palestine and a follower of Jesus during His public ministry. He was the living link between Jesus and the emerging Johannine community. At a later time, a writer in this group composed the Gospel, relying on the

The Beloved Disciple in John

The following passages make clear references to the beloved disciple:

John 13:23: "One of his disciples—the one whom Jesus loved—was reclining next to him" [next to Jesus at the Last Supper].

John 19:26: "When Jesus [on the Cross] saw his mother and the disciple whom he loved standing beside her, he said to his mother, 'Woman, here is your son.'"

John 20:2: "So she [Mary Magdalene] ran and went to Simon Peter and the other disciple, the one whom Jesus loved, and said to them, 'They have taken the Lord out of the tomb, and we do not know where they have laid him.'"

John 21:7: "That disciple whom Jesus loved said to Peter, 'It is the Lord!' When Simon Peter heard that it was the Lord, he put on some clothes, for he was naked, and jumped into the sea."

John 21:20: "Peter turned and saw the disciple whom Jesus loved following them; he was the one who had reclined next to Jesus at the supper and had said, 'Lord, who is it that is going to betray you?'"

In the following passage, the reference may very well be to the beloved disciple, but it is not as clear:

John 18:15-16: "Simon Peter and another disciple followed Jesus [after Jesus' arrest]. Since that disciple was known to the high priest, he went with Jesus into the courtyard of the high priest, but Peter was standing outside at the gate. So the other disciple, who was known to the high priest, went out, spoke to the woman who guarded the gate, and brought Peter in."

beloved disciple's testimony (see 19:35; 21:23-24).[2]

Unique Features of the Gospel of John

■ Simplicity and Complexity

The Greek syntax and vocabulary of the Johannine writings are perhaps the easiest in the New Testament. However, behind the relatively simple language and sentence structure there lurks a sophisticated and profound theology, which is the genius of this Gospel. The opening line of the Gospel is a good example: "In the beginning was the Word, and the Word was with God, and the Word was God" (1:1). Thirteen of the 17 words in the Greek text of this verse are monosyllabic. The sentence structure is simple and straightforward. Several words are repeated two or three times. Though grammatically simple, it has challenged the thinking of countless exegetes and theologians over the centuries.

■ Structure of the Gospel

The structure of this Gospel is unique compared to the Synoptics. It starts out with a **prologue** (1:1-18), which is unlike anything in the other Gospels.

Following the prologue, the first major section of the Gospel —often called the "Book of Signs" —recounts the ministry of Jesus in the world (1:19—12:50). Interwoven in this material are seven miracles or signs that Jesus performs. Most of these are unique to John.

The next major section (13:1—20:31)—often called the "Book of Glory"—focuses on the glorification of Jesus, which includes His death and His resurrection. This section starts with the Last Supper and moves on to a lengthy farewell discourse and prayer (chaps. 13—17) in which Jesus prepares His disciples for His departure. Next comes the Passion narrative (chaps. 18—19), which has many parallels to the Synoptics. The section concludes with the resurrection of Jesus and His appearances.

The final section (21:1-25) is an **epilogue** in which the resurrected Jesus appears again to some of His disciples on Lake Tiberias and has a dialogue with Peter. It is considered an epilogue because it appears to have been added after an earlier conclusion at the end of the previous chapter (20:30-31). The chapter ends with an attestation of the truthfulness of what has been narrated in the Gospel.

■ The Prologue

The uniqueness of the Gospel of John is immediately noticeable from the very first section, the prologue (1:1-18). This is a hymn-like meditation on *logos,* the Word. The first-time reader, unfamiliar with the Christian message, would have no idea until the very end of the prologue that this "Word" is Jesus Christ (1:17).

Unlike the Synoptics (see the opening chapters of Matthew, Mark, and Luke), John starts from "the beginning," which is an echo of Genesis 1:1, "In the beginning God created the heavens and the earth" (NIV). The uniqueness of the prologue becomes even more striking when we note some of its details. It is clear that John is stressing the deity of Jesus Christ: "the Word was God." However, John just as emphatically declares that Jesus was truly human: "The

Word became flesh and made his dwelling among us" (1:14, NIV). The eternal Word has become human in the historical person of Jesus **(Incarnation).** Some early Christians were apparently so eager to underscore the deity of Jesus Christ that they almost denied His real humanity. In their view, Jesus merely *appeared* to be human, but in reality He was not **(Docetism** from the Greek verb *dokeo,* meaning "to appear" or "to seem"). John, in concert with mainstream Christianity, rejected this view as heretical.[3] Note also the polemic against Docetism in 1 John 4:1-3.

■ Chronology of Events

The chronology of events in the life of Jesus in John is different from the Synoptics. John places the cleansing of the Temple at the beginning of the ministry of Jesus (2:13-22) rather than during the last week as in the Synoptics. The reason is not that the evangelist was confused; rather, he had a literary and theological reason for doing so, as will be explored later.

John tells us that Jesus made three journeys to Jerusalem for Jewish festivals (2:13; 5:1; 7:10, 14) instead of the one journey recorded in the Synoptics. In fact, most of the ministry of Jesus in John takes place in and around Jerusalem, whereas in the Synoptics it is in Galilee.

Because of this difference between John and the Synoptics, the question has been raised as to the length of the public ministry of Jesus. The Synoptics seem to indicate that it was one year or less, whereas the Gospel of John seems to suggest two to three years.

From the 2nd through the 18th century, the assumption has been that John had full knowledge of

Chronology of Passion Week in John

An intriguing issue of chronology occurs in the Passion narrative in John. In biblical times, a day was reckoned from sundown to sundown. According to John 18:28, the Jewish authorities that took Jesus to Pilate early in the morning did not themselves enter his headquarters "so as to avoid ritual defilement and to be able to eat the Passover" (cf. 19:14, 31, 42). Since Jesus was crucified that same day, His death occurred on the day of Preparation, which is the day before Passover when the Passover lambs were slaughtered, that is, Nisan 14. But in the Synoptics, Jesus and His disciples had already eaten the Last Supper the night before His crucifixion clearly as a Passover meal (Mark 14:12-16), which means that Jesus was crucified on the day of the Passover, Nisan 15. Now, all four Gospels agree that the Resurrection occurred on Sunday, the death of Jesus on Friday shortly before the beginning of the Sabbath, and the Last Supper on Thursday. This means that John and the Synoptics disagree on the day of the week when Passover occurred. According to the Synoptics, the day of the Passover was from Thursday evening to Friday evening. But according to John, it was from Friday evening to Saturday evening. Thus in the Synoptics the Last Supper is a Passover meal, whereas in John it is not. This is not the place to resolve the apparent discrepancy between the Passion chronologies of John and the Synoptics. Equally credible scholars have taken opposite positions on the issue.[4] Later in this chapter we will explore John's theology of the Last Supper and the death of Jesus arising from John's timing of these events.

the other Gospels and wrote his account to supplement and complete what the others lacked, which meant that this Gospel was regarded as the most authentic of the four Gospels. In the last two centuries, however, critical scholars reversed this appraisal, with the result that John was regarded as having little historical value. More recently, the pendulum has swung into a more middle position that sees John as a viable historical source independent of but complementary to the other Gospels.[5] John's three-year span of Jesus' ministry implied by His several journeys to Jerusalem is not necessarily at odds with the Synoptic Gospels. Mark 10:1 tells us that Jesus "left that place and went to the region of Judea and beyond the Jordan" (cf. Matthew 19:1). Since Jerusalem was in Judea, Mark implies that Jesus may well have visited Jerusalem and its surroundings *before* His final journey that begins later (Mark 10:32-33).

■ Long Discourses

Whereas parables, proverbs, and brief sayings of Jesus abound in the Synoptic Gospels, they are nearly absent from the Gospel of John. In John we find long discourses on a given topic on the lips of Jesus. The occasion for these discourses varies. Some discourses arise from a dialogue that Jesus has had with someone (see, for example, Jesus' conversation with Nicodemus and the discourse that follows in chap. 3).[6] In other cases, the discourse is occasioned by a miracle that Jesus had performed. (See the healing of the sick man in chap. 5 and feeding of the multitude in chap. 6.)[7] Still other discourses have

their setting in an event in the life of Jesus. Regardless of the occasion, the discourses are theological reflections or commentary on what had transpired. John has so skillfully blended the original event with the discourse that it is often difficult to know where one ends and the other begins.

Given John's theological objective, it should come as no surprise that the content of these discourses is **Christological.** They present a theological reflection on the significance of the person of Jesus as the Son of God. For example, in the discourse that follows the healing of the sick man at the

Pool of Bethesda, where Jesus healed the sick man.

pool (5:19-47), Jesus says, "The works that the Father has given me to complete, the very works that I am doing, testify on my behalf that the Father has sent me" (v. 36). The healing of the sick man should have functioned as a sign pointing to the person of Jesus, but unfortunately, the onlookers only noticed that the healing was done on the Sabbath and sought to kill Jesus. Likewise, the feeding of the multitude is followed by a long discourse on Jesus himself being the bread of life.

The irony is that the people who were so eager to eat the bread turned away from Jesus when He said, "I am the bread of life" (6:41, 52, 60).[8] They wanted the bread that filled their stomachs but rejected the One who was the source of life itself.

Farewell Discourse and Prayer

The **farewell discourse** and prayer (chaps. 13—17) is the longest discourse of Jesus in John. Its setting is the Last Supper.[9] In the farewell discourse, Jesus reassures His disciples that He will come back after He has prepared a place for them (John 14:3). Yet His coming back takes on various shades of meaning in the next few verses. He promises that He will not leave them as orphans, that He is coming to them (v. 18). Just prior to that, He deals with the coming of the Holy Spirit. And in verses 19-20 he says, "In a little while the world will no longer see me, but you will see me; because I live, you also will live. On that day you will know that I am in my Father, and you in me, and I in you." In these verses the coming of Jesus seems to

mean that He will appear to them after His death and resurrection. Thus the future eschatological return of Jesus in the Synoptic Gospels and in Paul's writings takes on a different meaning in John. The return of Jesus in John becomes in large measure a present reality in the life and experience of the disciples through the work of the Holy Spirit.

The farewell discourse ends with a prayer in which Jesus makes three major petitions:

First, Jesus prays for himself (17:1-5) that the Father glorify Him, but not the kind of glorification that a puffed up ego strives for. This will be discussed later.

Second, Jesus prays for His disciples (vv. 6-19) that the Father protect them while they are in the world fulfilling the mission of Jesus. His petition is for their unity (v. 11) and their sanctification in the truth (v. 17). Third, Jesus prays for future generations of believers (vv. 20-26) that they may become completely one in Him and the Father.

Theological Themes in the Gospel of John

■ Favorite Words

One way we can capture the most important themes in John is to note frequently used words in the Gospel, particularly when these same words are much less frequent in the other Gospels. The most significant of these, in descending order of frequency, are the following: know, Father (as a reference to God), believe, world, life, testify or testimony, glorify or glory, Son (as a reference to Jesus), truth, light, Spirit.

In the prologue (1:1-18), John

uses all of these words with the exception of Spirit. But it is not long before "Spirit" appears in the text. In 1:32-33 John the Baptist sees the Spirit descending on Jesus as a dove to signify that He, Jesus, is the One who baptizes with the Holy Spirit, in contrast to John who baptizes with water.

What are we to make of John's fondness for these words? If one were to use all of these in a paragraph to describe John's theology, what could one say? Actually, John has done just that for us in the prologue. It is as if John strikes the major notes of the Gospel in an opening overture and then returns to these repeatedly throughout the rest of the Gospel.

John states in the prologue that the Word, who is Jesus Christ, is the source of light that shines in the darkness. Although the world came into existence through Him, the world did not know Him. John the Baptist came to testify to the light so that all might believe. All those who believe in the name of Christ become children of God. The Word became flesh and lived among us, and we have seen His glory. In Him we find the grace and truth of God. Christ, the only Son, who is close to the heart of God the Father, has made God known to us.

Although a lengthy discussion of these words would be beneficial, two points of clarification are necessary for a proper understanding of John's theology. First, in keeping with an Old Testament perspective, the verb "know" in John denotes more than intellectual perception. The knowledge of God is a relationship with God mediated through Jesus Christ.[10] Jesus himself knows God because

He is from God (7:29). He also knows those who belong to Him in the same sort of relationship as a shepherd knows the sheep and lays down his life for them (10:14-15). Likewise, the sheep know the shepherd and follow him (v. 4). Unlike the world, the disciples know the Holy Spirit, the Spirit of truth, "because he abides with you, and he will be in you" (14:17). In the prayer of John 17, eternal life is defined as knowing "you, the only true God, and Jesus Christ whom you have sent" (v. 3). To know God and Jesus Christ is not merely a cognitive or a mystical experience but a relationship of love and faithful discipleship.

Another word in John to be clarified is "world." In some passages, the world appears in an adversarial relationship to God and Jesus. Jesus says in His prayer of John 17, "Righteous Father, the world does not know you, but I know you" (v. 25). To Pilate he says, "My kingdom is not from this world" (18:36). On the other hand, the world is not hopelessly abandoned. The world was after all created through the Word (1:10). Furthermore, God has demonstrated His love for the world through Christ who has given himself for the life of the world (3:15; 6:51). Jesus came not to judge the world but to save it (12:47). Yet the coming of Jesus does involve judgment: "Now is the judgment of this world; now the ruler of this world will be driven out" (v. 31); "I came into this world for judgment so that those who do not see may see, and those who do see may become blind" (9:39). Salvation, which is God's purpose for Christ's coming, is at the same time a pronouncement of judgment on the sinful ways of the world. When the light comes, darkness is condemned; the ruler of this world is judged. "Adherence to Jesus, and so to God's action in the world, is not something that can be privately given so as to avoid the world's hostility."[11] God's judgment is that the light exposes the evil ways of the world and provokes its hostility. "For all who do evil hate the light and do not come to the light, so that their deeds may not be exposed" (3:20). Salvation and judgment are the two sides of the same act of God in Jesus.

■ Miracles as Signs

Another way to come to grips with Johannine theology is to look at these seven miracles of Jesus during His earthly ministry:

1. Turning water to wine at the wedding in Cana (2:1-11)
2. Healing of the official's son (4:46-54)
3. Healing of the sick man at the pool (5:1-9)
4. Feeding of the multitude (6:1-15)
5. Walking on water (6:16-21)
6. Healing of a man born blind (9:1-12)
7. Raising of Lazarus (11:1-44)

Cana—Site of Jesus' first miracle.

Five of these seven miracles are only in John. The two exceptions are the feeding of the multitude and walking on water. The feeding miracle is the only one in all four Gospels.

Earlier we have noted that John does not simply tell a miracle story but provides a theological commentary on it in the form of a discourse on the lips of Jesus. Now we will further explore John's theological outlook on miracles and their relationship to faith, a rather complex issue.[12]

In John, there are various levels of faith. Miracles can certainly function as a catalyst to bring a person to faith in Jesus. This is clear from the story of the healing of the royal official's son who is dying (4:46-54). When the official begs Jesus to come with him and heal his son, Jesus seems a bit irritated and says, "Unless you see signs and wonders you will not believe" (v. 48). However, when the official persists in his urgent plea, Jesus pronounces healing on the child. When the official arrives home and finds that the son is well again, he believes along with his whole household.

In another context Jesus says, "If I am not doing the works of my Father, then do not believe me. But if I do them, even though you do not believe me, believe the works, so that you may know and understand that the Father is in me and I am in the Father" (10:37-38). It is for this reason that John calls the miracles of Jesus signs. A miracle is not an end in itself but is a sign that points to Jesus as the Son of God (20:30-31).

On the other hand, John is painfully aware of those who see the miracles but still reject the person of Jesus. True faith is much more than believing that Jesus can work miracles. Although many passages in John make this point clear, the dialogue between the resurrected Jesus and Thomas illustrates it well. The resurrected Jesus had earlier appeared to the disciples while Thomas was absent. Thomas had said that he would not believe that Jesus was resurrected unless he saw, and put his finger in, the wounds of Jesus. When Jesus appears again, He tells Thomas to put his finger in His wounds, at which Thomas exclaims his declaration of faith, "My Lord and my God!" Jesus says to him, "Have you believed because you have seen me? Blessed are those who have not seen and yet have come to believe" (20:29). John does not invalidate the type of faith demonstrated by Thomas. However, true blessedness is for those who have not seen and yet have believed.

■ The Sacraments in John

One of the complexities of the fourth Gospel that has puzzled scholars is that of the **sacraments** of baptism and the **Eucharist**, or the Lord's Supper.

Baptism

John does not narrate the baptism of Jesus, even though John the Baptist appears prominently at the beginning of the Gospel, and even in the prologue. Furthermore, Jesus does not command His disciples to baptize anyone. This is in contrast to Matthew, which tells of Jesus' own baptism and His command to His disciples to baptize others (Matthew 3:13-15; 28:19). However, the Gospel of John does tell us something that is not in the Synoptics: Jesus himself baptized

people alongside John the Baptist, so much so that John the Baptist's disciples anxiously reported to their master that Jesus was baptizing and making more disciples than John himself (John 3:22-26). Yet a bit later, a parenthetical statement clarifies that "it was not Jesus himself but his disciples who baptized" (4:2). This comment, possibly by a later editor than the evangelist, makes the practice of baptism in the Church align with the practice of the disciples rather than with Jesus himself. John 4:1-3 states that when the Pharisees had heard that Jesus was making and baptizing more disciples than John the Baptist, Jesus left Judea and started back to Galilee, possibly because He wanted to escape the kind of scrutiny and censure that the Pharisees had inflicted on John (1:19-25).

The sacrament of baptism in John is best understood in the words of John the Baptist, who says, "The one who sent me to baptize with water said to me, 'He on whom you see the Spirit descend and remain is the one who baptizes with the Holy Spirit'" (1:33). It is Jesus, on whom the

Bethany beyond Jordan (see John 1:19-34).

Spirit descends, who baptizes with the Holy Spirit, the only real baptism. This does not mean that water baptism is invalid or unnecessary. It simply means that water baptism is a sign and symbol of an underlying spiritual reality accomplished by the Holy Spirit bestowed by Jesus. This juxtaposition of Spirit with water crops up in a number of places in chapters 2 to 5 and several other places in John. In every case, the point is that what Jesus bestows, namely, the Spirit, is decidedly superior to anything that the older ways of Judaism is able to provide, "for he gives the Spirit without measure" (3:34). We include two stories to illustrate this theological perspective of John.

In His encounter with the Samaritan woman at the well, Jesus offers to her water that would quench the woman's thirst so perfectly that she would never be thirsty again (4:4-42). What Jesus provides is superior to the Samaritan ways of worship and piety (vv. 21-24). Jerusalem and Samaria were rival places of worship. But worship, Jesus says, is not a matter of locale, whether Jerusalem or Samaria. "True worshipers will worship the Father in spirit and truth " (v. 23).

In chapter 7, on the last day of the festival of Booths or Tabernacles in Jerusalem, which lasted seven days, Jesus cries out, "Let anyone who is thirsty come to me, and let the one who believes in me drink. As the scripture has said, 'Out of the believer's heart shall flow rivers of living water'" (vv. 37-38). The background for Jesus' reference to water was the Jewish ceremony of carrying water from the pool of Siloam in a joyful procession to the Temple and pouring it on the altar to symbolize the hope of salvation overflowing with abundance.[13] Jesus uses the symbolism of water to offer salvation that quenches the spiritual thirst of one's inner being. John comments that Jesus "said this about the Spirit, which believers in him were to receive; for as yet there was no Spirit, because Jesus was not yet glorified" (v. 39).

In summary, John has gone to great lengths to contrast the ceremonial practices of Judaism to the spiritual vitality, saving grace, and gift of the Spirit offered by Jesus. However, a word of caution is necessary here. John is not simply contrasting Jesus and Judaism. His concern is just as much with Christian sacraments that over time tend to become routine rituals without spiritual vitality.

The Eucharist

The Eucharistic words of Jesus about bread and wine are absent from the Last Supper account in John 13:1-20. John, however, has not omitted the Eucharistic words of Jesus altogether. He has instead transposed them to a much earlier passage and made them part of the miraculous feeding of the multitude in chapter 6 and the long discourse connected to it. The words of verse 11, "Jesus took the loaves, and when he had given thanks, he distributed them to those who were seated; so also the fish, as much as they wanted," are reminiscent of the Eucharistic words of the Last Supper in the Synoptic Gospels and in 1 Corinthians 11:23-24. Likewise, in the miraculous catch of fish after Jesus' resurrection, early Christians heard sacramental overtones in the words of John 21:13, "Jesus came and took the bread and gave it to them, and did the same with the fish."

Following the miraculous feeding of the multitude, Jesus says that His own flesh is true food and His blood is true drink. "Those who eat my flesh and drink my blood abide in me, and I in them" (6:56). This language of abiding in Christ shows up again in chapter 15 in the discourse about Jesus being the true Vine, which may in fact be another allusion to the Eucharist. The disciples are branches. In order to be fruitful and full of love and joy, the disciples must abide in Christ and Christ in them (15:1-11). The power of the Eucharist is that it is an enactment and reminder of the spiritual reality of abiding in Christ.

The Gospel of John is not opposed to the liturgy of the sacraments. The sacramental elements, such as water, bread, and the fruit of the vine, are everywhere in John. Yet there seems to be no explicit reference to Christian baptism and the institution of the Eucharist. This Gospel is rather a theological reflection on the spiritual reality underlying the sacraments.[14]

◼ The Paraclete

The spiritual reality that John is concerned with can come about only through the ministry of the Spirit. Although there are many references to the Spirit throughout the Gospel, the farewell discourse is particularly significant in this regard. Here the Spirit is given the unique name **Paraclete,** which is the Anglicized form of the Greek *paraklētos,* variously translated as advocate, comforter, counselor, helper. Although the exact meaning of the word has

puzzled exegetes, the basic idea is that of "someone who offers assistance in a situation in which help is needed."[15] Jesus speaks of the work of the Paraclete in the following ways:

Being Present with the Disciples: "And I will ask the Father, and he will give you another Advocate, to be with you forever. . . . You know him, because he abides with you, and he will be in you" (14:16-17).

Teaching the Disciples: "But the Advocate, the Holy Spirit, whom the Father will send in my name, will teach you everything, and remind you of all that I have said to you" (14:26; see also 16:12-14).

Bearing Testimony to Jesus: "When the Advocate comes . . . he will testify on my behalf" (15:26).

Convicting the World Concerning Jesus: "And when he comes, he will prove the world wrong about sin and righteousness and judgment: about sin, because they do not believe in me; about righteousness, because I am going to the Father and you will see me no longer; about judgment, because the ruler of this world has been condemned" (16:8-11).

John's Portrait of Jesus

In the Gospel of John, Jesus speaks frequently about himself. This is in contrast to the Synoptic Gospels where the words of Jesus are mostly about the kingdom of God.

◼ "I Am" Sayings

In John, we find long discourses

JESUS ACCORDING TO THE GOSPELS

built around seven sayings of Jesus that begin with "I am." The predicates in the **"I am" sayings** are all familiar images for people in biblical times: bread, light, shepherd, vine, and so on. There are also several "I am" sayings without a predicate. In 8:58, for example, Jesus says, "Very truly, I tell you, before Abraham was, I am."

In the Old Testament, particularly in Exodus and Isaiah, we often find "I am" statements made by God in solemn declarations. God tells Moses that His name is "I AM WHO I AM" (Exodus 3:14), which in Hebrew is Yahweh. In several instances in Isaiah the "I am" is even repeated, such as in Isaiah 43:25, which literally reads, "I am, I am He who blots out your transgressions."

First-century hearers of the Gospel of John, familiar with the "I am" language of God in their scriptures, would not miss the point: Jesus speaks with the same authority and dignity as God. It is no wonder that when Jesus said, "Before Abraham was, I am," His hearers were about to stone Him for blasphemy.

■ Deity and Humanity of Jesus

John underscores the deity of Jesus in various other ways. Nearly 30 times the title Son or Son of God is used of Jesus. The Word, who is Christ, was in the beginning with God and was God (1:1). Jesus often speaks of God as Father. His statement, "The Father and I are one," occasions another attempt to stone Him (10:30-31).

The sole purpose of the Gospel, as stated by the author himself, was "that you may come to believe that Jesus is the Messiah, the Son of God, and that through believing you may have life in his name" (20:31). Because of this strong emphasis on Jesus as the divine Son, some theologians, both ancient and modern, have thought that the Gospel of John is docetic. That is, Jesus is really God, and His humanity is only in appearance. Yet, in spite of John's strong emphasis on the deity of Jesus, the Gospel just as seriously reckons with His humanity. "The Word became flesh and lived among us" (1:14). We have already noted the antidocetic stance of this Gospel. The humanity of Jesus is seen in various ways in John. He gets tired and thirsty and asks for a drink from a Samaritan woman (4:6-7). When Jesus sees Mary and others weeping at the death of Lazarus, He is so disturbed and moved that He weeps (11:33-35). As Jesus approaches Jerusalem, acutely aware of the prospect of His

---

L Seven "I Am" Sayings of Jesus in John

1. "I am the bread of life" (6:35).
2. "I am the light of the world" (8:12).
3. "I am the gate for the sheep" (10:7).
4. "I am the good shepherd" (10:11).
5. "I am the resurrection and the life" (11:25).
6. "I am the way, and the truth, and the life" (14:6).
7. "I am the true vine" (15:1).

own death, He says, "Now my soul is troubled" (12:27).

John does not play down the human origin of Jesus even when it becomes an obstacle for people. People queried, "Is not this Jesus, the son of Joseph, whose father and mother we know? How can he now say, 'I have come down from heaven'?" (6:42). On another occasion His hearers asked, "How does this man have such learning, when he has never been taught?" (7:15).

The theological sophistication and subtleties of the Gospel of John must not be underestimated. It is precisely in the limitations of human existence that Jesus lives out His divine Sonship, and only in this manner the revelation of God the Father becomes visible through Him.

■ Death of Jesus

For John, the death of Jesus, more than anything else, is irrefutable evidence of His true humanity. However, John also portrays the death of Jesus as His glorification. His glorification is not limited to the Resurrection and Ascension. As absurd as this may sound, Jesus is glorified on the Cross. Indeed, His whole life is the working out of the glory of God. "We have seen his glory," John says (1:14). When Jesus prays, "Father, the hour has come; glorify your Son so that the Son may glorify you" (17:1), the glory He has in mind includes the Cross. In 12:32 Jesus says, "And I, when I am lifted up from the earth, will draw all people to myself." How will Jesus be lifted up? The Greek word used here for "lifted up" is the same one that is most often translated "exalted" in other places in the New Testa-

ment. It refers to Christ's glorious exaltation to the right hand of God. John, however, has intentionally given the word double meaning: Jesus will be lifted up on a cross and He will be lifted up to the right hand of God through the Resurrection and Ascension. The Cross is clearly in view in John 3:14 where Jesus says, "And just as Moses lifted up the serpent in the wilderness, so must the Son of Man be lifted up."

Earlier we have noted that the chronology of Passion week in John differs from the Synoptics. In the Synoptics, Jesus dies on Friday, the day of the Passover. According to John, Friday is the day *before* Passover. This means that in John Jesus was crucified at the time that the Passover activities were starting with the slaughter of the lambs at the Temple. John the Baptist had earlier pointed to Jesus as "the Lamb of God who takes away the sin of the world" (1:29). The fact that the legs of Jesus are not broken (19:33) and the comment in 19:36 that this fulfilled scripture may be a reminder of Old Testament regulations that the bones of Passover lambs were not to be broken (Exodus 12:46; Numbers 9:12). John seems to identify Jesus as the true Passover Lamb that takes the place of the older Jewish practices.[16] This may well be an early Christian tradition, since Paul also calls Jesus our paschal lamb (1 Corinthians 5:7).

John's understanding of the death of Jesus is that of a good shepherd who out of sheer love lays down his life for the sheep (10:11). "No one has greater love than this, to lay down one's life for one's friends" (15:13).

■ Resurrection of Jesus

As with Matthew and Luke, so also John ends his Gospel with the resurrection of Jesus and His appearances to His disciples. However, John's uniqueness can be seen here as well. John does not simply make the Resurrection the last chapter or two of the story of Jesus. The theme of resurrection and life is splashed everywhere in his Gospel (see this theme in 1:4; 5:21-29; 6:25-40; 10:7-10). The best example of the resurrection of Jesus working itself back into His earthly ministry is the raising of Lazarus in chapter 11. In His conversation with

Martha, Jesus emphatically proclaims: "I am the resurrection and the life. Those who believe in me, even though they die, will live, and everyone who lives and believes in me will never die" (vv. 25-26).

It is worth noting that Martha, along with most Jewish people in the time of Jesus, believed that there would be a final resurrection for the people of God on the last day in the distant future.[17] However, Jesus brings Martha to a new understanding, namely, that He himself is the resurrection and the life. The final resurrection in the distant future has become a present reality in Jesus.[18] Furthermore, Jesus' resurrection in the near future is already having a powerful impact during Jesus' earthly ministry. But what exactly does Jesus mean when He says that the one who believes in Him will never die? Lazarus, who was raised by Jesus, surely died again. Obviously, Jesus is now speaking of resurrection and life in a metaphorical sense rather than a literal, physical sense. Life, eternal life, or abundant life is much more than physical existence. Martha's response shows that resurrection life is rooted in the faith affirmation, "I believe that you are the Messiah, the Son of God."

We must include here a couple of other matters that are unique to John's Resurrection narrative. One of these is the story of Mary Magdalene. She is the first person to discover the empty tomb and later see the resurrected Jesus, who commissions her to go and announce to the disciples that He is ascending to the Father (20:17). As Gail O'Day observes, discipleship in John (and the other Gospels, for that matter) is not re-

Lazarus' tomb (interior).

stricted to men.[19] The Samaritan woman, Mary and Martha, and now Mary Magdalene all have significant roles in the life of Jesus and the ministry of the gospel.

The other unique feature of the Resurrection narrative in John is the final dialogue between Jesus and Peter. Three times Jesus asks Peter if He loves Him "more than these" (21:15-19), reminiscent of the three times that Peter denied the Lord (13:36-38; 18:17, 25-27). The point of this account is not to reprimand Peter but to reinstate him for a future ministry of shepherding Christ's sheep and for martyrdom, thus following in the footsteps of Jesus himself.

The Purpose of the Gospel of John

John has explicitly stated his purpose in 20:30-31 as follows: "Now Jesus did many other signs in the presence of his disciples, which are not written in this book. But these are written so that you may come to believe that Jesus is the Messiah, the Son of God, and that through believing you may have life in his name."

What appears to be a straight-forward statement contains many complexities. For one thing, the variants in the Greek manuscripts of verse 31 make it uncertain whether the verb should be translated "that you may come to be-lieve" or "that you may continue to believe." If the former, the Gospel apparently targets out-siders in order to bring them to faith. If the latter, its target audi-ence is people in the Church, and John's purpose would be to in-struct and strengthen them. If the target audience is taken to be out-siders, there is the added ques-tion as to whether they are Jews or Gentiles.

Since John contains so many debates between Jesus and "the Jews," some have argued that John's purpose is to make a case for Jesus as the Messiah to Jewish audiences that had trouble with such Christian claims. Was John's purpose to convince, evangelize, and convert Jews? At present there seems to be an emerging consensus that John's purpose cannot be established simply on the basis of two verses in 20:30-31, but that the whole Gospel must be kept in view.[20] Further-more, the issue of outsiders or in-siders as target audience is not the best way to understand John's purpose. In the words of Beutler, "The Fourth Gospel was written to deepen the faith of Christians in Jesus as Son of God and Giver of Life, but at the same time also to encourage them to confess this openly, even under circumstances in which this confession would endanger their social position or even their lives."[21]

Summary Statements

- The Gospel of John was composed in several stages, including the testimony of the beloved disciple, composition by the evangelist, and possibly later editing by others.
- John's prologue stresses the deity of Jesus Christ as the Word who was with God from the beginning.
- The real humanity of Jesus is equally stressed in the statement that the Word became flesh.
- John's chronology of the life of Jesus differs from the Synoptic Gospels at several points.
- A unique feature of the fourth Gospel is long discourses that function as theological commentary on a dialogue, a miracle, or an event from the life of Jesus.
- A good clue to John's theology is the frequent use of such words as "know," "believe," "life," "light," "glory," "truth," "world," "God as Father," "Jesus as Son," and "the Spirit as *Paraclete.*"
- The miracles of Jesus are called signs because their purpose is to bring people to faith in Jesus Christ, through whom there is eternal life.
- John is concerned to keep the sacraments from becoming mere ritual by focusing on believers' spiritual vitality in Christ.
- In the "I am" sayings Jesus speaks with the same authority and dignity as that of God known from Old Testament scriptures.
- Jesus willingly lay His life down for others, even though political and religious leaders conspired to get Him executed. His death was part of His being lifted up.
- The resurrection of Jesus at the end of the Gospel is repeatedly foreshadowed throughout His life, and its power is already at work even before it takes place.
- The purpose of the Gospel of John is to deepen the faith of Christians and encourage them to confess Christ even in the midst of opposition and persecution.

Questions for Reflection

1. Which is more important for your Christian life, to affirm that Jesus is divine or human?
2. When you ask God for a miracle, is it for the purpose of receiving a personal benefit or for exalting and glorifying Jesus Christ?
3. How has the Gospel of John deepened your understanding of your own baptism and participation in Holy Communion?
4. What does it mean for you to lay down your life for others, particularly in a culture that values ambition and self-advancement?

Resources for Further Study

Barrett, C. K. *The Gospel According to St. John,* 2nd ed. Philadelphia: Westminster, 1978.
Brown, Raymond E. *The Community of the Beloved Disciple.* New York: Paulist, 1979.
Morris, Leon. *Jesus Is the Christ: Studies in the Theology of John.* Grand Rapids: Eerdmans, 1989.
O'Grady, John F. *According to John: The Witness of the Beloved Disciple.* New York: Paulist, 1999.
Smith, D. Moody. *The Theology of the Gospel of John.* New York: Cambridge University Press, 1995.

UNIT III

THE BEGINNINGS OF THE NEW COVENANT COMMUNITY

Your study of this unit will help you to:

- Describe the story of the origin of the Christian Church in Jerusalem and the earliest days of its growth.
- Discuss the social and religious barriers to the spread of the Christian movement.
- Trace the spread of the Christian Church in the Roman world.
- Describe the method of Paul's ministry.

■ Acts 1—10

■ Acts 11—28

10 Acts 1—10

Objectives:

Your study of this chapter should help you to:
- Narrate the story of the spread of the gospel from Jerusalem to Samaria and Northern Africa.
- Discuss the relationship of other biblical stories to the Pentecost event and the sermons of Peter.
- Describe the complexities of the social and religious barriers to the spread of the gospel.

Key Words to Understand

Intertextuality
Microintertextuality
Macrointertextuality
Rereading
Self-text
Pentecost
Diaspora
Messianic expectation
Psalms of Solomon
Son of David
Traditional Jews
Jewish Christians
Gentiles
Proselytes
God-fearers
Sadducees
Hellenists
Samaritans

Questions to consider as you read:

1. How does Acts' story deal with ethnic and religious prejudice?
2. What would have been some of the community experiences of the participants of the early Christian movement?

The Writing of Acts

Acts is the continuation of the work begun in the Gospel of Luke. Our author, by tradition Luke the companion of Paul, wrote this work in the late 70s or early 80s A.D. The community for which he wrote favored the mission to the Gentiles and was probably very similar to, if not in fact, the church in Syrian Antioch, the church that commissioned Paul and Barnabas to go to the Gentiles. As in the Gospel, Luke writes to Theophilus, who perhaps sponsored the project.

The structure of Acts tells the story of Acts. The first seven chapters chronicle the establishment of the nascent movement in Jerusalem, probably over the period of a few years. Chapters 8—10 record the spread of the gospel to Samaria and North Africa and culminate with the conversion of the Gentile God-fearer Cornelius and his family. In this chapter of our study, we will focus on the content of Acts 1—10. In our next chapter, we will pick up the rest of the Book of Acts (chapters 11—28), which contains the story of the spread of Christianity from Syrian Antioch, across the Mediterranean basin, all the way to Rome.

The Inauguration of the Movement's Public Ministry (Acts 1—2)

The first chapter describes the presence of the resurrected Jesus among His followers, His ascension, and the selection of the replacement of Judas as apostle. Following the dramatic ascent of Jesus to heaven, the narrative turns to the first days of the new movement. The descent of the Holy Spirit on 120 people at **Pentecost**, a Jewish festival occurring 50 days after Passover, represents the birth of the Christian Church (Acts 2). This event is the shift from the *age of Jesus* to the *age of the Holy Spirit* in the Church. Both literal and symbolic meaning can be found in the great rushing wind, tongues of fire, and the many languages that

---

I

Reading Skills for Acts

There are three worlds to consider as we read any biblical text. The first is the social world of the author(s), that is, the realities of their particular cultural, political, and religious setting. The second is the literary world of the text. Here the focus is on the use of language, themes, characterization, plot, and other literary devices. **Intertextuality** is present when a biblical author makes reference to another part of the Bible or some other written source. A direct quotation of an earlier text by a biblical author can be called **microintertextuality.** That is, when an author wishes to invoke the meaning of a particular passage of Scripture for his reader, he will give a verbatim quotation of the passage and then expand on its meaning. When an author alludes *indirectly* to another passage or theme in the Bible, this is called **macrointertextuality.**[1] New Testament writers assumed their readers were intimately acquainted with the Old Testament and used this device frequently, especially given the importance of the *reinterpretation* of such passages for the preaching of the gospel. Scholars refer to such as **rereading.** Luke's record of the events of Pentecost shows significant evidence of rereading and microintertextuality/macrointertextuality.

The third world has been called the **self-text** of the reader. We, as readers, always bring our own assumptions and modern perspectives to the task of interpreting a biblical text. Being aware of our own self-text is part of responsible Bible reading and getting to know God through Scripture.

Chapel of Ascension, the traditional site of the ascension of Jesus.

the believers began speaking.

The great rushing wind in Acts 2:1-4 evokes the sweeping spirit of God in creation (Genesis 1:1) and is a good example of macro-intertextuality, the evocation of one biblical theme in a later passage. Fire is seen throughout Scripture as a symbol of God's presence. Some examples in the Old Testament are the burning bush in the story of the call of Moses (Exodus 3:2), the appearance of the glory of the Lord in fire on Mount Sinai (24:17), and the pillar of fire that led the people of Israel in the desert (13:21). In Acts 2:3 the appearance on each person of "divided tongues, as of fire" evokes the same palpable presence of God.

Some have suggested an allusion to the Genesis story of the Tower of Babel in Acts 2. In Genesis, God confounds the pride of the people by giving them different languages (11:1-9). This Pentecost event in Acts symbolically lifts that curse by having people praise God in all the languages of

the geographical areas in the ancient Near East: Parthia, Media, Elam, Mesopotamia, Judea, Cappadocia, Pontus, Asia, Phrygia, Pamphylia, Egypt, Libya, and Rome (Acts 2:9-11). The order is significant in that it moves from the distant east of Parthia to the western city of Rome. These believers at Pentecost proclaimed the gospel to the known world, an event that could be understood as the beginning of the global mission of early Christianity.

According to one Christian tradition, the site known today as the Upper Room at Mount Zion was the location of the events of the Day of Pentecost.

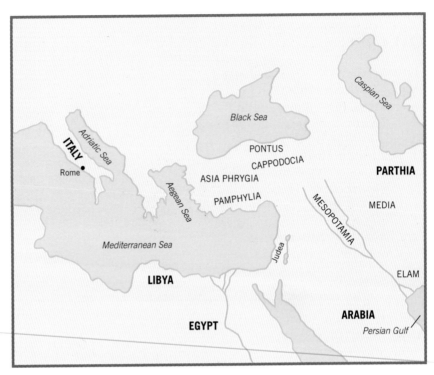

Geographical Locations of the Jewish Diaspora in the First Century A.D.

H The Jewish World in the First Century

The vehicle for the spread of the gospel by the first Jewish Christians was the network of Jewish synagogues and communities in the Mediterranean basin. To give some idea of the scale of the vision of Pentecost, it must be understood that there were large numbers of Jews living in communities from ancient Persia in the east to Rome in the west. There were at least 600,000 Jews in Palestine and an even greater number in the **Diaspora,** or those Jews living outside the Holy Land. In all of the areas mentioned in Acts 2:9-11, there were large, often prosperous, Jewish communities. There were likely several hundred thousand living in Mesopotamia and ancient Persia (Parthia), a holdover from the Jewish exile. Philo says there were 1,000,000 Jews in Egypt alone.[2] Many tens of thousands of Jews were also to be found in Asia Minor (modern Turkey) and Greece. A population of 60,000 Jews was in Rome at this time. Early Jewish Christian evangelists such as Paul of Tarsus traveled through these widely scattered communities preaching the gospel of Jesus' resurrection. It has been suggested that people present at the Pentecost event may have returned to Rome the fall of that same year proclaiming a primitive form of the Christian gospel. These traveling evangelists often encountered opposition from local Jews because of the radical implications a resurrected Messiah held for Judaism. The Roman historian Suetonius tells us the emperor Claudius expelled Jews from Rome (A.D. 49) for causing riots in the local Jewish community "at the instigation of Chrestus," most likely a reference to the followers of Jesus Christ.[3]

Peter's Pentecost Speech (2:14-36)

Peter's inaugural Christian sermon is worth close attention for two reasons. First, it gives us an account of the content of early Christian preaching. It is possible that Luke's narrative is based on eyewitnesses of Pentecost or those who were closely associated with them. By normal standards, this is historical reporting very close to the source. Even so, Luke probably does not preserve Peter's actual words, since no one wrote the speech down at the time. Most likely this sermon contains the essential elements of Peter's speech, rather than an exact rendering.

The second point of interest is how Peter's sermon demonstrates the principles of intertextuality and rereading. Many passages in Acts are indented in most Bible translations. These are quotations from the Old Testament (or occasionally another source). By looking at chapter 2 (vv. 14-22) it is possible to see that Peter preaches and then quotes the Old Testament, preaches and quotes, and so on. These quotations are a good example of microintertextuality. The way Peter *interprets* these texts is a good example of rereading. Specifically, Peter weaves together four different Old Testament passages in Acts 2 to answer four different questions: what age is this? (vv. 14-21); who is Jesus? (vv. 22-28); why was He raised from the dead? (vv. 29-36); what do we need to do now? (vv. 37-42). The sermon also shows that the earliest proclamation of Jesus centered on three issues: Jesus had been physically

T

The Christian Community in Acts

The Christian community in Acts was characterized by close-knit fellowship. They shared not only times of rejoicing and praise at the victories being won (2:47) but even their possessions, food, and land (vv. 44-46; 4:32-37). The communal nature of the movement must have strengthened the believers to endure times of persecution and doubt as they sought to be obedient to the gospel.

raised from the dead; He was the long-expected Messiah, the Son of David promised in 2 Samuel 7:12-13; and that He was not only the Messiah but also Lord.

What Age Is This?

Peter's sermon reveals his conviction that history is at a crossroads. He explains the chaotic situation to the crowd with a quote from the prophecy of Joel (Joel 2:28-32). Joel prophesied to the Jewish people (about 400 B.C.) in the wake of the devastation of Israel by a terrible plague of locusts. He announced this catastrophic time as the Day of the Lord (1:15; 2:1); that is, the Day of Judgment. Peter evokes this powerful image of devastation and seems to imply that Jesus' death was a parallel event inaugurating the end of one era and the beginning of another. In Joel's book, the prophet calls for repentance, followed by the promise of God's blessings and the outpouring of His Spirit upon all people at the end of the age (Joel 2:12-32). Peter rereads Joel (Acts 2:16), compares his own world to the one devastated by locusts in Joel, and finds hope for restoration of the land in the coming of Jesus and the outpouring of God's Spirit upon the disciples of Jesus.

One other interesting intertextual allusion can be gleaned from Joel 3:12: "Let the nations rouse themselves, and come up to the valley of Jehoshaphat; for there I will sit to judge all the neighboring nations." Tongues from every nation are being uttered at Pentecost, and this seems to further fulfill the prophecy from Joel. The valley of Jehoshaphat is traditionally understood to be the valley of the resurrection of the dead, known as the Kidron Valley in Jesus' day. It is a few hundred yards to the east of this scene in Acts 2. As in Joel, Peter calls his hearers to repentance and decision, this time by proclaiming Jesus as Messiah: "Multitudes, multitudes, in the valley of decision! For the day of the LORD is near in the valley of decision" (Joel 3:14). This fits well with Peter's call to repentance in Acts 2.

■ Who Is the Resurrected Jesus?

Peter now addresses the question of the identity of Jesus and the phenomenon of His resurrection for the first time publicly. Until now, the new believers had been in hiding in Jerusalem, fearful for their safety. Peter says that while Jesus was delivered up "according to the definite plan and foreknowledge of God," the residents of Jerusalem share guilt for this crucifixion by association and complicity. He tells them "you crucified and killed [Jesus] by the hands of those outside the law" (2:23), referring to the Roman role in the execution.

The Church's understanding of Jesus' identity was rooted in what is called **messianic expectation.** One version of this hope was the belief that a descendant of David would arise and restore Israel's shattered national expectations and usher in the final kingdom of

---

Son of David in Jewish Literature

The decline of Solomon's kingdom (922 B.C.) and the eventual destruction of the Northern Kingdom by the Assyrians (721 B.C.) and the Southern Kingdom by the Babylonians (587 B.C.) crystallized for Israel the hope in the coming of a messiah from the fallen house of David. The pseudepigraphal **Psalms of Solomon** contains statements that indicate that this expectation was strong by the middle of the first century before Christ. This non-canonical writing is actually the earliest known place where the phrase "Son of David" is used in Jewish literature. By the time of Jesus' ministry 100 years later, the phrase appears to be commonly known and connected to Jesus, "Jesus, Son of David, have mercy on me!" (Luke 18:38). This passage demonstrates how some expected the coming of the Son of David to be a new Jewish king and military deliverer from Roman oppression (Acts 1:6).

See, Lord, and raise up for them their king, the son of David, to rule over your servant Israel in the time known to you, O God. Undergird him with the strength to destroy the unrighteous rulers, to purge Jerusalem from Gentiles . . . to shatter all their substance with an iron rod (Psalms of Solomon 17:21-24).

God. The concept of Jesus as the **Son of David** is central to this expectation.

In his sermon, Peter rereads Psalm 16:8-10 and explains this psalm of David as a prophetic reference to Jesus' resurrection: "David spoke of the resurrection of the Messiah, saying, 'He was not abandoned to Hades, nor did his flesh experience corruption'" (2:31). This saying was one of the rare Old Testament statements about the immortality of life, but what is new is Peter's application of the text specifically to the resurrection of Jesus. Next, through macrointertextuality, he makes an allusion to God's covenant promise to David found in 2 Samuel 7:13. Peter's audience would have known these words of promise to David well: "He shall build a house for my name, and I will establish the throne of his kingdom forever." Because the throne of David was overthrown in 587 B.C. with the destruction of the first temple of Solomon, the people of Israel had been waiting for *the* son of David who would fulfill this promise. Peter tells his audience that David "knew that God had sworn an oath to him that he would put one of his descendants on this throne" (Acts 2:30). Peter then proclaims: "Let the entire house of Israel know with certainty that God has made him both Lord and Messiah, this Jesus whom you crucified" (v. 36).

It is difficult for the modern reader to understand how radical this would have sounded to Peter's audience. No Jewish interpreters had foreseen that Israel's Messiah would die and then be raised from the dead. Peter's audience was stunned by what they heard.

■ What Do We Do Now?

Peter's hearers were "cut to the heart" and responded, "What should we do?" (2:37). Peter's reply—"Repent!"—is familiar to any student of Luke's writings. Furthermore, Peter called for those who repented to be baptized and receive forgiveness of sins and the gift of the Holy Spirit. Three thousand were baptized in the coming months, and significantly, they continued to worship in the Temple daily, a reminder to us that these early believers were still a Jerusalem-based Jewish messianic sect.

The Jesus Movement Finds Its Voice (Acts 3—4)

In the aftermath of Pentecost, the nascent movement enjoyed a period of goodwill in the city. Their community of faith was characterized by signs and wonders through the apostles, by sharing and eating together with "glad and generous hearts," and by daily worship in the Temple (2:46). Even though they proclaimed Jesus as the Son of David, this group of believers would have been an integral part of Jewish faith and life in Jerusalem.

■ Peter's Second Speech (3:12-26)

Peter's second speech is occasioned by his healing of a 40-year-old man who had never walked. Nothing could improve on the drama of Luke's report of the event. In an exuberant scene, the healed man stands straight up and begins "walking and leaping and praising God" (3:8). Peter and John continue into the Temple ac-

Narrative Structure of Acts 2—4

Luke uses a literary device in Acts that requires comment. At points his narrative is structured as follows: the report of a miraculous event, an accompanying speech, and then a brief summary of the progress of the movement. This pattern appears in Acts 2 with the miraculous event of Pentecost (vv. 1-13), followed by Peter's first speech (vv. 14-42), a summary (vv. 43-47). In chapters 3 and 4 the pattern recurs, but in a somewhat expanded form (3:1—4:37).

companied by a large crowd of amazed Temple-goers. Peter makes a speech as the healed man is dancing about and clinging to the apostles in Solomon's Portico.

In this speech several familiar themes begin to emerge in the style and content of Peter's argument. Again, the people of Jerusalem are held accountable for Jesus' crucifixion (see also 2:23 and 3:13-14), even though it was due to ignorance. Peter begins to argue again that this should not have surprised them: "God fulfilled what he had foretold through all the prophets, that his Messiah would suffer" (3:18). According to Peter, the Law, Prophets, and Writings were beginning to manifest their prophetic meaning to the Church. Yet, in a sense, God had confounded *all* expectations with the death and resurrection of Jesus.

Peter again engages in rereading the Old Testament. He quotes the words of Moses that God would someday raise up a prophet like himself for Israel (3:22-23; see Deuteronomy 18:15-19). Peter claims that Jesus is this prophet and urges the audience to listen to the voice of this prophet. Even more significantly, the promise of the Messiah is seen in the word God gave to Abraham himself, a promise at the very heart of Judaism: "And by your offspring shall all the nations of the earth gain blessing" (Genesis 22:18; Acts 3:25). Peter believes Jesus is this Seed of Abraham, and this Seed holds the promise of salvation for Gentiles. Paul made the same argument on behalf of Gentiles years later in his letter to the Galatians (Galatians 3:16).

The far-reaching implications of these claims would not have been lost on Peter's audience in the Temple. While Peter anchored his message in the bedrock of Jewish self-understanding, he also signaled a shift in its center of gravity from Abraham and Moses to the Messiah, Jesus of Nazareth. Later, he makes this development explicit to the ruling elders by saying that Jesus is the rejected "cornerstone," and "there is salvation in no one else, for there is no other name under heaven given among mortals by which we must be saved" (4:12). Salvation, Peter argues, cannot come by Abraham, or by Moses, or by a high priest of the Temple, but only through Jesus. What began as a movement within Judaism is beginning to look more like a revolution within Judaism.

Growing Pains and Crisis (Acts 5—7)

■ Tensions Rise from Without: Sociological Tensions

The Jesus movement increased in prominence in Jerusalem as the number of baptized adherents grew. At Pentecost 3,000 were

Jews, Jewish Christians, Proselytes, and Gentiles

To be a Jew in Israel in the first century A.D. had ethnic, religious, and cultural dimensions. Ethnic identification as a Jew meant one was born to Jewish parents, but it also required participation in the religious traditions of Judaism. While it is recognized that Judaism had many competing streams and voices, there were three hallmarks of Jewish practice in this period: Temple, Torah, and synagogue.

To differentiate the majority of Jews from the relatively small number of Jewish followers of Jesus, we will refer to this majority as **traditional Jews,** though this term encompasses a wide variety of practice and belief. Jesus' first followers were Jews of this kind who had come to accept that Jesus was the promised Messiah. These believers could be called **Jewish Christians,** even though the term "Christian" did not arise until sometime later in Antioch (Acts 11:26). Their commitment to Jesus made them no less Jewish, of course, but they began a process of exploring what this new dimension of faith meant for their Jewishness.

The third group we will consider will be **Gentiles** or all non-Jews. Gentiles who had fully converted to Judaism were known as **proselytes,** such as Nicolaus in Acts 6:5. Other Gentiles who revered the God of Abraham but did not fully convert were known in the New Testament as **God-fearers.** Cornelius, one of Peter's early converts, is an example from Acts 10.

Finally, Gentiles who practice their own indigenous religions and cults are referred to in the Bible as "the nations" (see Isaiah 42:6). This does not denote people who were irreligious or atheistic, since such a category hardly existed at that time. Many highly developed religious systems and cults filled the ancient Near East, and almost everyone believed in some form of magic, superstition, or fate, as well as a multitude of deities and rituals.

baptized (2:41), with more added daily (v. 47). The number is then reported as having grown to 5,000 men (4:4), plus women and children. Luke tells us that "great numbers of both men and women" were added (5:14), and that a "great many of the priests became obedient to the faith" (6:7). There were "many thousands" of believers in Jerusalem during the time of Paul's visit in the late 50s (21:20). Jerusalem's permanent population was around 25,000. Imagine if a quarter of them or more had become Christians! The followers of Jesus were meeting in the Temple in large numbers (2:46; 3:1; 5:12), and a challenge to Temple authority may have emerged among Jewish priests who had accepted the Christian faith. While Acts does not say how long this period of growth was, it leaves the impression that it was short and intense. Whether it was several months, or even much longer, the effect on the social fabric of the city must have been profound. Many relationships, both private and public, were no doubt cast into turmoil by the growth in number of Jesus' followers.

■ Religious Tensions

The movement was mounting a theological challenge of growing proportions to traditional Judaism. The **Sadducees,** a hereditary class of prominent conservative Jews, disagreed with the doctrine of resurrection from the dead being promulgated by the Jesus movement (4:2; compare 23:6). Our analysis of Peter's preaching has also shown a fundamental challenge to the centrality of Moses and Abraham for Judaism. As we shall see shortly, Stephen will call into question the validity of Temple Judaism. While these differences initially had the flavor of sibling rivalry, the theological gap was widening. One author has noted that such intra-family rivalries are "fiercest when the siblings have an inheritance to share."[4] Theological debate on topics such as Moses and the Temple led the same scholar to observe: "Once we understand how worldviews function, we can see that the Jewish neighbors of early Christians must have regarded them, not as a lover of Monet regards a lover of Picasso, but as a lover of paintings regards one who deliberately sets fire to galleries—and who claims to do so in the service of Art."[5] This movement was no longer a small group of frightened provincial Galileans causing a ripple of trouble; rather, it was a mass movement posing significant challenges to Judaism at the heart of the Jewish capital.

■ **Political Tensions**

Given the political atmosphere that led to the Passover execution of Jesus, such a large movement would have been viewed with alarm by both Jewish and Roman authorities. The level of tension was such that after the healing of the man born lame, the very highest Jewish authorities were called together to consider the case of these "uneducated and ordinary men" (4:13). After the arrest of Peter and John, the authorities were forced to release them "because of the people" (v. 21). The atmosphere became so charged with tension that few disciples dared to enter the Temple with Peter and John (5:13).

■ **Tensions Rise Within the Movement: Jewish Christians and Hellenists**

Stephen, the first Christian martyr, is now introduced in the narrative of Acts. He is the leader of a group of **Hellenists** who are given responsibility for the daily distribution of food to the widows (chapter 6). In response to complaints of unfairness from the Hellenists, Peter appoints a team of seven individuals to manage the distribution: "men of good standing, full of the Spirit and of wisdom" (v. 3). Who were these Hellenists and why was there a conflict with "the Hebrews," as Luke calls the Jewish Christians? This question is not easy to answer, but it will have far-reaching implications for the young movement.

The seven all have Greek names (Stephen comes from the Greek *stephanos*, "crown") and most, but perhaps not all, would have been from outside of Israel. They all likely spoke Greek as their first language, as opposed to Aramaic and Hebrew for the locals, and would have been more tolerant of the ways of Greek culture, government, and leisure than the regional Jews. Hellenists seem to have been more open to the idea of spreading the messianic message beyond Jerusalem, and even beyond Judaism. The first to take the gospel outside of Judea to

Samaria was Philip, a Hellenist (8:5). For decades to come some Jewish Christians would view the mission to the Gentiles with suspicion, insisting on conversion to Judaism for all Christians. Stephen was the first visionary of this movement, and Philip the first evangelist. Paul would eventually become the most ardent proponent of the mission to the Gentiles. The story of Acts will now be primarily concerned with this issue—the emergence of the Jesus movement from its cloister in Jerusalem and its spread all the way to Rome.

■ Stephen

Jerusalem synagogues were undoubtedly the scene of many vigorous debates on the subject of the Messiah during this time. Luke tells us of a crucial dispute between Stephen and members of the Synagogue of the Freedmen that had a profound impact on the Jesus movement. Jews from Cyrene, Alexandria, Cilicia, and Asia worshiped at this synagogue while in Jerusalem, and Saul (later known as Paul), a native of Tarsus in Cilicia, was present during the dispute. When Stephen prevailed in the debate about Jesus, it was non-Christian Hellenists who took offense at his arguments. These opponents brought charges of blasphemy against him and said he spoke about destroying the Temple and changing Jewish customs (6:11, 13-14).

When brought before the council on these charges, Stephen rose to defend himself. His retelling of Israel's history is an example of macrointertextuality, and he invokes the broad sweep of God's interaction with Israel as the background for his argument that Jesus is the Messiah. Then Stephen turns to the prophet Amos whose writings contain a scathing denunciation of Israel's faithlessness to God and her corrupt Temple practice. The quotation of Amos 5:25-27 in Acts 7:42 lays a charge of idolatry against the Jerusalem Jews, and Stephen enters dangerous territory with his audience. He then recites Isaiah 66:1-2 as evidence for his assertion that: "The Most High does not dwell in houses made with human hands" (7:48). Finally, he

The Theodotus Inscription

An inscription from an ancient synagogue was found in the bottom of a well in Jerusalem in 1913. Its style of writing and the fact that no new synagogues were built after the destruction of Jerusalem makes it virtually certain the inscription is pre-A.D. 70. It has been suggested that this inscription came from the very synagogue mentioned in Acts 6:9, the Synagogue of the Freedmen. While this intriguing possibility cannot be established for certain, read the text below and consider its plausibility:

Theodotus the son of Vettenus, priest and ruler of the synagogue, son of a ruler of the synagogue, son's son of a ruler of the synagogue, built the synagogue for reading of the law and for teaching of the commandments, also the strangers' lodging and the chambers and the conveniences of waters for an inn for them that need it from abroad, of which (synagogue) his fathers and the elders and Simonides did lay the foundation.

lays the responsibility of Jesus' death at the feet of the high priest and rulers (vv. 51-53), just as Peter had done repeatedly.

The resulting outcry led to a mob action, and Stephen was killed by stoning. This first martyrdom marked a turning point for Christian history. Stephen understood the gospel had a mission field far beyond its Jewish setting in Jerusalem. He also seems to have understood that the Temple's role was now altered, perhaps even ended by the coming of the Messiah. These views made him the most radical visionary of the early Jesus movement. Just as anti-Temple rhetoric was one cause of Jesus' death (Mark 15:29), so it was with Stephen. And like the great prophets before him (Amos, Isaiah, and Jonah), he saw that all nations were to receive the good news of the Messiah. Stephen's execution led to a persecution in which everyone except the apostles were scattered. It is an irony that this seemingly tragic scattering was actually the means by which the movement would take on fresh vigor. The Temple-based messianic Jewish sect had broken out of Jerusalem and begun its dramatic spread to Rome.

Samaria— columns of Herod's palace.

The Movement Breaks Out of Jerusalem (Acts 8—9)

■ Philip: The First Evangelist

In the wake of Stephen's death, both Christian Jews and the Hellenists fled the city for a time. The apostles refused to be uprooted, however, and the Jewish Christian heart of the Church remained centered in Jerusalem until the Great Revolt of the Jews against Rome in A.D. 66. Philip was the colleague of Stephen and one of the seven Hellenists appointed to look after the distribution of the food (6:5). Luke tells us: "Philip went down to the city of Samaria and proclaimed the Messiah to them" (8:5). Samaria is a symbolically important location for the first evangelistic mission outside of Jerusalem (see sidebar). Luke said that Jesus as a traditional Jew had a poor reception in Samaria (Luke 9:52-55) and advised the 70 to not enter any towns there (Matthew 10:5). Yet, He always showed compassion to **Samaritans** and spoke of them often in His teaching as pious outcasts (see the stories of the Good Samaritan in Luke 10:29-37; the 10 lepers in Luke 17:11-19; the woman at the well in John 4:1-42). That Philip began his preaching there demonstrates the power of the gospel to bridge cultures and heal ethnic division. It may also have a sense of reuniting the kingdom of David that was torn apart many centuries earlier. In any case, the gospel of Jesus Christ and His message of love for one's neighbor was preached first to Judah's neighbors, the hated Samaritans.

Samaria

Samaria was the region north of Judea and Jerusalem and the center of the historic Northern Kingdom of Israel. Omri (876-869 B.C.) established the city of Samaria as his capital for the Northern Kingdom. One hundred and fifty years later, the Assyrians conquered the Northern Kingdom and carried away into exile 27,000 of its inhabitants. Assyria repopulated the cities of Samaria with her own residents and pagan worship flourished (2 Kings 17:24-41). Years later, the Judean king and reformer Josiah (633 B.C.) reoccupied parts of Samaria and tore down the pagan altars (1 Kings 13:1-2). When the Jews returned from exile in Babylon (539 B.C.), the Samaritan governor Sanballat refused to help Nehemiah restore Jerusalem (Nehemiah 6:1-14). Eventually, a mixed ethnic group loyal to Yahweh established a temple on Mount Gerizim (Shechem) as a center of worship. This is the place Abraham first visited in the Promised Land and where Joshua pledged support for Yahweh earlier in Jewish history (Genesis 12:6-7; Joshua 24:1 ff.). This Samaritan temple was destroyed by the Maccabean leader John Hyrcanus in the early second century B.C., after a year-long siege. Given all these factors, it is easy to understand the deep animosities between Samaria and Judea, even under Roman occupation. The Samaritans even had their own version of the Torah (the Samaritan Pentateuch). By Jesus' day its main city, now known as Sebaste, was famous as a center for magic and was the home of the magician Simon from Acts 8:9-24.

Peter and John were sent up from the Jerusalem church to impart the Holy Spirit to the Samaritans in a second Pentecost. The revolutionary importance of the Samaritan conversions for the growing movement required the blessing and validation of the Jerusalem church. If Peter had not endorsed the salvation of the Samaritans, then a fissure would have developed between the Hellenists and Jerusalem's Jewish Christians. Ironically, John had been the one who wanted to call down fire from heaven on the Samaritans for refusing Jesus entry to their village (Luke 9:51-56). They eventually received the fire of the Holy Spirit at his hand.

■ The Ethiopian Eunuch—the Gospel Spreads to Northern Africa

The story of Philip's encounter with the Ethiopian eunuch is rem-

Samaria and Galilee.

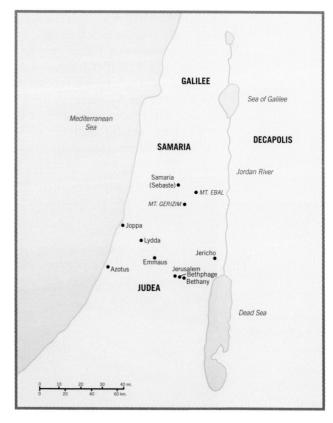

iniscent of the Old Testament prophets. An angel directs Philip to the road to Gaza where he encounters the chariot of the treasurer to the queen of Ethiopia. Like Elijah, who could also outrun chariots (1 Kings 18:46), Philip overtakes the eunuch, who is reading a manuscript of Isaiah 53:7-8. When Philip asks him if he understands the text, the eunuch says, "About whom, may I ask you, does the prophet say this, about himself or about another?" See Acts 8:32-33 for the famous quotation from Isaiah about the Suffering Servant, "Like a sheep he was led to the slaughter." This astute question offers Philip the opportunity to share the Christian rereading of this passage in light of the Jesus event. The Suffering Servant had been identified by some readers as Isaiah, as the eunuch notes, or possibly a king of Israel or even Israel itself. The text in Isaiah is not really clear on this point. Philip equates the text to the death of Jesus, and he goes on to speak of His resurrection and the "good news about Jesus." After the eunuch believes and is baptized, he continues on his way to Africa, taking the good news of Jesus with him. Philip is "snatched away" by the Spirit of the Lord to Azotus 20 miles away (compare 1 Kings 18:12). In a short period of time after the dispersion from Jerusalem, the gospel was already taking root in Samaria and northern Africa.

■ The Conversion of the First Gentiles (Acts 10)

A pious Gentile God-fearer named Cornelius lived in Caesarea by the sea. This story is the first conversion of a Gentile to the gospel of Jesus. Two visions are involved, one in which Cornelius is bid by an angel to send to Joppa for Peter, and one in which Peter is shown ritually unclean animals and encouraged to eat by an angel. When Peter refuses, citing his Jewish practice of eating nothing that is "profane or unclean," the angel responds, "What God has made clean, you must not call profane" (10:15). As Peter puzzles over the vision, men from Cornelius call at his door. It is interesting to note that Peter is staying in the home of a Jewish tanner, an unclean profession in itself! Even Cornelius's messengers will not enter the premises. Perhaps they

Peter was a guest at the house of Simon, who resided in this coastal town of Joppa.

do not want to offend Peter's Jewish sensibilities by Gentiles entering a Jewish house. Or maybe the smell from tanning was too unpleasant! In any case, they call out for Peter (vv. 17-18). Later, Peter invites them in to lodge (v. 23), and under the influence of the visions, Jewish Christians and God-fearing Gentiles have their social and religious barriers challenged and breached. When Peter addresses Cornelius and his family, he notes that it is unlawful for him to associate with a Gentile, but goes on to say, "I truly understand that God shows no partiality, but in every nation anyone who fears him and does what is right is acceptable to him" (vv. 34-35). This event opens the door to a much wider reach for the Jewish Christian gospel. Now the apostle Paul is ready to burst on the scene and spread the gospel throughout the Mediterranean basin.

Summary Statements

- The three worlds of a biblical text are the social text, the literary text, and the self-text.
- Macrointertextuality and microintertextuality are important to the understanding of Luke's use of the Old Testament.
- The descent of the Holy Spirit on 120 believers at Pentecost is the birth of the Church.
- The resurrected Jesus was central to the preaching of Peter, as was the theme of messianic expectation in the line of David.
- Tensions within and without the movement eventually led to its banishment from Jerusalem at the martyrdom of Stephen.
- The conversion of the first Gentiles in Acts 10 marks the beginning of the Gentile mission.

Questions for Reflection

1. The spread of the gospel in Acts came through the death of Stephen. Reflect on the role of tragedy in our lives and the role it can play in a spiritual journey.
2. The religious and racial barriers to the spread of the gospel were profound, yet God overcame these and even worked through them. How can such barriers be breached by the preaching of the gospel in your context?

Resources for Further Study

Albright, W. F., and C. S. Mann. *The Acts of the Apostles* in *The Anchor Bible.* Trans. J. Munck. New York: Doubleday and Company, Inc., 1973.

Bruce, F. F. *Commentary on the Book of Acts.* Grand Rapids: William B. Eerdmans Publishing Co., 1976.

Tannehill, R. C. *The Narrative Unity of Luke-Acts: A Literary Interpretation.* Vol. 2: *The Acts of the Apostles.* Minneapolis: Fortress Press, 1990.

11 Acts 11—28

O bjectives:

Your study of this chapter should help you to:
- Trace the spread of the gospel by Paul from Antioch to Rome.
- Explore some of the issues the early Christians faced as the gospel spread through the Jewish communities of the Dispersion.
- Describe Paul's life, message, and method of ministry.

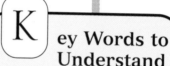

K ey Words to Understand

Asia Minor
Jerusalem Council
Tarsus
Hagiography
Nazirite vow
Sanhedrin
Client king

Q uestions to consider as you read:

1. Where does Paul fit in Judaism in the days of the Early Church?

2. The spread of the gospel in the Mediterranean basin was somewhat chaotic and characterized by conflict. Why would the leading of the Holy Spirit result in such conditions for the early missionaries of the Church?

The first 10 chapters of Acts tell the story of the spread of the Jesus movement within Jerusalem and outward to Samaria. The remainder of Acts (chapters 11 to 28) relates how the nascent movement began to spread throughout the Mediterranean basin following the martyrdom of Stephen. The book concludes with Paul imprisoned in Rome while awaiting an appeal on charges brought against him in Jerusalem several years earlier. We will now look at this second section of the Book of Acts.

While this latter portion of Acts contains many personalities, the focus is on Christianity's missionary to the Gentiles—Paul. In fact, these chapters of Acts could be called the chronicles of Paul. More specifically, the narrative relates events in the aftermath of Stephen's death in Jerusalem. These events include the following:

Peter defends his ministry
  among the Gentiles—11:1-18
The establishment of the
  Church at Antioch—11:19-30
Herod Agrippa's persecution of
  the Christians—12:1-25
Paul's first missionary journey
  to **Asia Minor,** modern-day
  Turkey—13:1—14:28
Gathering of Christian leaders
  in Jerusalem, which gives affirmation to the Gentile mission—15:1-41
Paul's second missionary journey—16:1—18:28
Paul's third missionary journey—19:1—20:38
Paul's final visit to Jerusalem
  and his arrest on charges of
  sedition—21:1-40
Paul's legal battle and appeal
  for justice to the Roman emperor—22:1—26:32
Paul's journey to Rome—27:1—
  28:31

The theme of Acts chapters 11 to 28 is the spread of the gospel among the Gentiles. Luke begins this section with a criticism leveled against Peter by the "circumcised believers" who wanted to preserve the Jewish customs and separation from the Gentiles (11:2-3). Peter responded to this charge with a recounting of his vision and his subsequent ministry among the Gentiles (vv. 4-18). The Jewish Christians of Jerusalem acknowledged the salvation of the Gentile Cornelius, saying, "God has given even to the Gentiles the repentance that leads to life" (v. 18).

The establishment of the church at Antioch on the Orontes in Syria further paved the way for the mission to the Gentiles (vv. 19-26). Barnabas, a native of Cyprus (see 4:36-37), who became a key leader in Jerusalem, came to Antioch and later introduced Paul to the believers there. Luke adds the historical fact that the disciples came to be known as "Christians" at Antioch (11:26). Persecution of the Christians during the reign of Herod Agrippa I, grandson of Herod the Great, and Peter's miraculous escape from jail are key events narrated in chapter 12. The rest of the book shows how ministry unfolds among the Gentiles. Following the so-called **Jerusalem Council** (see chapter 15), Paul declared the evangelization of the Gentiles as his main purpose (see 15:19; 18:6; see also 13:46). In Rome, where Acts concludes, Paul says that in response to Jewish intransigence "the salvation of God has been given to the Gentiles" (28:28; see also 22:21).

The narrative of Acts 11—28 concerns itself primarily with three issues. The first is the content and method of the preaching by Paul on his journeys. Paul's extensive activities on three journeys across Asia Minor and Greece are the narrative framework for seven speeches or sermons. The second issue is related to the first but will require separate attention: the matter of the intense persecution Paul's activities aroused, mainly among Jews in the synagogues of Asia Minor, Macedonia, and Greece. This will be the key to understanding how Paul differed from his fellow Jews and why the gospel generated so much resistance. The third issue is the appearance of Paul before both Jewish and Roman authorities on charges of sedition against the Roman state. These charges are first brought on Paul's final visit to Jerusalem, and he fights them for several years in Roman custody as they are vetted by a series of officials—in various locations. This part of the narrative is the subject of the last seven chapters, a quarter of the book!

Before we turn to these three issues, a look at Paul's personal background and experience will help to set the context more fully.

Paul the Man in Acts

■ Paul the Pharisee

Paul was a Cilician Jew raised in the sophisticated city of **Tarsus** (Acts 22:3). His father was a tentmaker and passed this vocation on to his son, who used these skills to support himself while working as a missionary (18:3). The family's service in this trade to the Roman authorities in Cilicia likely accounts for Paul's birth as a Roman citizen, this status having been awarded to his father for his loyalty to Rome (22:25-28).

It also means that Paul's family had social position in Tarsus.

By his own account, Paul was prominent among Jerusalem Pharisees prior to embracing Jesus as the Messiah. It is a sign of the affluence of his upbringing that he was sent to Jerusalem at an early age to study under the famous Rabbi Gamaliel (22:3 ff.; 5:34). His lifelong commitment to Pharisaic doctrine never wavered, as his words at the end of his ministry show: "I am a Pharisee, a son of Pharisees. I am on trial concerning the resurrection of the dead" (23:6; 26:5; Philippians 3:5). Thus, his belief in the resurrection of Jesus accords with his religious roots in Pharisaism (compare Galatians 1:14). In a sense, the story of Acts and Paul's personal correspondence preserved in the New Testament are an account of his journey from traditional Judaism to messianic Judaism. Paul never ceased to think of himself as Jewish; rather, he appears to have thought of himself as more fully Jewish having embraced Jesus of Nazareth.

■ Paul's Encounter with the Risen Jesus

As if to emphasize its importance, Luke includes three accounts of Paul's life-altering encounter with Jesus on the road to Damascus (9:1-22; 22:4-16; 26:9-18; compare Galatians 1:13). The beginning point of Paul's preaching was often his *personal experience* of the risen Jesus. No doubt Paul had heard a great deal about Jesus' earthly life and teachings, yet almost nothing of Jesus' life would be known to us if Paul's correspondence were our only source. Interestingly, he does preserve a single saying of Jesus not contained elsewhere in the New Testament: "It is more blessed to give than to receive" (20:35).

Students of Paul's life have debated the meaning of his so-called conversion on the road to Damascus. Yet "conversion" may not be the best word to describe his encounter, since he did not cease to think of himself as Jewish. His profound experience that day convinced him that Jesus was indeed the Messiah, an idea he had vigorously sought to suppress (9:1-2; 22:4-5). Paul's midlife reversal on this matter altered not only his own life but the history of Christianity as well.

The Method and Content of Paul's Preaching

■ Paul's Travels

Paul had an inveterate desire to

take the gospel to places it had never been preached. This meant that his life as an evangelist was a life of travel and hardship. As mentioned briefly above, three journeys are recorded in Acts. The first occurred in the mid-40s to late 40s, the second in the late 40s and early 50s, and the third in the mid-50s. Paul and Barnabas were first commissioned to undertake a missionary journey by the church in Syrian Antioch, the largest and most energetic church outside of Judea at that time. The church was full of the Spirit and had an aggressive view about spreading the gospel throughout the cities of Asia Minor. The evangelists traveled from Antioch to Cyprus, and from there to Perga, Antioch of Pisidia, Iconium, Lystra, and Derbe (13:1—14:28). John Mark also accompanied the evangelists, but he returned home when they reached Perga in Pamphylia. At Cyprus, they presented the gospel to the proconsul, Sergius Paulus, who became a believer, though a local magician attempted to turn the proconsul away from his faith.

Paul initiated the second journey and selected Silas as his traveling companion. This journey took the evangelists through the regions of Cilicia and Galatia to the western seaport of Troas. Paul recruited Timothy to join the team while he was passing through Lystra. Luke reports that a vision of "a man of Macedonia" that Paul saw while at Troas gave the evangelists the urgency to go over to the Macedonian province of Greece (16:6-10).

At Philippi, the evangelists met with some devout Jewish women, exorcised a demon-possessed fortune-teller, and were thrown in

I
Is Luke's Account in Acts Reliable History?

The issue of Luke's historical reliability was briefly discussed in the chapter on the Gospel of Luke. Acts also has been the subject of debate on this issue. Some have argued that Luke's representation of early Christianity was so skewed by his Christian agenda that the account has little value as a historical source. Many scholars find that assessment certainly too severe and difficult to accept. While most scholars believe Acts contains elements of **hagiography,** the tendency to portray individuals and events in a biased and favorable light, Luke should not be held to standards of modern historical reporting that were never part of his intent or literary age. Luke wrote Acts not only to lionize Paul as God's missionary to the Gentiles but also to fill a real vacuum in the record of the history of the Christian movement. Given these realities we can read Acts critically but also gratefully as an important source of information on the growth of the early Christian movement.

Gangitis river, possible site where Paul met his first converts at Philippi.

jail on charges of breaking the Roman law. A midnight vigil by the evangelists led to their miraculous escape from prison and the subsequent conversion of the jailer. The city magistrates urged them to leave the city without causing further trouble, and they went on to Thessalonica. Paul's preaching caused an uproar among the Jews in Thessalonica, which prompted the evangelist to leave town and go on to Beroea where they found hospitality among the Jews. Paul had to leave the city again because of the opposition of the Jews who followed him from Thessalonica. He traveled from Beroea to Athens where he met with Epicurean and Stoic philosophers and debated with them as a Christian philosopher. He addressed the Athenian crowd from Mars Hill (Areopagus) on the nature and existence of the one true living God.

From Athens, Paul traveled to Corinth where he met with Aquila and Priscilla, a devout Jewish couple who were also tentmakers by trade. Paul spent 18 months preaching and teaching the gospel at Corinth. Luke also reports opposition to Paul's preaching at Corinth and the Jewish complaint before Gallio, proconsul of the region of Achaia. From Corinth, he returned to Antioch via Ephesus, Caesarea, and Jerusalem (16:1—18:22). The third journey took him to Eph-

Mars Hill.

Acrocorinth
(the acropolis of
ancient Corinth),
the site of several
shrines, including
a temple of
Aphrodite.

...esus where he spent three years, before making a final tour of the Macedonian and Corinthian churches and returning to Jerusalem (19:1—21:16).

■ Synagogue First

There is a pattern to Paul's preaching activity as it is recorded in Acts. At Cyprus, Paul and Barnabas "proclaimed the word of God in the synagogues of the

Paul's First Journey.

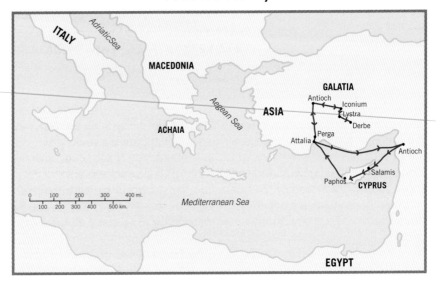

Paul's Second Journey.

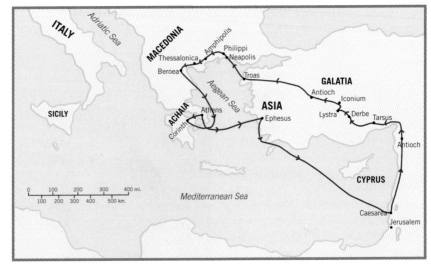

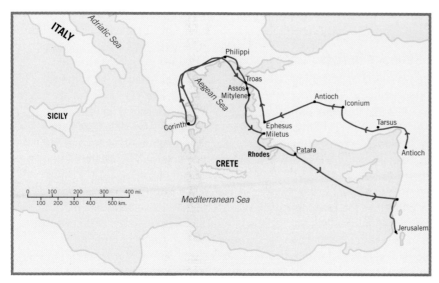

Paul's Third Journey.

Jews" (13:5). Beginning their preaching in each city in the local synagogue became their modus operandi and demonstrated Paul's fundamental belief that the gospel was intended, in the first instance, for the Jews (compare Romans 11:1-6).

■ The Content of Paul's Preaching

Seven sermons of Paul are recorded in Acts. They are as follows: in Antioch Pisidia on the first missionary journey (13:16-41); in the Areopagus in Athens on the second journey (17:22-34); to the Ephesian elders on the third journey (20:18-36); to a mob in the Temple in Jerusalem (22:1-29); before the chief priests in Jerusalem (23:1-11); to Tertullus in Caesarea (24:10-21); and before Agrippa, again in Caesarea (26:1-29). In these sermons Paul emphasizes his conversion (two times), his faithfulness to Judaism, the resurrection of Jesus from the dead, the arguments from Scripture for the Messiah, and that his

Ancient Jewish Synagogue Worship

The account of synagogue worship contained in Acts 13:13-15 is the earliest literary evidence for Jewish synagogue practice in the Dispersion in the first century. After the reading of the Law, a prominent teacher would sometimes be asked by the official of the synagogue to bring a homily. Similar to the event with Jesus in the synagogue in Nazareth (Luke 4:16 ff.), this speaker was often a distinguished visitor. A typical synagogue service would also include prayers and readings from the so-called Writings (for example, the Psalms) and the Prophets.

I Paul's Sermons in Acts

The similarity between Paul's sermons and Peter's sermons in Acts has led some to observe that Paul's preaching in Acts is not very Pauline. They cite, for example, the absence of the theme of justification by faith (characteristic of Paul's teaching in Romans 4 and Galatians 3) from his sermons in Acts (but see Acts 13:38-39). Also lacking in Acts is Paul's usual argument from Genesis 15:5 on the promise of salvation to Abraham and his "seed" (KJV) (again, Romans 4; Galatians 3:6-18), although he does call his hearers "descendants of Abraham" (13:26).

Luke's representation of Paul's preaching in similar terms with Peter and Stephen creates a seamless portrait of the preaching of the early Christian movement. His purpose, however, was not the creation of a technical précis of Paul's actual theology, and Luke had no written sources for any of the sermons as far as we know. The device of creating speeches for heroic figures is well documented for Luke's time.[1] Nevertheless, while there is evidence of Luke blending the messages of his main characters to accomplish this goal, the fundamental message of Jesus as Messiah in the Acts sermons is consonant with what we know of Paul's teaching from his other correspondence.

H A Chronology of Paul's Life

The details of Paul's life will always be debated, but the general dates are well documented and the following is intended as a guide for the reader.[2] In 10 years of intense activity from A.D. 47 to A.D. 56, Paul was able to establish churches in Galatia, Asia Minor, Macedonia, and Achaia. In his own thinking, he had exhausted the opportunities for evangelization in those areas and longed to travel to Rome to complete his work.[3]

10-15	Birth
34	Damascus Road event
34-36	In Arabia—the Transjordan area (Galatians 1:17)
36-46	Cilicia
47-48	First missionary journey
48	Jerusalem Council
49-52	Second missionary journey
50-51	Corinth
52-56	Third missionary journey
56	Arrest in Jerusalem
56-58	Caesarea
59-61	Rome
61	Martyrdom

enemies in Jerusalem are persecuting him, not for subversion, but for declaring the doctrine of the resurrection of the dead. The sermons are a fascinating representation of Paul's message by Luke, and the gospel of Jesus is clearly sounded throughout.[4]

Paul's first sermon in Acts (13:16-41) was delivered in Anti-

Paul's Dates: Acts or Epistles?

Different time lines of Paul's life arise from differing accounts of his visits to Jerusalem—namely, the depiction in Acts versus that in the Pauline Epistles.

Luke describes five visits to Jerusalem in the Acts of the Apostles:
- 9:26 (Immediately after his vision on the way to Damascus)
- 11:29-30 (Sent from the church in Antioch with Barnabas to take gifts to the famine-stricken church in Jerusalem)
- 15:2-4 (Sent by the church in Antioch with Barnabas to discuss the issue of whether a person needed to be circumcised to be saved)
- 18:22 (Implied visit, the verse says he went down to Caesarea, then went up [to Jerusalem] and greeted the church)
- 21:17 (Final visit and arrest)

Paul only refers to three Jerusalem visits in his letters:
- Galatians 1:18 (Three years after his Damascus vision when he went to Jerusalem to visit Cephas [Peter] for 15 days.)
- Galatians 2:1 (Fourteen years later, in response to a "revelation," he went with Barnabas and Titus to a private meeting with the "acknowledged leaders" to make sure that he had not run "in vain.")
- Romans 15:25 and 1 Corinthians 16:3 (Planned trip to Jerusalem to deliver resources/gifts for the poor saints in Jerusalem.)

Some scholars assume that Galatians 2:1-10 refers to the Jerusalem Council in Acts 15. Thus Paul's understanding of the conclusion of the council was that James, Cephas (Peter), and John gave him and Barnabas the right hand of fellowship, agreeing that they should go to the Gentiles, asking only that they remember the poor (or the saints in Jerusalem). While Luke reports in Acts 15:20 that Christian Gentiles were to "abstain only from things polluted by idols and from fornication and from whatever has been strangled and from blood."

Other scholars think Galatians 2:1-10 refers to the visit by Paul and Barnabas to the famine-stricken church in Jerusalem in Acts 11. It is supposed that an informal meeting took place, which came to the conclusion of Galatians 2:9-10 and that Paul's confrontation of Peter (Cephas) in Galatians 2:11 took place before the formal Jerusalem Council in A.D. 48.

och Pisidia during his first missionary journey. It bears considerable similarity to sermons by Peter and Stephen (Acts chapters 2 and 8 respectively).

Both Paul and Peter focus on the promise of a Messiah in the line of David (2:29-31; 13:22-23)—not a characteristic Pauline theme but undoubtedly crucial to the early proclamation of Jesus as Messiah. Both find the proof of Jesus' identity as the Messiah in His resurrection from the dead (2:24-32; 13:30-37), which is familiar from Paul's letters. Both blame the Jewish leaders of Jerusalem for complicity in the death of the Messiah (2:23; 13:27-28). Paul's and Stephen's sermons are similar in that they both start with a long recitation of Israelite history.[5]

Paul's Activities Arouse Intense Persecution

As Paul went from city to city, some responded positively to his message but others rejected it—sometimes violently. Luke often summarizes the response of the people in a specific locale. For example, on his first missionary tour Paul arrives at the synagogue at Antioch in Pisidia with his companions (13:13-16), and his preaching about Jesus (vv. 16-41) results in Jewish opposition to the gospel (vv. 42-52): "But when the Jews saw the crowds, they were filled with jealousy; and blaspheming, they contradicted what was spoken by Paul" (v. 45; compare other similar passages in Acts: 14:1-7, 8-20; 17:1-5, 22-34; 18:5-11). Paul often had to relocate outside the synagogue or simply flee the area altogether (13:51; 14:5-7, 19; 18:5-7). This constant opposition is a theme in Luke's narrative and serves to heighten the sense of drama and danger that were no doubt common to Paul's travels.

To be fair, it was not only Jews that Paul upset! In two cases Paul angered local Gentiles by eroding their economic livelihood. In Philippi a local slave girl was rendered useless to her owners by Paul's exorcism (16:16-19), and in Ephesus the local silversmith industry was negatively affected by Christian preaching against idols (19:23-27).

■ Why Was Paul Persecuted?

The conflict between Paul and his fellow Jews in Acts had three main causes: the dispute about the reinterpretation of Hebrew Scriptures, the conversion of Gentiles and their relationship to the Jewish Law, and the debate within Judaism about the doctrine of the resurrection of the dead.

Paul and other Christians reread the Old Testament and saw abundant evidence of prophecy about the suffering, death, and resurrection of Jesus. In his great final defense before Festus and King Agrippa in Acts 26 Paul says: "To this day I have had help from God, and so I stand here, testifying to both small and great, saying nothing but what the prophets and Moses said would take place: that the Messiah must suffer, and that, by being the first to rise from the dead, he would proclaim light both to our people and to the Gentiles" (vv. 22-23).

Many traditional Jews took exception to what they perceived as errant reinterpretation of their Scriptures in regard to the Messiah. For example, both Paul and Peter cite Psalm 16:10 in their message (Acts 13:35; 2:27): "You will not let your Holy One experience corruption." Both apply this passage to Jesus as evidence that a resurrected Messiah was prophesied in Scripture. While this seemed self-evident to Christians, not all Jews accepted this interpretation of that psalm, and similar rereadings of many of the other biblical passages Christians drew on for their scriptural proof of Jesus' identity. This fundamental issue was to plague the relationship of Christians with traditional Jews for decades and would eventually lead to an acrimonious split between church and synagogue.

The most controversial aspect of Paul's teaching was his contention that God saves Gentiles without requiring formal conversion to Ju-

Paul's Letters and the Acts Narrative

The narrative of Acts has long been of interest to students of Paul's letters as an independent source of information on his missionary activity. For example, Paul's earliest letter in the New Testament, Thessalonians, is *primary* evidence of his activity in Thessalonica, whereas Acts provides valuable *secondary* information (17:1-9). Likewise, Paul's specific activity in Philippi, Corinth, and Ephesus is discussed at length in the narrative of Acts (16:11-40; and chapters 18 and 19). Such comparative intertextual analysis is a valuable source of information in attempting to understand the life and message of Paul through his letters. While critical issues do arise, there is general agreement in these independent sources for the framework of Paul's activity.

daism (13:46-48; 15:1-11; 18:5-6; 22:21; 26:23). This was one of the issues that led to a perception among traditional Jews that Paul's vision of messianic Judaism was leading people to disregard the Law (21:20-21; 28:22). According to the Book of Acts, Paul's teachings in this matter were poorly understood by his fellow Jews, and the charge that he taught that the Law was to be completely disregarded was unfounded.

Finally, throughout his appearances before Jewish and Roman authorities (see Acts 23:6; 24:15, 21; 26:23) Paul contends that the real reason the Jewish authorities are persecuting him is because of his Pharisaic beliefs on the doctrine of the resurrection of the dead. Traditional Jews in Jerusalem were divided on this issue, pitting Pharisees, who believed in resurrection, against Sadducees, who did not. Paul claims that his affirmation of this doctrine is the real reason false charges of sedition have been laid against him by the Jewish authorities.

■ The Jerusalem Council of Acts 15

The debate was also raging within the Jewish Christian movement about whether a Gentile who believes in the resurrected Messiah must convert to Judaism. In practical terms this would normally require circumcision for males and full observance of Jewish life and customs. The answer to this difficult question is central to the narrative of Acts and was important for the future of the Jesus movement. On the one hand, if the decision went in favor of formal conversion for Gentiles, the movement may have stalled permanently within the family of Judaism. On the other hand, the spread of Christianity among the Gentiles would flourish, perhaps even taking on a life of its own separate from Judaism.

In chapter 15 the Jerusalem Council, sometimes called the Apostolic Council, gathers to consider this question. Some Jewish Christians from Jerusalem had traveled to Paul's home church in Syrian Antioch (v. 1) and were teaching that salvation without circumcision was not possible. Lest we think this was a minority opinion in Judean Judaism, the elders of the Jerusalem church advised Paul that his life was in danger from "many thousands of believers" who were "zealous for the law" (21:20). A plot to kill Paul was only narrowly averted (23:12-35).

After "no small dissension" with these visitors from Jerusalem, Paul and Barnabas were appointed to go up to Jerusalem for a ruling on the matter from the elders of the Church. This gathering included all the leaders of the new movement, including Peter, James, the brother of Jesus, and other local elders. In Luke's account, Peter argues that no circumcision should be required for Gentiles, thus opening the door to salvation based on faith alone (15:6-11). After all, the Gentile Cornelius had been saved through Peter's preaching. On that occasion Peter had said, "I truly understand that God shows no partiality, but in every nation anyone who fears him and does what is right is acceptable to him" (10:34-35). James, the leader of the Jerusalem church, added his approval to the Gentile mission (15:13-21; 21:25). All agreed that everyone is saved "through the grace of the Lord Jesus" (15:11). There follows the text of a letter from the assembly to be carried to the church at Antioch conveying this momentous decision for the Church and for the ministry of Paul (vv. 23-29).

The seeming harmony in Luke's account does not mean the issue was permanently settled that day. In fact, the dispute continued for decades and is often evidenced in Paul's writings and later in Acts (Galatians 2:9 ff.; 5:12; Philippians 3:2; Acts 21). From a literary perspective, Luke's description of this great council sets the stage in Acts for the movement to proceed with a clear two-pronged mission of salvation to *both* Jews and Gentiles. Paul becomes the head of the Gentile mission and Peter and James the mission to the Jews. Immediately following this policy victory for the Gentile mission, Paul and his companions depart on the second evangelistic journey (15:36).

■ Appearance Before the Chief Priests (Acts 21 — 23)

At the end of his third journey Paul went up to Jerusalem against the advice of coworkers and supporters. He had described himself to the Ephesian elders as "captive to the Spirit" (20:22) and drawn to the city. On the advice of the local Jewish church leaders in Jerusalem he joined some disciples fulfilling a seven-day temporary **Nazirite vow** (Numbers 6:1-21). This

---

L   The "We" Sections of Acts

A notable feature of Acts is the occasional change from third-person narrative (they) to first-person narrative (we). This occurs in 16:10-17; 20:5-15; 21:1-18; 27:1—28:16. The change would seem to indicate that the author actually traveled with Paul during parts of his journeys. This creates a vivid and lively presence to the narrative, as well as supplying an intriguing connection between the world of the Gospel literature and the world of the apostle Paul. It is remarkable to think that the author of Luke-Acts was actually a companion of Paul.

time "Jews from Asia" stir the crowd into a riot (Acts 21:27 ff.) charging Paul with bringing Gentiles into the Temple precincts. Paul addresses the crowd (22:1-21) and is taken into custody by the tribune of the Antonia Fortress, the soldier barracks overlooking the Temple court (vv. 22-29). An appearance before the chief priests and "entire council," presumably the **Sanhedrin** or so-called Council of the Seventy, leads to a division of opinion on the subject of the resurrection of the dead. Astutely exploiting the doctrinal difference between the Sadducees and Pharisees on this topic, Paul brings the assembly to an uproar and is rescued by the tribune (23:6-10). The resulting plot for his assassination by some of his opponents leads Paul to appeal to the tribune for safe passage from the city (vv. 12-35).

Paul's Legal Battles and the Trip to Rome

A lengthy series of legal proceedings follow in Acts 23 to 28 in which various groups and authorities bring charges of agitation against Rome, profanation of the Temple, and being a "ringleader of the sect of the Nazarenes" (21:28; 24:5; 25:7). Paul vigorously and repeatedly defends himself in the presence of mobs, the Jewish authorities, Felix, the Roman governor of Judea, his successor Festus, and even Herod Agrippa II, the **client king** of northern Palestine (22:1—23:10; 24:10-21; 25:8; 26:1-29). The Roman authorities ultimately can find no chargeable offense, and Paul is forced to appeal to the emperor to avoid being returned to the jurisdiction of the council in

Via Appia, the ancient road that Paul traveled in Rome.

Jerusalem (25:9-12). Ironically, it is Paul's Roman citizenship that saves him, since no citizen could be condemned without due process and all Roman citizens had access to a direct appeal to the emperor.

The final two chapters of Acts record Paul's journey to Rome and give a detailed account of his travels by ship from Caesarea to Rome. They are battered by winter storms, shipwrecked, rescued, and eventually arrive in Rome, where Paul is placed under house arrest (28:16, 30-31). He has considerable latitude to meet with local Jews and finds himself once

again at odds with those who oppose his message (vv. 25-28). For
two years Paul proclaims the
kingdom of God in Rome "with all
boldness and without hindrance"
(v. 31). Luke's chronicle of the early history of the Christian movement ends here without resolution of Paul's legal situation.
Tradition holds that Paul was
martyred in Rome in the early
A.D. 60s.

Summary Statements

- The second part of the Book of Acts may be called the Chronicles of Paul.
- The spread of the gospel among the Gentiles is a key concern of Acts chapters 11—28.
- Paul carried out three missionary journeys to take the gospel to the Gentiles.
- Synagogues were the first place of Paul's preaching of the gospel during his missionary journeys.
- Paul faced severe opposition and persecution as a result of his preaching of the gospel.
- Jesus as Messiah is a central theme in the sermons of Paul in Acts.
- Paul taught that God saves the Gentiles without requiring their conversion to Judaism.
- Paul's legal battles led to his journey to Rome as a prisoner who appealed his case to the emperor.

Questions for Reflection

1. Given the turbulent history of the early spread of Christianity, what do conflict and persecution teach the Church about life in the Spirit?
2. Early Christianity was spread by courageous and inspired leaders. How could their example inform the life of the Church today?

Resources for Further Study

Bruce, F. F. *The Book of Acts*. Grand Rapids: William B. Eerdmans Publishing Co., 1976.
Conzelmann, Hans. *Acts of the Apostles*. Philadelphia: Fortress Press, 1987.
Dibelius, Martin. *Studies in the Acts of the Apostles*. London: SCM Press Ltd., 1956.
Goodspeed, Edgar J. *Paul: A Biography Drawn from the Evidence in the Apostle's Writings*. Nashville: Abing-
don Press, 1947.
Hengel, Martin. *Acts and the History of Earliest Christianity*. Philadelphia: Fortress Press, 1980.
Keck, Leander, and J. Louis Martyn, ed. *Studies in Luke-Acts*. Philadelphia: Fortress Press, 1980.

UNIT IV

PAUL'S MINISTRY AND INFLUENCE THROUGH HIS LETTERS

Your study of this unit will help you to:

- Describe the significance of Paul to the Christian faith.
- Identify the structure and characteristics of Paul's letters.
- Discuss the occasion and purpose of Paul's letters.
- Describe the key theological themes of Paul's letters.

- Paul and His Letters
- Romans
- 1 and 2 Corinthians and Galatians
- Ephesians, Philippians, and Colossians
- 1 and 2 Thessalonians
- 1 and 2 Timothy, Titus, and Philemon

12 Paul and His Letters

Objectives:

Your study of this chapter should help you to:

- Describe the significance of the apostle Paul to the Christian faith.
- Discuss the religious and cultural background of Paul.
- Understand the structure and classification of Paul's letters.
- Identify central theological concepts found in Paul's letters.

Questions to consider as you read:

1. In what ways did Paul's background as a devout Jew as well as a Greco-Roman citizen shape his theological thinking as a Christian?

2. What are the similarities and differences between a typical Greek letter and the letters of Paul?

3. Why did Paul write his letters?

4. How did Paul apply his central theological convictions to the needs of the church or person to whom he was writing?

Key Words to Understand

Tarsus
Gamaliel
Soteriological letters
Eschatological letters
Christological letters
Pastoral letters
Letters
Epistles
Salutation
Thanksgiving
Body
Paraenesis
Diatribe
Conclusion
The center of Paul's
  theology
Kyrios
The work of Christ
The Body of Christ
Realized eschatology

The apostle Paul was an influential, complex, and controversial person. He pioneered Christian missionary activity, planted and pastored churches in many major cities throughout the Roman Empire, and wrote powerful and authoritative letters to the various congregations he had visited or hoped to visit. He was a well-recognized and respected leader of the Christian Church in the first 35 years of its history.

The extent of Paul's influence on New Testament Christianity can hardly be overstated. Of the 27 books in the New Testament canon, 13 are attributed to Paul. In addition, Hebrews was placed in the New Testament canon because of a Christian tradition that attributed this letter to Paul. The letter of James probably includes a response to a misunderstood Pauline theology. First Peter echoes significant elements of Pauline theology, and 2 Peter reflects a clarification of Paul's theology, even mentioning him by name. The impact of Paul upon Luke and his writings extends Paul's sphere of influence much farther. Nearly 70 percent of the New Testament carries a major imprint of Pauline influence.

This impact is significant enough to have caused some scholars to claim that Paul "invented" Christianity. Though this claim is an exaggerated distortion, it does point to the profound influence Paul has had upon Christianity. Paul's articulation of the gospel is contained in the letters that the Church preserved. This Pauline gospel has profoundly shaped the thought of many of the most significant theologians through 20 centuries of Christianity, including Augustine, Aquinas, Martin Luther, John Calvin, James Arminius, John Wesley, and Karl Barth.

So who is this major player in the early years of the Christian faith? In Paul's own words, he

Tarsus city under excavation.

was a Jew, "from **Tarsus** in Cilicia, a citizen of an important city" (Acts 21:39), who was brought up in Jerusalem "at the feet of **Gamaliel**" with strict training in the law of his ancestors, with extreme zealousness for God (22:3). Tarsus was a frontier city. To the West was the Hellenistic world of the Greco-Roman culture dominated by Rome; to the East lay the Hebrew world of Judaism. His parents were devout Jews who circumcised their son according to the Law on the eighth day (Philippians 3:5). He was from the tribe of Benjamin and was named after the first king of Israel, Saul, the most celebrated member of the tribe of Benjamin and a great hero of the nation who died in the battle against the Philistines. He adopted the Greek name Paul

(Paulos) and never refers to himself by his Jewish name Saul in his letters. How Paul gained Roman citizenship is not known. This may have been a privilege gained by his father or grandfather for some outstanding service to Rome.[1] Paul also identifies himself as a Pharisee (see Acts 23:6; 26:5; Philippians 3:5). He was trained in Jerusalem under the great first-century teacher Gamaliel. He was well versed in both the Hebrew Scriptures and the Greek Septuagint. He was also a student of Greco-Roman philosophy and a master debater skilled in both Greco-Roman rhetoric and the traditional Jewish Midrash.

First introduced in the New Testament as Saul of Tarsus, this zealous young Jew was a willing

Tarsus or Jerusalem?

Where did Paul receive his formal education and training? Was he educated at Tarsus, the capital city of the province of Cilicia, a cosmopolitan Hellenistic city known for its rich social, cultural, political, and intellectual heritage? Or, as the son of pious and wealthy Jewish parents, was he trained at Jerusalem, away from the influences of his native city? Scholars are divided on the answer to this question. At the end of the 19th century William Ramsay suggested that Paul's training and education at Tarsus prepared him well for his vision of a worldwide church. According to Ramsay, this Tarsus background also is seen in his "extraordinary versatility and adaptability . . . and his quickness to turn the resources of civilization to his use."[2] Some modern scholars continue this perspective and claim that Paul's training in the Septuagint (the Greek translation of the Old Testament) at Tarsus and the Greco-Roman cultural influence of his native city is evident in some of his letters.[3] There are others who seem to think that though Paul was a native of Tarsus, much of his education and training took place at Jerusalem. F. F. Bruce, by citing evidence from the Book of Acts and Paul's letters, holds the view that though Paul was a born in the Greek-speaking city of Tarsus, he was brought up in a strict Jewish family in which Aramaic was the language spoken at home. Bruce also thinks that his parents would have sent Paul to Jerusalem at an early age to grow up there under the Jewish cultural influence and to attend the school of Gamaliel.[4] Though we cannot argue with certainty where Paul received much of his educational and cultural training, one thing is clear. His Jewish religious heritage and Greco-Roman cultural understanding made him a most suitable candidate to be an apostle to the Gentile world.

accomplice to the stoning of Stephen. He was fiercely hostile to the early believers in Jesus as the Christ until his dramatic encounter with the resurrected Christ Jesus on the road to Damascus. After this revelation of God, the persecutor of Christians became a preacher of the gospel, and he began to proclaim that the resurrected Jesus was in fact God's Messiah, the living Lord.

Paul was convinced that his calling was to preach the gospel to the Gentiles. His commission was to proclaim throughout the Roman world that Jesus, the Galilean carpenter crucified by Pontius Pilate, had been raised from the dead by the power of God and thus was God's Messiah for all humanity. At a time when virtually all believers in Jesus as the Christ were Jews, this was a radical concept, and it required major rethinking for those Jewish Christians, not to mention the larger Jewish community who could not accept at all the notion of a crucified Messiah. This message was a scandalous stumbling block to Jews and pure foolishness to the wisdom of Greco-Roman Gentiles.

Paul's Letters

Paul apparently was a much more gifted writer than public speaker. The New Testament preserves 13 letters attributed to Paul. Some of these are letters that he wrote to the churches he established during his missionary travels. These letters show various aspects of Paul's theology—his understanding of sin, salvation, the end-time, the work of Christ, the Christian life, the nature and mission of the Church, and so forth.

Paul's letters provide us with a great deal of information about the cultural, social, and religious context in which Christians lived in the first century A.D. Each letter contains profound and timeless truth combined with specific practical life application. Individually and collectively, Paul's letters make a major theological contribution to Christian thought.

Paul's Epistles are collected in the New Testament in two basic groups. The first group consists of nine letters to specific churches, with the longest letter first, followed by the shorter letters. The second group follows with four letters addressed to individuals, again with the longest letter first and shorter letters following thereafter. Chronologically, the order of the letters would be quite different. The Thessalonian letters and Galatians were probably written first. The Corinthian letters would have been written next, followed by Romans, Philippians, Colossians and perhaps Philemon, followed by Ephesians. First and Second Timothy and Titus would likely be the last Pauline Epistles written.

Some scholars have used key theological themes found in these letters as a basis for classifying Paul's letters. Accordingly, Romans, 1 and 2 Corinthians, and Galatians are called **soteriological letters,** since salvation (Greek *sōtēria* means "salvation") is a primary theme in these letters. The Second Coming and the end-time (eschatology or the end-time events) are key issues in 1 and 2 Thessalonians; thus, they are called **eschatological letters.** Ephesians, Philippians, and Colossians emphasize the theme of the person and work of Jesus

Letter Writing in the Greco-Roman World

The following two Greek papyrus letters show the pattern of letter writing in the Greco-Roman world. The first letter is dated to about A.D. 25, and the second letter comes from the second or third century A.D.[5] Both letters show resemblance to the structure of the letters of Paul; the second letter in particular shows salutation, prayer, body, and final greetings—all found in Paul's letters.

Theon to the most honoured Tyrannus very many greetings. Heraclides, the bearer of this letter, is my brother, wherefore I entreat you with all my power to take him under your protection. I have also asked your brother Hermias by letter to inform you about him. You will do me the greatest favour if you let him win your approval. Before all else I pray that you may have health and the best of success, unharmed by the evil eye. Goodbye. [Addressed] To Tyrannus the dioecetes.

Irenaeus to Apollinarius his dearest brother many greetings. I pray continually for your health, and I myself am well. I wish you to know that I reached land on the sixth of the month Epeiph and we unloaded our cargo on the eighteenth of the same month. I went up to Rome, on the twenty-fifth of the same month, and the place welcomed us as the god willed, and we are daily expecting our discharge, it so being that up till today no body in the corn fleet has been released. Many salutations to your wife and to Serenus and to all who love you, each by name. Goodbye. Mesore 9. [Addressed] To Apollinarius from his brother Irenaeus.

Christ (Christology) and so are called **Christological letters.** Duties and responsibilities of pastoral leaders is a key theme in the **pastoral letters** (1 and 2 Timothy and Titus).

Scholars also classify the letters of Paul based on their similarity to various types of Greco-Roman letters. Accordingly, 1 Thessalonians and 1 Corinthians are called *exhortational or paraenetic letters,* since these letters are mostly Paul's instructions or exhortations to his readers. Philemon could be an example of a *letter of recommendation,* since the apostle is requesting Philemon to welcome his runaway slave Onesimus as a Christian brother. Second Corinthians is an example of *self-commendation,* or Paul's defense of his apostolic authority. Galatians is an *apologetic letter* that follows the style of self-commendation. Philippians, though it is paraenetic in form, also follows the style of a *family letter,* with its reassurances about both the sender and the recipients. Romans may be considered an *ambassadorial letter,* since it was written in anticipation of his visit to Rome.[6]

■ Structure and Characteristics of Paul's Letters

We now turn to an examination of the structure and characteristics of these letters that are attributed to Paul in the New Testament.

The Pauline Epistles in the New Testament are occasional correspondence, written at a particular point in time to specific congregations or individuals to address distinct situations in their given historical context. Their similarity to Greek papyrus letters has led some scholars to maintain the view that Paul's writings should be labeled as **"letters"** and not as **"epistles,"** since the latter refers to intentionally created literary works for wider reading.[7] As occasional correspondence dealing with specific situations, these writings can be called "letters." However, as Schreiner has shown, Paul's writings are much more than personal letters intended for a specific audience.[8] Though specific circumstances may have contributed to the writing of these letters, they demonstrate careful development of thought, use of language with precise meaning, and structure that are found in a well-planned literary composition. Thus the label "epistle" can be rightfully applied to these writings. Moreover, these letters are presented as correspondence from an apostolic authority and hence were intended for public reading and circulation within the churches in a geographical region (see Colossians 4:16).

Paul's letters follow the pattern of letter writing in the ancient Greco-Roman world. A typical Greek papyrus letter begins with a salutation, which includes the name of the sender, recipients, and greetings. Occasionally one may find a thanksgiving as a part of the salutation. This is followed by the body of the letter, which contains the message being communicated by the sender. The letter usually closes with some final remarks and a formal conclusion. The conclusion contains a peace wish, final greetings, and farewell.

All Pauline Epistles generally follow a similar structural pattern consisting of five basic sections,

and the exceptions are usually notable. The first section is the **salutation**, consisting of the sender, the recipient, and a brief greeting. Paul identifies himself as the sender of the letter with some qualifications or descriptions attached to his name, such as an "apostle" or "servant." Eight of the 13 letters (exceptions: Romans, Ephesians, 1 and 2 Timothy, and Titus) contain the names of some other individual or individuals along with Paul's name as the sender of the letter. The recipients are usually associated with the Christian communities to which they belonged (Rome, Corinth, Galatia, etc., with the exception of 1 and 2 Timothy, Titus, and Philemon). The greeting utilizes both the traditional Greek and Hebrew forms of greeting. Grace *(charis)* is the Pauline adaptation of the traditional Greek *chairein* (meaning "greeting"). Peace (Greek *eirene*) is the equivalent of the Hebrew greeting *shalom*. The greeting tends to be longer and more detailed when Paul is writing to a congregation that he has not yet visited.

The second section is the **thanksgiving** section, where Paul typically thanks God for the recipients and shares with them his prayerful remembrances of their mutual faith. This section, not found in Galatians, 1 Timothy, or Titus, often concludes with a doxological prayer of joy and thanksgiving. In some of the letters, the thanksgiving section alludes to the main concern expressed in the letter.

The third section, usually the longest and most substantial, is the **body** of the letter. Here we find various elements such as Paul's reasons for writing, his concerns for the recipients, responses to questions that have come to his attention, and major doctrinal and theological issues that need to be discussed with them. The theological concerns expressed in this section vary according to the particular needs of the recipients. This section usually begins with a request or disclosure or an expression of astonishment.[9] This section also often concludes with a doxological prayer.

The fourth section, which may sometimes rival the third section in length, is technically called the **paraenesis.** The mode of the verb is the imperative, which presents an urgent challenge to respond in order to set things the way they ought to be. The material presented in this section includes ethical

Diatribe in Paul's Letters

Paul utilized a conversational method in some of his letters to communicate with his audience. In this method of communication, the writer anticipates a possible question or objection from the audience directed at what he or she intends to state as a primary argument. The writer then states that objection or question and then gives a response. Scholars label this method of communication **diatribe,** a literary feature in some Pauline letters. This is illustrated below:

Paul's statement

Romans 2:25 Circumcision indeed is of value if you obey the law; but if you break the law, your circumcision has become uncircumcision.

26   So, if those who are uncircumcised keep the requirements of the law, will not their uncircumcision be regarded as circumcision?

27   Then those who are physically uncircumcised but keep the law will condemn you that have the written code and circumcision but break the law.

28   For a person is not a Jew who is one outwardly, nor is true circumcision something external and physical.

29   Rather, a person is a Jew who is one inwardly, and real circumcision is a matter of the heart—it is spiritual and not literal. Such a person receives praise not from others but from God.

Question anticipated from the audience

3:1   Then what advantage has the Jew? Or what is the value of circumcision?

See other such questions in Romans

3:9   What then? Are we any better off?

4:1   What then are we to say was gained by Abraham, our ancestor according to the flesh?

6:1   What then are we to say? Should we continue in sin in order that grace may abound?

6:15 What then? Should we sin because we are not under law but under grace?

7:7   What then should we say? That the law is sin?

Paul used this conversational method as an effective way of getting a message across to the readers. Scholars have recognized diatribe as a common teaching method in the classroom in the Greco-Roman world. Paul may have borrowed this method and adapted it to his particular need to give instruction to his audience.[10]

exhortations and practical considerations, often blended together. Some instructions are given as moral maxims; others as lists of virtues and vices; yet some others are in the form of long exhortations or homilies on certain topics.[11] The emphasis of this section is on application to life based upon information and reflection. The paraenetic material is concerned with the answer to the question: What then should we do and how then should we live in response to the truth that we have heard and believed? Some letters—such as 1 Thessalonians, 1 Corinthians, and Philippians—are either entirely or mostly in paraenetic form.

The fifth section is the **conclusion**, which typically includes travel plans or other personal situations, a commendation of co-workers, a pronouncement of peace, personal greetings, some final instructions, and a benedictory prayer. Not all of these are found in every conclusion, and some are repeated or ordered differently in particular letters.

While Paul generally followed this pattern, he sometimes departed from it, adapting various forms to suit his needs. Paul worked dynamically within the letters, utilizing a broad, diverse variety of literary constructs to communicate his message. He includes within his letters formal and informal prayers and benedictions, domestic codes, slogans or unique views held by some of his readers, hymns and homilies, wisdom sayings and aphorisms, metaphors and similes, creedal and baptismal formulas. He passes along traditions that he had received, recites words of the Lord, quotes and paraphrases scripture

passages, raises and answers rhetorical questions, and pronounces both blessings and judgment without equivocation. He is kind and gentle in dealing with young converts, yet at times caustic and sarcastic with veterans. He encourages, consoles, and comforts a struggling church, yet also challenges, confronts, and commands that same congregation.

■ **Key Theological Themes in Paul's Letters**

When Paul's occasional letters are collected and read together within the larger Christian canon, two things become readily apparent. First, there is a coherent theological core or center that appears in some form in the majority of his letters. Paul did not state this theological core in any single place. Rather, it must be discovered by investigating both the arguments and the assumptions that are found in the letters. Second, the way Paul expressed and drew upon this theological core varied from letter to letter. How the apostle made use of the theological core was contingent on the specific goals that he had for each letter. This variety in the way he applied the core has occasionally led to accusations of inconsistency on Paul's part. It is certainly possible that the apostle was not always consistent or that he changed his mind on some issues. However, careful study of his letters suggests that he had a strongly consistent core theology from which he drew in differing ways to meet the various needs of the churches and individuals to whom he wrote.

Scholars have often tried to identify **the center of Paul's the-**

ology. By this they mean the single theological concept upon which all his letters depend. This represents an oversimplification of Paul's thought. Rather than focusing on a single theological concept, Paul's theological vision incorporated a cluster of important theological ideas. Because he never directly identified these theological concepts, they must be discovered by an inductive study of his letters. Because Paul did not directly discuss these ideas, any way of organizing and prioritizing his central theological concepts is arbitrary and reflects something of the bias of the modern author. Nevertheless, the following concepts should be included in any discussion of Paul's theology.

The Old Testament Foundation

Paul rarely discussed God in an abstract way. Seldom did he speak of the nature and means of God's self-revelation. Rather, Paul assumed an understanding of God and Scripture that was the shared heritage of Judaism and the Old Testament. The holiness of God, the mercy of God, the power of God, the wisdom of God, the notable persons and the major events of the Old Testament all appear in Paul's letters without introduction. He simply assumed that his readers would understand these concepts from the Old Testament and from the Jewish theological perspectives that were part of his heritage.

Christology

Though based on the Old Testament and Judaism, Paul's view of God was not identical to that found in those sources. Paul clearly believed that the coming

Beroea—Mosaic of Paul's call to Macedonia.

of Jesus and the understanding of Jesus in the earliest church shed new light on the activity and even the nature of God. With the earliest church Paul believed that Jesus was the long-awaited Jewish Messiah. This meant that God had acted in history to fulfill the promises that He had made to His people Israel in the past. Specifically, the coming of Jesus as the Messiah meant that the final age of human history had begun. (See below under Eschatology.)

With the earliest church Paul confessed Jesus as Lord (Romans 10:9 and 1 Corinthians 12:3). This confession opened up several avenues of understanding for the apostle. The Greek word for "Lord" is **kyrios.** The secular meaning of *kyrios* was a "(slave) owner" or "master." Thus when Paul taught the Gentile converts of his churches to declare "Jesus is Lord," they were affirming the right of Jesus to "own" them and thus to direct every aspect of their lives. However, Paul also thought of Jesus as a cosmic Lord. Thus Jesus was master or owner not just of believers but of the entire universe (*cosmos* in Greek). The way in which Paul

Beroea—Mosaic of Paul teaching the Beroeans.

described Jesus as cosmic Lord raises the question of the relationship of Jesus and God.

The word *kyrios* was also used by the translators of the Septuagint for the God of Israel, Yahweh. Thus the Scriptures read in the earliest churches spoke of Yahweh, the God of the Old Testament, as Lord. The earliest church also proclaimed Jesus as Lord. In some passages written by Paul it is difficult to determine whether the word "Lord" referred to the God of Israel or to Jesus. The apostle often quoted Old Testament passages referring to the Lord (meaning the God of Israel). It is clear, however, from the flow of Paul's thought that he was referring to Jesus (Romans 10:13). Scholars debate whether Paul ever actually called Jesus "God" in his letters. It would be a few centuries after Paul before the Church clearly articulated the doctrine of the deity of Christ. However, regardless of whether the apostle used the actual word "God," it is clear that he was thinking in the terms that would lead the Church to confess that Jesus was God.

Paul also understood Christ as a Second Adam. This is especially clear in Romans 5:12-21 and 1 Corinthians 15:20-49. This understanding of Christ built on theological speculations about Adam by Jewish rabbis of Paul's time. They spoke of Adam as both a historical individual at the beginning of time and as the entirety of the human race throughout time. In Romans 5:12-21 Paul noted that Adam's disobedience brought death to the entire human race. In a similar fashion Christ's obedience brought life to a renewed or restored humanity. Thus Christ's obedience reversed the effects of Adam's disobedience and offered hope for God to restore human beings to the holy relationship with himself He had originally designed for them. In a symmetrical fashion Paul saw Adam and his disobedience bringing ruin upon the human race at the beginning of time, while Christ and His obedience brought restoration to the human race at the end of time. This Adam-Christology may have been an original contribution to Christian theology by Paul.

Trinity

Neither Paul nor any other New Testament author ever used the word "Trinity" with reference to God. However, as was the case with the deity of Christ, one can find some of the "building blocks" of the doctrine of the Trinity in Paul's writings. One can say that Paul experienced God as Trinity even though he did not use the word "Trinity" to describe God.

Though the apostle does not often use the full title, Son of God (Romans 1:4; 2 Corinthians 1:19; Galatians 2:20; and Ephesians 4:13), he frequently described Christ as "his Son" or "the Son" in contexts where it was clear that

God is the Father. These passages make clear the distinction in persons between the Father and the Son. For example Romans 8:3 and Galatians 4:4 speak of God sending "his Son" into the world.

Many passages in Paul speak of Christ and the Holy Spirit, and sometimes these are brought into such proximity that it is difficult to determine if Paul really distinguished between the two. However, the distinction between the Son and the Spirit was clear for the apostle. He never spoke of the Spirit being crucified or raised. First Corinthians 6:11 clearly distinguishes between Christ and the Spirit.

There are also a series of texts in which Paul mentioned God (or the Father), Christ (or the Son), and the Spirit in a way that identified the three distinct persons of the Trinity. Romans 5:1-5; 8:14-17; 15:30; 1 Corinthians 2:7-16; 6:11; 12:4-6; 2 Corinthians 1:21-22; and 13:13—all suggest that Paul's experience of God was Trinitarian.

Salvation

Beyond the nature of God and the person of Christ Paul proclaimed the transforming effects of Christ. This is often called **the work of Christ** in theological discussions. The apostle showed little interest in the teachings or miracles of Jesus. His emphasis was on the death and resurrection of Christ. Through that death and resurrection God made possible the gift of salvation to all who by faith would receive it.

Paul used a broad array of metaphors describing this saving result of Christ's death and/or resurrection. One of the common terms was "salvation" with the corresponding verb "to save."

The root idea of this word was rescue or deliverance from danger. Some scholars believe Paul derived his use of the word "salvation" from the Old Testament passages that described Yahweh saving Israel from her enemies. Others argue that Paul derived his use of this word group from the Greco-Roman world where a number of deities were described as "saviors" for people in need.

Another common metaphor describing the results of Christ's death and resurrection is "justification" or "righteousness." This term was derived from the language of law and was used to describe a person in right relationship with other persons. The related word "just" or "righteous" was often used in the Old Testament to describe both God and persons in right relationship with God and/or with other persons. Paul's justification language was most common in Romans and Galatians where he declared that a person could be put into this right relationship with God through faith in Christ.

The language of interpersonal relationship was the source of another common Pauline metaphor for salvation, that being "reconciliation." This image assumed that sin causes a broken relationship with God and that through Christ's death and resurrection God has taken the initiative to restore that relationship.

The practice of sacrifices in the ancient world provided Paul another metaphor for salvation. The most important word appears in Romans 3:25 and is now usually translated "sacrifice of atonement." In previous decades translators debated whether to use the term "expiation" (the covering of

Paul's ship stopped at Rhodes harbor (Acts 21:1).

ery in Egypt. In the Greco-Roman world these words referred to the process by which the freedom of slaves was purchased.

The full list of metaphors Paul used to describe the saving work of Christ is quite long and varied. Different clusters of these metaphors have been influential and popular at different periods of church history. Paul's rich variety of images for salvation provided a resource by which every person, in every culture, in every period of history can find a meaningful way to understand the saving results of Christ's death and resurrection.

The Church

Paul also referred to the Church in a variety of ways. The very use of the word "church" (*ekklēsia* in Greek) suggests continuity with the Old Testament congregation of Israel. "The people of God," "the saints," and "the elect" are all terms Paul used to describe the Church that are also found in the Old Testament. The apostle was also aware of the image of the Church as the family of God and the fellowship (*koinōnia* in Greek) of the Spirit. All of these are images of the Church that Paul shared with other first-century believers.

sin) or "propitiation" (appeasing God's wrath against sin). In a certain sense Paul understood both expiation and propitiation to have taken place as a result of Christ's death. However, the propitiation was not the result of human action but the grace of God in giving His Son as a sacrifice of atonement.

Paul drew another set of images from the reality of slavery in the ancient world. The words "redemption," "redeem," "freedom," and "free" portray sin as an enslaving power (or rival "Lord") and salvation as freedom from the power of sin. The words "redemption," "redeem," and "redeemer" were used in the Old Testament to describe Yahweh's deliverance of Israel out of slav-

One of Paul's distinctive ways of referring to the Church was to identify it with Christ. There are passages such as Romans 6:3 in which one could easily substitute the word "church" for the word "Christ" and the meaning would not significantly change. This understanding appears to flow out of Paul's Second Adam Christology, in which the distinction between Adam and the human race was somewhat blurred. Similarly, the distinction between Christ (the Second Adam) and the Church could fade into the background of the apostle's thought.

The most significant expression of this understanding of Christ appears in Paul's description of the Church as **the Body of Christ.** Greco-Roman philosophers and politicians often used the image of the body to describe society, but their purpose was to argue that the lower classes should be satisfied with their place in the social order. Paul used the Body of Christ image to describe every believer participating in a meaningful way in the full reality of Christ incarnate through the Church. Particularly in Romans 12 and 1 Corinthians 12 Paul used the picture of the Church as the Body of Christ to plead for both unity and diversity within the Church. The image of the Church as the Body of Christ became especially influential in a number of renewal movements arising in Christianity in the last half of the 20th century.

Eschatology

The term "eschatology" refers to our understanding of last things—the final events of human history. This has both individual implications (such as death and eternal destiny) and universal implications (such as the second coming of Christ, the final judgment, and "the end of time"). While Paul alluded to most of these eschatological issues, he did so from a perspective that was typical of the first-century church. Present-day Christians tend to think of these eschatological concerns as matters of the future. Paul and the first Christians believed they were present-tense issues as much as future-tense concerns.

Most first-century Jews and thus most early Christians believed the last days would be ushered in by the coming of the Messiah. Thus, when the first believers began to proclaim Jesus as the Messiah they also understood that the last days had begun in Jesus' ministry. This view is often called **realized eschatology,** and it can be seen in 1 Corinthians 10:11 where Paul said "the ends of the ages" had come to the first believers.

In addition to believing that the first coming of Christ brought about the last days, Paul also looked forward to the second coming of Christ and the final fulfillment of all the eschatological promises of God. He described both Christ and the Spirit as "first fruits" of the final glory. He saw Christ and the Spirit as "down payments" or guarantees in the present that the end of time had both begun and would come to a swift consummation. Thus eschatology was an "already-not yet" issue for Paul. Each eschatological statement he made must be read carefully to determine the degree of "already" versus the degree of "not yet."

In a very profound sense this "already-not yet" understanding of eschatology permeated all Paul's theology. It linked directly to his confidence that Jesus was the long-awaited Messiah. It related to his understanding of the Holy Spirit. Both salvation and the church were seen in the framework of the "already-not yet" fulfillment of God's final promises. This perspective was often forgotten through church history but was rediscovered in 20th-century biblical scholarship, offering the Church a way to affirm the world-changing effects of Christ's first coming and still look forward in hope to what God will yet do in Christ's final coming.

The ways in which Paul drew upon these core theological concepts varied a great deal from letter to letter. The differing problems of each local church and the changing circumstances of Paul's own life made every letter different from the others. However, it is clear that what the apostle was doing was contextualizing these central theological convictions to the particular needs and circumstances of the churches and individuals to whom he was writing. Thus Paul's letters are examples of practical theology, applying the truth of Christ to the real problems of people and churches.

Summary Statements

- Paul's letters contribute to a significant part of the New Testament literature.
- Paul's theology has influenced key Christian theologians in the history of Christianity.
- Paul was well versed in the traditions of Judaism.
- Paul's letters show influence of the Greco-Roman culture on his method of communication.
- Paul's letters were occasional in nature, written in response to specific needs that existed in various churches he established.
- Paul's letters follow a five-part arrangement: salutation, thanksgiving, the body of the letter, paraenesis or instructions, and conclusion.
- There is a strong theological coherence and consistency to the letters of Paul.
- Paul related his theology to the varying circumstances of his readers.
- Paul's letters need to be understood in the historical context of the first-century Christian church.

Questions for Reflection

1. In light of your understanding of Paul's conversion story and his life and contributions as a Christian disciple, discuss the impact of Christian conversion (its goal, intended result, etc.).
2. How is the Lordship of Jesus at work in your personal life? Relate it to Paul's teaching on "Jesus is Lord."
3. What does it mean to be a member of the Body of Christ today?

Resources for Further Study

Bruce, F. F. *Paul: Apostle of the Heart Set Free.* Grand Rapids: William B. Eerdmans, 1977.
Roetzel, Calvin J. *The Letters of Paul: Conversations in Context.* Louisville, Ky.: Westminster/John Knox Press, 1991.
Schreiner, Thomas. *Interpreting the Pauline Epistles.* Grand Rapids: Baker Book House, 1990.

13 Romans

Objectives:

Your study of this chapter should help you to:

- Discuss the significance of the letter to the Romans to the Christian tradition.
- Describe the context of Paul's letter to the Romans.
- Summarize the major theological themes of Romans.
- Evaluate Paul's ethical instructions and apply them to contemporary Christian life.

Questions to consider as you read:

1. What does Paul mean when he states, "All have sinned and fall short of the glory of God"?
2. What is faith? What role does it play in one's salvation?
3. What is justification and sanctification?

Key Words to Understand

Martin Luther
Protestant Reformation
John Wesley
Augustine
Corinth
Erastus
Phoebe
Rome
House churches
God's righteousness
Wrath of God
Circumcision of heart
Justification by faith
Grace
Baptism
Slaves to righteousness
Sanctification
Holiness
Torah
Law of sin
Law of God
Adoption
Glorification
Remnant of Israel

Paul's letter to the church at Rome has been called "the Gospel in its purest form."[1] The richness and diversity of the profound theological expressions set forth in this letter have exerted great influence upon the Christian Church for centuries. **Martin Luther**'s expositions of Romans that he began in November 1515 brought him to a clear understanding of Paul's emphasis on justification by faith, which later became a key principle of the **Protestant Reformation.** On May 24, 1738, **John Wesley** wrote in his journal the following words: "In the evening I went very unwillingly to a society in Aldersgate Street, where one was reading Luther's preface to the Epistle to the Romans. About a quarter before nine, while he was describing the change which God works in the heart through faith in Christ, I felt my heart strangely warmed. I felt I did trust in Christ, Christ alone for salvation. And an assurance was given me, that he had taken away my sin, even mine, and saved me from the law of sin and death."[2] Wesleyan scholars trace the beginning of the Evangelical Revival in the 18th century to this experience of John Wesley.

Augustine and the Letter to the Romans

    Augustine (A.D. 354—430), the greatest theologian of Western Christianity, was converted after reading Romans 13:13-14. Though he was raised by a devout mother, young Augustine pursued a life of worldly pleasures and evil. His intellectual pursuit led him to become an ardent defender of Manichaean philosophy and its teachings of material dualism and moral irresponsibility. At the age of 29, he moved from Carthage to Milan to teach rhetoric, where he came under the influence of the kind and saintly bishop Ambrose. Though he wanted to be freed from the evil pleasures of life, he could not escape them. He recounts for us what happened as he was sitting at the garden of his friend and former student Alypius, deeply agonizing over the power of evil upon his life.

        I heard the voice as of a boy or a girl . . . coming from a neighboring house, chanting and oft repeating, "Take up and read; take up and read." . . . So, restraining the torrent of my tears, I rose up, interpreting it no other way than a command to me from Heaven to open the book, and to read the first chapter I should light upon. . . . So quickly I returned to the place where . . . I put down the volume of the apostles. . . . I grasped, opened, and in silence read that paragraph on which my eyes first fell,—"Not in rioting and drunkenness, not in chambering and wantonness, not in strife and envying; put ye on the Lord Jesus Christ, and make no provision for the flesh, to fulfill the lusts thereof." No further would I read, nor did I need; for instantly, as the sentence ended,—by a light, as it were, of security infused into my heart,— all the gloom of doubt vanished away.

This text from Romans 13:13-14 led him to his conversion at the age of 33.[3]

Date and Context

This is the first of the Pauline Epistles that is addressed to a church that was established by someone other than the apostle. Though he had never visited the congregation prior to the writing of the letter, he knew a great deal about them, and the church also had heard a great deal about him. He makes it clear within the letter that he desired to see them face-to-face, and "be mutually encouraged by each other's faith" (1:12). In fact, he includes in his letter his plan to stay with the congregation for a little while, during his journey to Spain (15:22-24). It is thus likely that he intended this letter to help pave the way for a productive and enjoyable time together when he would arrive at Rome. He accomplishes this goal by sharing with the church his spiritual insights, the content of his faith, and his preaching of the gospel. Paul spells out in this letter in great detail the message and implications of his gospel, and clarifies aspects of that gospel that had likely been misunderstood by others. He also includes in his letter an immediate application of that gospel to his readers' situation as he understood it.

Paul wrote this letter during the final days of his third missionary journey (A.D. 55-56). Some scholars date this book to A.D. 57 or even 58, depending on their reconstruction of the chronology of Paul. Toward the end of his third journey, he returned to the churches in the region of Macedonia and Corinth to receive a relief offering for the poor saints at Jerusalem (1 Corinthians 16:1-6; see also Acts 20:1-2). Paul's mention of this collection and his im-

Martin Luther.

John Wesley.

pending journey to Jerusalem to deliver this offering strongly suggests that he wrote this letter from **Corinth** (Romans 15:25-28). In 16:23 Paul makes reference to Gaius, who was his host at Corinth (see also 1 Corinthians 1:14), and Erastus the city treasurer. Scholars identify **Erastus** with the person mentioned in an inscription found on a section of a pavement found at Corinth (see photo on page 243). It is very likely that **Phoebe,** a member of the church at Cenchrea, near Corinth, carried the letter to the church at Rome (16:1-2).

The city of **Rome,** the capital of the Roman Empire, was the premier city of the first-century world. Nero Claudius Caesar (54-68) was the emperor when Paul wrote his letter to the church at Rome. The early years of his rule were considered to be among the best within the empire since the death of Augustus in A.D. 14. It was only in the last half of Nero's rule that he became known as a brutal, murderous tyrant.

Rome, as the capital of the empire, attracted large colonies of diverse people from all around the Mediterranean region. Many of these people brought with them their particular cultural customs and religious practices. While there is evidence of a Jewish population in Rome dating back to the second century B.C., their numbers became more significant following the Roman occupation of Judea in 63 B.C. The Roman army took many Jewish slaves back to Rome, and in time many of them would have become free citizens of the empire. The native Romans, however, generally had a negative view of Jews in the first century, and Christians as such were scarcely mentioned in Roman sources until near the end of the century.

The Christian church in Rome likely began very early, possibly with some Jewish believers that were present in Jerusalem during the Pentecost festival when God poured out His Spirit upon the believers in the Upper Room (see Acts 2). When these Jewish Christians returned to Rome, they would have continued to worship within the synagogues and eventually in the **house churches** in their community. In A.D. 49, the Roman emperor Claudius expelled all the Jewish community from Rome, and these Jewish Christians would have been among the Jews forced to leave the city. The only remaining Christian community in Rome would have been the remnant of Gentile God-fearers that had been attracted to the Jewish Messiah Jesus, who had previously worshiped with the Jewish Christians.

With the death of Claudius in 52, many Jewish Christians legally returned to Rome over the next several years. However, the church they returned to was different from the church they had left behind at Rome. Gentiles had a much more prominent role than previously, and there was bound to be some friction in blending the congregations back together again.

The Jews would have understood themselves to provide the primary leadership within the church, as they had from the very beginning. But the Gentiles, emboldened by the news of Paul's ministry among the Gentiles, and the nature of the gospel that he was preaching, were not willing to take a secondary or subordinate role in the church. The letter implies a sharp disagreement that existed between these two groups concerning the believers' relationship to certain aspects of the Mosaic Law (see 14:1—15:13). It is thus likely that Paul wrote the letter to deal with the Jewish-Gentile tension and to bring about healing to a divided congregation. However, as Douglas Moo points out, we cannot limit the purpose of this letter to this issue alone.[4]

It is obvious that Paul needed this congregation's support of his plan to evangelize Spain (15:24). He also needed to defend his theological understanding of the gospel he was preaching among the Gentiles. Thus Paul may also have intended this letter as a statement of his faith to win the favor of the church and to clear up any misunderstanding caused by those who tried to slander him (see 3:8). William Greathouse describes this letter as "an ecumenical theology designed (1) to show and insure the *true meaning* of the Torah in light of God's final word in Christ, and (2) to liberate the message of Christ from its Jewish trappings in order 'to win obedience from the Gentiles' (15:18)."[5] Regardless of the reasons why he wrote this letter, this work is considered to be the most profound theological treatment of Paul on the matter of sin and salvation.

Content

For the purpose of our study, we follow a simple outline, though the content may be divided into numerous subunits based on Paul's treatment of the relationship of the gospel to the Mosaic Law.

Salutation and thanksgiving
1:1-10

God's righteousness
1:11—11:36

Exhortations and admonitions
12:1—15:13

Conclusion and final greetings
15:14—16:27

■ Salutation and Thanksgiving

The letter opens with the longest salutation found in any of Paul's Epistles. The opening verses (1:1-6) give a detailed introduction of Paul as a servant and apostle of Jesus Christ. These verses also hint at a number of significant theological issues that Paul will discuss at length in the letter. Paul begins with a strong claim that God had called him to be an apostle and that he was "set apart for the gospel of God, which he promised beforehand

Paul's statue in Rome at St. Paul's Outside the Walls, a basilica built over the apostle's tomb.

through his prophets in the holy scriptures" (vv. 1-2). He also affirms that Jesus is the Messiah, born of the Davidic line, as well as the Son of God, raised up from the dead. Jesus Christ is also Lord, the one who provides grace to bring about the obedience of faith among all the nations for His name's sake. After a brief notation of the recipients and the standard "Grace and peace" greeting in verse 7, Paul moves quickly through a short thanksgiving section in verses 8-10 to the body of the Epistle.

■ God's Righteousness

Most scholars agree that **God's righteousness** is the theme that Paul develops in the body section of the letter that runs from 1:11 to 11:36. This section begins with statements that convey Paul's longing and desire to visit the church in Rome in order to impart a spiritual gift to them, and to encourage and further establish them in their faith (1:11-13). The apostle also expresses here his conviction that he is under obligation to preach to both Greeks and barbarians, and the wise and the foolish. Paul emphatically states that he is not ashamed of the gospel because "it is the power of God for salvation to everyone who has faith, to the Jew first and also to the Greek" (v. 16). This motif that gives priority to the Jew but equal status to the Gentile will recur throughout the body section of Romans. The reason that Paul can so boldly declare this all-inclusive gospel is clearly disclosed in verse 17. This powerful gospel is the vehicle through which the righteousness of God is faithfully revealed "from faith to faith" (NASB). Paul draws support for this proclamation from the book of the prophet Habakkuk in the Old Testament scriptures where this principle is clearly stated: "The one who is righteous will live by faith" (1:17; Habakkuk 2:4). This is the foundation upon which Paul builds his subsequent arguments.

Paul's focus then shifts immediately to the **wrath of God** against all ungodliness and unrighteousness. In careful rhetorical fashion, he argues that the primary human sin is idolatry, the intentional and deliberate suppression of true knowledge about the sovereign Creator God that has been available to all humanity from the beginning of creation. In the refusal to honor and acknowledge God as Creator, creatures set up alternative objects of worship, taking to and for themselves the role that rightly belongs to the sovereign God alone. What results from the creature's efforts to supplant the right and true with the "lie" of self-sovereignty is the shattering of "right-relatedness" with the sovereign Creator. When creatures inexcusably deny what can be known about God and refuse to grant to Him the honor that He is due, then God gives them up to the darkness, lust, and depravity of their lies. The ultimate consequences of such actions are degradation, abandonment, and death (vv. 18-32).

In chapter 2, Paul reminds the Church that judgment belongs to the One Lord God alone and that God's impartial judgment is righteous and as such will fall upon all who do evil, the Jew first and also the Greek. He subtly argues

Righteousness of God

Throughout the Bible God is described as a righteous God. This attribute of God is essential to our understanding of God as a holy God. The Bible portrays God's righteousness revealed through His saving actions. H. Ray Dunning describes God's righteousness as "salvific," that is, His actions to bring salvation to those who are oppressed or to "put things right."[6] God as a holy God comes to the aid of those are weak and helpless by nature or by social condition and extends to them His help. Dunning connects this meaning of righteousness with the Pauline view of God's righteousness. He states: "The apostle Paul makes use of the idea of the righteousness of God to refer to His justifying activity toward those who were undeserving, thus preserving the essentially salvific connotation of the idea from the Old Testament."[7] This understanding of righteousness as God's "free bestowal of mercy upon the believing sinner" is a significant contribution of Martin Luther to Christian theology.[8]

against the Jewish notion that since Jews have the Law, they will be exempt from the righteous judgment of God. On the contrary, having the Law puts them under the closer scrutiny demanded by that very Law. The essence of the Law would demand that the Jew first and foremost have no other gods before God. So, to place themselves in the role of judge over the Gentiles is to replace their God with themselves. The only value of the Law for the Jew in relationship to righteousness before God comes when they in fact keep and maintain the "right-relatedness" with God that the Law was intended to provide. That would include above all else having no other gods before Yahweh. This kind of lawful obedience to the commandments of God requires not an external circumcision of the flesh in accordance to the Law but rather an internal **circumcision of heart** through the Spirit. This is what brings praise from God, and what it means to be truly Jewish. Paul also counterar-

Wrath of God

We often hear people asking the question, "How can a loving God also be a God of wrath?" The Bible clearly expresses the view of God as a God of holy love. However, the Bible also describes the wrath of God. How can this be? It is important to note that the wrath of God is God's response to human sin. However, this cannot be understood as His anger toward sinful humanity. The Bible does not portray God as an angry God who expresses His angry attitude and emotion toward humanity. However, the sinful humanity is subject to God's wrath, which is His holy response to sin and sinners. Willard H. Taylor describes God's wrath as "His steady, holy displeasure at sin." He further states that the goal of God's wrath is to "maintain the created order and to punish those who rebel against His providences and redemption and who persist in acting wickedly."[9] The good news of the gospel is that His wrath is not forever. Though Paul often speaks of God's wrath in Romans, he also speaks of the redemptive work of Christ on the Cross that brings deliverance and salvation from God's wrath. God's purpose is not to condemn sinners to their eternal judgment but rather to draw them toward himself and thus enable them to be the object of His holy love.

Natural Revelation

The Bible makes clear that all things that God created stand as a testimony to the majesty and glory of God. God's existence is clearly revealed through His creation. Psalm 19 is an excellent example of this affirmation of biblical faith. The psalmist states:

The heavens are telling the glory of God; and the firmament proclaims his handiwork. Day to day pours forth speech, and night to night declares knowledge. There is no speech, nor are there words; their voice is not heard; yet their voice goes out through all the earth, and their words to the end of the world. In the heavens he has set a tent for the sun, which comes out like a bridegroom from his wedding canopy, and like a strong man runs its course with joy. Its rising is from the end of the heavens, and its circuit to the end of them; and nothing is hid from its heat *(vv. 1-6)*.

This beautiful, poetic expression of the psalmist's faith in God invites us to see God's glory revealed all around us in the beautiful things He has made.

Circumcision of the Heart

The ritual act of circumcision, which God established for Abraham and his descendants as an external sign of the covenant, receives a spiritual meaning in later biblical texts. Moses challenged the people of Israel to circumcise their "heart" (Deuteronomy 10:16), and later promised that God will circumcise their "heart" and the "heart" of their descendants (30:6; see also Jeremiah 4:4; 9:26). Gerhard Von Rad sees in these texts in Deuteronomy the ideas of cleansing and one's commitment to live on God's terms.[10] The Wesleyan doctrine of entire sanctification finds its Old Testament pattern and promise in these passages.

In the New Testament, circumcision of the heart is a spiritual circumcision (Romans 2:29; Colossians 2:11-12; 3:14). Paul also equates true circumcision with the "circumcision of the heart" evident through faithful and obedient living (Romans 2:29). Spiritual circumcision is thus the circumcision of heart through which we receive deliverance and cleansing from our rebellious and disobedient nature. God's gracious work of cleansing our sinful hearts gives us a new disposition and a new commitment to live a life of wholehearted love for God and humanity.

gues that when the Gentiles without the Law do what the Law requires in matters of the heart, their uncircumcision will be considered as circumcision by God, and that they will stand in judgment upon the physically circumcised but Law-breaking Jews.

In chapter 3, Paul declares that while the Jew has many advantages over the Gentile, they are alike in that both live under the power and influence of sin. "There is no one who is righteous, not even one" (3:10). Works of the Law cannot make a person righteous before God. However, now apart from Law, the righteousness of God has been revealed through the faithfulness of Jesus Christ for all who believe, Jew and Gentile alike. The God of Jews and Gentiles is One God, the Lord, who "justifies" or makes people righteous on the basis of faith in Jesus Christ, who has demonstrated God's faithful righteousness. This concept is il-

lustrated further in chapter 4, where Paul reminds the Romans that Abraham was reckoned righteous by God on the basis of his faith prior to his circumcision, becoming thereby the father of all who would come to God by faith, the Jew first but also the Gentile.

Chapter 5 brings the first part of the body of the letter to a logical conclusion, yet also works as the foundation for the heart of the Epistle, which is found in chapters 5—8. Chapter 5 further illustrates and amplifies the implications of **justification by faith.** Justification provides for sinners peace and reconciliation with God. They are no longer under the wrath and judgment of God. Moreover, they have the hope of sharing God's glory. They enjoy not only new life in Christ Jesus but also God's love that has been poured out into their hearts—love that God demonstrated for the sinful world through the death of Christ.

Roman Colosseum, as seen from the Arch of Titus.

To further illustrate his gospel of justification by faith, Paul contrasts the disobedience of Adam with the obedience of Jesus Christ and shows how both have impacted the world (5:12-21). Sin entered the world through "one man," or Adam, bringing with it a universal infection and the ultimate consequence of death to all humanity. However, the good news of the gospel is that through "one man," Jesus Christ, has come "the free gift of righteousness" (v. 17). This is God's **grace,** an unmerited favor from God. Sinners can do nothing to merit the righteousness and the life that comes through this free gift. Moreover, God extends this grace to all humanity. Though sin continues to proliferate in the world, God continues to extend this grace without limit to sinful humanity. The goal of God's grace is to lead sinners under the dominion of death to "eternal life through Jesus Christ" (v. 21).

Though Paul's proclamation of justification by faith is really good news for both Jews and Gentiles, this gospel also raises some significant questions. In chapters 6—7, Paul addresses two significant questions, one from each side of the spectrum of the diverse Roman congregation. He then pulls both sides into a climactic conclusion in chapter 8. In chapter 6, Paul addresses a question from the Gentile perspective with a carefully crafted rhetorical argument. If grace increases beyond the increase of sin (5:20), why not continue in sin so that more grace might be extended to them (6:1)? Paul's answer is a resounding *no.* He reminds those who misunderstood the full implications of justification by faith that in their baptism they have died to sin. **Baptism** is one's identification with the death of Jesus. Those who have been crucified with Him cannot go on living in sin, and they should no longer be slaves to sin. Christ died to sin once and for all; sin and death no longer have any power over Him. He was raised from the dead by the power of God unto life, and the life that He now lives is a life lived unto God. Therefore, those who are baptized into Christ also should consider themselves to be dead to sin but alive unto God in Christ Jesus (vv. 3-11). As a result, sin is no longer to reign and rule over their bodies in unrighteousness (vv. 12-14). Instead, they are to present themselves to God as **slaves to righteousness** (v. 19). Though Paul has spoken of righteousness in the previous chapters as right relationship with God, the call here is for moral and ethical conduct and behavior. The result of this decision to become servants of righteousness or "enslaved to God" (v. 22) is **sanctification,** or **holiness** (NIV). Holiness is one's conformity to the character of God. The ultimate outcome of being slaves to righteousness is "eternal life in Christ Jesus our Lord" (v. 23).

The primary question that Paul addresses in Romans 7 is a question that would have been of great concern to the Jewish Christians. What about the Law? The typical Jewish Christian may have had little interest in the case Paul had made previously about the sinfulness of humanity and the righteousness of God, since they believed that they already had an adequate way to deal with sin in the careful observance of the **Torah**/Law.

So what did Paul say to those who know the Torah? In 7:1, he states the well-known principle that the Law has jurisdiction over a person as long as that person lives. However, he explains further that death frees and releases an individual from the Law and enables that individual to be joined to another without viola-

tion of the Law. Thus a woman whose husband has died is free to be joined to another man without being adulterous. In the same way, those who are baptized into the death of Christ have died to the Law and are now free to belong to Christ. Those who are thus joined to Christ are free from the old covenant, which once held them captive. They are now in a new covenant relationship with Christ and are free to serve Him in the newness of the Spirit (vv. 1-6).

In verses 7-13, he illustrates the point by dealing with the Law in relationship with sin. Though the Law had been given to reveal sin or to make known what sin is, sin seized the holy, righteous, and good Law and perverted it into an instrument of death. He emphatically states that the Law is not sin (v. 7). Sin took advantage of the Law, contorted and twisted it into an instrument for its own purposes. In verses 14-25, Paul suggests that the result of sin's perversion of the Law of God creates an opposing law that sets itself against God. This **law of sin** is in diametric opposition to, even open warfare against, the **Law of God.** Working upon humanity through the flesh, it brings bondage and ultimately death to those captured under its dominion. The whole problem of this "anti-law" in conflict with the Law of God is brought to a climax in verses 24-25. The problem is that the Law is weak through the flesh (8:3), and in and of itself it is powerless to overthrow the law of sin. Yet 7:25a is a hymn of praise for deliverance that comes through Jesus Christ. He ends the whole section begun in chapter 5: "Thanks be to God through Jesus

Christ our Lord!" Thus chapter 7 not only explains the relationship of the Law to death and to sin but also points to God's gracious provision of the new life in the Spirit discussed in chapters 6 and 8.

Chapter 8 opens with a clear message. "There is therefore now no condemnation for those who are in Christ Jesus" (v. 1). Why? Because God has acted in the death and resurrection of Jesus to set them free from the law of sin and death. What is now at work in the life of those who are in Christ is the Spirit of God who dwells in them. Christ's death makes it possible for those who are in Him to live a life being led by the Spirit. This Spirit is a life-giving Spirit, and the ultimate outcome is peace that comes from God. Moreover, they no longer live in fear and bondage, but rather live in the inner assurance that they are children of God, adopted by Him as His heirs and "joint heirs with Christ" (v. 17).

Paul reminds his readers that **adoption** as God's children does not mean that the Christian life will be free from suffering. God's plan is to liberate the whole creation from the decay brought upon it by human sin. What awaits the children of God is yet another "adoption," which is the final "redemption of our bodies" (v. 23) and sharing of the glory of God. This restoration of humanity to their true destiny will also mean the restoration of the whole creation. Christians live with this hope in their future glory and release from all suffering (vv. 18-25). This life they live with the full awareness that the Spirit helps them in their "weakness." They are also confident in their faith that "all things work together for

good for those who love God" (v. 28). They know full well that God's purpose for them is not only their justification but also their **glorification** (vv. 26-30). Nothing in the whole creation can separate them from this hope they have in God and God's love experienced in their lives (vv. 31-39).

In chapter 9, Paul addresses his profound concern for his own people, Israel, and explains his understanding of the gospel to the Jew first and also to the Greek. Israel indeed is a blessed nation because of the covenant, the Law, and the promise to the patriarchs. God's word of promise to Abraham did not fail even if not all of Abraham's children have proven to be his true descendants. Some of Abraham's children have denied their calling, and thus could not be considered true children of the promise (vv. 6-18). However, in Paul's thinking, both Jews and Gentiles who are faithful to their calling from God are indeed the children of the promise and thus the true heirs of Abraham (vv. 22-29). He concludes that Gentiles attained righteousness through faith in God's faithfulness, even though they were not striving for it. Israel, however, failed to achieve righteousness before God because they pursued it through the works of the Law and not through faith. More than that, in their intense pursuit of the Law, they stumbled over the "stone" (which is Christ) that God has placed in their path for their salvation (vv. 30-33).

Paul continues the theme of righteousness that comes from God in chapters 10—11. He affirms that Christ is the completion of the Law, providing righteousness unto salvation for everyone who believes, the Jew first but also the Gentile (10:1-13). Israel failed to embrace Jesus as Messiah. Though they did hear the word of Christ, they did not obey what they heard (vv. 14-21). Yet chapter 11 makes it clear that Israel's rejection is neither total nor permanent. As there was a remnant during the time of Elijah, even so there remains a **remnant of Israel** (vv. 1-6). If they abandon their unbelief, they, too, will be saved, just as branches broken off can be grafted again to an olive tree. In their unbelief, they were broken off, but in their faith they will be grafted again as God's people (vv. 23-24). Paul ends the discussion with a beautiful vision of the ultimate salvation that will embrace all of the new true Israel, including Gentiles that have been called by faith to experience the mercy of God extended to all humanity (vv. 25-32). The hymn in verses 33-36 brings the entire body section of the Epistle to a close and makes an excellent transition to the paraenesis that follows.

◼ Instructions

Chapter 12 begins with a powerful admonition to the Roman Christians, Jew and Gentile alike, to present their bodies as living, holy sacrifices to God. They are not to be conformed to the world. But they are to be a renewed, transformed people whose very lives display God's goodwill completely (vv. 1-2). The practical implications of this life are spelled out in the remainder of chapter 12. He reminds his readers that though they are diverse in their makeup, they are indeed "one body in Christ." They are also re-

cipients of a variety of gifts given to them by God's grace, and these gifts are to be used for the community. He concludes this chapter with an admonition that love must be the basis of all Christian conduct and relationships (vv. 3-21).

Chapter 13 continues the theme of love, extending it into the areas of civic duty and responsibility. Respect for civil authorities and paying taxes are all part of Christian civic duty. Paul reminds his audience that the essence of the commandments is love and that the one who loves thus fulfills the Law. Christians must live an honorable life, free from the deeds of evil and other sinful influences. Salvation has already dawned upon them, and the day of the Lord's coming is near. Therefore they must clothe themselves with the life that comes to them through Christ, a life in which there is no room for the desires of the flesh.

In chapter 14, Paul revisits the problem of judgment and judging within the Body, reminding Jewish and Gentile Christians alike that God alone is the ultimate and final Judge before whom all humanity will one day stand. He instructs the strong in faith to be patient with weaker brothers and sisters, and do nothing that would cause another to stumble.

In chapter 15, Paul urges harmony among all in the Christian fellowship, with special praise to God for His good plan to bless all humanity beginning with the Jews and extending that blessing to include Gentiles as well (vv. 1-21). He ends chapter 15 with a summary of his travel itinerary, which includes his plan to visit Rome on his way to Spain (vv. 22-33). The final chapter includes his recommendation of "Phoebe, a deacon of the church at Cenchrea" (16:1) to the church at Rome and his greetings to several friends and coworkers. He concludes the letter with a benediction, an expression of praise to the eternal God, who in His wisdom revealed the mystery of Jesus Christ to the Gentiles, "to bring about the obedience of faith" (v. 26).

Summary Statements

- Paul's letter to the Romans had profound influence on the lives of Augustine, Martin Luther, and John Wesley.
- Paul wrote this letter to the church at Rome to share the content of his preaching of the gospel of Jesus Christ.
- God's righteousness is a major theme in the letter to the Romans.
- Both Jews and Gentiles stand under the judgment of God.
- Trust/faith in the faithfulness of God demonstrated through Jesus Christ is necessary for one's right relationship with God.
- Justification is a free gift of God's grace that God extends to all humanity.
- Justification calls for one's commitment to live as servants of righteousness.
- God's provision for a justified believer is a new life in the Spirit, free from the power of sin and death.
- A justified believer can have hope in the sharing of God's glory.
- Christians must practice love in all areas of human relationships.

Questions for Reflection

1. What perspective do you gain about humanity in the early chapters of Romans?
2. What perspective do you gain about God and His attitude toward humanity, based on your reading of this Epistle?
3. What should be our proper response to God's demonstration of righteousness in our lives?
4. What are the ways by which you practice hospitality toward others?

Resources for Further Study

Greathouse, William. *Wholeness in Christ: Toward a Biblical Theology of Holiness*. Kansas City: Beacon Hill Press of Kansas City, 1998.
Moo, Douglas. *Romans*. In *The NIV Application Commentary*. Grand Rapids: Zondervan, 2000.
Stulmacher, Peter. *Paul's Letter to the Romans*. Louisville, Ky.: Westminster/John Knox Press, 1994.

14

1 and 2 Corinthians and Galatians

 bjectives:

Your study of this chapter should help you to:

- Describe the context of Paul's letters to the Corinthians and Galatians.
- Discuss Paul's relationship to the churches of Corinth and Galatia.
- Describe the key theological issues in 1 and 2 Corinthians and Galatians.
- Relate the meaning and message of 1 and 2 Corinthians and Galatians to the Christian Church today.

 ey Words to Understand

Corinth
Julius Caesar
Nero
Achaia
Aquila
Priscilla
Claudius
Gallio
Dialectical parallelism
Parousia
North Galatian theory
South Galatian theory
Judaizers
Justification

Questions to consider as you read:

1. What are the problems that existed in the church at Corinth?
2. What does Paul say about unity and diversity in the Church?
3. What is the relationship between Christian faith and the surrounding culture?
4. What is the relationship between the Law and the gospel in the letter to the Galatians?

Ancient Corinth

The ancient city of **Corinth** was located approximately two miles from the Gulf of Corinth at the foot of Acrocorinth, a rocky hill rising to about 570 meters above sea level. The city has a long history that goes back to at least 3000 B.C. It had been a great Greek city at the zenith of the Greek Empire. Romans destroyed the city in 146 B.C. and later rebuilt it as a Roman colony under the order given by **Julius Caesar** before his death in 44 B.C. Its strategic location on the Isthmus of Corinth with the port of Lechaion on the Gulf of Corinth and the port of Cenchreae on the Saronic Gulf gave the city significant opportunities for trade and commerce. Goods were transported from East to West across the isthmus. There is evidence that smaller vessels were once dragged over the land at the narrowest part of the isthmus, thus making a shipway across the land. Though many—including Alexander the Great, Julius Caesar, and Caligula—planned to cut a canal through it, it was **Nero** (A.D. 66-67) who began the work, which he later abandoned. The Corinthian canal was not actually cut until the 19th century. Corinth gained its wealth primarily through its commerce; another source of wealth was the Isthmian Games, which brought large numbers of people into the city. Though a wealthy city, it had its share of poverty also.[1]

The Corinthian canal that connects the Gulf of Corinth with the Saronic Gulf.

Corinth was a truly cosmopolitan city. In Paul's day, it was the capital of the Roman province **Achaia,** and the leading and the most prosperous city in Greece. The city that Paul visited was the Roman Corinth rebuilt by the Romans. As a Roman colony, the city's population was primarily made up of Roman citizens who were retired members of the Roman army and other citizens who relocated to Corinth from Rome. The city also had a large number of Greeks, a significant Jewish population,[2] and many entrepreneurs from the Middle East. The Greek inhabitants who remained in and around the city were not counted as citizens, and they did not have the same privileges held by the colonists. The government of the city was patterned after the Roman system of government. In architecture, the city's buildings were patterned after the Roman style, and it would have looked more like a typical Roman city.[3]

Religion played a significant role in the life of the Corinthian population. Romans at Corinth incorporated Greek gods and goddesses into their religious worship. Corinth had a large number of pagan temples and shrines to honor a variety of deities such as Apollo, Asklepios (a god of physical and emotional health), and Hera Argaea (a goddess of marriage and sexual life). The city also had massive temples built to honor Aphrodite and Venus, the Greek and Roman goddesses of love. The temples in Corinth were centers of sacred prostitution and other sexual activities in connection with temple meals. The orgies that marked the temple practices included liberal imbibing of intoxicating drinks,

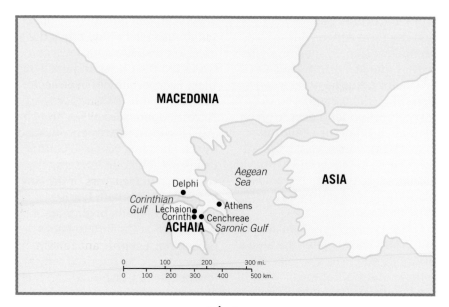

Achaia.

as well as consorting with temple prostitutes, both male and female. So famous was Corinth for such behavior that Corinthians were typically cast in Greek drama as drunks and profligates, and the term "to Corinthianize" meant to engage in prostitution. The city also promoted the imperial cult in which the citizens played a prominent part, since such activities helped them gain status in the society.

Paul at Corinth

Acts 18:1-17 gives us a summary report of Paul's arrival and

Temple of Apollo at Corinth.

work at Corinth. Paul came to this city from Athens during his second missionary journey. Luke tells us that at Corinth Paul met a Jew named **Aquila** and his wife, **Priscilla**, who were forced to leave Rome under a decree given by Roman Emperor **Claudius** (A.D. 41-54). Some scholars place this decree in the ninth year of Claudius's reign, which would place the arrival of Aquila and Priscilla around A.D. 50.[4]

It is very likely that Paul arrived at Corinth shortly after the arrival of Aquila and Priscilla. Luke also reports that **Gallio,** the brother of the Roman philosopher Seneca, was proconsul of Achaia, the Roman province in the southern part of Greece. Extrabiblical sources indicate that Gallio took office no earlier than A.D. 51.[5] Paul's stay at Corinth for 18 months (Acts 18:11) would have taken place around A.D. 50-52.

When Paul first arrived at Corinth, he joined with Aquila and Priscilla in the business of manufacturing tents (v. 3). Paul in his letter reminds the Corinthians that he worked with his own hands while he was among them (see 1 Corinthians 4:12). Luke re-

ports that Paul attended the local synagogue every Sabbath and tried to persuade both Jews and Greeks to the Christian faith (Acts 18:4). He proclaimed Jesus as the Messiah to the Jews, which brought opposition to his preaching. However, he was encouraged by the Lord in a vision to continue his preaching at Corinth, which brought many Corinthians to the Christian faith (vv. 5-11). Scholars trace the beginning of the church at Corinth to Paul's preaching. According to Paul's own account, he baptized only a few people (1 Corinthians 1:14-17; compare with Acts 18:8), but he makes the claim that he "planted" the seeds of faith at Corinth (1 Corinthians 4:6). The Jews brought charges against Paul and brought him before the tribunal when Gallio was proconsul. Gallio dismissed the charges since they were complaints made on the basis of Jewish Law and not matters that concerned Roman law. The angry mob seized Sosthenes, an official of the local synagogue, and beat him in front of the tribunal (Acts 18:12-17). It is likely that the Sosthenes mentioned in 1 Corinthians 1:1 is this former synagogue official who later became a trusted coworker of Paul.

Paul wrote his letters to the Thessalonians during his stay at Corinth. Silas and Timothy joined him at Corinth and gave the good report that the Macedonian churches were growing in their faith and love (see 1 Thessalonians 3:6). After 18 months of stay at Corinth, he left the city, accompanied by Aquila and Priscilla, and crossed the Aegean Sea to Ephesus in Asia Minor, perhaps in late 51 or early 52. From there

Remains of the Bema, the Roman tribune, where Paul stood before Gallio.

he traveled to Jerusalem and on to Antioch (Acts 18:12-23).

Setting and Date

During Paul's stay in Ephesus in A.D. 52-55 (his third missionary journey), he remained in frequent dialogue with the church at Corinth, writing them several times and returning for a brief visit as well. This ongoing communication provided unique opportunities for Paul to deal with some issues that were reported to him by members of the church (see 1 Corinthians 1:11; 5:1) as well as to respond to the questions the church asked him on various matters (7:1). These communications show that the church was divided on various issues, which in turn led to a real crisis in the life of the church. These letters also offer to us personal, intimate insights into the stormy relationship Paul had with this troubled and divided church.

The major critical problems that emerge from reading the Corinthian Epistles relate to the timing, sequence, structure, and availability of Paul's correspondence with the church. In both Epistles, references are made to other letters that apparently no longer exist as independent letters. Both letters also have some structural irregularities. The composition of 2 Corinthians is particularly problematic; the letter does not follow the standard letter outline that Paul follows in his other letters. A brief synopsis of the likely sequence of events is helpful in setting the context for each Epistle.

After settling in Ephesus, Paul wrote an initial letter to the Corinthians, in which he stated that they were not to associate with immoral people. He mentions this letter in 1 Corinthians 5:9, but nothing else about it is known to us; so we regard this letter as "lost" or not preserved by the Christian tradition. After hearing back from the church, Paul wrote a second letter, in which he addresses both written and oral questions from the congregation. This letter is preserved in the New Testament as 1 Corinthians. Paul then sent Timothy to the church to resolve some of the problems there, but his efforts were not successful. Consequently, Paul himself made a brief, painful visit to Corinth. It was a failure, and he returned to Ephesus in humiliation (2 Corinthians 2:1-2; 12:21). Paul then wrote a third letter, which is described in 2 Corinthians 2:3-9 and 7:8-12 as painful, written with a heavy heart, which brought great sorrow to the church. This third, harsh letter has also been "lost," although some scholars have speculated that part of it may be included in 2 Corinthians 10—13. Paul sent that third letter to the church with Titus, who later met Paul in Macedonia with encouraging news about the church's response to his third letter. That prompted Paul to send a fourth letter to the church from the Macedonian region (A.D. 55/56), a letter of reconciliation, which would include the first nine chapters of 2 Corinthians, if not the entire Epistle. The rift between Paul and the church must have been healed, because Paul later returned to Corinth to receive an offering from the Gentiles for the poor of the Jewish Jerusalem church.

This brief synopsis demonstrates the occasional nature of Paul's letters and also makes clear that what is collected in the Pauline Epistles provides only a portion of what Paul wrote, certainly not everything. It also demonstrates that the Early Church had to develop and grow in the midst of hostile environments, as well as learn how to deal with conflict within. Paul's letters to the Corinthians address real people dealing with significant problems in the process of learning to live together in Christian community.

1 Corinthians

Content

The structure of 1 Corinthians fits the standard model reasonably well. We outline the content of this letter as follows:

Salutation and thanksgiving
1:1-9

Main body of the letter
1:10—4:21

Paraenesis section 5:1—16:18

In the salutation (1:1-3), the language used to describe the recipients as "those who are sanctified in Christ Jesus, called to be saints" (literally, "holy ones") is noteworthy. As the letter unfolds, that will prove to be a most interesting designation of the members of the church at Corinth. The thanksgiving (vv. 4-9) is typical, with some early hints of major theological discussion to follow relating to themes of grace, speech, knowledge, spiritual gifts, and ultimate confirmation as blameless at Christ's Parousia.

In the body of the letter that runs from 1:10 to 4:21, Paul addresses a number of issues that have splintered the congregation,

treating major issues in **dialectical parallelism.** The rifts and disputes over theological and practical matters created the appearance of a divided, chaotic congregation instead of a united church. Over the next several chapters, Paul contrasts knowledge and ignorance, wisdom and foolishness, power and weakness, the spiritual and the natural, holiness and sexual immorality, the "puffed up" and those who build up others. Aligning several of these issues into the most significant of all issues, Paul unpacks the implications of the gospel of the Cross that brought the congregation into existence from the very beginning.

Paul contended that baptism should make all believers united into one new created order in Christ, rather than dividing them into separate parties, tied to the individual leader who baptized them (1:10-16). He was commissioned by Christ to proclaim the gospel without the usual "words of wisdom" (2:4; see 1:17). However, he declares that the proclamation of the gospel should not empty the Cross of its power (1:17). In ironic fashion, Paul redefines the meaning of the Cross, which to the ancient Greco-Roman mind was a symbol of shame and humiliation. The gospel of the Cross he preached at Corinth was "foolishness" to the wise and a scandalous "stumbling block" to the Jews who could not grasp the concept of a crucified Messiah (vv. 18, 23). But the wise of this world are ignorant of the wisdom of God; therefore, they are perishing in their foolish ignorance (vv. 18-25). So, God saw fit to redeem humanity not through His wisdom but through the foolishness of preaching a crucified Messiah. This foolishness of God proved to be wiser than the wisdom of humanity. The crucified Christ is true "wisdom from God, and righteousness and sanctification and redemption" (v. 30).

The apostle's own determination was to preach the crucified Christ, not with eloquent words, but "in fear and in much trembling" (v. 3) and in the power of the Spirit (v. 4). Paul invites Corinthians to follow his model by living their lives in pursuit of the true wisdom of God, instead of following the wisdom of the world as "people of the flesh" (3:1; see 2:6—3:15). He brings that discussion to a powerful climax by utilizing the image of the collective church body as the holy temple of God, which is marked by the presence of God's Spirit (3:16-17). Paul concludes his discussion of wisdom and foolishness with the reminder that the wisdom of this world is foolishness before God. It is divine wisdom that brings together the community of faith. And that community of faith belongs to Christ and not to any human leaders (vv. 18-23).

In chapter 4, Paul contrasts arrogance with humility and considers the impact of these upon the Body. The arrogant are "puffed up," proud of the gifts that they have received and contemptuous of others within the Body. Paul sarcastically suggests that the apostles, including himself, are unfortunately a cut below those gifted Corinthians who love to blow their own horns loudly. As slaves and stewards of Christ, true apostles are not kings but powerless. They are condemned to death, a spectacle to the world,

fools for Christ's sake, hungry and thirsty, homeless and poorly clothed, and the dregs of society. And then, Paul invites the Corinthians to become imitators of them! He challenges the arrogant to remember the source of their gifts, encouraging them to use those gifts for building up and edifying the Body as a whole instead of being puffed up with self-pride. The Body section of 1 Corinthians ends not with a typical prayer-wish but with a direct challenge to the power of the arrogant instead.

The paraenesis section (instructions and exhortations) extends from 5:1 to 16:18, making it nearly three times the length of the body of the letter in 1:10—4:21. Given the circumstances that necessitated the letter, that should not come as a major surprise. Paul had spent enough time with the church from the beginning to lay a solid theological foundation. The conflicts emerged from the problems they had in putting their faith into practice in the arena of daily living.

Paul shames the Corinthian believers first for their blatant refusal to remove a sexually immoral man from among them and then for lawsuits against fellow Christians (chapters 5—6). He is deeply concerned that the Corinthians do not discern between wicked and righteous behavior; so he spells out for them that the unrighteous, sexually immoral, idolaters, adulterers, perverts, homosexuals, thieves, drunkards, and other such people shall not inherit the kingdom of God (6:9-10). He reminds them that they once were that kind of people, but now they have been washed, sanctified, and made righteous as new

Marriage and Celibacy

T Paul's treatment of marriage and celibacy in 1 Corinthians 7 is best understood if we approach it from the context of marital and family relationships in the Roman world. Roman marriages were mostly arranged, and as such they were nothing more than social and economic contracts between a man and a woman to live together in peace and harmony. Husbands, usually much older than wives, held power and authority and dominant position in the family. The marriage did not require a formal ceremony; neither did it require a legal procedure to dissolve a marriage.[6] Paul's instructions in 1 Corinthians 7 give the church at Corinth a Christian perspective on the issue of marriage and celibacy among Christians. Paul begins with a popular slogan of those who were ascetic ("It is well for a man not to touch a woman"), which cannot be taken to mean that Paul is advocating celibacy for Christians. This is clear from the way he deals with various contexts of marital relationships in this chapter. Though he prefers single-ness for the sake of greater devotion to the Lord, he does not devalue marriage or consider sexual relations as sinful. On the other hand, he holds a very high view of the sanctity and sacredness of the marriage relationship. Against the Roman view of the dominance of the husband over his wife, Paul teaches that just as the body of a wife belongs to her husband, so does the husband's body belong to his wife. Husbands and wives should mutually respect and yield to their partners' conjugal rights. His strongest argument against ascetics, who consider sexual relations as sinful, is his instruction that in a marital relationship sex should be abstained only by mutual agreement for a time of prayer. The emphasis on marriage is reiterated again in his instructions to the betrothed and the widows.

to Christ should not bring dishonor to God by engaging in sexual immorality whether or not it is sanctioned by their culture. Paul reminds the Corinthians that their bodies are the temple of the Holy God and the dwelling place of His Holy Spirit. They no longer belong to themselves but to the God who has redeemed them from the slavery of sin.

Chapters 7—14 seem to contain Paul's response to the questions from the Corinthians (see 7:1). He begins with a discussion on the sanctity of marriage and then gives instructions on various issues, including divorce, remarriage, and celibacy (vv. 1-40). Some of these instructions are personal perspectives, but others he attributes to the Lord. The question of whether a Christian should eat food offered to idols is discussed in chapter 8. He admonishes those who possess superior knowledge on this issue to be sensitive to the weak among them (those who find it offensive to eat food offered to idols). What builds up the community is not knowledge but love for others. Giving up personal freedom and rights may be necessary for the building up of community. Paul illustrates this principle by his own conduct among the Corinthians (9:1-27). Though he was an apostle, he gave up his rights as an apostle and made himself "a slave to all" for the sake of the gospel (v. 19). He warns his readers to "flee from the worship of idols" (10:14) and denounces a believer's participation in pagan religious rites (vv. 6-22). He reminds them that while all things may now be lawful to them in Christ Jesus, not all things are profitable, and he will do everything within that

creatures in the Lord Jesus Christ. In verses 12-20, he stresses the importance of embodying the reality of their salvation as members of Christ. Those joined

Paul's Letters to the Corinthians in Their Social and Cultural Setting

Witherington notes a number of possible connections between Paul's letters to the Corinthians and the social-cultural life of the Corinthian citizens. These include the following:

1. Civic and individual pride displayed in the inscriptions found at Corinth show that at Corinth people often sought public recognition of their accomplishments. Such efforts included financing building projects or erecting inscriptions to promote one's significance in the society. The topics of boasting and pride are issues that Paul often deals with in his letters to reorient the believers at Corinth to the Christian culture and value system that are based not on one's social standing but on one's relationship with Christ.
2. Athletic contests in Corinth were open to women, which provided women greater freedom of expression. Paul's statements about women in these letters may be viewed as the apostle's response to the Christian women from Greek and Roman background who were used to greater freedom in the Greco-Roman culture than what was permitted in the Christian churches.
3. Sexual activities were a part of the temple meal at Corinth. Women companions often accompanied the elite and the rich in the society at the temple meals. Paul warns the Christians not to indulge in this idolatrous way of life, which included eating, drinking, and dancing (1 Corinthians 10:7).
4. The sanctuary of Asklepios was a popular place for dining and exercise and other forms of relaxation. First Corinthians 10:27-30 may be viewed as Paul's instructions to Christians who may be invited to eat food that had been offered to gods in the pagan temples.
5. Instructions in 1 Corinthians concerning marriage and divorce may be viewed as Paul's response to those who may have had questions concerning their previous sacred marriage relationship with Hera, a goddess of marriage and childbirth.
6. The oracle at Delphi, located about 50 km. from Corinth, may shed light on the Corinthian phenomenon of speaking in tongues and prophecy. It is possible that 1 Corinthians 14:34-36 may be Paul's response to the problem of Corinthian church women interrupting male prophets with their questions, similar to the questions about childlessness, and so forth, asked of the Delphi oracle.[7]

freedom in Christ to the glory and honor of God (vv. 23-33). He concludes with a denunciation of their worship practices, especially in relation to the Lord's Supper. The sacred time of communal meal (the Lord's Supper) had become the context for gluttony and drunkenness for some in the church. Paul gives clear instructions on how the Lord's Supper should be properly observed, and he warns them of the consequences of eating the bread and drinking the cup without respect for the "body and blood of the Lord" (11:17-34).

In chapters 12 and 14, Paul directly addresses the issue of spiritual gifts and graces within the Body of Christ. God is the giver of all gifts to individual members of the Body of Christ. Though members of the believing community may show evidence of a variety of gifts, they all proceed from one Spirit, one Lord, and one God (12:4-11). Paul implies that the unity within the three persons of the Godhead is a model for the Church, the recipient of diversity of spiritual gifts. He points out that Christ is the head of the Body, the Church, and that everything that flows out graciously from that head has one primary function—enhancing, sustaining, and nurturing the entire Body for the sake of the whole Body. Paul makes it clear that not all have the same specific gifts and that there is not any single gift that is shared by all within the Body, except for the more excellent way—the gift of love. It seems that some members of the Corinthian church may have promoted "special languages" and frenetic worship as marks of their spirituality. Paul encourages thoughtful proclamation and order and community-building during public worship. He carefully places the great love chapter (chapter 13) between the chapters devoted to spiritual gifts (12 and 14). Nothing is more essential to the life and practice of the church than the gift of God's gracious love extended to and through His people. That love in action is the true mark of the presence of God's living Spirit among His people.

Chapter 15 provides significant autobiographical material about Paul, tied to a major theological treatise that deals with the resur-

T Prophecy and Tongues in 1 Corinthians 14

Paul's treatment of prophecy and tongues in 1 Corinthians 14 give us insight into how Paul viewed these two spiritual gifts, which were very popular in the church at Corinth. At the outset, we must note that Paul's treatment of these phenomena focuses on which of these two serves to edify and build up the church. He is also concerned with an overemphasis given to the spiritual gifts by the Corinthians, which led to confusion and lack of order in the worship service. He begins his argument with the instruction that love should be the governing principle of the exercise of all spiritual gifts (v. 1). Prophecy is a gift for all believers, since it is given for upbuilding, encouragement, and consolation of others. Prophecy is given in an intelligible language understood by all who hear it, whereas those who speak in tongues speak to God in a language others do not understand. Prophecy did not require interpretation, whereas tongues needed someone to interpret the unknown things. He urges his readers at Corinth to strive for the gift of prophecy, the spiritual gift that would build up the church. It is obvious that Paul does not equate prophecy with the phenomenon of prophecy in the Old Testament where God spoke through some specially called individuals to communicate an urgent word from Him. Prophecy in Corinth seems to be a Spirit-inspired speech given spontaneously for the upbuilding of others. Paul also makes clear that tongues are a sign not for the believers but for the nonbelievers, "a sign of judgment that they are out of touch with God."[8] In contrast, prophecy is a sign for believers of "the gracious presence of God in the community in which it occurs."[9] We must also keep in mind Paul's treatment of the limited and temporary nature of these spiritual gifts (see 1 Corinthians 13:8-11). Paul's concluding instruction is that whatever spiritual gifts are exercised in the Christian community, they all must show evidence of peace and order because "God is a God not of disorder but of peace" (14:33)

rection of the dead. Verses 1-11 give the foundational core of Paul's gospel and the affirmation of his apostolic authority. He sums up the essence of the Christian faith that Christ died for our sins, was buried, and was raised on the third day. In the retelling of the appearances of the risen Christ to His disciples, Paul includes the story of Christ's encounter with him, a persecutor of the Church, one "unfit to be called an apostle" (v. 9), as a sheer display of divine grace. He goes on to claim that it is "by the grace of God I am what I am" (v. 10; see vv. 3-11).

The remainder of chapter 15 is devoted to a discussion of the resurrection of Christ Jesus from the dead. There were some skeptics in Corinth who did not believe in the resurrection from the dead. Paul logically develops his argument that if resurrection from death is impossible, then Christ could not have been raised from the dead. If that is true, then Paul's witness is false and his preaching is vain. He then asserts that the faith of the Corinthians would be worthless, for they would all still be dead in their sins. Even worse, those who have died in Christ have perished without hope. He contends in verses 12-19 that if the only hope for the Christian is found in this life, then Christians are pitiable fools! But that is not what the gospel proclaims. He asserts that Christ has been raised as "the first fruits of those who have died" (v. 20). Christ's resurrection is the proof that God has commenced the activity in human history that will one day demonstrate His total sovereign rule over all creation. The resurrection of Christ further

shows that the power of death has been conquered. He ends this chapter with a discourse on the nature of the resurrected body as spiritual, imperishable, and immortal.

The final chapter of 1 Corinthians includes some practical requests concerning the collection for the poor in Jerusalem, Paul's future travel plans, and final exhortations. He ends this letter with greetings, his personal signature, and a benediction (16:19-24).

2 Corinthians

As stated earlier, Paul wrote this letter of reconciliation from the Macedonian region around A.D. 55-56, after hearing encouraging news from Titus about the Corinthian church. The content of this letter is somewhat unorganized, and therefore it is difficult to follow the apostle's development of thought. We give the following outline to the content of this letter:

Salutation and blessings 1:1-11
Paul's defense of his ministry 1:12—7:16
Collection for the church at Jerusalem 8:1—9:15
Paul's defense of himself and his work 10:1—13:10
Final greetings and benediction 13:11-14

Second Corinthians begins in very typical epistolary fashion, although the salutation (1:1-2) is quite brief. In place of the typical thanksgiving immediately following the salutation, Paul pronounces praise and adoration to God (vv. 3-11; "Blessed be the God . . ."), a pattern also found in Ephesians 1. The object of Paul's praise is God, Father of our Lord

Jesus Christ, who is also "the Father of mercies" and "the God of all consolation" (v. 3). Paul uses the noun and verb form of the Greek word *parakaleo* (meaning "to comfort or to console") 10 times in verses 3-7 to emphasize God's provision of consolation or comfort for a people facing severe sufferings and trials. There has been suffering, both on Paul's part and in the life of the Corinthian congregation. Paul is confident, however, that those who share in the suffering of Christ will find comfort and consolation that comes through Christ. He assures the church of his solidarity with them in their suffering, as well as the sufficiency of God's grace necessary to endure suffering.

In verses 12-14, the apostle reminds the congregation how he had walked in holiness and godly sincerity while he was with them. They, too, are to model such conduct until the **Parousia**, the coming of the Lord Jesus Christ. Paul then defends his change in plans concerning another visit to Corinth; he decided to wait until such time as they were ready to receive and acknowledge his authority as an apostle (vv. 15-24). He reveals his passion and concern for the church in chapter 2 and exposes the pain and agony that he felt even as he produced the powerful letter that brought them great sorrow and pain. Paul makes it clear in 2:17—3:18 that he is not a mere peddler of the gospel for the monetary gain that it could bring. There is no need for him to bring letters of reference when dealing with the Corinthians because they are in fact the true "letter of Christ," written in his heart with "the Spirit of the living God" (3:3).

In chapter 4, he reminds them that despite everything that has happened to him and to them, he does not lose heart. He is confident that the light of the gospel will prevail despite the dominant darkness of the age. But he also realizes the limits and weaknesses of human beings that God has chosen as vessels of His revelation. He recounts being afflicted, perplexed, persecuted, struck down, given up to death, while carrying within himself the death of Jesus in his decaying body. But he also affirms that he has not been crushed, forsaken, or destroyed by the power of death. He does not lose heart because the inner humanity is being renewed day by day through the power of God's Holy Spirit, given as the pledge and guarantee of God's ultimate and final salvation for those who are in Christ (4:16—5:10).

In 5:11-21, we find some of the most powerful, profound theology in the New Testament. Paul asserts that the love of Christ compels those who belong to Christ to live "no longer for themselves, but for him who died and was raised for them" (v. 15). If any person is in Christ Jesus, old things have passed away, new things have begun—a new creation comes into existence (v. 17). And all of this comes about directly through God's reconciling ministry of the entire world brought about through Christ, the One who was made sin on our behalf that in Him we might become the righteousness of God (vv. 19-22). In 6:1-10, Paul discusses the badge of true discipleship. Opposition and difficulties do not negate what God had accomplished through His word and power in the daily lives of His

This inscription on a section of a pavement found at Corinth indicates that Erastus paid for this pavement. Paul in his letter to the Romans, written from Corinth, mentions "Erastus the city treasurer" (see Romans 16:23).

faithful apostles. Paul challenges the Corinthians to open wide their hearts to him even as he had opened wide his heart to them. 6:14—7:1 seems to interrupt the flow of that thought, which is resumed in 7:2, but the challenge addressed within that text is one that Paul dealt with previously in 1 Corinthians. He challenges the Corinthians to be partnered with fellow believers in all of their relationships. Believers must remember that they are the temple of the living God, and therefore they must live in holiness and the sanctity of flesh and spirit, "making holiness perfect in the fear of God" (v. 1).

Paul returns in 7:2-16 to the issue of the pain that his powerful letter had caused them, and he rejoices that the sorrow brought on by that letter led them to repentance and to restoration of their broken relationships. In chapters 8—9, Paul details the importance of the offering that he wanted to take to the poor in Jerusalem. The Gentiles who once were lacking in terms of spiritual riches and wealth had now by God's grace become heirs of the rich spiritual heritage that once was exclusively Jewish. He urges the predominantly Gentile churches to be generous in their giving to the poor saints in Jerusalem as an expression of their gratitude to God. Paul closes this section with a prayer of thanks to God for His indescribable gift of grace to the church.

The tone changes dramatically in chapters 10—13, and the transition from chapters 1—9 is very rough and abrupt. In chapters 1—9, the addressees are those who had repented and who were seeking to repair the strained relationship with the apostle. However, in chapters 10—13, he moves to a confrontation with his most vocal opponents. These so-called superapostles had mocked and defied Paul, ridiculing and deriding him for his strong letters but weak performance when he was present with them on the failed visit. Paul declares that he would boast only in the Lord and not according to the fleshly standard of his opponents. Since these superapostles compare themselves to another, Paul decides to indulge in a bit of foolishness with them (10:12—11:6). Sarcastically turning the tables on them in the process, he suggests that they were right by earthly and fleshly standards to consider themselves superior apostles and Paul an inferior apostle. After all, they were strong, wise, handsome, and respected by all! Paul on the other hand was weak, foolish, had been beaten, imprisoned, stoned and left for dead, and was in constant danger as he traveled for the sake of the gospel. But in that process, Paul made a most crucial discovery. God's grace is sufficient in the midst of the most trying times, and His power is made perfect in the midst of human weakness (12:9). Paul ends where he had begun. The gospel of a crucified Messiah on the surface is a gospel of weakness and failure, scandal and foolishness, to the wise and strong of this world. But when the gospel is heard and believed, then the weakness of God proves stronger than the strength of humanity and the foolishness of God proves far wiser than the wisdom of human-

ity. And that gospel builds up the Body of Christ instead of tearing it down. That indeed is the true test of apostolicity.

Letter to the Galatians

Paul's letter to the Galatians is addressed to an audience that includes Gentiles who appear to be under heavy pressure to become Jewish in their belief, behavior, and practice. Apparently some Jewish Christians insisted that the Gentiles must obey the Law of Moses in order for them to be considered truly Christian. This letter seeks to address this issue by boldly claiming that the Gentile believers are free from the Law of Moses. Paul reiterates in this letter his understanding of the gospel of Jesus Christ. Along with Romans, this letter also emphasizes the justification of a believer by faith and not by works of the Law. The letter is often referred to as the Magna Charta of Christian liberty because of its

L

Location of the Churches of Galatia

Scholars hold two different theories about the identity of the recipients of this letter. Some regard that Paul wrote this letter to the Christians in the district of Galatia, an actual territory in north central Asia Minor **(North Galatian theory).** The name Galatians comes from Gauls who established themselves in this area by the end of the third century B.C. The inhabitants of this area may have thus belonged to a distinct ethnic group. This district was also a part of the Roman province of Galatia in central Asia Minor. Though there is no clear evidence in the Book of Acts, these scholars think that Paul would have done some preaching in this district during his second missionary journey, after the Holy Spirit forbade him to take the gospel to Asia (see Acts 16:6). Others think that Galatia in Paul's writing refers to the Roman province by that name and not the district in the northern part of the province. This theory thus views the "churches of Galatia" and "Galatians" as the churches that Paul established in the southern part of the province of Galatia during his first missionary journey **(South Galatian theory).**[10] These churches are Antioch of Pisidia, Iconium, Lystra, and Derbe, mentioned in Acts 13:13—14:28.

overriding emphasis on the freedom of Christians from the Law of Moses.

Date and Setting

Paul addresses the recipients of his letter as "the churches of Galatia" (1:2) and as "Galatians" (3:1). The location of the audience plays a role in determining the date of this letter. Those who favor the South Galatian theory propose a date either before the Jerusalem Council (see Acts 15) or a year or two after the council. This would place the letter around A.D. 48 or 50/51. Those who support the North Galatian theory think that Paul wrote the letter from Ephesus around A.D. 53-55, during his third missionary journey. The choice made concerning date and region has little effect on the message of Galatians.

Galatians clearly reflects a strong and powerful Jewish influence within the early Christian church. Apparently some preachers had come to the region after Paul had left and had persuaded the churches that Gentile converts had to become completely Jewish to be truly Christian. These **Judaizers** undermined the message of the gospel of freedom that Paul had preached, and their perspective became dominant in the churches of Galatia. Paul, in this letter, responds to this distortion of the gospel message in an eloquent and powerful way, at times with expressions of his anger and frustration at those who have been misled by the Judaizers.

Content

Paul's tone and approach in Galatians clearly demonstrate his agitation with those who were preaching a radically different gospel. He skips the customary thanksgiving section and moves to defend his apostolic authority and then challenges the strange teaching that the Galatians had embraced. We give the following outline to the letter:

Introduction and occasion of the letter	1:1-10
Defense of Paul's apostolic authority	1:11—2:21
Justification by faith	3:1—4:31
Christian liberty	5:1—6:10
Conclusion and benediction	6:11-18

The opening statements make clear the context of Paul's letter to the Galatians. The recipients of this letter have deserted the "one who called [them] in the grace of Christ" and have turned to "a different gospel" (1:6). He rejects the notion of "another gospel" and pronounces a solemn curse (anathema) on those who create confusion among the Galatians by perverting "the gospel of Christ" (v. 7).

In the next section, Paul establishes his authority as an apostle (1:11—2:21). He declares that his gospel came directly from God and that his mandate to go to the Gentiles was not a mere human endeavor. Here he inserts a brief autobiographical sketch, which includes his former life as a zealous Jew who violently persecuted the church in an attempt to destroy it. He reflects on his call and commission as part of God's sovereign plan for his life even before his birth (1:15-16; see also Jeremiah 1:4). God not only called him through a special revelation but also gave him the charge to proclaim Christ among the Gentiles. He reinforces the divine authority behind his mission by claiming that everything he did was in response to God's special revelation to him. He neither conferred with the Jerusalem leaders nor did they send him out on his ministry to the Gentiles. Eventually, when he met with the Jerusalem leaders and shared with them his calling to the Gentiles, they acknowledged "the grace that had been given" (2:9) to him by God to take the gospel to the Gentiles (vv. 1-10). He cites one occasion when he confronted Peter, who broke fellowship with the Gentiles because of pressure from Judaizers, though he (Peter) himself was convinced that there was no distinction between Jews and Gentiles. Peter's inconsistent behavior led many other Jews, including Barnabas, to join him in their hypocrisy (2:11-14).

The major foundation of Paul's gospel is that "a person is justified not by the works of the law but through faith in Jesus Christ" (v. 16; see vv. 15-21). **Justification** is God's act of declaring and making persons righteous. This gracious divine act is possible because of the faithfulness of the crucified Messiah Jesus. Paul claims that his life is centered on the crucified Christ who loved him and gave himself for him as a demonstration of God's grace to sinners. He proclaims his solidarity with the crucified Christ ("I have been crucified with Christ" [v. 19]), and asks the Galatians to reconsider the implications of their demands upon Gentile converts.

Chapter 3 begins with Paul's rebuke of the Galatians who have become victims of the misguided teachings of those who pervert the gospel. He argues that Abraham had believed God and that

faith was the basis of his being reckoned righteous by God, totally apart from any works of the Law. Thus Abraham was blessed, and in Christ Jesus that same blessing has now been extended to Gentiles who receive the promise of the Spirit through faith (vv. 5-14). He contends that the Law served as a tutor to lead all to Christ, that they might be made righteous by faith in the new order that no longer consists of Jew and Gentile, slave and free, male and female. Instead, there is one new humanity in Christ Jesus, and all who believe are Abraham's true children (vv. 24-29). Jesus Christ came into this world to bring freedom to those who live under the Law and to bring them to a relationship with God as His children and His heirs (4:1-7). They are no longer bound as slaves to the flesh but are now free to serve God in the Spirit by faith working through love (4:8—5:6). The argument concludes sharply with his cutting advice to those who would nullify the scandal of the Cross by submitting to circumcision of the flesh (5:10-12). After contrasting deeds of the flesh with the fruit of the Spirit in verses 19-23, Paul declares that those who live by the Spirit shall also walk by the Spirit, having crucified the flesh in Christ Jesus (vv. 24-25). The Law of Christ must be the guide for one's life in the society (6:1-10).

Paul concludes his letter to the Galatians with a final reminder that the cross of Christ is the true mark of a Christian and that the scandal of the Cross cannot be avoided. What is crucial to the Christian life is the newness of life that comes neither through circumcision nor through uncircumcision, but through the cross of Christ. He describes the Cross as the "marks of Jesus branded on my body" (v. 17; see vv. 12-17). He ends the letter with a formal benediction (v. 18).

Summary Statements

- Paul established the church at Corinth during his second missionary journey and wrote his letters to this church during the third missionary journey.
- Paul wrote his letters to the Corinthians to deal with various issues that contributed to a crisis in the life of the church.
- Paul reminded the Corinthians that they belonged to Christ and not to any human leaders.
- Spiritual gifts should not become a source of pride, but in humility they must be used for the building up of the Body.
- Giving up of one's freedom may be necessary for the building up of community life.
- Paul called for proper conduct and order in Christian worship.
- In 2 Corinthians, Paul characterizes the Christian life as a new creation through Christ.
- Paul urged the Gentile churches to give generously to the poor saints in Jerusalem.
- The letter to the Galatians claims the freedom of the Gentiles from the Law of Moses.
- Paul emphasized the doctrine of justification, God's act of declaring and making persons righteous by the faithfulness of Christ.
- Christians are called to live by the law of Christ, being guided and led by the Holy Spirit.

Questions for Reflection

1. What are different ways to promote unity within the Christian community today while celebrating diversity within the church?
2. How do you distinguish between nonnegotiable matters of Christian faith and culturally conditioned practices that have no bearing on one's salvation experience?
3. What are various expressions of legalism today? What does it mean to live in freedom from the Law but in subjection to the law of Christ?

Resources for Further Study

Barrett, C. K. *A Commentary on the First Epistle to the Corinthians.* New York: Harper and Row Publishers, 1968.
Guthrie, Donald. *Galatians.* Grand Rapids: William B. Eerdmans, 1973.
Witherington, Ben, III. *Conflict and Community in Corinth: A Socio-Rhetorical Commentary on 1 and 2 Corinthians.* Grand Rapids: William B. Eerdmans, 1995.
_____. *Grace in Galatia: A Commentary on Paul's Letter to the Galatians.* Grand Rapids: William B. Eerdmans, 1998.

15 | Ephesians, Philippians, and Colossians

Objectives:

Your study of this chapter should help you to:

- Describe the context of Paul's letters to Ephesians, Philippians, and Colossians.
- Discuss the content and message of Ephesians, Philippians, and Colossians.
- Describe the key theological themes of Ephesians, Philippians, and Colossians.
- Relate the meaning and message of Ephesians, Philippians, and Colossians to the Christian Church today.

Questions to consider as you read:

1. What is the portrait of Christ and His Church that Paul presents in his letter to the Ephesians?

2. What is the source of joy and contentment to Paul while he wrote his letter to the Philippians?

3. What was the Colossian heresy? What instructions does Paul give to his readers at Colossae to help them overcome the influence of heretical teachings?

Key Words to Understand

Christological Epistles
Christology
Prison Epistles
Captivity letters
Ephesus
Rome
Artemis
Lysimachus
Apollos
Tychicus
Ecclesiology
Philippi
Via Egnatia
Lydia
Epaphroditus
Praetorian guard
Kenosis hymn
Kenotic theory
Halakah
Colossae
Laodicea
Hierapolis
Epaphras
Gnosticism
Colossian heresy

Christological Epistles is a term that may be applied to Paul's letters to the churches at Ephesus, Philippi, and Colossae. These short but powerful letters contain some of Paul's highest and finest expressions of **Christology** (i.e., his understanding of the nature and person of Jesus Christ). These letters, along with Philemon, are also called **prison Epistles** or **captivity letters** because Paul was in prison at the time of their writing. The Book of Acts recounts two lengthy imprisonments of Paul, one in Caesarea (Acts 23—26) and another in Rome while awaiting his trial before Caesar (chap. 28). In addition to these two instances, he may have been in prison at other locations for shorter periods such as his overnight jail experience at Philippi (16:19-40; see 2 Corinthians 11:23). Some recent scholars think that one or two of these prison letters originated during Paul's imprisonment at **Ephesus.** Though Paul spent three years at Ephesus during his third missionary journey, there is no record of this imprisonment in Acts or in the Pauline writings. Most scholars think either Caesarea or Rome would have been the setting of these letters. If he wrote these letters from Caesarea, then we may assign A.D. 56-58 as the date of writing. The traditional view assigns **Rome** as the place of writing, which means the writing of these letters would have taken place around A.D. 59-62.[1]

Each of the Christological letters has a bold affirmation of the gospel and a significant expression of Jesus as the exalted Christ. These letters also include joyful and thankful reflections upon the community of faith and a clear call to live all of life in love as holy people in the power of the Holy Spirit.

The Letter to the Ephesians

Ephesus

Ephesus was located along the coastal region in the southwest part of Asia Minor. Scholars trace the Greek settlement of this area to 1000 B.C. In the mid-first millennium B.C. (around 550 B.C.), the city came under the control of the Lydian kingdom. The Temple of **Artemis** at Ephesus was built by the support of the Lydian king Croesus. The conquest of Cyrus brought the city under Persian rule. Later, around 290 B.C., the city came under the rule of Alexander the Great's successor **Lysimachus.** Lysimachus relocated the city to its present site and built an impressive wall around it, parts of which still remain in their original place. The city became part of Roman rule in 133 B.C. Under the reign of Augustus (27 B.C.—A.D. 14), Ephesus enjoyed a period of prominence and prosperity. As the provincial capital of the province of Asia, it received the title "First and Greatest Metropolis of Asia." Ephesus served as a major commercial and political center for the entire region of Asia. This prosperity continued through the reign of various emperors until the late second century A.D.

In addition to the much-renowned temple dedicated to Artemis, one among the pantheon of pagan gods, the city also had its share of imperial temples, such as the temple of Roma and Julius Caesar, Domitian's temple, and the temple of Augustus. Though Ephesus was the primary cult center of the Ephesian Artemis, the city also became a leading center for Roman emperor worship in the first century. Other pagan shrines in the city include temples dedicated to Hestia, Serapis, and Zeus. These temples show that it was a prominent center of pagan worship in Asia. The city was also a center for many Gnostic religious groups and groups that practiced magic and astrology. Though Judaism was among the city's many religions, archaeology has not yet yielded any physical evidence of its Jewish population in the Greco-Roman period.[2] Acts 18:19 indicates that there was a Jewish synagogue in the city.

Paul at Ephesus

Based on the accounts in Acts 18—20, we may conclude that Paul was the earliest Christian leader to exert Christian influence in this city known for its pagan temples and imperial cult. Paul's first recorded visit to Ephesus took place during his second missionary journey (18:18-21). He stopped at Ephesus, preached in the synagogue, and had discussion with the Jews at the conclusion of his second journey (A.D. 52). After promising his audience that he would return to them, Paul left Ephesus and went on his way to Jerusalem. According to Luke 18:24-26, after Paul's departure, **Apollos,** a Jewish Christian from Alexandria, arrived at Ephesus and preached about Jesus in the synagogue. However, Apollos left there and went over to Corinth to preach the gospel in that city.

It is likely that Paul undertook his third journey to fulfill his promise to the Jews at Ephesus. He departed Antioch in Northern Syria and traveled through the interior land (modern Turkey) and arrived at Ephesus perhaps around early 53. He preached in the synagogue for three months and then continued his ministry in the public marketplace for two years (Acts 19:1-20). Paul's ministry at Ephesus may be placed between A.D. 53 and 56. At Ephesus, he first encountered some disciples who have never heard of the Holy Spirit; they have only been taught of the baptism for repentance that John the Baptist preached. Under Paul's ministry of teaching, these disciples were baptized in Jesus' name and they also were filled with the Holy Spirit. Though he preached in the synagogue for three months and "argued persuasively about the kingdom of God," opposition from some Jews prompted him to take the gospel to the "lecture hall of Tyrannus" where he continued his preaching for two years (19:8-10). Luke tells us that "all the residents of Asia, both Jews and Greeks" heard the gospel proclaimed by Paul (v. 10).

At Ephesus, Paul performed many miracles, including healing and exorcism of evil spirits (Acts 19:11-12). Paul's ministry led many who practiced magic and sorcery to give up their profession and become believers (vv. 13-20). While at Ephesus, Paul made plans to travel through Macedonia and Achaia, before departing for Jerusalem (vv. 21-22). Before he left Ephesus, he was faced with an uproar in the city instigated by Demetrius, a silversmith who regarded Paul's message against human-made gods as a threat to the vocation of those who made statues of Artemis and as a potential threat

An Ephesian Imprisonment?

Was Paul ever imprisoned at Ephesus during his ministry there? This question cannot be answered with confidence. A large number of scholars think that he wrote the letter to the Philippians during his imprisonment at Ephesus. They cite reference to the "imperial guard" (Philippians 1:13) and "the emperor's household" (4:22) to the Roman garrison and imperial property at Ephesus. The Book of Acts indicates that he endured some trials at Ephesus (20:19). Paul makes reference to his struggle with "wild animals at Ephesus" (1 Corinthians 15:32); however, this might be a figurative use of the phrase rather than an actual incarceration in an Ephesian jail.

he was exiled to Patmos, an island not too far from Ephesus, from where he wrote the Book of Revelation. The church's existence in the early second century is evident from the Epistle of Ignatius to the Ephesians.

Our understanding of the nature of the Christian community at Ephesus comes from the content of Paul's letter to the Ephesians. Paul describes the community as formerly of the Gentile background. They were once "aliens from the commonwealth of Israel, and strangers to the covenants of promise" (Ephesians 2:12); now they are "no longer strangers and aliens, but . . . members of the household of God" (v. 19; see vv. 11-22).

against the majesty of the great goddess herself (vv. 23-41). On his return from a final tour of Macedonia and Achaia, Paul sent word to Ephesus and asked the elders of the church to meet him at Miletus. In his farewell speech, he reminisced on his ministry among them and gave them the charge to be faithful in their work as overseers of the church at Ephesus. Luke concludes the narrative with a farewell scene filled with prayer and sorrowful embraces of the apostle by his beloved followers (20:17-38). No doubt, there existed a strong emotional bond between Paul and the church at Ephesus.

The Church at Ephesus

It is quite clear that Paul played a crucial role in the spread of Christianity at Ephesus. Tradition also associates the apostle John with Ephesus. Second-century Christian tradition places John at Ephesus in the latter years of his life. It was during this period that

Context

The Epistle to the Ephesians contains one of the best portraits of the Church and life within that community that God has established through His Son Jesus Christ. Unlike other letters in the Pauline corpus, the letter to the Ephesians does not show any clear evidence of the context that prompted the writing of this letter. Many of the significant theological concepts found in the letter are stated in more general terms than is typical in the earlier letters. The style is lofty and the language of worship and praise is present throughout the letter, which has been called "the quintessence of Paul's thought." There are no indications of heresy or other major problems in the church. The focus seems to be on the essential place of the Gentile believers as the people of God and the intimate relationship between the Church, the Body, to

Who Wrote Ephesians?

Scholars who question the authenticity of a number of Pauline Epistles place Ephesians among the "deutero-Pauline" collection of letters in the New Testament (other so-called deutero-Pauline letters are Colossians, 2 Thessalonians, 1 and 2 Timothy, and Titus). Though Ephesians bears a clear letter structure very similar to all other Pauline Epistles, the author may have composed it as a circular letter with a much wider audience in mind than a single congregation. There are some Greek manuscripts that lack the name of a specific recipient in 1:1, and not a single individual within the congregation at Ephesus is mentioned anywhere within the letter itself. This would seem most unusual in a letter addressed to the congregation that Paul pastored longer than any other, unless he intended this message to be given to multiple congregations in and around Ephesus as well as to the specific congregation within Ephesus itself. Scholars think that the author was someone other than Paul because of some apparent vocabulary and stylistic differences between Ephesians and other letters credited to Paul. The letter also bears a remarkable similarity in thought and language to the Epistle to the Colossians, so much so that some scholars have speculated that an anonymous author used the latter as a blueprint to write Ephesians. Yet Ephesians has numerous unique features and characteristics, typical of the diversity found within all of the Pauline letters. The similarity to Colossians may be due to the fact that both letters come from the same period of Paul's imprisonment either at Caesarea or at Rome. It is likely that **Tychicus** was the bearer of both Ephesians and Colossians to their respective recipients (6:21-22; see also Colossians 4:7; 2 Timothy 4:12).

Christ who is the Head of the Church. Does this mean that there was divisiveness or lack of unity between Jewish and Gentile Christians in the Church? We do not have an answer to this question.

Content

The letter may be outlined as follows:

Salutation	1:1-2
Thanksgiving section	1:3-23
Jews and Gentiles: heirs to God's promises	2:1—3:21
Exhortations	4:1—6:20
Conclusion and benediction	6:21-24

After the rather typical salutation in 1:1-2, Paul utilizes a blessing as the foundation of his thanksgiving section. This blessing sums up Paul's Christology. He be-gins with the proclamation that believers are the recipients of all the spiritual blessings of heaven that come through Christ. Paul then recounts the numerous implications of redemption through Christ. God's purpose is to unite all things in heaven and on earth through Christ. He is the ultimate vehicle of God's grace to us, through whom believers have an inheritance with God. The Holy Spirit is the pledge of that inheritance of God's people (vv. 3-14). Paul concludes the thanksgiving section with the bold proclamation that Christ is seated at God's right hand in the heavens, above all rule and power and authority and dominion, with the name above all other names that have come or that ever will come (vv. 15-21).

Building upon that exalted Christological blessing, Paul pro-

Hadrian's temple
in Ephesus.

vides his most comprehensive treatment of the nature of the Church **(ecclesiology)** in the next several chapters. Christ, who sits at the right hand of God, is the Head of the Church, which is His Body (vv. 22-23). That concept is unpacked in detail in chapter 2, where Paul describes the work of Christ as that which takes two totally different and distinct entities, Jews and Gentiles, and unites these two into one new, transformed people to the glory of God. Using the powerful image of the wall of separation in the Temple compound that once differentiated the outsiders (Gentiles) from the insiders (Jews), Paul declares that in Christ the two groups were welded into one new and unique people of God. Strangers, aliens, and people without God and hope in the world have become citizens and members of the household of God through Christ. They now constitute a new temple of God, built upon the foundation of

prophets and apostles with Christ Jesus as the Capstone that holds this entire new structure together. This is what the Church now looks like through Christ. On the basis of this understanding of the Church, Paul challenges Christians to a way of life that demonstrates unity of the Spirit and to the confession that there is indeed "one body and one Spirit . . . one hope . . . , one Lord, one faith, one baptism, and one God and Father of all" (4:4; see vv. 1-6). To His Body Christ has graciously given a variety of gifts to perform different functions within the Body. However, the goal of these gifts is to bring "unity of the faith and of the knowledge of the Son of God" (v. 13) and maturity and growth in Christ, who holds the entire body together and builds it up in love (vv. 7-16).

Paul challenges the new kingdom people, in the very familiar language of "walking the walk," to live as God's people. In a number of places in Ephesians, Paul illustrates the concept of the walk as a way of life. In 2:1-10, he provides a vivid contrast between the former walk, which was according to the course of this world, and the new current way of life that is now an actual reality in Christ who provided redemption. Paul portrays the former walk as a state of being dead in trespasses, sins, and transgressions, a walk according to the influence of this world, a life of indulging in the lusts of the flesh. He contrasts this walk with the walk of believers who have been made alive with Christ, those who have been saved by grace through faith. The community of faith is God's workmanship, created in Christ Jesus for good works. Later, in chapter 4, Paul exhorts the Ephesians to walk in a manner worthy of the calling with which they had been called (v. 1). He adds that this walk should be characterized by humility, gentleness, patience, forbearance in love, and in the unity of the Spirit and the bond of peace (vv. 2-3). This way of walking is further amplified in verses 17-24, where Paul admonishes the Ephesians to stop walking as the heathen walk. Heathen walk in the futility of their mind, with a darkened understanding, having been excluded from the life of God, characterized by ignorance and hardness of heart. The entire chapter of Ephesians 5 is a description of the walk of a holy people set in contrast with the walk of those who are disobedient and unrighteous. The command to walk in love in Ephesians 5:2 is set in context by the command to be imitators of God, and the reminder that Christ loved them and gave himself up for them.

The Christian walk is set in op-position to sexual immorality, impurity, greed, filthiness, empty chatter, and coarse jesting, none of which is considered appropriate behavior (vv. 3-5). The sexually immoral, the impure, the covetous, or the idolater has no share in the kingdom of God (v. 5). In verses 6-14, he contrasts those who walk in the light with those who walk in darkness. Again, he admonishes the Ephesians to look carefully how they walk, not as fools, but as the wise who understand the will of the Lord (vv. 15-18). God's will for His people is that they would go on being filled with the Spirit rather than dissipating themselves in drunkenness.

The theme of walking in love also finds further expression in this letter. In 3:14-19, Paul's prayer expresses the wish that the Ephesians would be rooted and grounded in love, able to know the love of Christ so that they may be filled up to all the fullness of God. In 4:2, the walk in a manner worthy of their calling includes showing forbearance to one another in love. This call is even more direct in 5:2, where Paul commands the Ephesians to walk in love, just as Christ loved them. Paul describes the self-giving love of Christ as the foundation of the relationship between Christ and the Church, His Bride (vv. 25-26).

Paul also draws a major contrast between two distinct kinds of humanity (4:17-32). The old humanity that the Christian is to lay aside (v. 22) is akin to the life still being lived by Gentiles ignorant of God's saving activity (vv. 17-18). The old humanity is characterized by hardness of heart, sensuality, impurity, greed, lust, corruption, deceit, lies, theft, bitterness, wrath, anger, slander, and malice. In Christ, that kind of humanity and selfhood is to be taken off and put away (v. 22). A new humanity and selfhood is to be put on by those who have been redeemed in Christ Jesus (v. 24). The new humanity is characterized by truth, spiritual renewal of the mind, righteousness and holiness, diligent labor, edifying speech, kindness, tenderheartedness, and forgiveness.

Paul's concluding admonitions include instructions for proper life and relationship within the faith community, addressed to wives, husbands, children, fathers, slaves, and masters (5:21—6:9). Submission, sacrificial love, obedience, and discipline are essential to proper relationships within the community of faith. It is important to note that Paul introduces these instructions given to individuals of various family and social relationships with the keynote admonition, "Be subject to one another out of reverence for Christ" (5:21). This mutual submission is the key to unity in the family of God.

Paul closes his final admonitions with the charge to put on the whole armor of God so that God's people might be able to withstand the forces of evil and darkness arrayed against them (6:10-17). Truth, righteousness, faith, salvation, and the Word of God—these are the weapons and implements of defense that will enable the Church to prevail and prepare her to continue to proclaim the gospel that brings peace to humanity. He also instructs the church to "pray in the Spirit" and be alert in their prayer for those who are engaged in the proclamation of the gospel, and

particularly for Paul who is an "ambassador in chains" for the sake of the gospel (vv. 18-20). The letter concludes with a typical benediction, which invokes God's peace, love, and grace for the community of faith (vv. 23-24).

Letter to the Philippians

Philippi

The site of **Philippi** in northern Greece was once known as Krenides, possibly because of the springs and other sources of water in this area (*krēnē* in Greek means "spring" or "well"). The earliest known occupants of this city were Greek colonists from the island of Thasos. Philip II of Macedon brought Krenides under his kingdom in 356 B.C. and gave it the name Philippi after himself. Rome incorporated the Macedonian region as part of its empire in the 2nd century B.C. Philippi was an outpost of the Roman province of Macedonia on the **Via Egnatia,** the ancient Roman road that connected the east with Rome. From the port of Neapolis on the Aegean Sea, this road went through Macedonia and Illyricum to Dyrrhachium on the Adriatic Sea. The plain of Philippi was the site of the battle fought by the troops of Octavian and Antony in 42 B.C. against the legions commanded by Brutus and Cassius. After their victory, Octavian and Antony established Philippi as a Roman colony made up of army veterans. Later, after Octavian's (who took the title Augustus) victory over Antony at the battle of Actium (30 B.C.), more retired veterans settled at Philippi. Augustus renamed the city and gave it its full legal name *Colonia Augusta Julia Philippensis.* As a Roman colony, the city adopted Latin as its official language, and Roman law provided the basis of the city's judicial system. During Paul's time, this city was the principal city in the Roman province of Macedonia (see Acts 16:12).[3]

Philippi most likely had a sizable population of Roman citizens. In addition to the colonists, there were also those who legally gained citizenship, which entitled them to full legal rights as citizens of Rome. These rights included exemption from scourging and illegal imprisonment, and the right to appeal to the emperor.[4] The Book of Acts indicates that there was a small population of Jews in the city, not large enough to maintain a synagogue as the place of prayer. The city also had many Greeks as well as Asians as part of its population.

Acropolis at Philippi.

Paul at Philippi

Paul arrived at Philippi from Neapolis, the port city on the Aegean Sea. Luke informs us that he arrived here in response to the Macedonian call he received while he was at Troas during his second missionary journey (Acts 16:6-10). Here he met a woman named **Lydia,** a dealer in purple-dyed cloth, and won her to the Christian faith. Members of her house

The traditional site of Paul's imprisonment at Philippi.

also were baptized, and they became the first Christian family at Philippi. During his stay at the city, he exorcised a slave girl possessed with the spirit of divination, who was a source of income to her owners. This led to the beating and imprisonment of Paul and Silas on charges that they were disturbing the city and promoting customs not lawful for Romans to practice. At midnight, while Paul and Silas were praying, the doors of the jail were opened and their chains were unfastened. This miraculous event eventually led to the conversion and baptism of the jailer and his family. When the city magistrates decided to let the evangelists go free, Paul claimed his Roman citizenship and complained about his illegal imprisonment and beating by these authorities without a trial and guilty verdict. After gaining an apology from the city magistrates, the evangelists left the city and went on to Thessalonica (vv. 11-40). Acts 20:1-6 indicates that Paul returned to Philippi twice during his third missionary journey.

The Church at Philippi

Based on Luke's narrative, we may conclude that Paul established the church at Philippi around A.D. 49-50. From the standpoint of early Church history, this was an important event, since the congregation he established here was the first Christian church on European soil. Many scholars think that Paul and Silas left Luke in charge of this fledgling congregation (the "we" section in Acts that begins in 16:10 ends at the end of this chapter). Despite a difficult beginning for the church, with Paul and Silas being publicly beaten and imprisoned, the congregation grew and became a strong church in the Macedonian region.

Remains of the Byzantine Basilica at Philippi.

Context

Why did Paul write this letter to the church at Philippi? A cursory reading of this letter shows that this is more like a personal note from the apostle to the congregation at Philippi. Paul describes this church as an exemplary partner with him and a source of financial support for the traveling apostle (4:15-16). He had received gifts from the church several times before, and most recently the church had sent a gift through **Epaphroditus**, which Paul describes as "a fragrant offering, a sacrifice acceptable and pleasing to God" (v. 18). This letter then is most likely a "thank you" note from the apostle to one of his most beloved congregations for its faithful partnership and support of his ministry (see Paul's description of the church as his "joy and crown" and his "beloved" in 4:1). Evidently Epaphroditus became ill to the point of death and the church at Philippi was concerned about their messenger. Paul felt it was necessary for him to send his "brother, and co-worker and fellow soldier" (2:25) back to Philippi so that the church may rejoice at seeing him again (vv. 25-30). Epaphroditus was the carrier of this letter to the church at Philippi (v. 29). The letter was also aimed to prepare the church for an upcoming visit by Timothy and perhaps by Paul himself (vv. 19-24).

However, this letter is more than a personal thank-you letter. The content of this letter shows that Paul also wrote this letter to deal with some problems that existed in the church. Evidently the Christian community at Philippi was not free from opposition to the preaching of the gospel (1:28). It is also likely that there was division within the church. Paul urges the church more than once to be of one spirit and mind (v. 27; 2:2). This lack of unity is also reflected in his appeal to Euodia and Syntyche "to be of the same mind" (4:2). Evidence also seems to indicate that those who preached the necessity of circumcision for one's salvation (Judaizers) have had some influence on the Christians at Philippi (3:2 ff.). Paul may have heard about these issues through Epaphroditus, and the letter contains his instructions to the church on these matters.

Content

This brief letter may be outlined as follows:

Salutation and thanksgiving
1:1-11
Paraenetic section   1:12—4:9
Expression of gratitude for
the gift   4:10-20
Doxology and final greetings
4:21-23

The customary salutation section in 1:1-2 indicates that Timothy was with Paul at the time of the writing of this letter. The recipients of this letter include the Christian community at Philippi along with "bishops and deacons" (1:1). The thanksgiving section in verses 3-11 is noteworthy for the profound sense of joy and affection that Paul has for the Philippians. Paul is grateful because the Philippians stood with him as his fellow workers and partners in the gospel enterprise "from the first day until now" (v. 5). He commends them for standing firm despite his imprisonment and encourages them to increase and abound in love so that they

Philippians: Three Letters?

The Pauline authorship of the letter to the Philippians is not widely disputed by scholars today. However, some scholars have maintained the view that the present form of the letter is a combination of two or three originally independent letters or fragments of the Pauline Epistles. They cite 3:2—4:3 as a separate letter to the Philippians because of the abrupt transition from a call to rejoice in the Lord (3:1) to warning and exhortation (v. 2—4:3). The theme "rejoice" is continued again in 4:4. Scholars also note 4:10-20 as another letter that Paul wrote to the Philippians as a thanksgiving epistle. Though there is no consensus on the order in which Paul might have written these letters to the Philippians, they think that someone has joined these letters together to give the book its present form. Those who favor the unity of the Epistle point out several consistent motifs such as joy, thanksgiving, and contentment in life, appearing throughout the book. The overall evidence does not seem to support the argument that the letter is a composite of two or three letters.[5]

may stand before Christ as a blameless people. He is confident that the God who began the good work in them through the gospel would bring it to completion through Christ Jesus.

The next section of the letter can rightly be called a paraenetic body, extending from 1:12 through 4:9. Paul begins this section with a statement of his confidence in the power of the gospel. Even the **praetorian guard**, the specially chosen soldiers to guard the emperor's palace and provincial palaces, have come to know that he is in prison for the sake of the gospel of Christ. Though he is critical of the questionable motives of some who were proclaiming it, he rejoices in the fact that Christ is being preached even in the midst of his imprisonment. In life or in death, Paul's desire is to exalt Christ. Though his desire is to die and to be with Christ, for the sake of the Church, he would rather live and continue to labor

Kenosis Hymn

Many scholars think 2:6-11 is an early Christian hymn. This text is called the **kenosis hymn** because Jesus, according to Paul, "emptied himself" (Greek *ekenōsen*) to take the form of a servant. Paul describes this emptying *(kenosis)* of Jesus as the example in his exhortation to the Philippians for unity and oneness of mind through humility. The primary focus of this text is on humility, which in Paul's thinking is a Christian virtue.

The idea of Christ emptying himself has led some to ask the question, "Of what did Christ empty himself?" The so-called **kenotic theory** explains that he emptied himself of the divine attributes such as omnipotence, omniscience, and omnipresence. Most recent scholars do not see this text in light of the above question. The NIV translation "but made himself nothing" perhaps best explains the thought of Paul in verses 6-7. Though He was "in the form of God," He "made himself nothing" (NIV). This self-emptying does not mean that at any time in His earthly life, Christ ceased to be God or relinquished His divine attributes. Hooker states, "It is in his [Christ's] self-emptying and his humiliation that he reveals what God is like and it is through his taking the form of a slave that we see 'the form of God.'"[6] God is love, and this is the nature of God that we see in the person of Jesus Christ. Paul makes very clear in this hymn that the Cross is the greatest display of the self-emptying of Christ.

for Christ. He concludes this section with an admonition to the Philippians to be united together for the cause of Christ and in their struggle against those who are their opponents (1:12-30).

In chapter 2, Paul's Christology reaches its highest peak as he exhorts the church to set their minds upon the will and word of God following the servant example of Christ Jesus. In the beautiful hymn found in 2:6-11, often called the kenosis hymn, he declares the "emptying" of Christ. Though Christ was "in the form of God," He exemplified humility by emptying himself to become fully human, a servant obedient to the point of death upon the Cross. It was this faithful servant Jesus that God raised up from the dead, and to whom He gave the name that is now above all other names. At the exalted name of Jesus Christ, every knee in all creation will bow, and every tongue will confess that He is indeed the Lord. This discovery of the revelation of God in the resurrected Messiah enables Paul to proclaim the surpassing value of the righteousness attained through the faithfulness of Christ. It is this faith in the exalted Christ that compels Paul to press on toward the upward and higher calling of God and the ultimate reward that is found only in Him (3:7-14). He does not put any confidence in attaining righteousness through the traditions he kept as a zealous Jew and a Pharisee, but rather he counts all those requirements of the Law as worthless. He is, however, confident in the righteousness that comes through faith and through his knowledge of Christ and the power of His resurrection.

Paul calls upon the Philippians to recognize that they are now citizens of the new heavenly kingdom. Therefore, they must live lives worthy of that Kingdom and walk in a manner that reflects the One who called them (1:27; 2:1-4, 12-15; 3:20—4:1). The understanding of the Christian life in terms of the walk is found in all of the Christological Epistles. In rabbinic Jewish thought, the Hebraic understanding of **halakah** was a typical metaphor for the life one leads, including the expected behavior flowing out from what one believes. The Greek term *peripateō* embodies the same metaphor and can well be translated "live the life" in verbal form or "lifestyle" in noun form. Paul urges the Philippians to "walk the walk" in harmony and unity with the mind-set of Christ as the standard. He also encourages them to discover the ultimate contentment of a life that is completely committed to the Lordship of Christ (4:1-14). Paul is well aware of the anxiety of the Philippians over the welfare of their beloved apostle. So he urges them to join with him and rejoice in his sufferings for the sake of the gospel (4:4; see 1:19). He is confident that through prayer the believers can experience "the peace of God, which surpasses all understanding" (4:7) in the midst of their anxiety-filled life. This peace *(shalom)* will stand as a guard, a soldier on duty, over the hearts and minds of believers.

He concludes the letter with commendation and gratitude to the Philippians for their gifts and offering to him, the customary final greetings, and benediction (vv. 15-23). The Philippians have fully rewarded him for his faithful service among them. The gifts that he received from them are a "fragrant offering" to God. He expresses his wish that just as the Philippians "satisfied" the apostle, God would "satisfy every need" of his beloved congregation.

Letter to the Colossians

Colossae

The town of **Colossae** was a small market town during the days of Paul, and far less significant than many of the other places where Paul had established churches during his missionary journeys. The town was located in the region of Phrygia, about 120 miles east of Ephesus, in the upper valley of the Lycus River, a tributary of the Meander. The town was situated near other well-known cities such as **Laodicea** and **Hierapolis.** In the fifth and fourth centuries before the Christian era, Colossae was a great and prosperous city, attested by the reports of Herodotus and Xenophon. The city seems to have lost its significance in the Roman period, particularly due to the elevation of Laodicea as the most important city in the Lycus valley. Colossae enjoyed prosperity through the textile industry and was known for the purple color of its wool. The strategic location near a highway also contributed to its prosperity. The coins from Colossae indicate that the Gentile population here worshiped a number of deities, among whom the Ephesian Artemis and the Laodicean Zeus were the most prominent. There is also evidence of the worship of Egyptian deities such as Isis and Sarapis. The city was most likely destroyed by an earthquake around A.D. 60 or 64.[7]

The Church at Colossae

The letter to the church at Colossae is unique in that here we have a letter that Paul has written to a church that he had never visited before the writing of the letter. However, it is possible that he may have traveled through this area on his way to Ephesus. The origin of the Christian communities in Colossae, Laodicea, and Hierapolis may be traced to the work of Christians who were once a part of the communities that Paul had established in larger cities of Asia Mi-

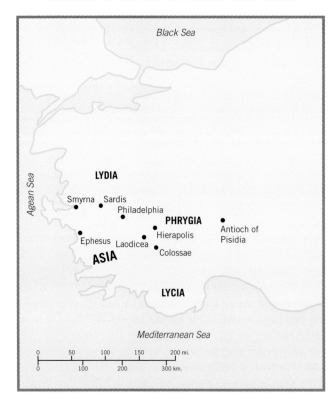

Locations of Churches in Western Asia Minor.

Black Sea

Agean Sea

LYDIA

Smyrna Sardis
        Philadelphia
                    PHRYGIA
Ephesus Laodicea Hierapolis   Antioch of
                                  Pisidia
ASIA   Colossae

LYCIA

Mediterranean Sea

0   50   100   150   200 mi.
0   100   200   300 km.

nor.[8] Most scholars think that the church at Colossae was established by **Epaphras,** who "has worked hard" for the Colossians as well as for the believers in Laodicea and Hierapolis (4:12-13). Colossae was the home of both Philemon and his runaway slave Onesimus (Colossians 4:9; Philemon 10).

The congregation was made up mostly of Gentiles, despite there being a notable Jewish population in the city. Paul makes reference to their heathen past in 1:21 and 2:13. He also describes the Colossians as those who hold their faith in Christ and love all the saints (1:4). They are a people among whom the gospel has been "bearing fruit" (v. 6).

Context

Paul wrote the letter to caution and give warning to the Colossians concerning false teachers and their deceptive teachings. This warning is clearly seen in 2:8. It seems that these false teachers who promoted their teachings through "philosophy and empty deceit" were adherents of some kind of **Gnosticism.** The strange combination of Gnostic elements with Jewish rituals suggests a unique kind of heresy that confronted the Colossians (vv. 16-23). Scholars are still uncertain as to the precise make-up of the opponents of the gospel. However, it is clear that Paul responds to this heresy with the strong affirmation of Christ as

---

The Colossian Heresy and Heresies Today

The location of Colossae with its trade route linking east and west was a fertile ground for the growth of Gnosticism and Oriental mystery religions. To what extent these Greek philosophical speculations or Oriental cults influenced the church at Colossae is not clearly known. Most scholars think that there was a blending of the philosophical speculations of Gnosticism, Judaism, and Christianity at Colossae. In chapter 2, Paul makes reference to a number of the teachings promoted by false teachers who were promoting this syncretistic Christian faith. These teachers held the view that knowledge of the divine realm and the spiritual world can be attained through secret revelation. According to Paul, this "philosophy" or religious perspective has no truth in it. These teachers also demanded observance of festivals, new moons, Sabbath, strict regulations on food and drink, and worship of angels. Asceticism, self-imposed piety, and false humility were also characteristics of this teaching.

How do we confront heresies in our day? Paul's instructions to the Colossians are worth following when we encounter attempts to mix elements of other religious perspectives with the Christian faith. Paul confronts the **Colossian heresy** with the bold proclamation that true knowledge is the knowledge of Christ as "the image of the invisible God, the firstborn of all creation" (1:15), the one in whom "the fullness of God was pleased to dwell" (v. 19). God has "rescued us from the power of darkness, and transferred us into the kingdom of his beloved Son, in whom we have redemption, the forgiveness of sins" (vv. 13-14). Through Christ "God was pleased to reconcile to himself all things, whether on earth or in heaven, by making peace through the blood of his cross" (v. 20). This is the true knowledge of God, the true "philosophy" of the Christian faith.

Lord over the world and as the head of the Church (1:15-20).

Content

The Letter to the Colossians may be outlined as follows:

Salutation	1:1-2
Thanksgiving	1:3-8
Body of the letter	1:9—4:6
Final greetings and instructions	4:7-18

Paul includes Timothy as a sender of this letter along with the apostle (1:1). The thanksgiving section in verses 3-8 is filled with joy and praise for the Colossian community's response to the gospel, which was proclaimed to them by Epaphras.

The body section of the letter begins with Paul's prayer that the Colossian community would be filled with the knowledge of God's will and that they would live a life pleasing to God (v. 9). He also prays for God's strength for them when they face opposition. God had rescued them from the realm of darkness that once marked their lives. They are now citizens in the kingdom of Christ, who is the Source of their new life (vv. 9-14).

The high Christological language of verses 15-20 has led some scholars to conclude that these verses were taken from an early Christian hymn.[9] In this hymnic section, Paul speaks first of Christ as the image of the invisible God, the Firstborn of all creation (v. 15). All creation, both the earthly and the heavenly, has been created by Him and for Him (v. 16). Moreover, Christ has preeminence over all creation, and the entire created order is held together in Christ (v. 17). Christ is the Head of the Church, the beginning point of everything, and through His res-

urrection from the dead, He has priority over everything (v. 18). This Messiah Jesus has within himself all the fullness of God, and through Him God was pleased to reconcile all things to himself, having made peace through the blood of His cross (vv. 19-20). The Christ-hymn is followed by a challenge to the Colossians that they must stand firm in the faith so that Christ might present them as a holy people before God (vv. 21-23). Paul makes it very clear that the primary mystery of the universe has now been revealed in Jesus and in His redemptive work that includes all of the created order (1:24—2:15). The implications of this Christ-centered salvation are many, and Paul unpacks them throughout the remainder of this letter in his exhortations to live the Christian life.

Paul uses a variety of terms and concepts to communicate the essential components of this new life. While there is a great deal of overlap among all of these concepts, there are three major ideas that express Paul's primary concern. The first is the concept of walking worthy of God. The second is the idea of increasing and abounding in love for God and for all humanity and living according to that principle of love. The final concept is that of living a holy life, a life in the power of the Holy Spirit.

The concept of the walk as a life that is worthy of the God who calls is taken up in great detail in Colossians. Paul's prayer in 1:9-14 centers on his desire for the Colossians to walk in a manner worthy of the Lord. Such a walk will be pleasing to the Lord in all respects and will be obvious in the fruit that is borne in every good work. As a people redeemed in Christ from the dominion of darkness, their lives are to reflect the reality of the God of light to His honor and glory. Paul instructs the Colossians to walk in Christ just as they have received Him, and that such a walk should naturally flow from those who have been firmly rooted, built up in Him, and established in the faith (2:6-7).

One final admonition to walk the walk is found in 4:5, where Paul commands the Colossians to be wise in their conduct toward outsiders. Outsiders are those who are outside of the community of faith. Believers must live in such a way that would demonstrate to those who are not part of the circle of faith the manifestation of their holy God within their lives.

Closely related to this instruction for a Christian walk worthy of God is the idea of the Christian life characterized by ever-increasing love (3:12-17). The concept of love is both dynamic and relational. Love must continue to grow or the love relationship will begin to wither and may eventually die. Love can be understood as a gift from God made known through the preaching of the gospel of Christ. Yet the human response to this gift of God's love is itself called love. Loving God means entering into and maintaining a dynamic love relationship with God. It is love that keeps the Christian walk from becoming nothing more than a religious legalism or sentimental moralism. Paul suggests several things that Christians should put on as fitting for those who are holy and beloved of God (vv. 12-14). Beyond all other things, they should put on love, which is the perfect bond of unity

(v. 14). Love is the culmination, the most significant binding and uniting aspect of their experience as new creatures in Christ.

The holy life for the Christian is often referred to as life in the Spirit, a new way of holy living that is in striking contrast to the former way of life. Paul utilizes a variety of images to describe this new life in the Spirit. The major metaphor that Paul uses to depict living the new life in Christ is that of putting off the "old self" or humanity and putting on the "new self" or humanity. Paul draws a sharp contrast between these two radically different kinds of humanity in verses 1-17. The old humanity, characterized by earthiness, sexual immorality, impurity, passion, evil desire, greed, idolatry, anger, wrath, malice, abusive speech, lies, and bigotry has been stripped off (v. 9). The Christian has now been clothed by the new humanity, marked by a new mindset, a new master, and a new way of life (v. 10). The mind of the Christian is to be set on things above (vv. 1-2), constantly being renewed in true knowledge by the Christ who is all in all (vv. 10-11). The new life is to be marked by compassion, kindness, humility, gentleness, patience, forbearance, forgiveness, love, peace, and thanksgiving. In the new humanity, created by God in His image, there is no racial or religious or social preferences or distinctions. Moreover, in this new community, whatever is said and done should be done in the name of the Lord Jesus as an expression of thanks through Him to God the Father. Paul's instructions on the new life concludes with admonitions to wives, husbands, children, slaves, and masters (3:18—4:6). In all of these family and social relationships, Paul urges the Christian community to conduct themselves as members of the new humanity that God has created through Jesus Christ.

The letter concludes with personal messages and greetings and some final instructions (4:7-18). He includes greetings sent by his coworkers and special commendations of Tychicus, the courier of this letter, and Epaphras, who may have started the church at Colossae. The letter ends with Paul's personal signature and a request to remember him, a prisoner for Christ.

Summary Statements

- Paul wrote Ephesians, Philippians, and Colossians while he was a prisoner either at Caesarea or at Rome.
- The letter to the Ephesians describes the Church as the Body of Christ made up of both Jews and Gentiles that God has brought together as His people.
- Paul states in Ephesians that the goal of all gifts from God is to bring unity in the Church.
- Paul states in Ephesians that in Christ believers put on a new humanity, a way of life that is distinctly different from the old one.
- Philippians is a "thank you" note from Paul to one of his most beloved congregations.
- Paul states in Philippians that Jesus, though He was in the form of God, made himself nothing and became fully human, a servant obedient to the point of death on the Cross.
- Paul called the Philippians to seek contentment in life through complete commitment to Christ.
- Colossians is a letter written to warn the church at Colossae about false teachers and deceptive teachings.
- In Colossians, Paul declares that all things in creation are held together in Christ, who is the image of the invisible God.

Questions for Reflection

1. Through Christ, God has broken down the wall that divided the Jews and the Gentiles. What are the areas in our social life where humanity continues to erect walls of separation? What does it say to you about the mission of the church today?
2. Throughout the prison letters, Paul calls us to imitate Christ and follow His example. What actions do you need to take in your life to follow Christ completely?
3. Compare and contrast contentment that Paul advocates in his letter to the Philippians with the type of contentment that our culture promotes through consumerism and possession of wealth.

Resources for Further Study

Barth, Markus. *Ephesians: Introduction, Translation, and Commentary*, 2 Vols. New York: Doubleday, 1974.
Hooker, Morna D. *Philippians*, in *The New Interpreter's Bible*, Vol. XI. Ed. Leander E. Keck. Nashville: Abingdon Press, 2000.
Lohse, Eduard. *Colossians and Philemon*. Trans. William R. Poehlmann and Robert J. Karris. *Hermeneia: A Critical and Historical Commentary on the Bible*. Philadelphia: Fortress Press, 1971.

16 1 and 2 Thessalonians

O bjectives:

Your study of this chapter should help you to:

- Discuss Paul's relationship to the church at Thessalonica.
- Describe the context of Paul's letters to the Thessalonians.
- Identify the key theological concerns found in 1 and 2 Thessalonians.
- Relate the message of Paul found in 1 and 2 Thessalonians to the life of the Christian Church today.

K ey Words to Understand

Parousia
Thessalonica
Politarchs
Silas
Timothy
Corinth
Eschatology
Sanctification
Theophany
Day of the Lord
The rebellion
The lawless one

Q uestions to consider as you read:

1. How does Paul describe the church at Thessalonica? What are some of the characteristics and qualities of the Thessalonian church?

2. What is sanctification and its relation to sexual purity, according to Paul?

3. What does Paul say about the second coming of Jesus Christ? How should Christians conduct themselves while waiting for the Second Coming?

The Thessalonian letters are addressed to a predominantly Gentile audience where Paul gives a clear answer to the question: How shall Christians live until the **Parousia**—the second coming of Christ? These letters reflect Paul's pastoral concerns for the congregation at Thessalonica. Paul's primary concern for them was the strength of their faith under persecution and the quality of character that they should display in their lives until the coming of the Lord Jesus Christ. In these two letters, Paul instructs the believers at Thessalonica to live, work, and walk in a manner worthy of their calling, in holiness and sanctity as befitting the Lord Jesus Christ so that they would be ready for His arrival and presence.

Thessalonica

The city of **Thessalonica**, located about 90 miles west of Philippi, was founded in 316 B.C. by Cassander, who named it in honor of his wife, Thessalonike, a stepsister of Alexander the Great. Romans gained control of the Macedonian kingdom around 168 B.C. and made Thessalonica the capital of the province of Macedonia in 146 B.C. Cicero spent six months of his exile in Thessalonica in 58 B.C. Thessalonica enjoyed favor from Octavian and Antony in return for its cooperation against the forces of Brutus and Cassius. They made the city a "free city" with the government in the hands of an assembly of people, and magistrates **(politarchs)** were chosen from that assembly. In the first century, the city of Thessalonica was a large prosperous community. The city's proximity to the Via Egnatia and its natural harbor and seaport on the Aegean Sea facilitated its commercial prosperity. The city was also the seat of much ancient culture. The city's population in the first century A.D. included mainly Greeks, but there was also a large Roman and Oriental presence, including a colony of Diaspora Jews. The Book of Acts indicates that there was a Jewish synagogue in the city (Acts 17:1).[1]

Arch of Galerius in Thessalonica.

Paul at Thessalonica

The church in Thessalonica was the second church established in Macedonia by Paul. He came to this city, after leaving Philippi, during his second missionary journey. He carried out his preaching and teaching ministry in the Jewish synagogue for three weeks. The focus of his teaching was the suffering, death, and resurrection of Jesus the Messiah. Those who believed the message of Paul were mostly Greeks, including some leading women. The Jews who opposed Paul's message started a tumult in the city and brought Jason and some believers before the city authorities (politarchs). The charge against Jason was that he welcomed Paul and his colleagues, who were preaching a message "contrary to the decrees of the emperor" and promoting "another king named Jesus." Because of opposition, the believers sent the evangelist off to Beroea for his own safety. While the total amount of time that he spent in the city is unknown, it appears that Paul had to leave before he was able to fully establish the new church (Acts 17:1-15).

Context

Paul was concerned about the young church's ability to withstand affliction and persecution. So when he left Beroea, he left behind **Silas** and **Timothy** to oversee the work in the Thessalonica-Beroea area (Acts 17:14-15). It is possible that Timothy soon joined him at Athens; however, Paul sent him back to Thessalonica to encourage and strengthen the believers (1 Thessalonians 3:1-5).

Thessalonica Rotunda.

From Athens, Paul went over to Corinth, where Timothy joined the apostle from Thessalonica. This chronology of events seems to suggest that Paul wrote his first letter from **Corinth** after the arrival of Timothy from Thessalonica. This letter is a response to "the good news" that Timothy had brought from Thessalonica (3:6). At the time of writing 1 Thessalonians, both Silas and Timothy were with Paul (see 1:1).

Paul's first letter to the Thessalonians makes it clear that the church had remained true and faithful to the gospel, but this new congregation did have some major questions that Paul needed to address. Paul commends the believers for their faith, love, and hope and for becoming "an example to all the believers in Macedonia and in Achaia" (1:7; see vv. 2-10). In 2:1-16, Paul explains at length his ministry and conduct among them. It seems that here he is defending his apostolic ministry against those who brought charges of flattery, heresy, and greed. He reminds the readers that he worked hard to support

Thessalonica Church of St. Demetrios.

himself while preaching the gospel at Thessalonica. The first letter also indicates that Paul was concerned about those Christians who were under persecution at Thessalonica (2:14-15; 3:3-4). The church also needed instructions on holy living, sexual conduct, moral and ethical responsibility, and issues related to the Second Coming. The second letter clarifies more fully Paul's perspectives on the Second Coming and the question of how to conduct oneself while waiting for the "coming" of the Lord Jesus Christ.

Traditional dating places 1 Thessalonians around A.D. 50-51, although some contemporary scholars suggest a date in the early 40s and others suggest a date around 54-56. If the traditional dating were accepted, then Paul would have written 1 Thessalonians from Corinth where he remained for 18 months during his second missionary journey; 2 Thessalonians may have followed

shortly thereafter, from the same location. Some scholars see a radical shift in the **eschatology** between the letters, and so they argue that 2 Thessalonians reflects a post-Pauline perspective. Such a view is not necessary, however, to account for the differences and similarities found in the two letters. The major issues addressed remain the same in both, including the need for further clarification about eschatology and the need for love and patient endurance of persecution and suffering within the community. Both letters also contain Paul's challenge to the slothful, and his call to develop and maintain a holy life.

Content

The Thessalonian letters may be outlined as follows:

1 Thessalonians

Paul begins the first letter with the usual epistolary introduction, which includes a detailed thanksgiving section. He addresses a community of faith that has its existence in "God the Father and the Lord Jesus Christ" (1:1). His thanksgiving reflects his extreme joy for the community of faith at Thessalonica. In his thanksgiving, Paul commends them especially for their "work of faith," their "labor of love," and their loyal perseverance in hope. He describes the Thessalonians as a people who have not only received the gospel "with joy" in the midst of persecution but also imitated the apostle by their participation in the work of evangelism. Paul commends the believers for their remarkable conversion, their turning away from idolatry to worship "a living and true God" (v. 9), and for their hope in the coming of Christ (vv. 2-10).

In chapter 2, Paul reminds the congregation of the example he has set before them. His mistreatment by the authorities at Philippi did not detract him from preaching the gospel at Thessalonica, though he was faced with great opposition in that city also. The goal of his preaching was not to gain approval from his human audience but to please God who entrusted him with the gospel. He dismisses the accusation of his opponents with a strong claim of the integrity with which he preached the gospel and the impeccability of his conduct among the Thessalonians. He had not lorded it over them but had worked hard among them, both as a gentle, nursing mother on the one hand and as a diligent, loving father on the other. He staunchly defends the character and integrity of the apostolic party while they were present in Thessalonica; they worked "night and day" so that they would not be a burden to others. Paul practiced what he preached and challenged the Thessalonians to do the same. The people of God must walk in a manner worthy of the God who is calling them into His own kingdom and glory. That walk is described as "holy, righteous and blameless" (2:10, NIV; see vv. 1-12).

Verses 13-16 resemble a thanksgiving section, often found in the beginning of Paul's letters. Some scholars view this section as a later addition to the letter because of its dissimilarity to the typical Pauline Epistle structure and its anti-Jewish expressions. The writer expresses thanks to God because they have received the gospel not as human words but as "the word of God" that is at work in the believers. He further describes the suffering they have experienced from their own countrymen as similar to the persecution of the churches in Judea by the Jews. Paul's longing to see the Thessalonians "face to face" (v. 17) is vividly expressed in verses 17-20. Though the apostle wanted to visit the church at Thessalonica, Satan blocked his way and he was unable to fulfill his desire. Paul views obstacles to his travel plans as the work of Satan.

Chapter 3 begins with an explanation of why Paul had sent Timothy from Athens to Thessalonica. Timothy's mission was to "strengthen and encourage" the believers at Thessalonica to remain faithful during their persecution. While he was with them, Paul had forewarned them that suffering would come because of their Christian faith. He sent Timothy because of his concern that some may have fallen victim to the tempter's strategy to dissuade believers from their Christian commitment (vv. 1-5). However, Timothy's return from Thessalonica and his good report about the faith he witnessed there and their love for Paul revived the apostle's spirit. Paul once again expresses his desire to see the believers at Thessalonica so that he may continue to build them up in their faith (vv. 6-10).

The closing prayer in chapter 3, which echoes the thanksgiving in chapter 1, expresses Paul's desire for the church to increase in her love for others (vv. 11-13). This prayer also serves as a good transition to the paraenesis that follows in chapters 4 and 5. He prays that God would establish their hearts "in holiness" and that they may be "blameless" before Him at the Parousia.

The paraenesis section combines several commands and admonitions. It is clear that these instructions have an urgency, since they are given in the context of Paul's own expectation of the near return of Jesus Christ. These instructions are authoritative because they are given in the name of the Lord Jesus Christ (4:1). The goal of his instructions is to teach the Thessalonians the manner of life that is pleasing to God. He be-

Holiness and Sexual Purity

Contemporary views on sexuality and sexual behavior promote a lifestyle contrary to the biblical ideals of holy living. There is indeed a "holiness code" in the Bible that calls the community of faith to pursue a life of moral and ethical integrity in the area of sexual conduct. Human freedom and pursuit of individual happiness are central to modern perspectives on human sexual behavior. In this mode of thinking the interests of the self become more important than the value and human dignity of others. Marital unfaithfulness, premarital sex, bisexual and homosexual relationships—all of these involve bondage and slavery, exploitation and manipulation, self-fulfillment and self-gratification. Such relationships, no matter how responsible and committed they claim to be, have no moral and ethical integrity. The "holiness code" that Paul promotes in 1 Thessalonians 4:1-8 calls for purity of motive and sacrificial love as the basis of human relationships. Holy conduct involves abstinence from all immoral activities. Paul makes it clear that without holiness in life, it is difficult to maintain integrity in sexual conduct.

gins his instructions with an explicit affirmation that **sanctification** is God's will for His people (v. 3). God's people have been called into the sphere of sanctification because God is a holy God. Sanctification refers to the act of separation from the world and the act of consecration to God. That the believers cannot be made holy by their own act of separation and consecration is clear from Paul's reference to the activity of God in 1 Thessalonians 5:23. Believers are called here to pattern their lives as a holy people. Because holiness is God's will for His people, they are to abstain from all manner of sexual immorality. Moreover, they must honor and sanctify their marriage relationships and conduct all personal relation-

ships with godly love. Paul concludes his instruction on holiness and sexual purity with the warning that those who reject this instruction indeed reject God who gives His Holy Spirit to believers to live a holy life (4:1-12).

Paul commends the Thessalonians for the love they have for fellow Christians, but he urges them "to do so more and more" (4:10). Christians should strive to live a quiet life, minding their own business. They should also earn their livelihood through the work of their own hands, without being dependent on others (vv. 9-12).

These instructions set the stage for his discussion of the Parousia (4:13—5:11). It seems that Paul is responding here to the questions the Thessalonians had about

I Rapture

In 1 Thessalonians 4:13-17, Paul speaks like a prophet and announces future events associated with the Second Coming. A key event in this text is the descent of the Lord and the resurrection of those Christians who have died in their faith. Paul explains that following this event, "we who are alive, who are left, will be caught up in the clouds together with them to meet the Lord in the air" (v. 17). We find a similar expression in Acts 8:39, where the Spirit of the Lord is said to have "snatched" Philip the evangelist away; however, later Philip found himself at Azotus in the nearby region. Paul relates his acquaintance with a person who was "caught up to the third heaven" (2 Corinthians 12:2, 4), which most likely is an account of his own temporary ecstatic experience. See also the reference to the snatching activity in the account of the woman, the child, and the dragon in Revelation 12:5. However, it is only here in this text that we find this event in the context of the Second Coming. This idea of the living being "caught up in the air" has given rise to many speculations in the Christian church. The Latin Bible translated the Greek word used here as *rapio,* which is the source of the English word "rapture."

Some Christians view this event in relationship to the idea of a seven-year period of tribulation. According to some, the Rapture will precede this tribulation, and thus the Church will be removed from the earth. Some think that the Church will experience tribulation for three and a half years and then the Rapture will take place. For some others, Rapture will happen at the end of the Tribulation. Various perspectives like these do not have clear biblical foundation. However, we can confidently say that at the coming of Christ, both the dead in Christ and the living who are faithful to God will be taken up to be with the Lord.

those who die before the Parousia, and the time of the coming of the Lord. He makes it clear that the death and resurrection of Jesus Christ is the foundation of the Christian hope in the resurrection. Since Christians have this hope, they do not need to be concerned about those who die before the Second Coming. Paul comforts his readers with the declaration that no one who dies before Christ's return will miss that glorious event. The language of 4:16-17 contains apocalyptic imagery. These verses also reflect the Old Testament **theophany** narratives, which describe God's coming to meet with His people (see Exodus 19:16-20). The text affirms the certainty of the Second Coming; however, the symbolic language of the text cannot be interpreted literally.

Though Paul confidently expresses his faith in the Second Coming, he stops short of giving a specific timetable for this event. This event will occur suddenly, without warning. God's people do not live in darkness but in the light of God's revelation shining through the gospel of Jesus Christ. Therefore, when the day of the Lord comes, it will not be a surprise to them. Paul urges the believers to continue living and walking as children of the day, because the dawning **Day of the Lord** lies just ahead (1 Thessalonians 5:1-11). Faith, hope, and love are essential trademarks of the people of God who anticipate the coming of the Lord.

Verses 12-22 contain Paul's final instructions to the church at Thessalonica. His pastoral concerns are clearly evident in this

T Entire Sanctification

"May the God of peace himself sanctify you entirely; and may your spirit and soul and body be kept sound and blameless at the coming of our Lord Jesus Christ" (v. 23). This prayer is parallel to Paul's prayer in 3:13 ("And may he so strengthen your hearts in holiness that you may be blameless before our God and Father at the coming of our Lord Jesus Christ with all his saints"). Ernest Best notes: "'May God sanctify you' (v. 23) balances 'sanctify yourselves'" (4:3a). Though the Thessalonians "need to strive for holiness (4:3) God alone can produce holiness in them."[2]

In the Wesleyan tradition, this text (5:23) has been understood as the classic New Testament passage that provides the biblical foundation for the phrase "entire sanctification."[3] Sanctify you "entirely" means sanctify you "through and through," "completely," or "wholly." H. Ray Dunning describes verse 23 as "the climactic statement of a series of exhortations designed to emphasize the sanctity of the whole of life. It emphasizes the whole person's involvement in the holy life."[4] The phrase "spirit and soul and body" does not mean three distinct components of a human person, as in the Greek thinking. Paul is referring here to the whole person. Sanctification in the Bible, on the one hand, is one's separation from the world and complete belonging to God. Equally important is the idea of one's conformity to the character and likeness of God. This ethical transformation within a believer, which involves one's whole being, is the prayer-wish that Paul expresses in verse 23. The apostle is confident that the God who calls us to belong to Him is also faithful to accomplish this work of salvation in us (v. 24).

text. He calls for respect and love for leaders, peace, care for the weak, and other basic Christian principles. God's will for His people is that they live a life of joy, prayer, and constant thanksgiving. Above all else, they must live a life free from evil.

Paul closes the letter with a grand theological summary in verses 23-24 that connect his concern with their concerns. "May the God of peace himself sanctify you entirely; and may your spirit and soul and body be kept sound and blameless at the coming of our Lord Jesus Christ. The one who calls you is faithful, and he will do this." God's plan for His people is to bring them into complete conformity to a lifestyle that is fitting for a Christian disciple. This means the activity of God's grace to transform our whole being—body, soul, and spirit—to God's character that is made known to us through Jesus Christ. The letter concludes with the typical Pauline greetings and benediction (vv. 25-28).

2 Thessalonians

Second Thessalonians reflects many of the same concerns and issues found in 1 Thessalonians. It is likely that Paul wrote this letter to address three specific issues. The opening chapter makes reference to intense persecution of believers. Chapter 2 indicates that there was a mistaken view among some in the church at Thessalonica that the day of the Lord had already come. Chapter 3 contains a strong admonition to those who were living in idleness, not doing any work. As mentioned earlier, Paul may have written this letter from Corinth not too much

Agora in ancient Thessalonica.

longer after his first letter to the Thessalonians.

In his opening thanksgiving section, Paul commends the believers at Thessalonica for their display of faith and love even in the midst of intense persecution and suffering (1:3-12). He reminds his readers that they are suffering for the kingdom of God. He comforts them with the assurance that at the Parousia, God the righteous Judge will punish those who do not know Him and those who do not obey the gospel. Paul concludes this section with a prayer for the Thessalonians that they would continue in their faithful response to God's call in their lives.

Questions about the Parousia persisted at Thessalonica. Paul responds to these questions in 2:1-12. It is likely that the Thessalonians have misunderstood or misinterpreted Paul's previous letter or his teaching while he was at Thessalonica (v. 2). It is also possible that the source of their misunderstanding was a prophetic word from some other individual(s) or a letter attributed to Paul. The primary concern that Paul deals with is the mistaken view that the day of the Lord has already come. He assures his readers that that day has not come. Certain things such as **the rebellion** (literally, "the apostasy") and the appearance of **the lawless one** must precede the coming of the Lord. The word "rebellion" perhaps indicates a large-scale increase in ungodliness and immorality in the world. "The lawless one" (NIV, "the man of lawlessness," or "the man of sin" in some manuscripts) seems to refer to a human being. Obviously Paul had given some previous instructions on "the lawless one" to the Thessalonians (vv. 5-6). It is thus possible that the readers had some understanding of what Paul meant by this label. Interpreters have taken this label to mean the Roman Empire with its demand for emperor worship, or a supernatural power, or Satan. In the absence of specific identity, we may think of this as a reference to the power of evil that is already at work in the world, a power that will appear in its full force in the end-time.[5] God will bring His judgment upon this power and on all who refuse "to love the truth" that leads to salvation.

The power of evil cannot nullify the reality of God's gracious work of salvation and sanctification for those who stand firm in the faith and hold fast to the teaching of the gospel (2:13-15). Paul expresses his gratitude to God for the Thessalonians for their salvation "through the sanctifying work of the Spirit and through belief in the truth" (v. 13, NIV). He concludes his thanksgiving with a prayer for the Thessalonians.

Chapter 3 includes Paul's closing appeals and final exhortations. The apostle seeks the prayer support of his readers as well as offers his prayers for them (3:1-5). Paul concludes the

T Second Coming and the Signs of the Time

In Christian history, there has been a great deal of interest in the Second Coming and events that might occur in the end-time. Paul's letters to the Thessalonians clearly show that the believers at Thessalonica were concerned about the timing of the Parousia. At the center of this concern is the question: How could we be prepared for an event if we do not know when it is going to take place? In our own contemporary period, we have witnessed a resurgence of interest in the end-time events. The overwhelming success and popularity of the Left Behind series of books and movies attest to this growing interest in the Christian Church today. Behind every major event in history in the past, some Christians have attempted to see the signs of the time. Many have even speculated on a specific date for the Second Coming.

What does Paul say to us concerning the Second Coming? Are we to keep a constant vigil for particular signs, which will prompt us to shape our life in conformity to God's will, so that we will be found worthy to be participants in this event? Or are we to live our lives daily in the hope of the Second Coming, so that regardless of the timing, we will be found ready for that glorious day? A preoccupation with the signs of the time may lead us to unnecessary worry and concern. It may even lead us to think that that day is far away in the future, a thinking that might lead us to become slack in our Christian commitment. Paul challenges us to be ready at all times.

letter with some strong admonitions to those who refused to remain productive within the community because of their concerns about the Parousia (vv. 6-15). He does not want preoccupation with last things to prevent meaningful, productive life in the present. The best way to prepare for Christ's return is to live, walk, and work in the manner that is worthy of the One who has created the new people of God in His own image. The letter concludes with the typical Pauline greetings and benediction (vv. 16-18).

Summary Statements

- Paul established the church at Thessalonica during his second missionary journey.
- Paul wrote the letters to the church at Thessalonica from Corinth, after hearing the good news from Timothy about the faith, hope, and love of the Thessalonian believers.
- Paul instructs the Thessalonians to remain faithful in the midst of their suffering for Christ.
- Sanctification is God's will for His people.
- Holiness calls for moral and ethical integrity in the area of one's sexual conduct.
- Both the dead in Christ and the living who are faithful to God will participate in the Second Coming.
- God's gracious plan for His people is to transform our whole being—body, soul, and spirit—to His character and likeness that is made known to us through Jesus Christ.
- Christians should not be concerned about the time and signs of the Second Coming; rather, they should be ready for that great eschatological event.

Questions for Reflection

1. How does faith, hope, and love work in your personal life?
2. What are your concerns about the Second Coming? What answers do you find in Paul's instructions to the Thessalonians?
3. What does it mean to live a holy life in the 21st-century context of moral relativism and cultural changes?

Resources for Further Study

Best, Ernest. *A Commentary on the First and Second Epistles to the Thessalonians.* New York: Harper and Row, 1972.

Marshall, I. Howard. *1 and 2 Thessalonians: The New Century Bible Commentary.* Grand Rapids: William B. Eerdmans, 1983.

Wanamaker, C. A. *The Epistles to the Thessalonians.* Grand Rapids/Exeter: William B. Eerdmans/Paternoster, 1990.

17

1 and 2 Timothy, Titus, and Philemon

Objectives:

Your study of this chapter should help you to:

- Describe the context of Paul's letters to Timothy, Titus, and Philemon.
- Discuss the content and message of Paul's letters to Timothy, Titus, and Philemon.
- Summarize the key theological themes of 1 and 2 Timothy, Titus, and Philemon.
- Relate the message of 1 and 2 Timothy, Titus, and Philemon to contemporary Christian life.

Questions to consider as you read:

1. What are the responsibilities of a faithful church leader?
2. What is sound doctrine?
3. How does Paul model true Christian leadership to his younger pastors?
4. How did Paul view the master-servant relationship?

Key Words to Understand

Pastoral Epistles
Crete
Ephesus
Nicopolis
Jewish Gnosticism
Overseer or bishop
Lois
Eunice
The First Epistle of
   Clement
Colossae
Apphia
Onesimus
Tychichus

In the final four Pauline Epistles in the New Testament, Paul addresses individuals rather than congregations, with specific, personal letters. These letters share some common structural features with the previous letters and with each other; however, they also show some characteristic features that are unique to each letter. In this chapter, we will examine each letter to study the contributions it makes to the New Testament and the Christian faith.

The two letters to Timothy and the letter to Titus are often grouped together under the designation **Pastoral Epistles.**[1] These letters include Paul's pastoral concerns for Timothy and Titus; they also address issues related to congregational life within the churches where these men were serving as leaders. However, that designation should not obscure the reality that each letter has its own context and setting, which are important considerations for the interpretation of these letters. The shortest Pauline letter, the Epistle to Philemon, which belongs to the prison Epistles, will be examined last even though it may well have been written prior to the Pastoral Epistles.

Context

We encounter several critical issues when we try to determine the time and historical setting of each of the Pastoral Epistles. All three are internally attributed to Paul as the sender. However, the historical setting reflected in these letters is difficult to fit into all of the details that we know about Paul's life and ministry as recorded in Acts and corroborated in Paul's other letters. Many scholars in the last two centuries have argued that the language and style of these letters is different from the other Pauline Epistles and that the opponents addressed within the letters seem to match up with the kind of opposition that the church experienced in the second century rather than the middle of the first century. There is also an apparent established hierarchy of leadership understood within the letters that seems to reflect later development within the churches. These issues have led many scholars to conclude that the Pastoral Epistles belong to a period decades later than Paul's lifetime, and that the writer(s) of these letters attributed the authorship to Paul.[2]

Simply stated, then, the time and actual historical setting hinges upon whether these Epistles were actually authored by Paul during his lifetime or were written later by some other Christian writers who have incorporated Paul's thought as well as interpretations of his thought to address issues that emerged in the Church after his death. Scholars who prefer to see the Pastoral letters as the work of Paul provide a reasonable explanation of the different situations and setting reflected in these letters. They argue for the possibility that these letters reflect Paul's changed perspective that would be consistent with a later Roman imprisonment of the apostle near the end of his life in the mid-60s.

The traditional reconstruction of events would suggest that after Paul's voyage from Caesarea (58-59), he went to Rome where he spent two years under house arrest facing charges placed against him by Jewish leaders in Jerusalem (59-61). The final chapters of Acts indicate that Paul's case appeared headed for favorable resolution and his release. After his release from house arrest, it is possible that he may have completed his goal of traveling to Spain (61-62; see Romans 15:24,

28). Later he may have returned to areas where he had previously established churches. It is possible that he left Titus in **Crete** (Titus 1:5) and Timothy at **Ephesus** (1 Timothy 1:3) as overseers of the work at these places. From Ephesus he may have continued his journey on to Macedonia. On that journey, he left his cloak, books, and parchments with Carpus at Troas (2 Timothy 4:13). He spent the winter of 63-64 in Nicopolis on the western part of Macedonia (Titus 3:12). Some scholars speculate that Paul wrote Titus and 1 Timothy during his travels in the Macedonian region, possibly from **Nicopolis.** Due to the turn of events in Rome and Nero's blaming of Christians for the fire that had destroyed much of the city, Rome became a very hostile environment for all Christians. At some point in Paul's travels, he was arrested again (65-66), this time as a Christian under indictment for treason, and returned to Rome where he was imprisoned for the final time. This reconstruction of the final days of Paul would thus place him back at Rome, from where he composed 2 Timothy, shortly before his martyrdom during the reign of Nero.

Apart from the historical issues, arguments about language and style in letters as brief as the Pastoral Epistles can cut both ways; there are as many or more similarities in the language of all the Pauline Epistles with the Pastorals as there are differences. As for structural differences, Paul utilizes a wide variety of styles within the earlier Epistles as well as in these later ones. And as a careful examination of each letter will demonstrate, the hierarchy and church order discussed within the Pas-

Remains of the ancient city of Ephesus.

torals does not require decades or centuries to develop, nor do the opponents radically differ from those Paul deals with in Galatia, Corinth, or Thessalonica.

What is more important than actual time of writing is the life setting of the Pastoral Epistles. These letters are addressed to younger men charged with the responsibility of setting in order the Christian church in and around Ephesus (Timothy) and Crete (Titus). They are given instruction concerning their own work and character as ministers, and guidelines for developing a Christian community that truly reflects the gospel of Christ.

As the era of the first generation of leadership in the Christian period moved to a close in the mid-60s, those who became followers of Jesus faced many challenges. People that believed Jesus was the Messiah were increasingly forced to separate from their Jewish roots and go in a distinctly different direction in their worship places, patterns, and practices, even though they still shared a common heritage and Scriptures with the Jews. This created opposition and tension within the church wherever there was a strong local Jewish presence.

Viewed with suspicion and contempt by Romans throughout the empire, Christians were often considered to be a menace to Greco-Roman customs. Christians became suspect in the Roman world because they refused to acknowledge the Roman pantheon of gods or participate in the imperial cult. Since many Christians also took Jesus' teaching on pacifism literally and refused to serve in the Roman army or even fight against those opposed to Rome, they were not considered good subjects or citizens. As a result, they suffered much persecution for their beliefs, at times even to the point of beatings, imprisonment, and death, especially after Nero turned against them.

These persecutions from both religious and civil leaders were especially hard for Christians to endure and understand because many of the early leaders indicated that Christ would soon return to relieve the pain and suffering of the Church. Compounding the problem was the imprisonment and death of many of the first generation of leaders. The persecution only got worse for the Christians. Furthermore, with the rise of new leaders, there was also an increase in false doctrines promoted by false leaders who distorted the truth of the gospel. These false leaders and their false teachings caused confusion and division within some local churches. Paul wrote the Pastoral Epistles (1 and 2 Timothy and Titus) to address these issues; his audience is the leaders of the Christian churches. The instruc-

tion he gives in these letters complements many things that he had communicated to the Christian community in person or through his letters.

Paul addresses the leaders because they were the ones who were faced with the challenge of confronting false doctrines and false teachers. The apostle displays his pastoral responsibility to these leaders whom he had appointed as overseers of the Christian communities. We may with some confidence attribute the differences between these letters and other Pauline letters to the fact that in these letters Paul is communicating as a "pastor in charge of pastors" of the Christian churches with encouragement, exhortation, and challenge.

In the Pastoral Epistles, Paul gives encouragement to those who are striving to remain faithful to his teaching. He also gives exhortation to his pastors to combat false teaching with sound doctrine. Finally, he challenges them to continue living in right relationships one with another in the Christian community. The Pauline gospel of encouragement, comfort, and hope is prominent in the Pastoral Epistles, where it is connected with instructions, admonitions, and reminders to young leaders to remain true to the faith despite opposition from many sources.

In terms of standard letter structure, it is clear that the thanksgiving section, so pivotal in several of the previous Pauline Epistles, is of lesser significance in the Pastoral Epistles, disappearing completely from 1 Timothy and Titus. In both of these letters, as in the case of Galatians, Paul goes right to the problem that confronts the church. Absence of thanksgiving thus reflects the severity of the crisis that prompted Paul to respond with such urgency in these letters. Also it is important to note that the body section is rather brief in each of the Pastoral Epistles. The paraenesis section, consisting of exhortations and admonitions, has been significantly expanded to include a great deal of material that would typically have been covered in the body section in other Pauline letters. This possibly reflects a serious need that existed in these churches for strong exhortations and instructions. In these letters, Paul addresses matters that concern him the most in the stronger mode of imperatives, rather than the more typical mode of indicatives. These issues thus make clear that in these letters we have a style of letter writing different from the typical style found in the rest of the Pauline letters.

1 Timothy

First Timothy contains elements of a personal paraenetic letter. Paul is the model to be followed, and Timothy is to be a similar model to the church. Paul gives instructions concerning Timothy's actions and sets them as opposite of the actions of those who are the opponents of Paul. These instructions give this Epistle its distinctive character. And while this letter is addressed to Timothy, it is written for public reading to benefit the whole church. This would provide support for Timothy as Paul's representative as well as establish a standard by which his ministry and effectiveness could be evaluated.

Content

First Timothy could be outlined as follows:

As the letter opens, the introduction is followed immediately with a reminder of Paul's admonition to Timothy when he asked him to remain at Ephesus. Timothy's charge was to instruct the false teachers to discontinue their teaching of strange doctrines (1:3-4, 6-7). These strange doctrines included "myths and endless genealogies" (v. 4), which may be a reference to elements of **Jewish Gnosticism.**[3] Paul contrasts such false teaching with sound doctrine that is based on proper understanding of the Law, which reveals all that is immoral and unjust (vv. 8-11). The goal of sound doctrine is to elicit love that flows from a pure heart, a good conscience, and a sincere faith (v. 5). This instruction is followed by personal testimony of Paul in which he describes himself as a former persecutor of Christ, who nonetheless is the recipient of mercy and grace from God. He considers himself as the foremost of sinners in whom Christ has manifested His patience to illustrate the truth that He came into the world to save sinners (vv. 12-17). Chapter 1 ends with a strong charge to Timothy to keep the faith with a good conscience and to fight the good fight against those who oppose the Pauline gospel (vv. 18-20).

Chapter 2 begins with instructions to pray, intercede, and give thanks for all who are in authority in recognition that God is the ultimate Source of all authority. God's plan is the salvation of all humanity and their knowledge of the truth of the gospel. Paul con-

T Women and Ministry in Paul's Letters

Some Christians have taken 1 Timothy 2:11-15 along with 1 Corinthians 14:34-35 as the biblical basis for their opposition to the preaching, teaching, and leadership position of women in the church. First Timothy 2:11-15 calls for women to be silent and have no authority over men. What makes the text difficult is the reason for this prohibition given in verses 13-14. These verses suggest that Adam was formed first and that the culpability of sin in the Garden belongs only to Eve and not to both Adam and Eve. Verse 15 then states that childbearing is a necessary means for a woman to experience salvation. First Corinthians 14:34-35 is also a prohibition against women speaking in churches.

How do we understand these texts? If we take these texts at face value without looking at the context, culture, Paul's overall theological perspectives on equality and freedom of all Christians, mutuality of genders, and his endorsement of women who were his trusted coworkers, then we might be tempted to agree with those who deny women any place of ministry in the Christian Church. We cannot support this perspective without violating all the rules of biblical interpretation.

In dealing with these difficult passages, one must look at the overall evidence in Scripture. Even in the Old Testament, God has called women to leadership positions (examples: Miriam, Deborah the Judge, Huldah the prophetess, etc.). Joel the prophet anticipated the outpouring of God's Spirit on all people and both "sons and daughters" becoming the vehicle through which God would speak His words (Joel 2:28). Women played a significant role in the life of Jesus and in the history of the Early Church. In Paul's letters, Paul mentions three women as leaders of house churches (see Chloe in 1 Corinthians 1:11; Nympha in Colossians 4:15; Apphia in Philemon 2). He also mentions Mary, Tryphena, Tryphosa, and Persis (Romans 16:6, 12) as those who worked very hard for the gospel. Priscilla and her husband, Aquila, were trusted coworkers of Paul (1 Corinthians 16:19; Romans 16:3-4). In Philippians 4:2-3, Euodia and Syntyche are grouped with Clement and the rest of Paul's fellow workers. Phoebe was a key leader in the church in Cenchrea and most likely the one who carried Paul's letter to Rome (Romans 16:1-2). Paul's statement in 1 Corinthians 11:5 suggests that prophecy and praying were activities women carried out in the Corinthian church. And most importantly, Paul emphatically claimed and taught the freedom of all believers in Christ. Paul's statement, "There is no longer Jew or Greek, there is no longer slave or free, there is no longer male and female; for all of you are one in Christ Jesus" (Galatians 3:28), should be our primary hermeneutical guideline with which we understand his perspective on women in ministry.

cludes this instruction with the affirmation of Jesus as the only Mediator between God and humanity, who gave His life as a ransom to save all humanity (vv. 1-7). Verses 9-15 reflect a domestic code for women.[4] Interpretation of verses 11-15 is difficult and there is no consensus among scholars. Some who hold the Pauline authorship of the Pastorals think that these verses are a later insertion to the letter.

Chapter 3 explicitly details appropriate conduct for those who are leaders in the church. Verses 1-7 describe the characteristics of one who would be an **overseer or bishop.** Such persons must be above reproach, monogamous, moderate in all things, worthy of respect, graciously hospitable, gifted teachers, even-tempered, gentle, not quarrelsome, and free from the love of money. They should be exemplary in their management of their household, mature Christians able to resist temptation, with a good reputation inside and outside the church family. Verses 8-13 set forth the charge for those who would be deacons or ministers. These persons must not be greedy but rather must be those who speak the truth plainly and clearly, who are moderate in all things, above reproach in faith and conscience, dignified, mature and well tested in service, monogamous, exemplary in their management of the home and family matters, faithful in all things entrusted to them. Verses 14-15 contain another statement of the goal of this letter; that is, to give instructions concerning one's conduct in the community of faith. Chapter 3 ends with a Christological hymn that affirms the content of the Christian faith (v. 16).

Ephesian ruins, Celsus library built in A.D. 135.

A strong warning is provided in chapter 4 against those who heed deceitful spirits or hold to "demonic doctrines" that pervert God's good creation by legalistically denying His gracious gifts (4:1-5). Here Paul connects the false teaching and other problems in the church with the work of Satan. Verse 3 may be a reference to Gnostic teachings, which promoted abstinence from marriage and certain foods. Verses 6-16 consist of encouraging words to meet the challenge of the opponents by being a true example of sound doctrine and godliness. Discipline is highly commended and recommended for the young leader so that he might persevere in word, thought, and deed as an exemplary model for the entire congregation.

Chapter 5 contains a good deal of practical advice on dealing with church matters with wisdom. Christian leaders should treat older and younger members, men and women alike, with respect and purity of heart. Verses 3-16 give detailed instructions concerning the treatment and conduct of widows. The church needs to provide communal support to those widows who are older and without anyone else to help them. Younger widows should marry and continue their family life. The church should regard in high esteem and respect the elders who are involved in preaching and teaching (vv. 17-20). Paul gives Timothy a personal charge to carefully keep these instructions in purity and upright conduct, avoiding sin of every kind (vv. 21-25).

Chapter 6 begins with instructions for the conduct of Christian slaves toward their masters (vv. 1-2). This is followed by final instructions to teach and defend the Christian faith against false and conceited teachers who associate

their godliness with material gain (vv. 3-5). Paul calls for godliness and contentment in life and warns against the danger of materialism in verses 6-10. The battle for the faith is the focus of verses 11-16, followed by instructions for the wealthy in verses 17-20 and the conclusion in verses 20-21. The final challenge to Timothy is to refrain from materialism and love of money and instead pursue the righteous life that is consistent with the true faith, and guard the instructions that have been given to him (vv. 6-21).

2 Timothy

The content of 2 Timothy may be outlined as follows:

Introduction, greetings, and thanksgiving   1:1-5
Exhortation to Timothy
                                   1:6-14
Onesiphorus's ministry to Paul   1:15-18
More instructions to Timothy
                                   2:1-13
Instructions on how to deal with false teachers
                                   2:14-26
Warning about apostasy
                                   3:1-9
Call to follow the pattern of life shown by Paul   3:10-17
Paul's final charge and testimony   4:1-8
Final instructions and greetings   4:9-22

Second Timothy echoes many of the same concerns that are found in 1 Timothy. The tone and setting are different, but the structure of these two letters is very similar. First Timothy reflects Paul's freedom and mobility in carrying on his work in areas around the Aegean Sea. Second Timothy reflects the grim reality

"I have fought the good fight, I have finished the race, I have kept the faith" (2 Timothy 4:7, NIV).

of a Roman imprisonment that does not seem to bode well for Paul's future. Second Timothy bears the structure of a personal paraenetic letter. Paul presents himself as a father to Timothy, evoking in his memory the model that he can and should imitate. He contrasts his behavior and by extension Timothy's behavior with that of the opponents and warns Timothy repeatedly to avoid their conduct and teaching. The theme of remembering, retaining, and calling back to mind (reminded) dominates the opening and middle sections of 2 Timothy (1:3, 4, 5, 6; 1:13-14; 2:1, 8, 14), and this connects well with the theme of 1 Timothy. Timothy is charged to remember, hold on to firmly, guard the faith, and never compromise with those who are opponents of the true faith.

Second Timothy begins with an address, salutation, and thanksgiving (1:1-5). In his thanksgiving, Paul recalls Timothy's faith heritage, faith that was evident in the life of his grandmother **Lois** and his mother **Eunice**. He reminds Timothy that he must continue to keep alive that gift of faith that is in him through the help of the Spirit that was bestowed upon him by Paul through the Christian tradition of ordination (vv. 6-7). In verses 8-14, he challenges Timothy not to be ashamed of the gospel but to embrace suffering that awaits all who have responded to the "holy calling" (v. 9) that comes from God to preach the gospel. Paul reiterates his conviction that God has called him to be "a herald and an apostle and a teacher" (v. 11) of the gospel and that his suffering is for the sake of the gospel. Paul is not ashamed of

Clement on the Order of Ministers

The apostles have preached the gospel to us from the Lord Jesus Christ; Jesus Christ [has done so] from God. Christ therefore was sent forth by God, and the apostles by Christ. Both these appointments, then, were made in an orderly way, according to the will of God. Having therefore received their orders, and being fully assured by the resurrection of our Lord Jesus Christ, and established in the word of God, with full assurance of the Holy Ghost, they went forth proclaiming that the kingdom of God was at hand. And thus preaching through countries and cities, they appointed the first-fruits [of their labours], having first proved them by the Spirit, to be bishops and deacons of those who should afterwards believe. Nor was this any new thing, since indeed many ages before it was written concerning bishops and deacons. For thus saith the Scripture in a certain place, "I will appoint their bishops in righteousness, and their deacons in faith" (**The First Epistle of Clement** to the Corinthians, chapter 42, ca. A.D. 96).[5]

the gospel of Jesus Christ, and he is certain that the God in whom he put his trust will keep him faithful to that gospel. He exhorts Timothy to "hold to the standard of sound teaching" (v. 13) and with the help of the Holy Spirit guard the gospel that has been entrusted to him.

Chapter 2 begins with instruction to Timothy to pass along to faithful people what he has received from Paul, so that they may in turn teach others what they have learned from Timothy. Though teachers do not comprise an order of ministry established in the Early Church, we find here the ministry of teaching as one of the key functions of Christian leaders. Using the metaphors of a faithful soldier, a dedicated athlete, and a hardworking farmer, Paul challenges Timothy to remain faithful to the gospel despite suffering, persecution, or hardship (vv. 3-13). Verses 14-19 contain numerous admonitions to avoid vain and empty discussions and debates that deny the reality of the essential gospel that has been established previously by Paul. The challenge is to be a loyal servant of Christ, honorable, dependable, and faithful in accurately handling the word of truth in order to correct and reprove those in error, even while living a life useful to the Master in every aspect. The rest of chapter 2 (vv. 20-26) is again an exhortation to avoid passion and controversy and to be patient and gentle with others. This section also includes a reminder that all who "cleanse themselves" will become "special utensils, dedicated and useful to the owner of the house, ready for every good work" (vv. 20-21).

The third chapter vividly describes the challenges that will come from evil persons who are bent on undermining the gospel that had been preached. Although these false teachers will succeed in leading some away from the true faith, such difficult realities will not negate the effect of the gospel so long as those who are faithful to the truth will stand firm and remain loyal to the faith they have received. Verse 10 through 4:8 is an exhortation to follow Paul's example in teaching and preaching the Word, with particular emphasis on sound teaching (3:10, 16; 4:2-3) and faithful preaching of the Word (3:15-16; 4:2; cf. 2:15). The challenge is to be ready and well prepared to proclaim and explain the true faith in the midst of difficult times. The final instructions to Timothy run from 4:9 to 4:18 and include a warning against those who opposed Paul's teaching (4:15; literally, it says they opposed his "words"). The letter closes with personal greetings to many of their mutual friends and a gracious benediction in 4:19-22.

Titus

Titus, the recipient of this letter, is known to us as a trusted companion of Paul, whom the apostle addresses as "my loyal child in the faith" (1:4). Some have attempted to identify him with Titius Justus mentioned in Acts 18:7. He was a Gentile, and most of our knowledge of this individual comes from Galatians and 2 Corinthians. Titus accompanied Paul when the latter went to Jerusalem after his conversion (Galatians 2:1-10). Though Judaizers insisted that Titus the Gentile Christian be circumcised, neither Paul nor the Jerusalem leadership yielded to their demand. According to 2 Corinthians, Paul sent Titus twice to bring about a peaceful resolution to the problems at Corinth (2 Corinthians 7:6-7, 13-14; 8:6, 16-17). We do not have any clear indication in the Book of Acts or at any other place except in Titus 1:5 that Paul and Titus made a journey to Crete. Scholars speculate that this journey may have taken place during the final phase of Paul's third missionary journey or after his release from Paul's first Roman imprisonment recorded in Acts 28. Second Timothy 4:10 indicates that Titus traveled to Dalmatia, in the southern part of Illyricum, on the eastern side of the Adriatic Sea.

The Epistle to Titus has many similarities to the letters addressed to Timothy and seems closest in historical context and structure to 1 Timothy, even though the church in Crete appears to be at a stage of development significantly different from the church in Ephesus at this time. Titus is commanded to model good deeds for the community rather than simply modeling or imitating Paul's example within the church. Titus is told to appoint leaders in the various cities; 1 Timothy presupposes leadership already in place, suggesting that Titus is dealing with a much more rudimentary Christian community than that which had been established in Ephesus. The opponents in Crete seem to have much stronger Jewish roots and elements, similar to the opponents Paul addressed in Galatians, and they appear to be making significant inroads into the primitive Christian community in Crete.

Content

Titus may be outlined as follows:

The Epistle to Titus begins with a long theological introduction of the sender in 1:1-3 as part of the opening in verses 1-4. The letter lacks the thanksgiving section typical to most Pauline Epistles. The introductory greeting section is followed by a discussion of the qualifications of church leaders. Paul left Titus at Crete primarily to "put in order what remained to be done" and to "appoint elders in every town" (v. 5). These leaders were to be above reproach, monogamous, good managers of their households and families, moderate in lifestyle, and even-tempered. They were to be models of discipline that would be worthy of discipleship and were expected to hold fast the faithful word according to the teaching and sound doctrine that Paul had established among them previously. Their responsibility included exhortation and encouragement of fellow believers as well as repudiation of those who contradict the message of the gospel. In verses 10-16, Paul instructs Titus to silence and rebuke the false teachers who deceive and disrupt the community of faith by teaching falsehood for the purpose of personal gain.

Chapter 2 spells out in detail what constitutes acceptable behavior for all age-groups within the Body. Characteristics and qualities of Christian life include patience, prudence, faith, love, self-control, submission to authority, respect for others, sound speech, and similar virtues. Paul concludes this chapter with a bold proclamation of the universality of salvation—God's grace at work in all humanity that leads us to reject the world-centered life and embrace a godly life (vv. 11-14). Christ is not only the Redeemer of the Church but also the One who sanctifies her to do good work for Him.

In the final chapter, there is additional exhortation to be submissive and obedient to those who rule and govern. All people, even those outside the community of faith, are to be treated with consideration and respect. Paul emphasizes that salvation is based solely upon the grace and mercy of God made known in Jesus Christ. On the basis of this, he challenges God's people to be engaged in good deeds and live a productive, righteous lifestyle. General exhortations in verses 1-7 give way to specific exhortations concerning heretics in verses 8-11, followed by a brief conclusion in verses 12-15.

Philemon

The last letter placed in the collection of Pauline letters in the New Testament is often referred to as a personal letter of Paul to a Christian named Philemon. Philemon is believed to have been an influential and wealthy person at **Colossae.** It is likely that he became a Christian through the ministry of Paul (see v. 19). However, the addressees include others as well, including **Apphia,** Archippus, and the church that met in Philemon's house (v. 2). Apphia is found nowhere else in the New Testament; Paul refers to her as "our sister." Some have assumed that she was the wife of either Philemon or Archippus. Evidently she was an influential Christian woman in the area of Colossae. Paul calls Archippus "our fellow soldier." He was most likely involved in some ministry at Colossae. Paul concludes his let-

ter to the Colossians with a charge to the church: "And say to Archippus, 'See that you complete the task that you have received in the Lord'" (Colossians 4:17). Though scholars have attempted to establish the identity of Apphia and Archippus, they remain to us as unknown individuals, most likely close friends and coworkers of Paul.

This letter is also commonly grouped together with Colossians since **Onesimus,** a key character in Philippians, is said to have returned to Colossae with **Tychichus,** the courier of Paul's letter to the church at Colossae (Colossians 4:7-9). Both letters also contain the names of Epaphras, Mark, Aristarchus, Demas, and Luke, Paul's fellow workers who are included in the final greeting section (Colossians 4:10-14; Philemon 23-24). Evidence seems to support Colossae as the location of Philemon and the house church mentioned in 1:2. It is also likely that both Colossians and Philemon were written from the same place and at the same time. We place Philemon among Paul's other prison Epistles, written most likely from Rome between A.D. 59 and 62. There is no reason to doubt the authenticity of this letter.

Context

Onesimus, once a slave owned by Philemon, ran away from him and left Colossae. Why he left Philemon is not clear. The suggestion that he ran away after a theft is not clear, though some see an implied reference to it in verse 18. The circumstance of Onesimus's meeting with Paul during his imprisonment is also not clear. It is possible that Onesimus may already have been acquainted with Paul through an association with him at Philemon's house. At any rate, Onesimus, the runaway slave, became a Christian through his contact with Paul, and the two established a very close personal relationship with each other (vv. 10-16). Paul describes this as a father-son relationship. Paul, however, recognized that his new convert was still a slave under the ownership of Philemon. Though he would have preferred to keep his new convert with him for his own service, the apostle decided to send him back to Philemon, perhaps because of the latter's legal claim over his runaway slave. He wrote the letter to urge Philemon to take Onesimus back and treat him as a "beloved brother" (v. 16). Onesimus himself would have been the bearer of this letter.

Content

This brief Epistle has the following outline:

Greeting   vv. 1-3
Thanksgiving for Philemon's
    love and faith   vv. 4-7
Appeal on behalf of Ones-
    imus   vv. 8-21
Final greetings and benedic-
    tion   vv. 22-25

Paul begins this letter with a prayer of thanksgiving for Philemon's love for "all the saints" (v. 5)—those who have membership in the community of faith. He is thankful also for this Christian's faith in Christ. Apparently, Paul had heard of these qualities of Philemon through other Christians (v. 5). These qualities are at work in the life of Philemon and have been instrumental in strengthening and encouraging others, including Paul.

It is clear that Paul makes his appeal on behalf of Onesimus on

Christianity and Social and Legal Customs

Paul worked within the context of the social and legal customs of his day. He would have preferred to keep Onesimus for his service, but he returned him to his master. For Paul, it would be a violation of Philemon's rights to keep Onesimus for his service during his imprisonment. He sees this opportunity, however, to make clear the point that the slave who is coming back to his master should be treated with forgiveness and Christian love. Both the master and the slave have one Lord, and they share the same faith. The master should therefore treat the slave as a brother who is useful not only to him but also to the Lord. Both are recipients of the same divine love (agape), and that love must be evident in human relations within the church. Paul thus sets forth in this letter a principle for conduct within the life of the church. He takes a social issue (slavery) and places it in the context of the life of the church and instructs both the master and the slave to deal with this issue on the basis of the transforming power of divine love. Love thus liberates the slave from bondage. The master is no longer an oppressive power but a brother in Christ. It is this liberating power of love at work in the church that gives him the theological legitimacy to speak the words "there is no longer slave or free . . . all of you are one in Christ Jesus" (Galatians 3:28). It is this gospel that challenges us to be agents of change in the world, which continues to oppress and exploit the powerless in the society.

the basis of these qualities that he finds in Philemon. Paul appeals to Philemon to let his faith and love work in his relationship with Onesimus, his runaway slave. It is important to note that he is not making this appeal on the basis of his apostolic authority (vv. 8-9). Though he has his rights as an apostle to direct a Christian follower to obey his apostolic command, Paul demonstrates love as the principle of his relations with Philemon and leaves the decision to his free choice.

Paul concludes the letter with an anticipation of a visit to Philemon's house. The letter ends with greetings from a number of co-workers and with a typical benediction (vv. 22-25).

Summary Statements

- The focus of the Pastoral letters is on the responsibility of pastoral leaders and their own conduct and character as ministers of the gospel of Christ.
- Pastoral letters reflect the context of false doctrines and false teachers in the Early Church.
- Sound doctrine is a key emphasis in the Pastoral letters.
- Overseers or bishops of the church should maintain exemplary character and thus be models of piety and godliness in the community to their congregation.
- Even in the final hour of his life, Paul was not ashamed of the gospel of Jesus Christ.
- In the letter to Titus, Paul proclaims the universality of the grace of God.
- Philemon calls for Christian love as the basis of all social relationships.

Questions for Reflection

1. What criteria would you use to distinguish between sound doctrine and false teaching?
2. Why is it necessary for a believer to be firmly grounded in the sound doctrines of the Bible?
3. In what ways should the Church be involved in bringing about social change in the culture in which we live today?

Resources for Further Study

Barrett, C. K. *The Pastoral Epistles*. Oxford: Clarendon Press, 1963.
Hanson, A. T. *The Pastoral Epistles: The New Century Bible Commentary*. Grand Rapids: Eerdmans, 1982.
Martin, Ralph P. *Colossians and Philemon: New Century Bible Commentary*. Grand Rapids: Eerdmans, 1981.

UNIT V

TRIALS AND TRIUMPHS OF THE NEW COVENANT COMMUNITY

Your study of this unit will help you to:

- Recognize the difficulties and tensions that developed within the early Christian community.
- Describe the steps taken by the Church to maintain faith while it encountered opposition and heretical teachings.
- Identify the key theological themes of the General Epistles.
- Discuss the occasion and purpose of the Book of Revelation.

■ The Letter to the Hebrews

■ The Letters of James, Peter, and Jude

■ The Letters of John

■ The Book of Revelation

18 The Letter to the Hebrews

Objectives:

Your study of this chapter should help you to:
- Describe the authorship problem of the letter to the Hebrews.
- Discuss the background of the original audience of the letter to the Hebrews.
- Identify the historical and theological issues relative to the Book of Hebrews.
- Evaluate the significance of the Christological emphasis in Hebrews.

Key Words to Understand

General Epistles
Catholic Epistles
Clement of Rome
Origen
Paul
Platonic thought
Hebrews
Hellenists
Qumran
Melchizedek
Word of exhortation
Homiletic midrash
High priest
Apostasy
Maturity
Perfection
Covenant
Faith
Discipline
Holiness

Questions to consider as you read:

1. What Old Testament symbols does the author use for Christ? How is Christ different from these symbols?

2. What dangers did the original readers of this book face? How does the author address those issues?

3. Why does the author say that there is no forgiveness for the sin of apostasy?

4. Why is the suffering of Christ important for the author?

5. How does the author define faith? What is its importance?

Introduction to General Epistles

Because of its lack of salutation or greeting, Hebrews is sometimes classified with the **General** or **Catholic** (meaning "universal") **Epistles.** However, many scholars place Hebrews in a category by itself. If one places Hebrews with the General Epistles, then there are eight letters in this group of New Testament books. Otherwise, this group has seven books with the Letter of James at the head of the list. Reference to this group as the General Epistles or Catholic Epistles goes back to the days of the Early Church fathers.[1] However, most of these fathers placed Hebrews with the Pauline Epistles.

> These letters are called "general" or "catholic" because they (except for 2 and 3 John) were written to a wider audience than to one particular church or person, like Paul's letter to the Romans, or Philemon. The term "epistle" is an old English word for "letter." "Epistle" did not originally mean a sacred letter, although today this is its usual meaning.

Origen on the Authorship of Hebrews

Eusebius in his *Church History* reports that Origen recognized the difference in style between Paul's Epistles and Hebrews. According to Origen, the language of Hebrews is "not rude like the language of the apostle [Paul]" but "the thoughts are those of the apostle [Paul]." He also thought that the "the diction and phraseology" are those of a student who was able to write those thoughts down "at leisure." He concluded that, although some have suggested that Clement of Rome or Luke wrote or translated Hebrews from the original Hebrew, "who wrote the epistle, in truth, God knows."[2]

The eight General Epistles are Hebrews; James; 1 and 2 Peter; 1, 2, and 3 John; and Jude. There is good reason to place Hebrews with the General Epistles since the author and audience are not stated. It is very likely that these Epistles were formally written for the purpose of being read publicly in the churches. The early Christian writers do not mention most of these Epistles until almost A.D. 200, although **Clement of Rome** seems to draw from the thoughts of Hebrews in a letter to the Corinthian church around A.D. 96.[3]

Authorship

Although early Christian tradition titled this book "The Epistle of Paul the Apostle to the Hebrews," the earliest manuscript of the New Testament that includes Hebrews does not mention Paul as the author. However, it does include the audience designation, "to the Hebrews."[4] The discussion on the authorship of Hebrews is one of the most disputed in the New Testament; the debate has been going on from before the days of **Origen,** a third-century Christian scholar.

The churches in the eastern part of the Roman Empire have usually regarded **Paul** as the author of Hebrews. Although the language does not resemble Paul, its theology, including an incarnate Savior, the preexistence of Christ, Christ as Creator, the importance of faith, and the gifts of the Holy Spirit, does resemble Paul's theology. The western churches, however, doubted that Paul wrote Hebrews and even excluded it from the canon at first.

Eventually Church tradition came to claim Paul as the author.

The book became part of the New Testament canon because of this claim and its theological relationship to the rest of the New Testament. However, since Paul's name is not found in the oldest extant manuscripts, very few modern scholars accept Pauline authorship.

Other suggested names for the author of this letter include the following: Barnabas, companion of Paul; Luke because of the good style of Greek; Clement of Rome; Apollos, an Alexandrian Jew associated with the churches at Corinth and Ephesus; Silvanus, companion of Paul; Philip, apostle and missionary to Samaria; and Priscilla, coworker of Paul and teacher of Apollos. It seems probable that the Epistle was written by someone closely associated with Paul, perhaps a student of Paul, an idea first suggested by Origen.

From the Book of Hebrews itself we can discern some characteristics of the author. The author was:

- thoroughly trained in Jewish Scriptures and tradition. (Note the extensive use of the Old Testament: 1:5-13; 2:6-7, 12-13; 3:7-11, etc.)
- eloquent or gifted in Greek rhetoric. The book is known for its high quality of Greek literary style.
- concerned to teach the gospel accurately, and passionate about proclaiming the gospel (1:3-4; 2:1-4; 3:12-14, etc.).
- capable of debating the Jews on the merits of Christianity over traditional Judaism (2:5-18).
- not an eyewitness of Jesus (2:3).

> ## I Platonic Thought
>
> Plato (427-347 B.C.) introduced a philosophical thinking that emphasized the material elements of the universe as nonreal and shadowy in existence. For Plato, what is real is ideas or concepts, such as what is true, what is beautiful, and what is good. This thought influenced some of the early Christian writers. The letter to the Hebrews seems to show the following correspondences with platonic thought:
>
> 1. The material world is imperfect and changing, a copy or shadow of the real world (7:18-19; 8:5; 9:23; 10:1).
> 2. Humans have access to the divine through the mind and reason (5:12; 13:15-16).
> 3. Education of the soul by giving milk (elementary teaching) to the immature and meat for the soul that seeks maturity or perfection (5:12—6:3).

- a student of **Platonic thought,** which was applied to Scripture by Jewish exegetes (especially Philo) in Alexandria.
- a strong proponent of the superiority of the Christian faith to the tabernacle ritual of Judaism (7:22, 28; 8:6; 9:10-11; 13:9).

F. F. Bruce describes the author of Hebrews as "a second-generation Christian . . . a learned man . . . mighty in the Scriptures." Bruce also thinks the author was a Hellenist who shared the theological perspectives of the Hellenists mentioned in Acts 6—8 and 11:19 ff.[5]

Audience

The earliest manuscripts all have the title "to the Hebrews," which Christian tradition has interpreted as Jewish Christians.

Some scholars claim that "to the Hebrews" in the earliest manuscript is an editorial addition and that the letter could have been written to Christian Gentiles as well as Jewish Christians.

In the Book of Acts, a distinction is made between the **Hebrews** and the **Hellenists.** Both groups are Jewish Christians, but the Hebrews are those who grew up in very devout homes, speaking Hebrew or Aramaic as their mother tongue. The Hellenists were Diaspora Jews who grew up speaking Greek. "To the Hebrews" implies that the readers came from devout Jewish homes.

The text of Hebrews itself reveals some things about these readers:

- They were Jews who believed in angels and were probably influenced by the teachings of Pharisees (1:1; 2:9, 16).
- They were very familiar with the Old Testament. The writer frequently quotes from the Old Testament (1:5-14; 3:7—

4:13; 8:7-13; 10:38).

- They had heard the gospel through eyewitnesses of Jesus' life and ministry (2:3).

Some scholars have suggested that these "Hebrews" were Jewish Christians that had come in contact with the **Qumran** community. The Dead Sea Scrolls from Qumran indicate special interest in a Messiah figure who would be a high priest. This community also had considerable interest in **Melchizedek** as well as the rituals of the Day of Atonement. However, these ideas are not unique to the community at Qumran. There seems to be no clear connection between the audience of Hebrews and the Qumran community.

Historical Setting and Date

So much of the historical setting and context that is important to the interpretation of Epistles are missing in Hebrews. Because we do not know for sure the identity

Model of Herod's Temple, which was standing until its destruction in A.D. 70.

of the author or the audience, it is impossible to date the letter with any certainty. Most scholars prefer a setting anywhere between A.D. 60 and 90. However, some argue for a period as early as A.D. 40 and some for a date later than A.D. 100. Some scholars prefer a date before the destruction of the Jerusalem Temple in A.D. 70. They call attention to the fact that the book contains no reference to the destruction of the Temple and the cessation of sacrifices.

There are several considerations in favor of a period between A.D. 60 and 90 as the possible setting of the writing of Hebrews. This was a period of increasing tension between Judaism and Christianity. Christians also faced severe persecution initiated at first by Nero in A.D. 65, and later by Domitian in A.D. 81-96.

The Jewish revolt that broke out in the Palestine area against Rome in A.D. 66 culminated in the destruction of the city of Jerusalem and the Temple by the army of Titus in A.D. 70. This period would have been a difficult time for the Jewish Christians who were still strongly loyal to their Jewish traditions and customs. For the Jewish Christians, the tension between loyalty to their parental religion and loyalty to the Christian faith continued

Roman Empire A.D. 70.

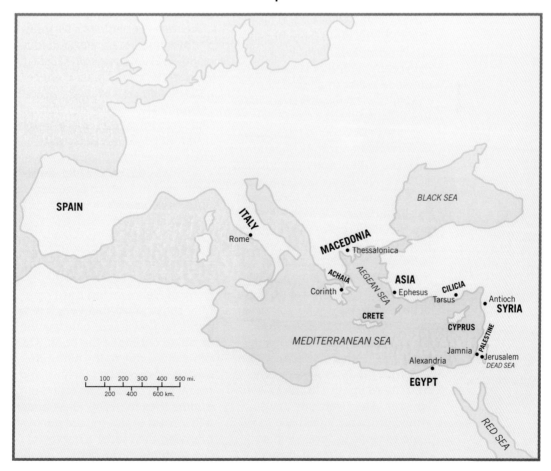

through the next two decades or more. This was intensified during the persecution of the Christians by the Roman Emperor Domitian.

During the second half of the first century A.D., Jewish Christians also encountered hostility from Judaism. These Christians were no longer welcome in the synagogue services. This was one more wedge between the Jews who did not believe in Christ and the Jewish Christians. They were living in a world where they had to choose between their Jewish heritage and their Christian faith. If they renounced Christianity, they could go back to their Jewish families and friends and enjoy protection against Roman persecution. If they renounced Judaism, they were cut off from family, friends, and traditions and faced deadly persecution. Though we are uncertain about the precise date of the setting of Hebrews, its message seems to address the Jewish Christians who lived under the difficult times of A.D. 60-90.

It is also difficult to determine the precise geographic location of both the author and the audience of this book. Some have suggested Alexandria, Egypt, because of its similarities to Jewish literature produced there. Another possibility for the location of the readers is Rome. The only place mentioned in Hebrews is Italy (13:24). The closing greeting reads, "Those from Italy send you greetings." Jerusalem is also a good likelihood since this was the center of the Jewish Christians. Conflict with the Jews would have been more intense in the Palestinian area. The "Hebrew" Jews would probably have tried to remain as close to Jerusalem as possible, even after its destruc-

tion in A.D. 70. Other places suggested for both the author and the readers include Spain, Antioch (Syria), and Corinth, or some other cosmopolitan city in the Roman Empire.

Form and Genre

Traditionally, Hebrews has been considered a letter, but it lacks the usual salutation, initial greetings, and thanksgiving or prayer found in the classical Greco-Roman letters or the letters of Paul. The author of Hebrews presents his writing as a **word of exhortation** (13:22). This phrase is used in Acts 13:15 for the sermon or message that traditionally followed the reading of the Law and the Prophets during the synagogue service.

Hebrews resembles a sermon or speech to which was added a traditional letter closing (13:22-25). It follows the form of alternating doctrinal teaching, practical application, and exhortation. Some recent studies suggest that it "might be a 'homiletic midrash' (a special Israelite sermonic interpretation) on the Old Testament Ps. 110," which also mentions Melchizedek, a key figure in Hebrews.[6]

Content

All scholars agree that the Book of Hebrews has been carefully constructed, but very few agree on how it was constructed or on an outline of the book. The difficulty is due to the alternate mixing of doctrinal teaching and moral application. The following outline tries to group ideas under a few main topics for the purpose of giving the reader a survey of the contents of the book.[7]

Hebrews examines two main roles of Christ: Christ as the divine Son of God and Christ as the heavenly **high priest** who both presides over the sacrifice and is the sacrifice itself. Its main purpose is to show the superiority of Christianity over the ancient traditions of Judaism as an antidote to **apostasy** (falling away from one's former beliefs) in the face of difficult circumstances.

■ God Speaks Through the Son (1:1 — 4:13)

The author begins this sermon with an introduction establishing the authority of Jesus Christ as the perfect One to communicate God's Word to His people. Jesus is the "reflection of God's glory," the "exact imprint" of who God is, the One who sustains "all things by his powerful word," and the One who provided "purification for sins" (1:3). As such, Jesus is not just an angel or messenger of God, He is *the* Son of God and as such *is* God, who "founded the earth" and the heavens (v. 10).

A warning to pay careful attention to Christ's message interrupts this address on the nature of Christ. If the message delivered by angels and prophets was binding—how much more important is the message delivered by Christ and divinely attested by signs and miracles (2:1-4)?

The author states that God placed everything under the Son's control. Jesus was sent in human form to be the pioneer or founder of our salvation, which was accomplished through His suffering and death. It was specifically through Jesus' death that He was able to destroy the devil, the one holding the power of death, and to free those enslaved to the fear of death. Because Jesus became human, was tempted, and suffered, He is able to help those who are tempted and suffer (vv. 5-18).

Jesus is greater than Moses because although Moses was faithful as a servant, Jesus was faithful as a son. As a result of Jesus' relationship to the Father, believers are also children of "his house" and not just servants (3:1-6). The author then warns the readers that the result of their rejection of God's word in the new covenant era will be much greater than the punishment of those who rebelled against Moses in the wilderness (3:7—4:13). Today is the time to respond to God's call, and "the word of God is living and active, sharper than any two-edged sword, piercing until it divides soul from spirit . . . it is able to judge the thoughts and intentions of the heart" (4:12).

Jesus as the Eternal High Priest (4:14—10:31)

This section is the main body of the sermon. The author presents Jesus as the great heavenly High Priest and then instructs the readers to hold firmly to their faith. Faith is the main theme in the second main section of the sermon.

In contrast to the practice of the selection of the high priest in the first century by the Roman government, the author says that no one can be a high priest unless God calls him. The high priest's task is to represent the people before God and to offer gifts and sacrifices for sins, and he must be able to deal gently with the ignorant and wayward (4:14—5:10).

In the setting of the first century these comments were radical critiques of the prevailing religious and political systems. The corruption, arrogance, and pride of these first-century Jewish high priests were a far cry from the original intent of God and very different from the nature of Jesus, the heavenly High Priest.

In the next section, the author encourages the readers to go on to **maturity** and **perfection** (5:11—6:20). They are babies in the faith and need to mature to the point of eating solid food. They should have been teachers by now but have remained immature, unable to distinguish between good and evil. According to the platonic worldview, this situation is abnormal because the soul always seeks for maturity and perfection.

Interpretation of Hebrews 6:4-6 is difficult. However, taking the Greek grammar into consideration, the meaning is clear. It says that those who have once known the salvation of God and fall away cannot be brought back to repentance, *while* they are crucifying the Son of God and *while* they are putting Him to open shame. There is no forgiveness of sins while one is actively participating in the denial of Christ. In the first-century context Jewish Christians had to choose between following Christ and their loyalty to Judaism. To leave the Christian faith and return to Judaism was a denial of Christ and His salvation.

After this stern warning against apostasy, the author then reminds readers of the certainty of God's promise. God is unchanging and He does not lie. This certain hope is the anchor of their souls, and it enables them to enter the inner sanctuary, where Jesus has gone before them as their eternal High Priest, "according to the order of Melchizedek" (6:20).

In chapter 7, the author recounts a Jewish tradition about Melchizedek that he was not born and did not die but remains a priest forever. Jesus is of the

Melchizedek in Jewish and Christian Traditions

Melchizedek is first mentioned in Genesis 14:18-19 where he is identified as the king of "Salem" (Jerusalem) and as "priest of God Most High." He blesses Abram and in turn Abram gives him a tenth of everything. The only other citation of Melchizedek in the canonical Old Testament is Psalm 110:4. Jesus quotes from this psalm (v. 1) to explain to the Pharisees that the Christ (Messiah) was more than just the "Son of David" or an earthly conqueror-king (Matthew 22:44; see parallels in Mark 12:36 and Luke 20:42). While Jesus is not recorded in the Synoptic Gospels as making reference to Psalm 110:4, the writer of Hebrews and probably many other Christians made the connection. The Messiah was to be a king and a "priest forever according to the order of Melchizedek" (Hebrews 6:20).

The author of Hebrews considers the priesthood of Melchizedek to be superior to that of Aaron, because Abram (Abraham) paid a tithe to Melchizedek and as such all of Abram's descendants (including Aaron and Moses) paid homage to this priest-king. Furthermore, in Genesis 14, Melchizedek appears and disappears with nothing said about his birth or his death. The writer to the Hebrews takes this to be an indication of a heavenly priesthood. He also relates to the historical fact that David's kingship in Salem (Jerusalem) and the Old Testament expectation that the Messiah would come from the line of David.

In the century surrounding the life of Jesus, Melchizedek is mentioned by Philo (a Jewish philosopher), Josephus (a Jewish historian), and in rabbinical literature. Most of the emphasis was on the fact that Melchizedek was a priest-king. The literature of the Maccabean period does not mention Melchizedek but does speak of the ruler of Israel as a priest-king. The intertestamental apocalyptic literature expected "a future priestly monarchy."[8] The author of Hebrews seems to connect this Jewish expectation of a future priest-king with the person of Jesus Christ, a descendant of David, who through His death entered heaven as High Priest forever.

same lineage and as such is superior to the earthly and time-bound priesthood of Levi. The author also states that when there is a change of priesthood, there must be a change of law (7:12). This means that the old law is set aside because it was weak and useless, that is, it was not able to bring one to perfection.

Because Jesus lives forever and has a permanent priesthood, He is able to save us completely. Jesus is "holy, blameless, undefiled, separated from sinners, and exalted above the heavens" (v. 26). In contrast to other high priests, he does not "need to offer sacrifices day after day, first for his own sins, and then for those of the people" (v. 27). Furthermore, Jesus sacrificed for our sins "once for all when he offered himself" (v. 27). Following platonic thought, the author says that Jesus' high priesthood is superior to the earthly priesthood because the earthly is only a shadow of the reality in heaven.

The author then claims that if the first **covenant** (promise or agreement) had been faultless, then God would not have offered a new covenant. He quotes Jeremiah 31:31-34 to support the assertion of the necessity of a new covenant. The new covenant has made the old covenant "obso-

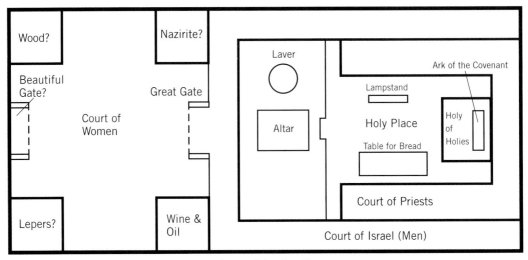

Jerusalem Temple Layout.

Court of the Gentiles

lete," something that will "soon disappear" (8:13).

In 9:1-8 the author describes briefly the regulations for earthly worship and the arrangement of the earthly sanctuary. He shows that the earthly gifts and sacrifices were not able to "perfect the conscience of the worshiper" (v. 9) because they were external regulations.

While the earthly sanctuary and priesthood mediated the old covenant, Jesus has come as High

Hebrews presents Jesus' death as a "once for all" sacrifice.

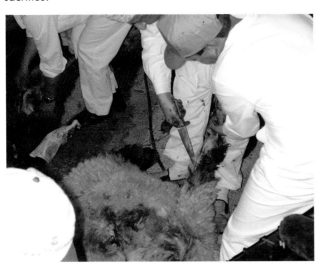

Priest of the great and more perfect heavenly tabernacle. Jesus is the Mediator of the new covenant, and those responding will receive an eternal inheritance, since He died as a ransom to set them free from their sins. The Law requires that for nearly everything there must be shedding of blood for forgiveness of sins. The shedding of earthly blood was necessary for the old earthly covenant. But a better sacrifice was needed for the new heavenly covenant. So, Christ offered himself as a sacrifice to take away the sins of humanity (9:15-25). In chapter 10, the author emphasizes another aspect of Jesus' death. Because the earthly law is only a shadow of the coming reality, it was not able to make worshipers perfect. But the sacrifice of Jesus Christ once for all offers not only forgiveness but also sanctification of the believer (v. 10).

The author then inserts another section of exhortations and warnings (vv. 19-39). Since believers have confidence to enter the holy

Hebrews and the Wrath of God

Hebrews 10:31 states: "It is a dreadful thing to fall into the hands of the living God" (NIV). Discussion or warning about hell and the wrath of God is not a popular topic today. However, in the first century and especially for the Jewish Christians who were very familiar with the Old Testament, the wrath of God was a reality and an important counterpart to the love and grace of God.

Although the love and sacrifice of God through Jesus Christ is enough to encourage one to live a God-pleasing life, the reality of punishment for sin must neither be forgotten nor ignored. If taken seriously, it will encourage one's daily walk and evangelism efforts. The author of Hebrews comes back to this reality of punishment again and again throughout the Epistle.

of holies through the blood of Christ and a great High Priest, they must persevere, encourage one another, maintain hope, and attend their regular meetings. This is followed by another specific warning against apostasy and the fact that a person cannot be saved while continuing to sin. The author sternly warns that because of the tremendous grace the readers have received in the blood of the new covenant, their punishment will be much greater than those of the old covenant, if they reject it.

■ Faith as Insight into an Alternative Reality (10:32– 12:29)

In transitioning to the topic of **faith**, the author of Hebrews reminds his readers of their past. They suffered persecution, stood side by side with those who were persecuted, sympathized with those in prison because of their faith, and joyfully accepted the confiscation of their property.

Chapter 11 begins with a definition of faith followed by several examples of faith from the Old Testament Scriptures. These peo-

ple were insulted, flogged, chained, imprisoned, tortured, stoned, sawed in two, killed by the sword, and destitute, but they never gave up their vision of the real, heavenly world—they never gave up their faith!

Hebrews relates to the suffering and afflictions of the faithful people of the Old Testament.

Faith Defined

Hebrews 11:1 is the only place in the Bible where faith is defined. Other biblical authors describe or illustrate faith, but the author of Hebrews defines it: "Now faith is the assurance of things hoped for, the conviction of things not seen." The author does so within the framework of the platonic system of two parallel worlds—the seen and the unseen, the earthly and the heavenly. Faith gives us access to the heavenly or truly *real* world.

The author defines faith in terms of hope and certainty. What is hoped for will certainly happen. This hope is hope in the things that are eternal—the promise of salvation that God offers to us. This hope is more than wishful thinking; it is a matter of certainty. This hope is founded on a conviction that God is faithful. We are certain of our salvation, because by faith we believe that the One who promises salvation will be faithful to deliver His promises.

Chapter 12 begins with the exhortation to "run with perseverance the race that is set before" the believer (v. 1). The capstone of the argument is a description of what Jesus endured so that the readers will not "grow weary or lose heart" (v. 3). Quoting Proverbs 3:11-12, the author challenges them to consider their suffering as **discipline** from God. Their present trials are an illustration of God's love for them.

Chapter 12 ends with the exhortation to pursue peace with everyone and holiness. The writer presents **holiness** not as an abstract idea but rather as a way of life essential to seeing God (v. 14). This is a call to live Christlike lives, free from bitterness, godlessness, and immorality. Holiness is God's requirement for those who expect to have fellowship with Him under the terms of the new covenant. The readers are not at Mount Sinai where the Israelites were barred from approaching the holy God who ap-

Hebrews' Faith Hall of Fame

Hebrews' Faith Hall of Fame includes the names of ordinary people—some with no reputation, including a prostitute and an illegitimate person. Abel, Enoch, and Noah belong to the pre-Israelite history. Their stories exemplify simple faith, an earnest desire to walk in fellowship with God. Abraham, Isaac, and Jacob are Israel's patriarchal figures. Against all odds, they trusted in the covenant promises of God. Joseph held the firm belief that God was with him even in the most difficult circumstances of life. Moses' parents defied the royal decree, and Moses challenged Egypt's capacity to challenge the authority of Yahweh, Israel's God. The Israelites saw God at work both at the Sea of Reeds and at the walls of Jericho. Rahab the prostitute, though a Canaanite woman, believed in the God of Israel, who brought His people to His land. Gideon, Barak, Samson, Jephthah, Samuel, and David—all fought heroic battles against overpowering enemies. The prophets, though they were ostracized by the nation, refused to surrender to the will of the people.

Here we have a list of people who put tremendous trust in God. Often they were lonely, rejected, and despised by their own people. All of them were confident, however, that God was on their side. This hall of fame contains the names of heroes who "chose to be in God's minority rather than with earth's majority."[9]

The author of Hebrews challenged his readers to run the race with perseverance.

peared on the mountain in the midst of smoke, fire, and thunder. They are at "Mount Zion and to the city of the living God, the heavenly Jerusalem" (12:22). Because the readers are receiving an unshakable kingdom—the *real* heavenly kingdom—they must be thankful and worship God with the reverence and awe that is due such a great and powerful God.

■ Practical Advice and Letter Closing (13:1-25)

Chapter 13 concludes Hebrews with advice on everyday living, intimate and public relationships, money, and church traditions. The readers must not drift into heresy, especially the teachings of the Judaizers who claim that salvation comes through the keeping of Jewish ceremonial laws. The suffering and sacrifice of Jesus makes His people holy, and it is through Jesus that Christians "continually offer a sacrifice of praise to God" (13:15).

After a short request for prayer, the letter ends with a benediction and encouragement to pay attention to the letter they just received. This is followed by an announcement about the release of Timothy, the writer's hope to visit the readers accompanied by Timothy, and final greetings.

Summary Statements

- Most General (Catholic) Epistles were written to a larger audience than one particular church or person. This group of letters traditionally includes James, 1 and 2 Peter, 1, 2, and 3 John, and Jude. Occasionally, Hebrews is placed in this category.
- The authorship of Hebrews is one of the most disputed in the New Testament. Church tradition eventually named Paul as the author, but this is accepted by very few modern scholars.
- The author of Hebrews, a second-generation Christian, was skilled in Greek and philosophy, was well-trained in the Hebrew Scriptures and ritual, and passionate about Christianity.
- The readers of Hebrews were also second-generation Christians, probably Jews in the Pharisaic tradition who knew the Hebrew Scriptures well and may have been influenced by the Qumran community.
- Hebrews is impossible to date with certainty, but many scholars place its writing between A.D. 60 and 90 when there was increasing tension between the Jewish Christians and the Jews, as well as persecution from Rome.
- The Book of Hebrews is a word of exhortation or sermon to which was added a traditional letter closing.
- The main purpose of Hebrews is to show the superiority of Christianity over the ancient traditions of Judaism as an antidote to apostasy.
- Hebrews 11:1 is the only place in the Bible where faith is defined: "Faith is the assurance of things hoped for, the conviction of things not seen."

Questions for Reflection

1. Based on your understanding of Hebrews, discuss some of the challenges that young converts into Christian faith might face in the 21st century.
2. Do you find Hebrews critical of the Old Testament? Why or why not?
3. If faith is "the assurance of things hoped for, the conviction of things not seen," how do we know that we "have faith"?
4. How would the author of Hebrews address those Christians today who want to return to the comforts of relativism or historical certainty for their salvation?

Resources for Further Study

Attridge, Harold W. *The Epistle to the Hebrews*. Philadelphia: Fortress Press, 1989.
Bruce, F. F. *The Epistle to the Hebrews*, rev. ed. Grand Rapids: William B. Eerdmans Publishing Co., 1990.
Hagner, Donald A. *Encountering the Book of Hebrews*. Grand Rapids: Baker Academic, 2002.

19 The Letters of James, Peter, and Jude

bjectives:

Your study of this chapter should help you to:

- Identify the primary suggested authors for the letters of James, Peter, and Jude.
- Describe the nature of the audience to whom these letters were written.
- Evaluate the significance of the Jewish Christian emphasis in these books.
- Discuss historical and theological issues relative to these books.

Key Words to Understand

James
Septuagint
Diaspora
Synagogue
Word of exhortation
Paraenesis
True religion
Silas
Amanuensis
Resident aliens
Testament
False teachers
Day of the Lord
Jude
Apostasy
Heresy
Invective rhetoric

uestions to consider as you read:

1. What are the literary forms of these letters and why are they in the New Testament?

2. What are the Jewish Christian contributions to the theology of the Early Church?

3. What dangers did the original audience of these letters face? How do these letters address those issues?

4. Why is suffering important for the authors?

James, 1 and 2 Peter, and Jude are part of the General Epistles in the New Testament (see chapter 18 for a discussion of the General Epistles).

James

The Book of James, five chapters in length, is full of advice on Christian living. However, the thought world of James is thoroughly Jewish in character. The book reflects the Jewish emphasis on good deeds as an important part of the Christian life. James's emphasis on good deeds seems to contradict Paul's theology of grace and faith. This may be one of the reasons why it was one of the last books to be placed in the New Testament canon.

Because of James's emphasis on good deeds, Martin Luther called this book "an epistle of straw," a book that has no value for the Christian Church. We must recognize the fact that this statement was an overreaction by Luther the Reformer, who insisted that "faith alone" is necessary for one's salvation.

Authorship

The Book of James begins with an identification of the author as **James,** a servant of God and of the Lord Jesus Christ (1:1). This introduction lacks any reference to the author's family background or apostolic position. We assume that the author was a person with significant authority in the Early Church.

The New Testament mentions several people named James: the son of Zebedee (Mark 1:19), the son of Alphaeus (3:18), the brother of Jesus (6:3), the younger (15:40), and the father of Judas (Luke 6:16). The letter of Jude refers to Jude as a brother of James (Jude 1). Of these names, James, "the Lord's brother" (Galatians 1:19), was a prominent authority figure in the early Christian church. The Book of Acts portrays James as a mediator of the Jerusalem Council and as head of the Jerusalem church (15:13-21; 21:18-26). James, the brother of Jesus, seems to be a good candidate for the authorship of this letter.

The text of James indicates that the writer was fluent in Greek and may have used the **Septuagint** (Greek translation of the Hebrew Old Testament). He was also deeply influenced by Jewish wisdom writings, which promote proper moral and ethical conduct.

Many modern scholars think that a Galilean, without much education in Greek, could not have written this book containing excellent Greek. They conclude that whoever wrote this book presents it as James's letter. Such pseudonymous authorship was a practice common in Jewish literature but not common in Christian literature of the first century A.D.

Ralph Martin suggests an attractive idea that a Hellenistic Jewish editor in Antioch reworked James's original text and this would account for the good Greek grammar and style.[1] Though we are uncertain about the precise identity of the author, it is clear that the author (or the editor) of this book understood the significance of religion to be worship of God and a commitment to superior moral conduct.

Audience

James greets the "twelve tribes in the **Diaspora**" (1:1, author's translation). Although Diaspora generally referred to the Jewish population dispersed from their homeland, the term is used here to address Jewish Christians. There are other indicators in the letter that suggest James was addressing Jewish Christians. The phrase "twelve tribes" denotes those of Jewish racial background. The assembly of worshipers in James is **synagogue** (2:2, author's translation), rather than "church" *(ekklēsia)* found elsewhere in the New Testament. Elders lead the community (5:14), a custom of the Jewish community life. The author also utilizes Jewish idioms like "Father of the lights" (1:17), "Lord of Sabaoth" (5:4, author's translation), and places significant emphasis on keeping the Law (2:10; 4:11-12) and belief in one God (2:19).

Historical Setting and Date

According to some traditions, James the brother of Jesus was martyred in A.D. 62. Some scholars place his death in A.D. 69 or 70. This would place the date of this book prior to A.D. 70. It is very likely that the book belongs to a period between A.D. 40 and 62, when James was the head of the church in Jerusalem.

Josephus, the Jewish historian, describes the time right before James's death as "anarchy, which was caused by the fact that Festus had died just at this time in Judea, and that the province was thus without a governor and head."[2] Josephus thus gives us some insight into the social and political conditions of the time.

The letter of James also reflects a change in the social structure of the Christian community described in the early chapters of Acts. Acts 4:32-35 indicates that community life with emphasis on caring for one another was characteristic of the Early Church. But James seems to be addressing a context and a people that failed to maintain the community ideals of the early 30s.

The letter of James is too general and the salutation is too vague for us to conclude with certainty the location of James's original audience. It is possible that they lived in Jerusalem where the author himself lived. It is more probable that they lived in large Roman cities in Syria and Asia Minor.

Form and Genre

James begins with the traditional salutation of a Greco-Roman letter; however, it lacks the typical prayer or thanksgiving that follows the greeting. It has no closing greeting or benediction. Some scholars think that James may have been a **word of exhortation** or sermon prefaced with a greeting.

The book follows a rhetorical style called **paraenesis** or exhortation (encouragement and confrontation on issues of right and wrong). The author does not offer the readers anything new but encourages them to follow what they have been taught and to keep that faith pure. It resembles a compilation of Jewish wisdom literature topics that revolve around a "pure and undefiled" religion (1:27).

Content

James is an exposition of early Jewish Christian piety. It gives practical advice on how to live a life that is pleasing to God in situations that require patience and perseverance. Because of the proverbial nature of James, there is rarely an agreement on an outline of James. The following outline attempts to group the numerous exhortations into 10 sections for the purpose of our study.

James begins his letter with an exhortation on the nature and value of trials in the Christian life. It is in trials ("testing of your faith") that character is developed and brought to maturity. Through trials, we also develop faith, which helps us to overcome our doubt (1:2-8). The author also distinguishes between trials of faith and temptations that originate in our evil desires. Overcoming trials of faith will lead us to receive the "crown of life" (v. 12). On the other hand, yielding to temptation will lead to sin and eternal death (vv. 13-15). Maturity that comes through trials enables a believer to regard every good thing as a gift from God (vv. 16-18).

The author sees no place for anger in the life of a righteous believer and urges his readers to get rid of all wickedness (v. 21). He admonishes them not only to be hearers of the word but also doers of the word (vv. 22-25).

James is the only book in the New Testament that defines religion. The author presents **true religion** as practical—something people should practice by caring for the orphans and widows in their need and by avoiding the immoral influences of the world (v. 27). True religion also involves

True Religion

True religion is a major concern throughout the Bible. Religion is not simply a matter of our faith or religious convictions. Religion that is lacking in duty to others is not true religion. Though there is much emphasis on keeping the Law in the Pentateuch, there we also find strong reminders about loving one's neighbor and one's obligation to care for the needs of the widows, orphans, and sojourners in the community (Leviticus 19:18; Deuteronomy 26:12). Isaiah called his audience to share their bread with the hungry, and offer shelter to the homeless, and clothe the naked (Isaiah 58:6-7). Jesus' concern for the poor is clearly evident in the Gospels. He reminds us that ultimately we will be judged by our obedience or disobedience to the law of love (Matthew 25:31-46). The religion of Jesus compels us to go wherever there is hunger, homelessness, nakedness, and loneliness in our world.

a commitment to treat everyone the same without showing partiality to anyone (2:1-4). God shows no partiality to the rich. Indeed He has chosen the "poor in the world to be rich in faith" (v. 5). Keeping the "royal law" of love is the right way to maintain proper relationship with God and one's neighbor (v. 8).

James reminds his readers that faith without works is "dead" (2:17). One cannot claim to have faith and refuse to pay attention to the physical needs of a brother or a sister. A true mark of maturity is one's ability to control one's tongue. James says that no one can tame the tongue. It takes a change of nature that only God can bring about. When the person is changed, then the behavior changes (3:1-18). True qualities of a changed life are humility, peace, submission, mercy, impartiality, and sincerity.

Divided loyalty is a key theme in chapter 4. The author reminds the readers that as long as they nourish their "friendship with the world" (v. 6), they cannot expect to receive what they ask for from God (vv. 1-6). A "friend of the world" is an "enemy of God" (v. 4, author's translation). The alternative is to totally submit to God in humility and repentance (vv. 7-10). Those who submit to God do not "boast" about tomorrow, for they know that their future is totally in the hands of God (vv. 13-17).

In chapter 5, James launches a typical Jewish prophetic warning against the rich oppressors who oppress the poor and refuse to pay their workers (vv. 1-6). These rich oppressors show no charity to the poor. They are now living in luxury, but their day of misery is coming.

The focus of verses 7-12 is on patience, a quality essential to the Christian life. James cites the prophets and Job as examples of patience and perseverance, and he reminds the readers that God is "compassionate and merciful" (v. 11) to those who are patient in the midst of suffering.

James closes his letter with a series of instructions. Christians should pray when in trouble and request prayer from the elders when sick. The tradition of anointing the sick with oil comes from verse 14. The sick person will not only be healed but, if a sinner, will be forgiven. Prayer by a mature Christian is powerful and effective.

The final words are those of love and reconciliation. The community is to care for the sinner and the one who "wanders from the truth" (v. 19) and gently bring him or her back to God (v. 20).

1 and 2 Peter

The letters of Peter also share James's concern on matters of proper behavior, social discrimination, and the need for patience in trials. But these letters are very different from James in writing style.

Authorship

Both the text and Church tradition cite Peter, also known as Simon Peter and Cephas, an apostle of Jesus Christ, as the author for 1 and 2 Peter.

A member of the original 12 disciples, Peter was often the spokesperson for the group. He was a Jerusalem church leader whose ministry was primarily to Jews. He did travel as a mission-

Christian tradition holds that Peter was crucified upside down.

excellent Greek found in the book and the lack of specific details about Jesus' life point us to someone other than a former Galilean fisherman and an eyewitness of Jesus. However, the author refers to **Silas** as his **amanuensis** or scribe (1 Peter 5:12). This would explain the good Greek. Although there are no specific references to Jesus' ministry, the author makes numerous references to the theological significance of Jesus' suffering and death. There are no convincing reasons to deny the authorship of this book to Peter the apostle.

However, we are not certain about the authorship of 2 Peter. The book makes no mention of an amanuensis. The Greek style of 2 Peter has been described as everything from good Asiatic Greek to cumbersome stilted Greek. A total of 57 words in 2 Peter do not occur anywhere else in the New Testament, and 32 do not occur in the Septuagint.[4] Due to its brevity and lack of citations in Early Church literature, many modern scholars doubt that it was written by Peter the apostle. However, it is entirely possible that 2 Peter was written by Peter himself or with the help of an unnamed amanuensis.

ary to Asia Minor (1 Peter 1:1) and Rome (5:13, "Babylon") and encountered Paul at the church in Antioch, Syria (Galatians 2:11). There is no scriptural reference to Peter's death, but tradition maintains that he was crucified in Rome about the time Paul was beheaded.[3]

Although many modern scholars accept Peter as the author of 1 Peter, there are some who question this view. They think that the

I

Resident Aliens

The term "resident aliens," which is translated "strangers" in the KJV and the NIV, is a specific word that identified them as noncitizens, permanently living in a foreign province. This term and its synonyms are used by Peter to indicate not only geographical dislocation but also political, legal, social, and religious limitations and separation.

Ancient literature indicates that these resident aliens included "slaves, serfs, . . . homeless strangers who lacked citizenship either in their previous homeland or where they currently resided. Although the cities had their share of such *paroikoi* [resident aliens], the far greater number was found among the rural populace of tenant, farmer, slaves and local artisans. . . . who provided the work force and economic basis of the community."[5]

Audience

Peter describes his first Epistle readers as **"resident aliens of the Diaspora in Pontus, Galatia, Cappadocia, Asia and Bithynia"** (1 Peter 1:1, author's translation).

It is very likely that 1 Peter is directed to both Jewish and Gentile Christians. Though Diaspora and resident aliens reflect the Jewish heritage, Peter also seems to be addressing the Gentile Christians (see phrases such as "desires that you formerly had in ignorance" [1:14], "Once you were not a people" [2:10], and "you have already spent enough time in doing what the Gentiles like to do" [4:3], which seem to address a Gentile audience).

Second Peter is written to "those who have received a faith as precious as ours through the righteousness of our God and Savior Jesus Christ" (2 Peter 1:1). This addresses a very broad general audience. However, if 3:1

Remains of an ancient house at Derbe in Asia Minor.

("this is now, beloved, the second letter I am writing to you") refers to 1 Peter, then the audience of both letters would be the same. The salutation indicates that even if Peter first sent the letter to northern Asia Minor, he intended it for the whole church.

Historical Setting and Date

Those who view the apostle Peter as the author regard a period

Circus Maximus in Rome, the large oval track where chariot races took place.

before A.D. 68 as the date of the writing of these two books. Scholars who reject the Petrine authorship of these Epistles prefer late first century and early second century (A.D. 90-150).

The time between 64 and 70 was extremely volatile between Jews and Romans. The Roman Emperor Nero blamed the Christians for the fire that broke out in Rome in A.D. 64. Many Christians and their leaders were arrested and put to death during this period.

Meanwhile Jewish riots broke out in Palestine against the Roman occupation in A.D. 66 with repercussions all over the empire. Since Christianity was still considered a sect of the Jews during this time, both Jewish and Gentile Christians became subject to Roman retaliation. These events would have increased the Christians' anxiety as "resident aliens" in the Roman world. They would have faced the temptation to blend in with society especially in the Roman-controlled coastal areas.

Form and Genre

Peter's letters follow the Greco-Roman letter form with a salutation and greeting at the beginning of the letter. First Peter ends with greetings and a short benediction. Second Peter ends abruptly with no greetings but final exhortations and a very short benediction.

First Peter 5:12 states the purpose: "I have written this short letter to encourage you and to testify that this is the true grace of God." The letter's rhetorical style is paraenesis or exhortation. The author does not present any new teaching but rather encourages his readers to stand in the "true grace of God."

Second Peter is a letter of instruction that resembles the **testament** genre of the Old Testa-

Spread of Christianity in the Roman Empire (see 1 Peter 1:1).

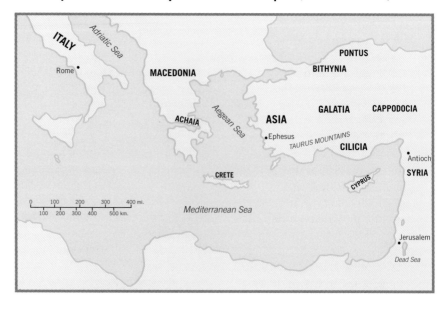

ment. It appears to be Peter's farewell speech before his death. Similar testaments occur in the New Testament (see Paul's words to Timothy in 2 Timothy 4:1-8, and Jesus' farewell discourses in John 14—17).

Content

The following outlines help us understand the literary structure of these two books.

1 Peter
I. Greeting (1:1-2)
II. Thanksgiving (1:3-9)
III. Exhortations on Christian living (1:10—5:11)
   A. The lifestyle of holiness (1:10—2:10)
   B. To resident aliens (2:11-17)
   C. Household relationships (2:18—3:12)
   D. Living and suffering as a Christian (3:13—4:19)
   E. To elders and young people (5:1-11)
IV. Final greetings (5:12-14)

2 Peter
I. Greeting (1:1-2)
II. God's power and the Christian's effort for salvation (1:3-11)
III. Peter's testimony (1:12-21)
IV. Prediction of false teachers and their destruction (2:1-22)
V. Prediction of scoffers (3:1-7)
VI. Prediction of the Day of the Lord (3:8-10)
VII. Living in anticipation of the new heaven and new earth (3:11-17)
VIII. Final benediction (3:18)

Peter writes to give encouragement and hope in the middle of persecution. He begins his letter with a celebration of the Christian hope, an "inheritance" in heaven (1:4). He reminds his readers that their faith is worth more than gold or any earthly gain. They are to keep their eyes on eternal salvation and not on the temporary persecutions (vv. 6-12). Quoting Leviticus 11:44, he charges them to live a holy life because God who has called them is a holy God (vv. 13-16).

In chapter 2, the author reminds the readers that they are a special people being "built into a spiritual house" (v. 5). They are "a chosen race, a royal priesthood, a holy nation, [and] God's own people" (v. 9). The Christian community inherited the same privileges and blessing that God extended to Israel at Mount Sinai

Household Code of 1 Peter

Peter's "household code" (2:13—3:7) contains typical Greco-Roman hierarchical values for submission to authorities, especially submission of slaves to their masters and wives to their husbands. Giving proper respect to authorities within first-century A.D. cultural setting was necessary for the Christians to avoid undue persecution.

The surprising element in light of the contemporary literature is Peter's exhortation to the husbands to be considerate of their wives and treat them with respect, and as "heirs [with them] of the gracious gift of life" (3:7). This emphasis on equality of respect and participation in life radically differed from the commonly accepted values of the Greco-Roman world. Paul also echoes this theme: "Be subject to one another out of reverence for Christ" (Ephesians 5:21). When the Body of Christ submits to one another and allows equal participation in the life of the community, then it can extend the kingdom of God most efficiently and powerfully.

(see Exodus 19:5-6). Therefore they have a responsibility to live as a people of God, a testimony to God's grace and mercy among the pagans around them (1 Peter 2:8-14). He reminds them that being good citizens is a testimony to God. He advises them that following and fitting into the cultural and hierarchical structure of the unbelieving world as much as possible wins unbelievers. Pagans will come to see that the church will not disrupt society, rather benefit society (2:13—3:7).

Peter urges his readers to show "good conduct in Christ" in their everyday life. This lifestyle includes a commitment to harmony with others, love, compassion, and presenting a good testimony of faith. Christ's suffering is a model for Christians to follow (3:8-22). Christians also have an obligation to live "by the will of God" (4:2), a lifestyle that is free from sinful behavior (vv. 1-6). One's good behavior in Christ also includes hospitality and sharing God's grace with others—all for the glory of God (vv. 7-11). The author returns to the theme of suffering in verses 12-19. A Christian's suffering is, in reality, participation in the suffering of Christ, for which one should be thankful.

First Peter closes with final exhortations to elders and young people (5:1-11). Elders must serve as shepherds of God's flock. Their reward waits for them at the Second Coming. Young people should live in submission to their elders. Christians should resist the devil who "like a roaring lion . . . prowls around" (v. 8) looking for its prey. The letter ends with greetings from fellow Christians in Rome and from Mark.

Second Peter encourages Christians to grow in grace. The virtues that promote growth are goodness, knowledge, self-control, perseverance, godliness, brotherly kindness, and love (1:3-11). The author reminds the readers that the stories about Jesus are not "cleverly devised myths" (v. 16) but eyewitness accounts. Believers can have confidence in the Scriptures because those who wrote them were inspired by God ("moved by the Holy Spirit" [v. 21]) (vv. 12-21).

Chapter 2 contains stern warnings about false teachers and their teachings (vv. 1-22). **False teachers** will always be around and will be known by their actions. They are bold and arrogant and do not recognize their ignorance and lack of understanding of spiritual things. Their judgment is certain. He concludes with an exhortation on the **Day of the Lord** and explains why Jesus had not returned (3:1-18). The delay in the Second Coming does not mean that God has broken His promise. Indeed the day will come "like a thief" (v. 10). The delay is nothing but a demonstration of God's patience and His will to save all who repent. The book ends with a challenge to the readers to remain blameless and at peace with God and to be on guard against false teachers.

Jude

Jude is probably the most neglected book of the New Testament. Much of Jude is found in 2 Peter, and the discussions continue over whether Peter used Jude or Jude excerpted part of 2 Peter or whether they both used an earlier source. Whether they borrowed from each other or from a third source, there was "no slavish copying; the borrower shaped what he borrowed to make it fit his purpose."[6]

The main purpose is to encourage Christians to be faithful to the earliest Christian teaching. Jude warns of godless people who have slipped into the church. They serve only themselves and do not have the Spirit. Whereas 2 Peter refers to these people as "false teachers," Jude calls them "ungodly" (v. 4).

Authorship

The writer of **Jude** describes himself as "a servant of Jesus Christ and a brother of James" (v. 1). There are four men named Jude (or Judas) in the New Testament: Judas Iscariot, who betrayed Jesus; Judas, son of James, one of the original 12 disciples (Luke 6:16; Acts 1:13; or Thaddaeus in Matthew 10:3); Judas (Barsabbas) who went to Antioch after the Council of Jerusalem with Paul, Barnabas and Silas (Acts 15:22); and Judas, the brother of Jesus (Matthew 13:55; Mark 6:3).

Of the four, only Judas, the brother of Jesus, had a brother named James who held a prominent place in the Early Church. Jude and James claim only to be a "servant of Jesus Christ" and not brothers of Jesus. Tradition suggests this means that they saw themselves as half-brothers and not worthy to be called brothers of Jesus.

We think the writer was most likely a Jewish Christian based on the references to the history of the Jewish people. The book also draws from *1 Enoch,* a Jewish

False Teachings

The letters of Peter and Jude include serious warnings about heresies and heretical teachers. A heresy is a false teaching or a distorted understanding of truth. Christians of the first and second centuries were especially victims of such teachings promoted by teachers who were influenced by pagan religions or philosophical ideas. The Christian Church has never been exempt from the influence of heresies. This tragedy continues to occur even in our present-day world.

How do we know what teaching is a distortion of biblical truth? Truth about God and His way of salvation is clearly described in the Bible. Therefore, it is important for a Christian to daily meditate on God's Word and seek the daily guidance of the Holy Spirit. When a new teaching is presented to us, we should examine and evaluate it in light of the clear testimony of God's Word. Studying the Scriptures diligently will save us from becoming victims of false teachings today.

apocalyptic writing (v. 14), and from a Jewish legend about Moses and the archangel Michael (v. 9). Many recent scholars believe Jude is a pseudonymous writing.

Audience

Jude is addressed to "those who are called, who are beloved in God the Father and kept safe for Jesus Christ" (v. 1). Although this is a "general" address, the writer is writing a personal letter, referring to his readers as "beloved" or dear friends (v. 3, *agapētoi*). This, coupled with the fact that Jude quotes freely from Jewish apocalyptic literature and makes allusions to the Old Testament, indicates that his friends were Jewish Christians as well.

Historical Setting and Date

There is no reference in the book that guides us to date this letter with any precision. Our major considerations come from the identity of the author. If we regard the author as the brother of Jesus, then the best date would be between A.D. 55 and 80. Those who consider the work to be pseudonymous date the letter between A.D. 100 and 125.

The text of Jude does not give any clues as to where the author was when he wrote the book, nor where the readers resided. Jude may have written from Palestine since tradition places him there between A.D. 60 and 80. There are no real historical events indicated in the book. The author seems to be addressing a situation in which there was **apostasy**—the problem of believers drifting away from the gospel, perverting it, and no longer acting like Christians.

Form and Genre

Brevard Childs notes that Jude is "a theological description of the phenomenon of **heresy** rather than attacking a specific historical form of error."[7] Other scholars find in this book **invective rhetoric** (arguments "characterized by verbal abuse and insults").[8] This characterization may seem harsh, but Jude's description of godless people as those who use the grace of God as a license for immorality and deny Christ also seems to be harsh.

Content

Jude encourages his readers to stay true to the gospel of Christ.

The author refers to those who have turned away from the gospel and as a result are empty and barren spiritually. The following outline shows the development of this theme in this letter.

  I. Greeting (vv. 1-2)
 II. Description of godless people (vv. 3-16)
     A. Godless people in history (vv. 3-7)
     B. Godless people in their congregation (vv. 8-16)
III. Encouragement to continue in faith (vv. 17-23)
 IV. Doxology (vv. 24-25)

Jude's greeting includes the words "mercy," "peace," and "love." The addition of "love" to the greeting sets the harsh condemnation of godless people in proper perspective. He writes that he would rather be writing about the salvation they share but finds it necessary to encourage them to "contend for the faith" (v. 3).

Following the greeting, the author reviews the history of God's deliverance, including the destruction of those who chose to rebel against Him. Jude describes these godless people as arrogant, rebellious, and selfish. Some of them are selfish leaders (shepherds) who grumble, boast about themselves, and flatter others to get what they want. Jude assures his readers that God will destroy these people.

The history Jude recounts comes from Jewish traditions with direct quotes coming from Jewish apocryphal books (vv. 9, 14b-15) and the prophecies of the apostles (v. 18).

Jude urges his readers not to give in but to build each other up and pray in the Holy Spirit. He also challenges them to keep themselves in God's love, be merciful to the doubting, and do every-

Jude and the Book of 1 Enoch

When the actual Greek is consulted for 1 Enoch 1:9 and Jude 14-15, it appears that Jude is quoting 1 Enoch almost word for word. Jude also alludes to 1 Enoch 1:1-9; 5:4; 18:12, 14-16; 27:2; 60:8; and 93:2.[9]

1 Enoch 1:9: "And behold! He cometh with ten thousands of His holy ones to execute judgement upon all, and to destroy all the ungodly: and to convict all flesh of all the works of their ungodliness which they have ungodly committed, and of all the hard things which ungodly sinners have spoken against Him."[10]

Jude 14-15: "Enoch, the seventh from Adam, prophesied about these men: 'See [Greek: Behold], the Lord is coming with thousands upon thousands [Greek: ten thousand] of his holy ones to judge everyone, and to convict all the ungodly of all the ungodly acts they have done in the ungodly way, and of all the harsh words [Greek: hard things] ungodly sinners have spoken against him'" (NIV).

thing they can to convert or reclaim those who are not following the faith.

Jude concludes his letter with a beautiful doxology. The author reminds his readers that no matter how strong the temptation is to turn away from the faith, God is able to keep them from falling and to present them "before his glorious presence without fault and with great joy" (v. 24, NIV).

Jewish apocryphal books like 1 Enoch were found among the Dead Sea Scrolls from these Qumran caves.

Summary Statements

- James, "the brother of the Lord," mediator of the Jerusalem Council and head of the Jerusalem Church is traditionally considered to be the author of the Book of James.
- James, 1 and 2 Peter, and Jude were written primarily to Jewish Christians in the Diaspora.
- The Book of James is a sermon, or exposition, on early Jewish Christian piety, giving practical advice on how to live a life that is pleasing to God.
- James reminds his readers that faith without works is "dead."
- Both the text and Church tradition consider the apostle Peter to have written both 1 and 2 Peter, using an amanuensis for either or both.
- Peter's letters follow the Greco-Roman letter form, with 1 Peter reminding and encouraging readers to stand in the "true grace of God" and 2 Peter resembling a farewell speech before his death.
- Both 2 Peter and Jude address the issue of false teachers who will always be around and can be known by their actions.
- Jude, the brother of James and half-brother of Jesus, is traditionally considered to be the author of the Book of Jude.

Questions for Reflection

1. How does James define true religion? Does it contradict the gospel of Paul? Why or why not?
2. What kinds of suffering does 1 Peter talk about? Which kind(s) should Christians expect and praise God for? Why?
3. According to Jude and 2 Peter, why should hypocrisy (false teachers/godless people) not be tolerated?

Resources for Further Study

Bauckham, Richard J. *Jude, 2 Peter,* in *Word Biblical Commentary.* Waco, Tex.: Word, 1983.

Elliott, John. *A Home for the Homeless: A Sociological Exegesis of 1 Peter; Its Situation and Strategy.* Philadelphia: Fortress Press, 1981.

Martin, Ralph. *James,* in *Word Biblical Commentary,* Vol. 48. Waco, Tex.: Word Books, 1988.

Perkins, Pheme. *First and Second Peter, James and Jude. Interpretation.* Louisville, Ky.: John Knox Press, 1995.

20 The Letters of John

Objectives:

Your study of this chapter should help you to:

- Understand the authorship issues of the letters of John.
- Discuss the background of the original readers of the letters of John.
- Identify the historical and theological issues relative to the letters of John.
- Evaluate the significance of 1 John's emphasis on the humanity of Jesus.

Questions to consider as you read:

1. What seems to be the problem or crisis in the Johannine churches?
2. Why was division in the Christian community a problem for the author of these letters?
3. John talks about two kinds of sin in 1 John. What are they and how are they forgiven?
4. Who are the readers of 2 John, and how do they relate to the issues in 1 John?
5. What seems to be the specific problem in 3 John, and how does it relate to 1 John?

Key Words to Understand

Papias of Hierapolis
Origen
Zebedee
Salome
Boanerges
Chosen lady
Gaius
Praenomen
Ephesus
Antichrist
Pre-Gnosticism
Diotrephes
Artemis
Cybele
Virgin Mary
Domitian
Exhortation
Docetism
World
Sarx
Teleios
Hospitality
Demetrius

Introduction to the Johannine Letters

The three letters of John are among the most beautiful and simply written books of the New Testament. First John, especially, is often the first book of the New Testament recommended to a new Christian to read. Yet it contains some of the most profound and important theological principles found in the Bible. First John is the longest of the three letters and includes the main message of the writer. Second and Third John confirm this message and add to our understanding of the readers.

Authorship

None of the letters claim to have been written by the apostle John, or any John for that matter. First John is really not a letter, but a sermon or tract, so does not have a salutation. Second and Third John are personal letters where the writer refers to himself as "the elder." Although most scholars agree that the same person wrote all three letters, they do not agree on who that person was.

Many modern scholars believe that there was a "school" of teachers in the Johannine churches who were disciples of the apostle John. The author seems to indicate that he was a member of this school when he uses "we" in 1 John 1:1-4.[1]

However, allusions in writings from the early second century (1 Clement, the *Didache,* and the Epistle of Barnabas) all indicate that the apostle John wrote these three letters.[2] There is no archaeological or other textual evidence to contradict this. Most of the scholars who believe the letters to have been written by a disciple of John do so "not on the hard evidence" but on "reconstructions of the development of the Johannine 'circle,' 'community' or 'school.'"[3] As a result, the possibility of the apostle John being the author is rejected by many modern scholars before the discussion starts.

Papias of Hierapolis in the middle of the second century was the first to refer specifically to the apostle John as the author of at least one of the letters. This was confirmed by other writers in the

John and his brother were fishermen who would have used a fishing boat like this one.

late second century, but **Origen** (died A.D. 253) was the first church father to mention all three letters.[4] Eusebius, the Church historian from the fourth century, who reports that Origen was convinced that John the apostle wrote all three letters, also records the fact that 2 and 3 John were disputed books.[5]

The apostle John was the son of **Zebedee,** a fisherman on the Sea of Galilee, who was wealthy enough to have hired hands (Mark 1:20). His mother, **Salome,** accompanied Jesus on some of His travels in Galilee, "cared for his needs" (15:41, NIV) and was one of the women at the opened tomb on Easter Sunday (16:1-2). At first John was a disciple of John the Baptist. But after Herod Antipas arrested John the Baptist, Jesus called John and his brother James to follow Him. They immediately left their fishing nets and their father in the boat and followed Jesus (1:19-20).

John was one of the Twelve and part of the inner circle of Jesus: Peter, James, and John. He is often thought to be one of the youngest of the disciples and in the Gospel of John is referred to as the beloved disciple.

Jesus may have been referring to an enthusiastic personality when he called both John and his brother, James, **Boanerges** or "Sons of Thunder" (Mark 3:17). John's Gospel tells us that John "knew" the high priest and so was allowed to accompany Jesus at His trial (John 18:15-16). John was also at the Crucifixion, and it was to John that Jesus (on the Cross) gave the responsibility to take care of His mother, Mary (John 19:25-27).

John was the first of the 12 dis-ciples to reach the empty tomb. The evidence of the facecloth folded up by itself apart from the linen that had wrapped Jesus' body was enough for him to believe that Jesus had been raised from the dead.

John spent his early ministry in Jerusalem with the Jerusalem church. Sometime, shortly before the destruction of Jerusalem (A.D. 70) and during the tension of the Jewish revolt (A.D. 66-70), he along with other Christians moved to Ephesus. There he spent the rest of his life in ministry to the churches in that area.

Carson, Moo, and Morris suggest that he was "The Elder" in this area with special authority claims because of his status as an apostle who actually traveled and lived with Jesus for the three years of His ministry. John, the elder, was not just any elder, but one who also "brands certain people as liars, deceivers, and antichrists . . . across congregations."[6]

Audiences

First John has no greeting and no specific address of his readers, other than calling them "my dear children" (NIV, 2:1, 12, 13, 18, 28; 3:7; 4:4; 5:21) or "beloved" (NIV, "dear friends") (2:7; 3:2, 21; 4:1, 7, 11).

Second John is written to "the **chosen lady** and her children" (NIV). The word "lady" is the feminine form of the Greek word *kurios,* which is usually translated "Lord," as in "Lord" Jesus Christ. This feminine form is used rarely in the New Testament and so has created some discussion about its meaning. Although it plainly refers to a highborn woman or patroness *(materfamilias)* and her children, most interpreters since the fourth century have taken it to mean a local church and its members.[7] The Greek word for "church" is feminine, and the ancients often personified a city or country as a woman. It is entirely possible that both interpretations are correct with "chosen lady" referring to the woman pastor or patroness in whose house the church met, as well as the church itself.

Third John is written to "my dear friend **Gaius**" (3 John 1, NIV). Gaius was a common Roman name and was "one of eighteen names from which Roman parents could choose a *praenomen* [first name] for one of their sons."[8] In the New Testament we know of two people named Gaius: Paul's host in Corinth (Romans 16:23; 1 Corinthians 1:14) and Paul's traveling companion from Derbe (Acts 19:29; 20:4). Al-

though there is no way to know for sure, it was probably one of these men whom John had come to know and trust in the churches of Asia Minor.

None of the letters of John indicate where the readers lived. But tradition indicates that John spent the last part of his life in **Ephesus,** ministering to the churches of Asia Minor.[9] So most scholars believe that all three were written to people in the churches of Ephesus and the surrounding area.

There is much discussion about the Johannine community, but the scriptures themselves indicate that there was division in the community. First John 2:19 says: "They went out from us, but they did not belong to us; for if they had belonged to us, they would have remained with us. But by going out they made it plain that none of them belongs to us." A few verses later we read, "Who is the liar but the one

Ephesian street and civic agora.

who denies that Jesus is the Christ? This is the **antichrist,** the one who denies the Father and the Son" (v. 22). Second John mentions deceivers "who do not acknowledge Jesus Christ as coming in the flesh" (v. 7, NIV) and these are also antichrists.

These statements indicate that a heresy had blossomed in the Ephesian area churches that denied the humanity or physicality of Jesus. This most certainly reflects the influence of Greek philosophy on the Christianity of Ephesus where the spirit of a person is seen as trapped in the physical body of a person. It also may indicate a further development of this thought, often called **pre-Gnosticism** and proto-Gnosticism. Classic Gnosticism does not really become a force until the second century, but pre-Gnostic elements are found in Jewish, pagan, and Christian sources of the first century.[10]

The readers of 1 and 2 John are struggling with division in their community and, like the readers of Peter's and Jude's letters, need direction on how to determine the truth and who is saying the truth. Whereas Peter and Jude emphasize the behavior of the false or godless people, John emphasizes their lack of love and their theological beliefs. However, they are not too different, for John remarks that the way a person loves God is to keep His commandments (1 John 5:3).

Third John reveals an internal church problem of a different kind. Here we encounter **Diotrephes,** "who loves to be first, will have nothing to do with us" (3 John 9, NIV). This leader is ambitious, selfish, gossiping, and inhospitable to traveling teachers

and evangelists. So in addition to the theological problems, there are issues of noncooperation and insubordination within the churches that are still a part of the "orthodox" community.

Historical Setting and Date

Ephesus was a major port city of Asia Minor in the first century and was situated at the crossroads of three important trade routes. A thriving urban center and the Roman administrative center for Asia Minor, it was also a major center for the worship of the Greek goddess **Artemis** (Roman: Diana). The strength of the worship of Artemis indicates that it had incorporated the great fertility mother-goddess **Cybele** of the ethnic groups in Asia Minor. The Temple of Artemis was one of the seven wonders of the ancient world, with a floor space of almost 10,000 square feet.[11] Ephesus also boasted a spacious theater, stadium, and well-designed public buildings. It was also known for its magic and publication of magical formulas.

The apostle Paul visited this city several times, was imprisoned there, and spent three years of his last missionary trip there. He along with Priscilla, Aquila, and Apollos helped to found the church in Ephesus in the A.D. 50s. It became a major center for Christianity, especially after the destruction of Jerusalem in A.D. 70. The letter in Revelation to the church in Ephesus indicates that the church was strong, worked hard, and was persevering. They also were active in denouncing heresies, especially the Nicolaitans. But they had "forsaken

St. John's Church
in Ephesus.

[their] first love" and were in danger, in spite of the denunciation of heresy and good works, of losing their "lampstand" or their relationship with God (Revelation 2:4, 5, NIV; see vv. 1-17).

In the early second century, Ignatius sent one of his epistles to Ephesus, and history shows that Ephesus and Antioch in Syria were the leading centers of Christianity for the first three centuries.[12] Ephesus later became a major center for the veneration of the **Virgin Mary** because tradition says that Mary moved with John to Ephesus.[13]

Most scholars date the letters a while after the Gospel of John, perhaps correcting some misreading of the Gospel. The most probable date is in the A.D. 90s, around the time of the writing of the Book of Revelation. Those who deny that John the Elder is the same as John the apostle tend to date the letters between 100 and 110 when Gnostic Christiani-

ty was beginning to threaten orthodox Christianity.

At the end of the first century, **Domitian** was trying to increase loyalty to the Roman government by enforcing emperor worship. The Jews were exempted from this practice, but since Christianity was no longer seen as a part of Judaism, the Christians no longer had that protection. Furthermore, by the time these letters were written, many Jewish Christians had fled Palestine in the wake of the Jewish revolt of A.D. 66 and the destruction of Jerusalem in A.D. 70. They were aliens in a foreign land and in need of community and identity. The recent exodus of some from their community was unsettling. Syncretism, a prevalent practice found in both the pagan and Jewish religions in Ephesus, began to creep into Christianity. We find John fighting heresy and establishing love and community as important doctrines of true Christianity.

1 John

Form and Genre

First John is similar to the Epistle to the Hebrews in that it does not have the regular features of a letter. There is no salutation indicating the author or the readers, there is no thanksgiving section at the beginning of the letter and there is no closing—not even a benediction.

But it is more than a tract written to Christians everywhere, for John addresses them as "dear children" and as "dear friends" or "beloved ones." He also addresses specific issues, and although many have tried, a clear structure or outline is hard to find.[14] Lack of clear structure makes it hard to categorize as a tract or sermon.

Perhaps the best way to understand 1 John is as the body of a letter John wrote to several churches in the Asia Minor area who were dealing with similar problems. He may have included a separate additional note to each individual church. However, there is no textual or archaeological evidence to support this.

The genre of 1 John is a letter of encouragement or **exhortation** *(paraenesis)*. John is not telling them anything new but is reminding them of what they already know so that they will not be led astray (see 1 John 1:1-5; 2:7, 26).

Content

Although there is no consensus on the structure of 1 John, most scholars would outline the letter into at least these four main sections:

Prologue	1:1-4
Walking in the light	1:5—2:29

I · Docetism and the Johannine Community

Gnosticism as a full-blown heresy does not appear until later in the second century A.D., but incipient forms of this belief system are known to have existed in the first century. One form of this is **Docetism,**[15] which came from the platonic worldview that everything was divided between matter and spirit. Matter was evil and transient, while spirit was good and eternal. This dualism allowed no interaction between spirit and matter. Thus God, who was spirit, could not create the world (matter); this was done by a lesser power. Resurrection was unthinkable. Why would the spirit, once it was released from the prison of the body, return to a new (although "spiritual") body?

It also caused problems with these Christians' view of Jesus. How could Jesus be equal with God and yet have a material body? F. F. Bruce describes one of these Christians:

> Cerinthus, a man trained in Egypt but resident in the province of Asia, accepted the general dualist world-view (including the creation of matter by an inferior power), but propounded a novel Christology. He distinguished the man Jesus (the son of Joseph and Mary, endowed with greater virtue and wisdom than other men), from "the Christ," who descended on Jesus in the form of a dove after He was baptized, empowering Him to perform miracles and proclaim "the unknown Father," but who left Him before He died, so that "Jesus suffered and rose again, while the Christ remained immune from suffering, since He was a spiritual being."[16]

The church father Irenaeus, in his book *Against Heresies*, writes that the apostle John knew Cerinthus and called him an enemy of the truth. He writes, "There are also those who heard from him that John, the disciple of the Lord, going to bathe at Ephesus, and perceiving Cerinthus within, rushed out of the bath-house without bathing, exclaiming, 'Let us fly, lest even the bath-house fall down, because Cerinthus, the enemy of the truth, is within.'"[17]

The prologue of 1 John has some similarities to the prologue of the Gospel of John. Notice the emphasis on the beginning, the use of the term "Word" for Jesus Christ, and the emphasis on hearing, seeing, and touching Jesus. Here John is emphasizing not only the physical and human nature of Jesus but His divine nature as well. The amazing thing for John and his community was that this divine person who was with the Father and who was "from the beginning" (1 John 1:1) was the very same Jesus who had physically lived on earth and was their friend.

John begins the body of his letter declaring that there are two lifestyles, one that walks in the light with God, because God is light, and one that walks in the darkness. Those who walk in the light have fellowship with God and with each other. The blood of Jesus purifies them from all sin if they confess their sin, because all have sinned.

The Meaning of "World" in 1 John

The author of 1 John uses the word **"world"** (Greek: *kosmos*) to mean several different things. In 1 John 4:9 and 17 it refers to the created universe or planet earth. In 1 John 2:2, "the whole world" means the whole human race. But in most of 1 John the world refers to a way of life that opposes God. The world opposes and is opposite of the children of God. The world is sinful and transient—the place where deceivers and *the* deceiver live. Those who are of the world are heard by the world and the world hates the children of God. This way of life is described in 1 John 2:16 as one that chases the desires of the body (flesh; Greek *sarx*), gives in to the lusts of the eyes, and trusts (boastfully) in earthly things.

Those who walk in darkness claim to have fellowship with God but hate their brother or sister and love the "world." They claim to be without sin and so have deceived themselves. Walking in the light is not just a matter of saying so but a matter of behaving as Jesus did. So if someone says that he or she is walking in the light but his or her actions don't testify to this, then he or she is walking in darkness.

John also refers to those who walk in darkness as "antichrists" (2:18). Specifically, these antichrists deny that Jesus is the Christ, the Messiah (v. 22). The issue is not just that Jesus is denied as the Messiah but that because Jesus is the Son of God, they are also denying the Father. Moreover, those who deny that Jesus was the Son of God, by saying that a spiritual being came down at Jesus' baptism and left before He died on the Cross, deny Jesus as the Christ as well.

John begins the second half of the body of this letter by exclaiming, "How great is the love the Father has lavished on us, that we should be called children of God" (1 John 3:1, NIV)! In this section he also explains that there are two ways of living, but this time he uses the metaphor of love instead of light. Those who break the law commit sin and do not do what is right. They hate their brother or sister. They have material possessions but do not share with those in need, and above all do not love. They do not know God and are not children of God.

Love for John is defined by God (1 John 4:16) and by what Jesus did in laying down His life for us (3:16a). Love comes from God and is made possible in our lives

Right and Wrong Beliefs

First John contrasts false teachings with true Christian faith:

Pre-Gnosticism/Docetism	Christianity
Sinning Religion	*Victorious Christian Living*
1:6: Believes a lie	2:20-23: Believes the truth
4:6: Spirit of falsehood	4:6: Spirit of truth
2:22-23/4:3: Denies Jesus	4:2: Confesses Jesus
1:10: Denies sin	1:9/2:1: Accepts forgiveness
1:6: Walks in darkness	1:7: Walks in the light
2:19: Division caused by spirit of the Antichrist	1:9: Has fellowship with God and others
2:4: Disobeys Christ	2:3, 17: Obeys Christ and does God's will
3:8: Sins continually	3:4-6: Freedom from sinning
5:19: Under the control of the devil	3:9-10; 4:4; 5:4-5: God's victory by faith

only because we live in God and God lives in us. John tells his readers "we ought to lay down our lives for one another" (v. 16b). He goes on to emphasize this action-based love when he says, "Dear children, let us not love with words or tongue but with actions and in truth" (v. 18, NIV). Thus his readers can tell who is from God and who is not by whether their actions are loving actions or hateful ones.

Toward the end of the section on God's love, John describes "perfect" love. This word for perfect comes from the Greek word *teleios,* which means "complete or mature." By living in God and God living in the individual, love is made complete, mature, or "perfect." This "perfect" does not mean that a person never makes any mistakes or sins, but that his or her motivations are godly and come out of the love that God gives. A person who is "perfect" or complete in love does not fear judgment. This is not because he or she never sins again but because his or her motivation is to

love; so when the Holy Spirit convicts him or her of an unloving action or motivation, the child of God quickly confesses that sin and is immediately restored to a right relationship with God.

Eros head, Roman period, in Pergamum museum.

In the middle of his discussion on love and how that works out in the lives of the children of God, John exhorts or encourages his readers to "test the spirits to see whether they are from God" (4:1). Apparently, in addition to loving actions, there is another way one can recognize the Spirit of God: confession that Jesus Christ has come in the flesh and is from God (v. 2). Here he is addressing again the problem of Docetism or pre-Gnosticism. Correct belief and loving actions are important characteristics of the true children of God.

First John concludes by stating that the purpose of the writing was to make sure that the readers knew they had eternal life so that they could live confident Christian lives.

2 John

Form and Genre

Second John follows the classical form of a first-century letter. The author, "the elder," is identified first; then the readers are described as "the elect lady and her children, whom I love in the truth" (v. 1). This salutation is followed by a prayer or wish for "Grace, mercy, and peace . . . from God" (v. 3). The body of the letter concludes with greetings

The Sin That Leads to Death

First John 5:16 deals with two kinds of sin: one that leads to death and one that does not. Now according to John, "all wrongdoing is sin" (1 John 5:17) and needs God's forgiveness to give life to the sinner. So how does one know which sin is forgivable and which is not? John does not go into much explanation; perhaps he is assuming that his readers know what he is writing about.

As we look back over the Bible we find a few places where certain kinds of sins are unforgivable. In Exodus 23:21, God announces to the people of Israel that He is sending an angel before them to guard their way and to bring them to the Promised Land. God warns the people not to rebel against him, because "he will not forgive your rebellion since my Name is in him" (NIV). Hebrews 6:4-6 states: "It is impossible for those who have once been enlightened . . . tasted the heavenly gift . . . shared in the Holy Spirit . . . tasted the goodness of the word of God and the powers of the coming age, if they fall away, to be brought back to repentance, because . . . they are crucifying the Son of God all over again and subjecting him to public disgrace" (NIV). The thought is continued in 10:26-27: "If we deliberately keep on sinning after we have received the knowledge of the truth, no sacrifice for sins is left, but only a fearful expectation of judgment and of raging fire" (NIV).

The conclusion of this brief survey of biblical texts that deal with unforgivable sins is that there is no forgiveness for those who have known the truth but have made a conscious choice to live in continual rebellion against God. Those who recognize their sinful way of life can always find life through repentance and forgiveness that comes from God. However, Scripture warns those who choose to continually rebel against God that they have no other recourse for salvation. Even then, we must recognize the truth that God is love and that He is the source of eternal life. Ultimately, this is the hope for even the most defiant sinner.

from "the children of your elect sister" (v. 13).

This brief letter is a letter of exhortation or strong encouragement *(paraenesis)* to continue in truth and in the teaching of Christ. Verse 12, "I hope to come to you and talk with you face to face," indicates this is a letter of friendship even though the reader's name is not given. It also gives advice on what to do if deceivers should come to her house.

Content

Second John is a very brief letter that covers the topics of truth, love, and obedience in just a few lines. It is basically a letter telling the reader that John hopes to come soon for a visit and to talk over these issues face-to-face. Apparently some of the chosen lady's children are "walking in the truth," and John reminds her that the command from the beginning was to "love one another." Here John defines love as walking in "obedience to his [God's] commands" (v. 6, NIV).

Second John again echoes the antidocetic concern about "deceivers, who do not acknowledge Jesus Christ as coming in the flesh" (v. 7, NIV). He calls them "antichrists" and advises her not to take them into her house or even welcome them.

3 John

Form and Genre

Third John also follows the classical letter form. Again the author is identified as "the elder," but this letter is written to "my dear friend Gaius" (v. 1, NIV). A typical prayer for the reader's good health and success follows the salutation. The body of the letter closes with a prayer for peace and greetings from friends.

The genre or type of letter is a friendship letter that uses praise and blame *(epideictic)* to make clear to the reader what behavior is considered proper in the church. John also gives specific advice to Gaius on how to treat visiting teachers.

Content

Following the salutation and prayer for Gaius's health and success, John tells of his joy in finding out that Gaius has been faithful to the truth. He praises Gaius for receiving the teachers of the truth, even though they were strangers to him. John advises him to send them on to the next church with plenty of food and money since they need it, and they are teaching the truth (v. 7).

He follows this praise of and advice to Gaius with criticism

John and the Antichrist

John acknowledges in 1 John 2:18 that the Antichrist will come in the last hour and since there are many antichrists, it must be the last hour. What is important for John is the spirit of the Antichrist that is a "spirit of opposition to Christ, denying that Jesus is the Christ and denying the Father-Son relationship. It is more than failure to believe: it is deliberate, reasoned rebellion."[18]

(blame) of Diotrephes who was not hospitable to these teachers. This individual loved to be first, spread evil words against John, and actually tried to stop other churches or leaders from extending **hospitality** to the traveling teachers.

John then gives advice in light of these examples of how to live and encourages Gaius to do good and not evil. Those who do good are from God and those who do evil have not seen God (v. 11).

Third John closes with a recommendation of **Demetrius**, who may have been the one who carried the letter to Gaius. He also wants to talk more with Gaius but does not want to write his thoughts; instead he hopes to see him soon and talk face-to-face.

Hospitality in the Early Church

Hospitality was a highly regarded virtue and a necessary gift for the advancement of the Early Church. Most respected people stayed with family or friends when they traveled. Staying in a roadside inn was only a last resort. It was considered dangerous, since one did not know the innkeeper or the people staying there.

Those who did not have family or friends in a city they needed to stay in would ask their friends for letters of introduction so that they could stay in a private home, rather than a public inn. Anyone who rejected someone with a letter of introduction without cause was considered to be an impolite and uncivilized person.

It was through traveling missionaries like Paul and the "brothers" or teachers referred to here in 3 John that the gospel spread quickly across the Roman Empire. The following excerpt from *Didache* (also known as *Teaching of the Twelve Apostles,* dated to the end of the first century A.D.) shows the guidelines for hospitality established by the Christians so that guests would not become a burden to their hosts.

12:1 Let every one that cometh in the name of the Lord be received, but afterwards ye shall examine him and know his character, for ye have knowledge both of good and evil.

12:2 If the person who cometh be a wayfarer, assist him so far as ye are able; but he will not remain with you more than two or three days, unless there be a necessity.

12:3 But if he wish to settle with you, being a craftsman, let him work, and so eat;

12:4 but if he know not any craft, provide ye according to your own discretion, that a Christian may not live idle among you;

12:5 but if he be not willing to do so, he is a trafficker in Christ. From such keep aloof (*"Didache,"* chapter 12).

Summary Statements

- First John does not follow the form of a letter and may have been a written tract sent to different local churches.
- Second and Third John are personal letters where the writer refers to himself as "the elder" and names a specific reader.
- First John says that each person has one of two lifestyles: one that walks in the light with God or loves others, because God is light and love, and one that walks in the darkness or hates his or her brother.
- Correct belief and loving actions are important characteristics of the true children of God.

Questions for Reflection

1. Can a person love God and hate his or her brother or sister? Why or why not?
2. The Scriptures say that perfect love casts out fear. Does that mean that if we have fears and worries, we do not love God with all our heart? Why or why not?
3. Is hospitality a virtue today? Is hospitality defined the same way today as it was in the first century?
4. Can a person be a Christian and not do something concretely to take care of the poor?

Resources for Further Study

Bruce, F. F. *The Epistles of John*. Grand Rapids: William B. Eerdmans Publishing Co., 1970.

Marshall, I. Howard. *The Epistles of John*. Grand Rapids: William B. Eerdmans Publishing Co., 1978.

Yamauchi, Edwin M. *Pre-Christian Gnosticism: A Survey of the Proposed Evidences,* 2nd ed. Grand Rapids: Baker Book House, 1983.

21 | The Book of Revelation

bjectives:

Your study of this chapter should help you to:
- Gain an understanding of Jewish and Christian apocalyptic literature.
- Describe the historical and theological issues relative to the writing of the Book of Revelation.
- Evaluate the practical and theological importance of the Book of Revelation.
- Describe the different types of interpretation of Revelation.

Questions to consider as you read:

1. What are some of the similarities and differences between Revelation and Jewish apocalyptic literature?
2. Why was Revelation written in apocalyptic style?
3. What do we learn about the nature of God and His relationship to His creation from Revelation?
4. Why was Revelation included in the canon?

ey Words to Understand

Revelation
Apocalypse
Apocalypticism
Dualism
Dionysius
Chiliasm
Patmos
Domitian
Ephesus
Artemis
Smyrna
Pergamum
Zeus
Thyatira
Sardis
Philadelphia
Laodicea
Eschatology
Montanists
Idealist
Preterist
Historicist
Futurist
Premillennial
Millennium
Amillennial
Postmillennial
Dispensational
   premillennial

Revelation is one of the most talked about but least understood books of the New Testament. Three factors contribute to the misunderstanding of this book: (1) Its literary style is not familiar to the modern reader. (2) Its historical context is drastically different from the modern context. (3) The original readers may have understood the meaning of many of the symbols in the book, but they remain unclear to its modern readers. In spite of these difficulties, it is possible to grasp the main message of hope the book gives to its ancient audience as well as its modern readers.

Revelation as Apocalyptic Literature

Revelation is the traditional translation of the Greek word *apokalypsis,* the first word in the Book of Revelation. It means an uncovering, or unveiling of something that was originally covered. An **apocalypse** reports things that were formerly hidden or secret, especially spiritual realities and future events. Revelation is the only book in the New Testament written entirely in an apocalyptic style. However, Revelation is not the only example of apocalyptic literature in the New Testament. Mark 13 is often referred to as the "little apocalypse." Other short apocalyptic statements are found in the Gospels as well as Paul's writings.

The Book of Daniel (especially chapters 7—12) is an example of apocalyptic literature in the Old Testament. Jewish apocalyptic literature flourished throughout the intertestamental period and in the first and second centuries A.D. The Jesus movement in the first century A.D. as well as the Early Church developed in a culture influenced by Jewish apocalyptic tradition and symbolism.

Authorship

The early Christian tradition regarded the apostle John as the author of Revelation. This view is attested by ancient Christian writers such as Papias, Irenaeus, Tertullian, Hippolytus, and Origen. Some scholars conclude that no New Testament book has a "stronger or earlier tradition about its authorship than does

I Apocalypticism

The characteristics of Jewish and Christian **apocalypticism** include the use of celestial and supernatural symbols or images. The prophecies of deliverance are clothed in the language of symbol. In contrast to most of the Old Testament prophecies, which focus on Israel, apocalyptic prophecies concern the whole earth and are thus universal in scope.

Apocalyptic literature is also characterized by the idea that evil will continue to grow and will lead to a cosmic catastrophe and universal judgment. Apocalyptic writers divide time into the present evil time and the future perfect time. The writers also subscribe to the idea of cosmic **dualism,** or the existence of material and spiritual worlds. Humanity is also sharply divided between good and evil people. A call to total commitment to God is also a key feature of this type of literature. God will reward the righteous and punish the unrighteous. The use of symbols to express these ideas is another characteristic of apocalyptic literature.

Revelation."[1] However, **Diony-sius,** bishop of Alexandria (A.D. 247-265), who did not believe in the commonly accepted doctrine of **chiliasm** (Christ would establish a thousand-year reign on earth), was a leading dissenter of this traditional view.[2] Many scholars today doubt that the apostle John wrote this book. They point out that the author does not claim to be an apostle but a brother and cosharer in the suffering of his readers. They also cite that there are significant theological and linguistic differences between the Gospel of John and Revelation.

In this study we follow the traditional perspective on the authorship of Revelation. According to tradition, John ministered in Jerusalem from A.D. 30 to 68 and in Ephesus from A.D. 68 to 98, where he died. Part of this time he was in exile on the Island of **Patmos,** the location of the visions of Revelation (1:9). It is possible that an editor may have been responsible for the final form of the book, as suggested by the reference to John in the third person (vv. 1-3). However, the content and the visions most likely belong to John the apostle.

Audience

Revelation is addressed to the seven churches in the province of Asia (v. 4): Ephesus, Smyrna, Pergamum, Thyatira, Sardis, Philadelphia, and Laodicea. The individual letters written to these churches indicate that there were a variety of issues that needed to be addressed in these Christian congregations. Some of these include apostasy, impending persecution and imprisonment, toleration of heresy, spiritual deadness,

spiritual apathy, and encouragement for those who are patiently enduring persecution.

Setting and Date

The common historical setting of all apocalyptic writings is that of oppression with no hope of liberation by earthly leaders. For the apocalyptic writer and his readers, only God breaking into history could change their situation. Since the writer uses symbolic language familiar only to his readers to communicate his message of hope and deliverance, there is little fear of retaliation by authorities.

Although the visions of John may have occurred earlier, most scholars date Revelation around

Emperor Domitian.

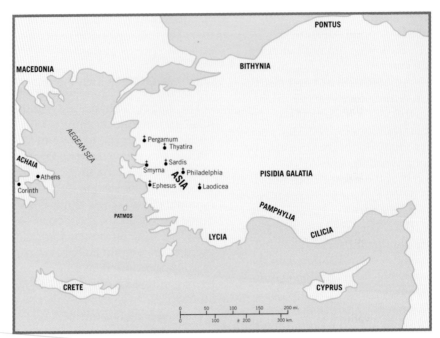

Seven Churches in the Province of Asia.

A.D. 95-96, during the reign of Emperor **Domitian** (81-96). Domitian, who was worshiped as a god in different parts of the empire, carried out an empire-wide and intense persecution of those who did not worship him, especially Christians.

John reports that he received his visions on the island of Patmos, just off the coast of Asia Minor near Ephesus. But the visions were probably written down in Ephesus where John spent the last part of his life. Ephesus was an important center of Christianity in the late first century.

The readers were located in Asia Minor along a circuit of seven important cities. They are addressed in the natural order that a messenger would take: from Ephesus, north to Smyrna and Pergamum and then east to Thyatira, then south to Sardis, Philadelphia, and Laodicea.

Form and Genre

We have already identified Revelation as an apocalyptic book. While the book presents itself as a "prophecy" (1:3; 22:10), it also has the form of a letter with a formal greeting at the beginning and a benediction at the end. Revelation has all the characteristics of an apocalyptic book, particularly visions, symbols, numbers, and dualistic language. Throughout the book, we also find numerous hymns that exalt the majesty and power of God and His Son Jesus Christ.

Content

The first line of Revelation is *Apocalypsis Iēsou Christou*—"A Revelation of Jesus Christ." One scholar points out that "in his title John also has given us the primary principle for interpreting his book . . . his desire to pro-

The Seven Churches of Revelation

Ephesus was a busy port city and the capital of the Roman province of Asia. It had an ethically mixed population and consequently many religious groups, including Judaism and Christianity. **Artemis,** the goddess of the hunt and women's fertility, boasted the largest temple, but there was also a temple to Domitian, which indicates that emperor worship was practiced there.

Smyrna, located about 40 miles straight north of Ephesus, was also a center for emperor worship. The city was "reduced to village status and off the map for three centuries (600-290 B.C.), but it was rebuilt on Mount Pagus (Kadifekale) because of a dream Alexander the Great had."[3] It recognized the value of allies and was known for being fiercely loyal. The wreath, a common impression on coins from Smyrna, was a crown of leaves given to those celebrating life events and victories in battle or games.

Pergamum, situated straight north of Ephesus and Smyrna, was a "spectacular city . . . rising 900 feet above the plain. . . . Its kings added the titles 'savior' and 'god' to their names."[4] It was famous for an altar to **Zeus** who was the king of the pagan pantheon. This altar is referred to in Revelation as the "throne of Satan."

Thyatira was the most insignificant city of the seven and was located about 40 miles southeast of Pergamum. It was known for its many trade guilds, which included "bronze workers, coppersmiths, tanners, leather workers, dyers (especially in purple; see Acts 16:14), workers in wool and linen, bakers, potters, and those who dealt in slaves."[5]

Sardis was located slightly north and east of Ephesus. At one time it was the capital of ancient Lydia, and in the first century A.D., the city had a Jewish community.

Philadelphia, located 30 miles southeast of Sardis and slightly northeast of Ephesus, had especially fertile volcanic soil that easily grew grapes. Around A.D. 92, Domitian required the citizens to replace half their vineyards with grain that did not grow, causing an area-wide economic disaster. The Philadelphians understood the importance of an all-knowing and wise ruler.

Laodicea, located 40 miles southeast of Philadelphia and about 100 miles slightly south and east of Ephesus, was extremely rich. It was a banking center and its medical facility was famous for its eye salve. Its water sources came via aqueducts both from hot springs and cold mountain waters, but by the time the water reached Laodicea, it was neither hot nor cold. The lukewarm water is symbolic for indifference, which for a Mediterranean person is "worse than hate."[6]

Fortifications of ancient Smyrna.

Altar to Zeus in Pergamum.

Jesus comes back in glory is not its purpose. Many books have been written on Revelation predicting the conditions and dates of the Second Coming but have missed the essential message of this book.

The content of Revelation can be outlined as follows:

1. Prologue   1:1-8
2. Letters to the seven churches   1:9—3:22
3. Visions of the throne of God and seven seals   4:1—8:1
4. Visions of the seven trumpets   8:2—11:19
5. Visions of the woman, dragon, and beast   12:1—14:20
6. Visions of the seven bowls of wrath   15:1—16:21

claim and expound the person of Jesus Christ."[7]

Since this title of Revelation reads, "a revelation of Jesus Christ," the prediction of when

The Meaning of Numbers in Revelation

The use of numbers in apocalyptic literature is quite common and is related to the ancient study of astronomy. In fact, ancient astronomers were called "mathematicians." Numbers were used not only to convey how many but also to describe quality.

The number 12 symbolizes completeness. Twenty-four (12 plus 12) elders seated on thrones before God, 12 gates in New Jerusalem, 12 different kinds of fruit from the Tree of Life, 12 foundations that are made of 12 different gemstones—all indicate completeness in Revelation.

Number 7, the number of perfection, is especially prominent in Revelation. The text is divided into 7 sections, there are 7 churches of the apocalypse, 7 seals, 7 trumpet blasts, and 7 angels with 7 plagues or bowls of wrath.

The number 6 has several interpretations. Most prominent is that of imperfection, since it is 1 less than 7. In Revelation, the best-known number is 666, the number of the beast (13:18). John tells us that this is a number of a human being. However, it is futile to try to determine the identity of this person.

A popular view regards 666 as the numerical equivalent to Nero Caesar. Robert Mounce points out: "What is not generally stressed is that this solution asks us to calculate a Hebrew transliteration of the Greek form of a Latin name, and that with a defective spelling."[8] The fact that Revelation was written in Greek and that Nero was never suggested by ancient commentators indicates that this interpretation is probably inaccurate.

The number 4 is related to the 4 corners of the earth and the directions from which come the 4 major winds. It also represents completeness or the "whole" of something specific on earth.

Three (3 angels in chapter 14) perhaps reflects 3 parts of the universe: the sky of fixed stars, the sky of planets, and the fixed earth. Three is more related to the cosmic whole or the essence of being.[9]

The introduction (1:1-2) presents the content of the book as the "revelation" of Jesus Christ from God, which an angel communicated to John. The book begins with a pronouncement of blessing to its readers and a formal greeting (vv. 3-5). This is followed by an announcement of the coming of Christ and the identification of God as the "Alpha and Omega"—the beginning and the end of all things (vv. 7-8). The writer identifies himself as a believer exiled to Patmos because of his faith and testimony. The visions came to him on the "Lord's day." He received the command to write in a book the content of the visions and send it to the seven churches (vv. 9-11).

For each church, there is a specific message. Each church is also

Ruins of Sardis.

given a commendation or a condemnation and a concluding exhortation and promise. The first church, Ephesus, receives the commendation as a church that endured hardships for the sake of Christ. Yet it has forsaken its first love (2:1-7). The second church, Smyrna, receives commendation as a church that experienced afflictions and poverty (vv. 8-11). The third church, Pergamum, receives the commendation for its faithfulness even in the midst of persecu-

Aqueduct and bathhouse ruins at Laodicea.

tion and martyrdom of its members. However, there are some in the church that follow false teachers and their teaching. They are called to repent or face the consequence of judgment (vv. 12-17).

The fourth church, Thyatira, receives commendation for its love, faith, and service; yet the church also tolerates false teachers (vv. 18-29). The fifth church, Sardis, receives a stern warning to wake up. Though they seem to be alive, they are on the verge of death. Only a few in the church have remained faithful (3:1-6). The sixth church, Philadelphia, receives commendation for its faithfulness and patience (vv. 7-13). The seventh church, Laodicea, receives condemnation for its lukewarm condition. The message urges the church to repent and enter into fellowship with Christ (vv. 14-22).

Chapter 4 describes the vision of God seated on His throne in heaven, surrounded by songs of praise and adoration of 24 elders and four living creatures. Chapter 5 contains the vision of the Lamb that was slain for the salvation of humankind. The four living creatures, the 24 elders, and all in heaven sing praise to the Lamb who is worthy to open the scroll sealed with seven seals. The opening of the first six seals is described in chapter 6. The opening of the first four seals announced destruction of various kinds, brought about by riders of four horses—white, red, black, and pale horses—respectively.

The two visions in chapter 7 announce protection to 144,000 from the 12 tribes of Israel during tribulation (7:1-8), and salvation to "a great multitude" from every nation, tribe, people and language" (vv. 9-17). The opening of the seventh seal leads to a fearful silence, anticipating the severe judgment that follows (8:1). The author recounts the sounding of seven trumpets by seven angels and the consequences that follow each trumpet sound in v. 6—11:19. The first four trumpets bring hail, fire, blood, water pollution, and darkness. The fifth trumpet brings the plague of fearsome locusts. The sixth trumpet unleashes a powerful cavalry to kill one-third of the human population. Before the seventh trumpet, the author sees two visions. In the first vision, the visionary is asked to eat a scroll (10:1-11). The second vision focuses on the prophesying activity, martyrdom, and resurrection of two prophetic witnesses in the holy city (11:1-13). The seventh trumpet announces that "the kingdom of the world has become the kingdom of our Lord and of his Messiah, and he will reign forever and ever" (v. 15).

Chapter 12 narrates the vision of "a woman clothed with the sun," a monstrous red dragon, and a male child that is born to the woman. A war breaks out in heaven, and Michael, the archangel, with his angels defeats the dragon and his angels, who are thrown out of heaven. Two beasts occupy the center of the visions in chapter 13. The dragon gives authority to a beast that comes out of the sea, and it becomes the object of worship of the whole earth. Another beast that comes out of the earth deceives and forces the people to worship the first beast. Everyone is forced to put a mark of the beast on their hand or forehead, showing their allegiance to the beast.

Chapter 14 contains a series of

visions, which give assurance to the faithful of their ultimate vindication by God. The visions also include the judgment of those who worshiped the beast and the defeat of Babylon (Rome).

Judgment of the earth is the key theme of the visions in chapters 15 and 16. Various kinds of judgments take place as seven angels pour out on earth "seven bowls of the wrath of God" (16:1). Visions in chapters 17 and 18 report the fall of Babylon (Rome). Chapter 19 narrates the victory celebration of Christ and the "marriage supper of the Lamb" (v. 9). Chapter 20 describes the temporary imprisonment of Satan, his release, the final conflict, the final overthrow of Satan, and the final judgment. The book closes with visions of the new Jerusalem (chapters 21 and 22). God creates a new heaven and a new earth. He makes His dwelling on earth. The Lord God will be light and life for His people and they will "reign forever and ever" (22:5).

Theology of Revelation

Although Revelation is fundamentally different in style from the rest of the New Testament books, its theology remains the same. God the Creator of the universe guides the course of history; He will overcome evil and bring an end to the suffering of His people. He is the "Alpha and the Omega," the One "who is and who was and who is to come" (1:8). The hymns in Revelation proclaim the majesty, greatness, and glory of God. He is holy and worthy to be worshiped because He "created all things" (4:8, 11). He is the "living God" and author of salvation (7:2, 10). "Blessing

and glory and wisdom and thanksgiving and honor and power and might" belong to God (v. 12). The kingdoms of the world belong to Him (11:15). His "judgments are true and just" (16:7). He reigns over the earth (19:6). He will create a new heaven and a new earth and establish His dwelling with humanity (21:1-4).

Jesus is the "faithful witness, the firstborn of the dead, and the ruler of the kings of the earth" (1:5). He is the "Alpha and the Omega" (v. 8) and holds the "keys of Death and of Hades" (v. 18). He is the "Son of God" "who has the seven spirits of God" (2:18; 3:1). He is "holy" and "true" and holds "the key of David" (v. 7). He is "the Lion of the tribe of Judah" and "the Root of David" (5:5). He is the "King of kings and Lord of lords" (19:16). He is the "lamb," or the one sacrificed for the sins of the world, but He is also divine and has the same nature as God, the Father (5:6; 22:12-13).

The people of God will experience the ultimate joy of God's salvation. They are servants or slaves of God, a kingdom, priests, saints, the blameless, the redeemed, and the bride of the Lamb. They are to continue believing in Jesus as the Word of God, being alert to perversions and deception, keeping God's commands, being holy, and doing the work God has assigned them to do.

Revelation is one of the main sources for **eschatology** or the study of the end-times. And its eschatology is consistent with the rest of the New Testament. Every believer can have the certainty of life after death. Christians also can be sure of their personal resurrection and reward for righteous living. The second coming

Interpretations of Revelation

Literal interpretation is the oldest known interpretation of Revelation. This method was popular among the second- and third-century **Montanists** who announced that the heavenly Jerusalem would descend near a certain village. The movement began in Phrygia, just east of the seven cities of the apocalypse.

Today, there are four classical views of the interpretation of Revelation. The **idealist** view interprets Revelation as a symbolic description of the ongoing struggle between God and the forces of evil. It emphasizes the final triumph of God over evil.

The **preterist** view sees Revelation as a message of hope for those being persecuted in the Roman Empire during the late first century. The city called Babylon is a code name for Rome, and the events represented symbolically were contemporary and not predictions of the future.

The **historicist** view builds on both the idealist and the preterist views, and sees Revelation as a symbolic description of the Church's history from its beginning to the return of Christ. The symbolic accounts are prophetic representations of past, present, and future events.

The **futurist** view interprets Revelation as a prophecy of future events. These events include a great tribulation lasting seven years, followed by Christ's second coming and the final judgment.

Insights on Revelation from Sociology

From a sociological perspective, scholars offer various suggestions on the possible contexts and interpretation of Revelation. Some scholars think that the book came out of the context of several social crises (examples: Christians' conflict with the Jews, their hatred and fear of the Roman government, and the crisis of wealth and poverty). They see Revelation as a literary work that sorts out these crises and brings comfort and meaning to the situation.

Others see the trauma and deprivation caused by the destruction of Jerusalem and the Christians' loss of social status in the Roman Empire as the context of Revelation. They perceive in the book not only the author's rationale for these crises but also the offer of a future resolution that would bring justice.

A third sociological interpretation seeks to show that the social crises would have led the Christians to the danger of compromise with the enemy in order to avoid persecution, and to adapt to the demands of business associations and social relationships. According to this view, Revelation is a call to the Christians to be radically committed to their faith.

of Christ will affect all of creation. Each person will be assigned to his or her eternal reward or punishment. And there will be the creation of a new heaven and a new earth. In the new Jerusalem, God will dwell with His people. They will be forever free from all suffering, mourning, crying, pain, and death.

This textbook holds no particular view on the interpretation of Revelation, except that it is the inspired Word of God communicated in apocalyptic symbolic language. Committed, born-again Christians have held all of the views discussed in this chapter. It is important to realize that the primary message of Revelation is

Millennial Views

Current discussions in evangelical churches concentrate on different millennial views.

The **premillennial** view relates the book to the history of the Church. Christ will deliver the Church from persecution and from the power of the Antichrist at His second coming. The dead in Christ will be raised up. This is followed by a thousand-year reign of Christ **(millennium).** After the thousand years, there will be a final judgment of unbelievers at the "great white throne" (20:11-15). God will then create a new heaven and a new earth, and He will establish His righteous rule forever.

The **amillennial** view does not hold to a literal thousand-year reign of Christ, but sees the millennium as being fulfilled spiritually in the ministry of the church. The persecution of believers will end with Christ's second coming. There will be a general resurrection of everyone, both saved and unsaved. After the great white throne judgment, a new heaven and a new earth will become the reward of the righteous. The unrighteous will be cast into the fiery lake of burning sulfur.

The **postmillennial** view sees the age of the Church as the millennium. This view maintains that through the preaching of the gospel, righteousness and justice will become more and more a reality on this earth. After the world has been saved, Christ will return in glory to the world He has saved. This view understands the events in Revelation to refer to John's time and not to future prophecies.

The relatively recent **dispensational premillennial** view maintains that the first three chapters of Revelation deal with the church age, after which the saints are raptured (taken directly to heaven) from the earth. According to this view, the middle section of the book (chapters 4—19) describes the trials of Israel on earth during a seven-year period of great tribulation. This tribulation does not affect the church because it is in heaven with Christ.

This view describes the gathering of armies in chapter 19 as the battle of Armageddon. Christ will bring the raptured Christians to rule with Him, and He will establish a Jewish millennium to fulfill the Old Testament prophecies. After a thousand years, Satan will be released from his prison; he will go out to deceive the nations but at the final judgment, he, his angels, and all the lost are thrown into the lake of fire. Finally, a new heaven and a new earth are created, and Christians enter into the eternal day of God's presence.

This millennial view comes in three versions: (1) pretribulation rapture (rapture of the believers before the tribulation); (2) midtribulation rapture (believers taken up in the middle of the seven years of tribulation); and (3) posttribulation rapture (rapture of the believers at the end of the seven-year period of tribulation).

about the *hope* we have in Jesus. What we do know for sure is expressed not only in Revelation but also in the rest of the New Testament: Jesus is coming again soon. He will come at an unexpected time like a thief in the night. God will triumph over all. God's people will dwell with Him for ever and ever. So, with the author of Revelation, we also pray, "Come, Lord Jesus" (22:20).

Summary Statements

- The first line of Revelation, *"Apocalypsis Jesu Christus,"* meaning a "revelation of Jesus Christ," expresses the primary principle for interpreting the book.
- Apocalyptic literature uses celestial and supernatural symbols to express its message, subscribes to a cosmic dualism, accepts that evil will grow and lead to a cosmic catastrophe, and calls for a total commitment to God.
- The traditional author of Revelation is the apostle John who was exiled to Patmos for his Christian beliefs and finished his lengthy ministry in Ephesus.
- The original readers of Revelation were seven churches in the province of Asia: Ephesus, Smyrna, Pergamum, Thyatira, Sardis, Philadelphia, and Laodicea.
- Most scholars date Revelation to A.D. 95-96 during the reign of Emperor Domitian, who was worshiped as a god and decreed an empire-wide, intense persecution of those who did not worship him.
- Revelation presents itself as a "prophecy" but is in the form of a letter and uses Jewish apocalyptic language.
- The number seven, symbolizing perfection, is prominent in Revelation: there are seven literary sections, seven churches of the apocalypse, seven seals, seven trumpet blasts, and seven angels with seven plagues or bowls of wrath.
- The primary message of Revelation concerns eschatology, or the study of the end-times. Although there are many different interpretations of Revelation, the message that remains constant is that no matter what happens the Christian's hope is in Jesus Christ.

Questions for Reflection

1. What do you think is the primary message of Revelation? Why?
2. In what ways is the message of Revelation relevant to the 21st century?
3. Does Revelation make a difference in how we live our lives daily, or is it just for the future? Why? Or why not?

Resources for Further Study

Collins, Adela Yarbro. *Crisis and Catharsis: The Power of the Apocalypse.* Philadelphia: Westminster Press, 1984.

Eller, Vernard. *The Most Revealing Book of the Bible: Making Sense Out of Revelation.* Grand Rapids: William B. Eerdmans Publishing Company, 1974.

Malina, Bruce J., and John J. Pilch. *Social-Science Commentary on the Book of Revelation.* Minneapolis: Fortress Press, 2000.

Metzger, Bruce. *Breaking the Code: Understanding the Book of Revelation.* Nashville: Abingdon Press, 1993.

Mounce, Robert H. *The Book of Revelation* in NICNT. Grand Rapids: William B. Eerdmans Publishing Company, 1977.

Epilogue
Keeping Faith Alive

We have come to the end of our discovery of the New Testament. This journey has taken us through the writings of the New Testament, which together with those of the Old Testament make up the Christian Scriptures. In this journey, we have discovered an intrinsic connection between these two Testaments. Within these Scriptures we see two communities of faith, though not all alike in their makeup and belief systems, coming into existence as God's people. The history of this people is shaped by a peculiar narrative that combines the narratives of the two faith communities. The narrative of Israel centered on their conviction that their destiny was to be a source of blessing to all humanity. It was for this purpose that God had called them and made a covenant with them at Sinai. That narrative, however, also contains their tragic failure to become a "light to the Gentiles." It is precisely at this point that the narrative of the Christian community finds its connecting link with the story of Israel. The early Christian community was formed around the simple, yet profound teachings of Jesus of Nazareth, the true Israel, who indeed fulfilled all the hopes and expectations of His nation Israel. Their narrative contained the profound truth about the identity of Jesus as God's Son, the Christ who is the Savior of all humanity.

It is this narrative of Jesus that not only brought the community of Christians together but also energized them to become a powerful religious movement in the first-century Roman world.

Continuing Formation of the Community of Faith

Though the story of the early Christian community, as it is found in the pages of the New Testament, ended in the last decade of the first century A.D., the faith it generated did not disappear from history. The New Testament writings, which preserve the story of the first-century Christian community, have become a powerful reservoir of faith in the succeeding centuries. These writings provided for the later communities of faith not only the historical documents of the first-century Christian community but also a resource for faith that was instrumental in the shaping of doctrines and community life. The story of the Christian Church over these past 2,000 years attests to the centrality of the faith transmitted through the pages of the New Testament. Even in the midst of divisions that took place in the history of Christianity, such as the division between the East and the West and the Protestant Reformation, Christians found in these writings the necessary faith to sustain them and even to bring about changes long-overdue.

What is central to the formation of Christian faith communities today is the simple gospel story. No community can call itself Christian if the story of Jesus as it is portrayed in the Gospels is removed from the narrative of that community. Many Christians may see the Gospels as too primitive and archaic for the modern world. Technologically advanced countries and cultures are increasingly becoming skeptical of the narrative of Jesus of Nazareth. It is nonetheless amazing to still see multitudes being drawn to the narrative of Jesus. Recently this has been demonstrated by the enormous success of the *JESUS* film that is being shown in many parts of world and by the worldwide interest in Mel Gibson's *The Passion of the Christ*. It is the story of Jesus that calls for a response. The first-century disciples' preaching of the Jesus story in the Book of Acts brought repentance and faith in Jesus the Messiah from their audience. This is precisely how Christian communities are being formed today. The story of the resurrected Christ and salvation through Him continue to be the center of the Christian community's faith.

A community of faith established through the narrative of Jesus of Nazareth participates in that narrative. In other words, Christian communities cannot remain spectators of the story of Jesus but must become participants in it. The story of Jesus must become the narrative framework in which the community exists. That means living the life of Jesus in a world fragmented by war, famine, competing political ideologies, economic and political oppression and injustice, and religious and cultural diversity. Living the life of Jesus in such a world, which in essence is not too far removed from the world of Jesus, means we must empty out ourselves to bring life to others, serving and not being served, seeking the lost, weeping with those who weep, and suffering the indignities that the world may throw upon us. This is the greatest challenge that the New Testament Gospels present to us today.

Faith Commitments

The early Christian community grappled with issues of faith and order. As we have seen in the study of Acts and the Epistles, grappling with issues of faith was not an easy task for the Early Church. This was particularly difficult for those who came from the Jewish religious background. They were born within a religious system that dictated a certain understanding of salvation and a particular way of life. To many early Jewish Christians, it was unthinkable to reject a faith that was so much a part of their ancestry. However, we see in the New Testament the development of a common core of faith that ultimately united both the Jews and the Gentiles. In spite of the differences in religious perspective, both the Jews and the Gentiles came to recognize the truth that Jesus is Lord and that there is no name under heaven in whom salvation can be found except in the name of Jesus. The New Testament calls for this confession of faith, which is central to the

Christian community's faith commitments. In a world in which many alternatives and religious ideologies exist, the idea of Jesus as the Way of salvation may sound obscurantist. However, this nonnegotiable standard of faith is the characteristic mark of a genuine Christian community. We become connected to the New Testament faith when this confession marks the center of our faith.

The Christian community also exists to offer hope to the world. The New Testament writings all project humanity as sinful and lost. However, these writings also offer a dynamic optimism of grace to the readers, which is also central to the Christian faith. In these writings no one is excluded from the offer of salvation. Jesus died to save all humanity, and the offer of God's forgiveness is extended to all. The Pauline statement "Where sin increased, grace abounded all the more" expresses the hope of humanity (Romans 5:20). This is a hope not only for deliverance from sin in the present but also for salvation in the future, with God through Christ. Central to this hope is the conviction that God raised up Jesus from the dead. It is upon this conviction that believers base their hope that they, too, shall be raised up. The culmination of all this is in the coming of God himself to dwell with His people, the New Jerusalem in which there will be no mourning or crying or pain or death (Revelation 21:1-4). The New Testament writings not only affirm this hope of our present and future salvation but also challenge us to participate in God's saving work through our faith commitment to Him. It is through this hope that we find our linkage with the early Christian community.

The New Testament does not promote a solitary Christian life. Life, as presented in the New Testament, is to be lived out in the community. The Book of Acts presents the earliest portrait of this community life. Togetherness was a characteristic of it. Whenever Christians met, there was prayer, praise, and a common meal. It is the community that tells the story, provides instruction, and preserves faith. The New Testament is a community document, and as such it is shaped by community beliefs and practices. It is precisely through our commitment to live in a Christian community that we hear the New Testament's message and recognize its call to live in faithful relationship with our brothers and sisters. And as faithful members of this community, it is now our responsibility to become faithful voices of the early Christian narrative, those who preserve the story for future generations. In other words, the Christian community today is entrusted with the memory of the past, and it is this past that we must preserve for the future. This task is not left for an individual to carry out alone. Again, it is in our community life that we find our connection with the New Testament community of faith.

Unity in Diversity

The Christian community in the first century was a diverse community, not only in its makeup but also in its attitude toward cultural practices, evangelistic goals, and even worship styles. Added to these complexities of the Church were issues such as divided loyalties, Jewish-Gentile controversies, questions of leadership and apostolic authority, and the infiltration and influence of false religious teachers. In the midst of these conditions that threatened the existence of this fledgling community of faith, we find the writers of the New Testament calling for a unity of faith and life. These writers developed metaphors such as the "Body of Christ" to challenge members of this diverse Christian community to see each other as belonging to this Body. In numerous places in his Epistles, Paul uses the phrase "one another" to challenge the Christians to strive for unity through forgiveness, compassion, humility, reconciliation, and other similar Christian virtues.

This model of unity in the midst of diversity compels us to view all Christians, whether Roman Catholic, Orthodox, Reformed, Wesleyan, Pentecostal, or any other Christian community, as part of the "one universal and apostolic Church." Christian faith that we find in the New Testament is neither parochial nor sectarian; rather, it is universal and inclusive. This faith goes beyond the boundaries of color, race, gender, age, social classes, economic conditions, and political preferences. In the world we live in, all too often we see Christians dividing over a particular way of reading and interpreting the Bible, particularly the New Testament writings. The message of the New Testament is not about a divided community of faith but about a community of "One Lord, one faith, one baptism, one God and Father of us all" (Ephesians 4:5-6). In this faith, indeed, all members are one in Christ Jesus. The challenge of the New Testament for us is to preserve this unity of faith. It is in preserving this unity that we preserve the memory of the early Christians that has been entrusted to us through the New Testament.

We hope that this journey through the New Testament has been a rewarding journey for you. Our prayer is that your discovery of the story and faith of the early Christian community will motivate you to remain faithful in your journey ahead, even when the path may take you through days of restlessness, anxiety, and uncertainty of faith.

Notes

Chapter 3

1. This historical overview is taken from John Bright, *A History of Israel,* 4th ed. (Louisville, Ky.: Westminster/John Knox Press, 2000), 417-27.

2. For a detailed summary of the history of the Jews, see Flavius Josephus, *Wars of the Jews* in *The Works of Josephus,* trans. William Whiston (Lynn, Mass.: Hendrickson, 1980), 429-605.

3. The following survey is taken from Merrill C. Tenney, *New Testament Survey* (Grand Rapids: Eerdmans, 1961), 66-68. Robert H. Gundry, *A Survey of the New Testament* (Grand Rapids: Zondervan, 1981), 35-37.

4. Flavius Josephus, *Antiquities of the Jews,* Book XIII, Chapter X in *The Works of Josephus,* trans. William Whiston (Lynn, Mass.: Hendrickson, 1980), 281.

5. Howard C. Kee, Franklin W. Young, Karlfried Froehlich, *Understanding the New Testament* (Englewood Cliffs, N.J.: Prentice-Hall, 1965), 39.

6. Josephus, *Works of Josephus,* 281.

7. Helmut Koester, *Introduction to the New Testament: History, Culture and Religion of the Hellenistic Age.* Vol. 1 (New York: Walter de Gruyter, 1982), 241.

8. Ibid., 235.

9. Ibid., 235-36.

Chapter 4

1. Several other early Christian writings outside the New Testament have "Gospel" in their titles as well, such as the Gospel of Thomas, the Gospel of Peter, and so forth. (See Bart D. Ehrman, *The New Testament and Other Early Christian Writings: A Reader,* 2nd ed. [New York: Oxford University Press, 2004], 116-42.)

2. Dennis C. Duling, *The New Testament* (Belmont, Calif.: Wadsworth, 2003), 294; cf. Craig A. Evans, *Mark 8:27—16:20* in *Word Biblical Commentary* (Nashville: Thomas Nelson, 2001), lxxxii-lxxxiii.

3. Raymond E. Brown, *An Introduction to the New Testament* (New York: Doubleday, 1997), 102-3; John Drane, *Introducing the New Testament* (Minneapolis: Fortress, 2001), 169-71.

4. Brevard S. Childs, *Biblical Theology of the Old and New Testaments* (Minneapolis: Fortress, 1993), 225-27; James H. Charlesworth and Walter P. Weaver, *The Old and New Testaments* (Valley Forge, Pa.: Trinity Press International, 1993); Fredrick C. Holmgren, *The Old Testament and the Significance of Jesus* (Grand Rapids: Eerdmans, 1999).

5. Werner H. Kelber, *The Oral and the Written Gospel* (Philadelphia: Fortress, 1983), 18.

6. Here the name "Luke" is used as an abbreviated reference to the author of this Gospel. Whether or not Luke the physician, Paul's coworker, referred to in Colossians 4:14, was the actual author of this Gospel is not relevant here and therefore is not discussed at this point.

7. *Theological Dictionary of the New Testament* (Grand Rapids: Eerdmans, 1964), 2:171.

8. Robert L. Cate, "Tradition," in *Holman Bible Dictionary* (Nashville: Holman Bible Publishers, 1991), 1359-61.

9. Brown, *Introduction to the New Testament,* 114.

10. See William R. Farmer, *The Synoptic Problem: A Critical Analysis* (New York: Macmillan, 1964).

11. H. Ray Dunning, *Grace, Faith, and Holiness* (Kansas City: Beacon Hill Press of Kansas City, 1988), 67-71; J. Kenneth Grider, *A Wesleyan-Holiness Theology* (Kansas City: Beacon Hill Press of Kansas City, 1994), 67-69.

12. Brown, *Introduction to the New Testament,* 365.

13. Edgar V. McKnight, *What Is Form Criticism?* (Philadelphia: Fortress, 1969); John H. Hayes and Carl R. Holladay, *Biblical Exegesis,* rev. ed. (Atlanta: John Knox, 1987), 83-91.

14. Norman Perrin, *What Is Redaction Criticism?* (Philadelphia: Fortress, 1969).

15. Mark Allan Powell, *What Is Narrative Criticism?* (Minneapolis: Fortress, 1990).

16. Jack Dean Kingsbury, *Matthew as Story* (Philadelphia: Fortress, 1986); David M. Rhoads, *Mark as Story* (Minneapolis: Fortress, 1999); William S. Kurz, *Reading Luke—Acts: Dynamics of Biblical Narrative* (Louisville, Ky.: Westminster/John Knox, 1993); Mark W. G. Stibbe, *John as Storyteller: Narrative Criticism and the Fourth Gospel* (New York: Cambridge University Press, 1994).

17. Powell, *What Is Narrative Criticism?* 6-10.

18. Kelber, *The Oral and the Written Gospel,* 23-26.

Chapter 5

1. For a brief but fair survey and evaluation of the quest of the historical Jesus, see Raymond E. Brown, *An Introduction to the New Testament* (New York: Doubleday, 1997), 817-30.

2. Johnnie Godwin, "Baptism," in *Holman Bible Dictionary,* 150.

3. Graham H. Twelftree, *Jesus the Exorcist* (Peabody, Mass.: Hendrickson, 1993), 22-52.

4. Bernard Brandon Scott, *Hear Then the Parable* (Minneapolis: Fortress, 1989), viii-ix.

5. Arland J. Hultgren, *The Parables of Jesus* (Grand Rapids: Eerdmans, 2000), vii-ix.

6. For a useful introductory text on the parables of Jesus, see Robert H. Stein, *An Introduction to the Parables of Jesus* (Philadelphia: Westminster, 1981).

7. Pheme Perkins, "Messiah," in *Harper's Bible Dictionary* (San Francisco: Harper and Row, 1985), 630.

8. Jouette M. Bassler, "Cross," in ibid., 194.

Chapter 6

1. Donald Senior, *The Gospel of Matthew* (Nashville: Abingdon, 1997), 20.

2. W. D. Davies and Dale C. Allison, Jr., *Matthew* in *International Critical Commentary* (Edinburgh: T & T Clark, 1988), 73-74.

3. Brevard S. Childs, *The New Testament as Canon: An Introduction* (Philadelphia: Fortress, 1984), 69.

4. http://www.ccel.org/fathers2/ANF-01/anf01-43.htm#P3502_597459.

5. Donald A. Hagner, *Matthew 1—13* in *Word Biblical Commentary,* 33A (Dallas: Word Books, 1993), xliii-xlvi.

6. Childs, *New Testament as Canon,* 78.

7. Donald Guthrie, *New Testament Introduction* (Downers Grove, Ill.: InterVarsity, 1970), 29-31.

8. Senior, *Gospel of Matthew,* 24-32.

9. Luke Timothy Johnson, *The Writings of the New Testament,* rev. ed. (Minneapolis: Fortress, 1999), 190.

10. Guthrie, *New Testament Introduction,* 32.

11. Ulrich Luz, *Matthew 1—7* (Minneapolis: Augsburg, 1989), 156-64.

12. Hagner, *Matthew 1—13,* lvi.

13. Daniel J. Harrington, *The Gospel of Matthew* in *Sacra Pagina* (Collegeville, Md.: Liturgical Press, 1991), 20-22.

14. Senior, *Gospel of Matthew,* 160-64.

15. For a brief discussion of this discourse see "Jesus' Olivet Discourse," in *The Second Coming,* ed. H. Ray Dunning (Kansas City: Beacon Hill Press of Kansas City, 1995), 55-77.

Chapter 7

1. Raymond E. Brown, *An Introduction to the New Testament* (New York: Doubleday, 1997), 114-16.

2. http://www.ccel.org/fathers2/ANF-01/anf01-43.htm#P3502_597459.

3. John R. Donahue and Daniel J. Harrington, *The Gospel of Mark* in *Sacra Pagina* (Collegeville, Md.: Liturgical Press, 2002), 38-39.

4. Brown, *Introduction to the New Testament,* 161-64.

5. Robert A. Guelich, *Mark 1—8:26,* in *Word Biblical Commentary* 34A (Dallas: Word Books, 1989), xli.

6. R. T. France, *The Gospel of Mark* in *The New International Greek Testament Commentary* (Grand Rapids: Eerdmans, 2002), 11-14.

7. Bruce M. Metzger, *A Textual Commentary on the Greek New Testament* (New York: United Bible Societies, 1975), 122-28.

8. Craig A. Evans, *Mark 8:27—16:20,* in *Word Biblical Commentary* 34B (Nashville: Thomas Nelson, 2001), lxx-lxxi.

9. Ibid., lxxxi-xciii.

Chapter 8

1. For New Testament Apocrypha see Willis Branstone, ed., *The Other Bible* (New York: HarperSanFrancisco, 1984). See also E. Hennecke, *New Testament Apocrypha: Gospels and Related Writings* (London: Lutterworth Press, 1963).

2. See *The New Oxford Annotated Bible with the Apocryphal/Deuterocanonical Books* (New York: Oxford University Press, 1991), 282.

Chapter 9

1. George R. Beasley-Murray, *John,* in *Word Biblical Commentary* (Waco, Tex.: Word Books, 1987), lxvi-lxxv; Vernard Eller, *The Beloved Disciple* (Grand Rapids: Eerdmans, 1987); Donald Guthrie, *New Testament Introduction* (Downers Grove, Ill.: InterVarsity, 1970), 258-61; Gail R. O'Day, "The Gospel of John," in *The New Interpreter's Bible* (Nashville: Abingdon, 1995), 9:498-504; Raymond E. Brown, *An Introduction to the New Testament* (New York: Doubleday, 1997), 368-69.

2. Brown, *Introduction to the New Testament,* 369.

3. Martin Hengel, *The Johannine Question* (Philadelphia: Trinity Press International, 1989), 68-72; Leon Morris, *Jesus Is the Christ: Studies in the Theology of John* (Grand Rapids: Eerdmans, 1989), 43-67.

4. For a review of the debate and suggestions for resolution see John P. Meier, *A Marginal Jew: Rethinking the Historical Jesus* (New York: Doubleday, 1991), 386-406; cf. Joachim Jeremias, *The Eucharistic Words of Jesus* (London: SCM Press, 1966), 15-105; Herman Ridderbos, *The Gospel of John: A Theological Commentary* (Grand Rapids: Eerdmans, 1997), 454-57.

5. John Drane, *Introducing the New Testament* (Minneapolis: Fortress, 2001), 211-12; Brown, *Introduction to the New Testament,* 362-63.

6. The discourse address to Nicodemus changes from singular "you" to plural "you," which indicates that the addressees of this speech have been shifted from a single person to a group of people, most likely the Jewish community that refuses to recognize Jesus as Messiah. See Ernst Haenchen, *John 1 (Hermeneia)* (Philadelphia: Fortress, 1984), 202.

7. For other examples of the relation between miracle and discourse see Morris, *Jesus Is the Christ,* 20-42.

8. John is well-known for his use of irony; see Paul D. Duke, *Irony in the Fourth Gospel* (Atlanta: John Knox, 1985).

9. The farewell discourse in John seems to be a substitute for the eschatological discourse of Jesus in the Synoptics (Mark 13, Matthew 24—25, Luke 21). In these Gospels, Jesus speaks of the last days, His own coming in the clouds with great power and glory, and the final judgment (Matthew 24:30; 25:31-46). There is nothing of this sort in John. This is not to say that John does away with Christ's return, the final resurrection, or the last judgment (see 5:28-29). John's eschatological outlook is that the hour of final resurrection and judgment is both future and present. There will be a future event, but that future event is already beginning to happen now in the life and ministry of Jesus. See C. K. Barrett, *The Gospel According to St. John,* 2nd ed. (Philadelphia: Westminster, 1978), 68.

10. Barrett, *Gospel According to St. John,* 85.

11. David Rensberger, *Johannine Faith and Liberating Community* (Philadelphia: Westminster, 1988), 130.

12. Graham H. Twelftree, *Jesus the Miracle Worker: A Historical and Theological Study* (Downers Grove, Ill.: InterVarsity, 1999), 230-33.

13. Ridderbos, *Gospel of John,* 272.

14. D. Moody Smith, *The Theology of the Gospel of John* (New York: Cambridge University Press, 1995), 158.

15. Ridderbos, *Gospel of John,* 503.

16. Barrett, *Gospel According to St. John,* 175-77, 545, 558. Other scholars have argued that the Old Testament reference to unbroken bones is Psalm 34:20, which reads, "He protects all his bones, not one of them will be broken" (NIV). If so, John's focus is not on Jesus as Passover Lamb but on God's faithfulness and victory even in Jesus' death. O'Day, "Gospel of John," 823, 834; Ridderbos, *Gospel of John,* 622-23.

17. N. T. Wright, *The Resurrection of the Son of God* (Minneapolis: Fortress, 2003), 200-206.

18. John F. O'Grady, *According to John: The Witness of the Beloved Disciple* (New York: Paulist, 1999), 124-25.

19. O'Day, "Gospel of John," 843.

20. Johannes Beutler, S.J., "Faith and Confession: The Purpose of John," in *Word, Theology, and Community in John,* eds. John Painter, R. Alan Culpepper, and Fernando F. Segovia (St. Louis: Chalice, 2002), 19-31.

21. Ibid., 31.

Chapter 10

1. This segment on macrointertextuality and microintertextuality, self-text, and rereading is derived from J. Bradley Chance and Milton P. Horner, *Rereading the Bible: An Introduction to the Biblical Story* (Upper Saddle River, N.J.: Prentice-Hall, 2000), 2-25. The Chance and Horne text uses this method throughout its introduction to biblical literature and is a useful resource.

2. Philo, *In Flaccum,* 45-46.

3. F. F. Bruce, *New Testament History* (New York: Doubleday and Company, 1972), 297.

4. N. T. Wright, *The New Testament and the People of God: Christian Origins and the Question of God* (London: SPCK, 1992), 450.

5. Ibid., 451.

Chapter 11

1. Martin Dibelius, "The Speeches in Acts and Ancient Historiography," in *Studies in the Acts of the Apostles* (London: SCM Press, 1956), 138-85.

2. Edgar J. Goodspeed, *Paul: A Biography Drawn from the Evidence in the Apostle's Writing* (Nashville: Abingdon Press, 1947), 222. The dates here are Goodspeed's, with some adjustments.

3. F. F. Bruce, *The Book of Acts* (Grand Rapids: Eerdmans, 1976), 26.

4. Hans Conzelmann, *Acts of the Apostles* (Philadelphia: Fortress Press, 1987), xliii-xlv.

5. E. Keck and J. L. Martyn, *Studies in Luke-Acts* (Philadelphia: Fortress Press, 1980), 208-16.

Chapter 12

1. F. F. Bruce, *Paul: Apostle of the Heart Set Free* (Grand Rapids: William B. Eerdmans, 1977), 38. Some modern scholars are skeptical of the historical authenticity of Paul's Roman citizenship. See Calvin J. Roetzel, *Paul: The Man and the Myth* (Columbia, S.C.: University of South Carolina Press, 1998), 19-22.

2. William M. Ramsay, *St. Paul the Traveler and the Roman Citizen* (London: Hodder and Stoughton, 1897. Reprint. Grand Rapids: Baker Books, 1962), 34.

3. See for example, Calvin J. Roetzel, *The Letters of Paul: Conversations in Context* (Louisville, Ky.: Westminster/John Knox Press, 1991), 19-25.

4. Bruce, *Paul,* 41-44.

5. See both of these letters in C. K. Barrett, *New Testament Background: Selected Documents* (Reprint, New York: Harper and Row, 1961), 28-29.

6. See descriptions of these various types and classifying letters using rhetorical critical method in William Klein, Craig Blomberg, and Robert Hubbard, *Introduction to Biblical Interpretation* (Dallas: Word Publishing, 1993), 355-58.

7. A view introduced by Adolph Deissmann in the early part of the 20th century in his *Light from the Ancient East: The New Testament Illustrated by Recently Discovered Texts of the Greco-Roman World* (London: Hodder and Stoughton, 1927), 228-41. This view is cited in Thomas Schreiner, *Interpreting the Pauline Epistles* (Grand Rapids: Baker Book House, 1990), 24.

8. Schreiner, *Interpreting the Pauline Epistles,* 24.

9. See ibid., p. 31, where he lists various introductory formulas found in the beginning of

the body section, taken from J. L. White, "Introductory Formulae in the Body of the Pauline Letter," *Journal of Biblical Literature* 90 (1971): 91-97.

10. See S. K. Stowers, *The Diatribe and Paul's Letter to the Romans* (Chico, Calif.: Scholars Press, 1981).

11. Roetzel, *Letters of Paul*, 65-66.

Chapter 13

1. This description does not minimize the significance of the Gospels as the authentic records of the life of Jesus Christ. Rather, this phrase conveys the idea that the Epistle to the Romans gives the most profound explanation of the content of the gospel message—the "good news" of what God has accomplished through His Son Jesus Christ.

2. John Wesley, *The Works of John Wesley*, Vol. 1 (Kansas City: Nazarene Publishing House, n.d.), 103.

3. J. G. Pilkington, trans., *The Confessions of St. Augustine*, Book VIII, Chapter XII. Philip Schaff, ed., *Nicene and Post-Nicene Fathers*, Vol. 1 (Peabody, Mass.: Hendrickson Publishers, 1995), 127.

4. For an excellent survey of the many reasons why Paul wrote the letter to the Romans, see Douglas Moo, *Romans*, in *The NIV Application Commentary* (Grand Rapids: Zondervan, 2000), 21-24.

5. William Greathouse, *Wholeness in Christ: Toward a Biblical Theology of Holiness* (Kansas City: Beacon Hill Press of Kansas City, 1998), 85.

6. H. Ray Dunning, *Grace, Faith, and Holiness* (Kansas City: Beacon Hill Press of Kansas City, 1988), 205.

7. Ibid., 206.

8. Ibid.

9. Willard H. Taylor, "Wrath," in *Beacon Dictionary of Theology*, ed. Richard S. Taylor (Kansas City: Beacon Hill Press of Kansas City, 1983), 552.

10. Gerhard Von Rad, *Deuteronomy: A Commentary*, trans. Dorothea Barton (Philadelphia: Westminster, 1966), 84.

Chapter 14

1. Otto F. A. Meinardus, *St. Paul in Greece* (New York: Caratzas, 1979), 61. For an excellent survey of the city of Corinth, see also J. Finegan, "Corinth," in George Arthur Buttrick, ed., *Interpreter's Dictionary of the Bible*, Vol. 1 (Nashville: Abingdon Press, 1962), 682-84.

2. Meinardus, *St. Paul in Greece*, 61.

3. See Ben Witherington III, *Conflict and Community in Corinth* (Grand Rapids: William B. Eerdmans, 1995), 5-19, for a detailed survey of the Roman Corinth.

4. Meinardus, *St. Paul in Greece*, 66.

5. Ibid., 66-67.

6. Witherington, *Conflict and Community*, 170-71.

7. Ibid., 5-19.

8. Ibid., 285.

9. C. K. Barrett, *A Commentary on the First Epistle to the Corinthians* (New York: Harper and Row Publishers, 1968), 324.

10. For an excellent survey of the discussion of these two theories, see Werner Georg Kümmel, *Introduction to the New Testament*, trans. A. J. Mattill Jr. (Nashville: Abingdon, 1966), 191-93; Donald Guthrie, *New Testament Introduction* (Downers Grove, Ill.: InterVarsity Press, 1973), 450-57.

Chapter 15

1. For an excellent survey of the place and time of the writing of the letter to the Philippians, see Werner Georg Kümmel, *Introduction to the New Testament*, trans. A. J. Mattill Jr. (Nashville: Abingdon Press, 1966), 229-35.

2. Richard E. Oster Jr., "Ephesus," in *Anchor Bible Dictionary*, Vol. 2, ed. David Noel Freedman (New York: Doubleday, 1992), 542-48.

3. For a detailed survey of Philippi, its history, culture, and religion, see Holland L. Hendrix, "Philippi," in *Anchor Bible Dictionary*, Vol. 5, ed. David Noel Freedman (New York: Doubleday, 1992), 313-17.

4. Meinardus, *St. Paul in Greece*, 10.

5. Kümmel, *Introduction to the New Testament*, 235-37.

6. Morna D. Hooker, *Philippians*, in *The New Interpreter's Bible*, Volume XI, ed. Leander E. Keck (Nashville: Abingdon Press, 2000), 508.

7. See the article on "Colossae" by Clinton E. Arnold in *Anchor Bible Dictionary*, Vol. 1, ed. David Noel Freedman (New York: Doubleday, 1992), 1089. Also Eduard Lohse, *Colossians and Philemon*, trans. William R. Poehlmann and Robert J. Karris. *Hermeneia* (Philadelphia: Fortress Press, 1971), 8-9.

8. Lohse, *Colossians and Philemon*, 2.

9. Lohse calls it "The Christ-Hymn." See Lohse, *Colossians and Philemon*, 41.

Chapter 16

1. See the history and culture of Thessalonica in Holland L. Hendrix, "Thessalonica," in *Anchor Bible Dictionary*, Vol. 6, ed. David Noel Freedman (New York: Doubleday, 1992), 523-27.

2. Ernest Best, *A Commentary on the First and Second Epistles to the Thessalonians* (New York: Harper and Row Publishers, 1972), 242.

3. See W. T. Purkiser, *Exploring Christian Holiness*, Vol. 1, *The Biblical Foundations* (Kansas City: Beacon Hill Press of Kansas City, 1983), 188.

4. Dunning, *Grace, Faith, and Holiness*, 350.

5. See I. Howard Marshall's excellent treatment of verses 6 and 7 in his commentary on *1 and 2 Thessalonians: The New Century Bible Commentary* (Grand Rapids: William B. Eerdmans Publishing Co., 1983), 193-200.

Chapter 17

1. The name Pastoral Epistles was attached

to these letters for the first time in the 18th century. See Kümmel, *Introduction to the New Testament,* 259.

2. For a detailed discussion of the authorship and the problem of dating and other historical elements, see A. T. Hanson, *The Pastoral Epistles: The New Century Bible Commentary* (Grand Rapids: Eerdmans, 1982), 2-51. Hanson is a strong advocate of a second-century date and the non-Pauline authorship of these letters.

3. Hanson, *Pastoral Epistles,* 57.

4. Ibid., 71.

5. A. Cleveland Coxe, "The First Epistle of Clement to the Corinthians" in *The Apostolic Fathers;* American ed., 2nd printing (Peabody, Mass.: Hendrickson Publishers, 1995), 16.

Chapter 18

1. Clement of Alexandria, Origen, and Dionysius applied the term "catholic" to all or a part of these seven Epistles and since the time of Eusebius this has become the common designation. http://www.ccel.org/fathers2/NPNF2-01/Npnf2-01-07.htm#P938_461218

2. Eusebius, *Church History,* Book VI, Chapter XXV, Verses 11-14. Christian Classics Ethereal Library, www.ccel.org.

3. There are a number of parallels between 1 Clement and the letter to the Hebrews. The following is a list of some of these parallel passages: 1 Clement 36:2-5//Hebrews 1:3-12; 1 Clement 17:7//Hebrews 11:37; 1 Clement 17:5//Hebrew 3:5.

4. Papyrus 46, from the 2nd-3rd century A.D. This manuscript contains only the Pauline Epistles, and Hebrews comes immediately after Romans. See Bruce M. Metzger, *A Textual Commentary on the Greek New Testament,* 2nd ed. (New York: United Bible Societies, 1994), 591.

5. F. F. Bruce, *Epistle to the Hebrews,* revised, *New International Commentary on the New Testament* (Grand Rapids: William B. Eerdmans Publishing Co., 1990), 20.

6. Dennis C. Duling, *The New Testament: History, Literature, and Social Context,* 4th ed. (Belmont, Calif.: Wadsworth/Thomson Learning, Inc., 2003), 284.

7. Adapted by author from Michael D. Coogan, ed., *The New Oxford Annotated Bible with the Apocrypha/Deuterocanonical Books,* 3rd ed. (New York: Oxford University Press, 2001), 370-85.

8. Gerhard Kittel, ed., *Theological Dictionary of the New Testament,* Vol. IV, trans./ed. Geoffrey W. Bromiley (Grand Rapids: William B. Eerdmans Publishing Co., 1967).

9. William Barclay, *The Letter to the Hebrews* in *The Daily Bible Study Series* (Philadelphia: Westminster Press, 1957), 186.

Chapter 19

1. Ralph Martin, *James,* in *Word Biblical Commentary,* Vol. 48 (Waco, Tex.: Word Books, 1988), lxiii-lxix.

2. Josephus, *Antiquities of the Jews,* from *The Works of Flavius Josephus,* trans. William Whiston, Book 20, Chapter 9, Verse 2. http://www.ccel.org/j/josephus/.

3. See Eusebius, *The History of the Church,* Book 2, Chapter 25, Verse 5.

4. Richard J. Buckham, *Jude, 2 Peter,* in *Word Biblical Commentary* (Waco, Tex.: Word, 1983), 135-36.

5. John Elliot, *A Home for the Homeless: A Sociological Exegesis of 1 Peter, Its Situation and Strategy* (Philadelphia: Fortress Press, 1981), 68.

6. D. A. Carson, Douglas J. Moo, Leon Morris, *An Introduction to the New Testament* (Grand Rapids: Zondervan, 1992), 437.

7. Brevard S. Childs, *The New Testament as Canon: An Introduction* (Philadelphia: Fortress, 1984), 493.

8. Stephen L. Harris, *The New Testament: A Student's Introduction,* 4th ed. (New York: Mc-Graw Hill, 2002), 385.

9. Ibid., 386.

10. R. H. Charles, "Book of Enoch" in *The Apocrypha and Pseudepigrapha of the Old Testament* (Oxford: Clarendon Press, 1913). http://wesley.nnu.edu/noncanon/ot/pseudo/enoch.htm

Chapter 20

1. Pheme Perkins, *Reading the New Testament,* 2nd ed. (New York: Paulist Press, 1988), 304.

2. Carson, Moo, and Morris, *Introduction to the New Testament,* 446.

3. Ibid., 450.

4. Eusebius, *History of the Church,* Nicene and Post-Nicene Fathers, Series II, Volume I, Book 6, Chapter 25, Verse 10 (http://www.ccel.org/fathers2/).

5. Ibid., Book 3, Chapter 25, Verse 3.

6. Carson, Moo, and Morris, *Introduction to the New Testament,* 449.

7. F. F. Bruce, *The Epistles of John* (Grand Rapids: William B. Eerdmans Publishing Co., 1970), 137.

8. Ibid., 147.

9. "The sojourn and death of the Apostle St. John at Ephesus are not mentioned in the New Testament, but both are attested as early as the latter part of the second century by St. Irenaeus (Adv. Haer., III, iii, 4), Polycrates, Bishop of Ephesus (Eusebius, Hist. Eccl., V, xxi), Clement of Alexandria, the 'Acta Joannis,' and a little earlier by St. Justin and the Montanists. Byzantine tradition has always shown at Ephesus the tomb of the Apostle." *Catholic Encyclopedia,* Article on Ephesus (http://www.newadvent.org/).

10. See Edwin M. Yamauchi, *Pre-Christian Gnosticism: A Survey of the Proposed Evidences,* 2nd ed. (Grand Rapids: Baker Book House, 1983), 13-28, 199.

11. Robert H. Gundry, *A Survey of the New*

Testament, 3rd ed. (Grand Rapids: Zondervan, 1994), 326.

12. *Catholic Encyclopedia.* Article on Ephesus (http://www.newadvent.org/)

13. "Ephesus was the site of the third ecumenical council of 431 A.D. at which the question of the Virgin Mary being the Mother of God was debated. In this council it was decided that Christ had a double nature as God and man, and the Virgin Mary was *theotokos,* god-bearer" (http://www.turkishodyssey.com/places/aegean/aegean3.htm).

14. "John takes up a number of themes and keeps returning to them in slightly different connections," Carson, Moo, and Morris, *Introduction to the New Testament,* 445. See also Bruce, *Epistles of John,* 25.

15. From the Koine Greek, *dokeo,* "to seem."

16. Bruce, *Epistles of John,* 17.

17. Irenaeus, *Against Heresies,* III, iii, 4, *The Ante-Nicene Fathers,* Vol. 1, AGES Digital Library Collections, ed. A. Roberts and J. Donaldson, Albany, Oreg.: Books for the Ages, Version 2.0, 1997.

18. Ralph Earle, Harvey J. S. Blaney, Carl Hanson, *Exploring the New Testament* (Kansas City: Beacon Hill Press, 1955), 418.

Chapter 21

1. Carson, Moo, and Morris, *Introduction to the New Testament,* 468, citing Gerhard Maier, *Die Johannesoffenbarung und die Kirche,* WUNT 25 (Tubingen: Mohr, 1981), 1-69.

2. Carson, Moo, and Morris, *Introduction to the New Testament,* 469.

3. Bruce J. Malina and John J. Pilch, *Social-Science Commentary on the Book of Revelation* (Minneapolis: Fortress Press, 2000), 54.

4. Ibid., 56.

5. Ibid., 58.

6. Ibid., 63.

7. Vernard Eller, *The Most Revealing Book of the Bible: Making Sense Out of Revelation* (Grand Rapids: William B. Eerdmans Publishing Co., 1974), 12.

8. Robert H. Mounce, *The Book of Revelation,* NICNT (Grand Rapids: Eerdmans Publishing Co., 1977), 264.

9. See Bruce J. Malina and John J. Pilch, *Social-Science Commentary on the Book of Revelation* (Minneapolis: Fortress Press, 2000), for more detailed information on the use of numbers in Revelation and the ancient first-century cultures.

Subject Index

A

Abraham
  and God's promise of a
    Messiah, 178
  and Peter's preaching, 180
  and the Promised Land in
    Samaria, 183
  God of, 179
  Jesus as Seed of, 178
  mentioned by Paul, 194
Achaia, 232
  believers in, 271
  location on a map, 233
  Paul returns to, 252
  Paul travels to, 251
  proconsul of, 234
Acrocorinth, 192, 232
Actium, 256
  battle of, 256
Adam, 47
admonition(s), 25
adoption as God's children,
  227
Adriatic Sea, the, 256, 291
Advocate, the, 163
Aegean Sea, 256
  location on a map, 233
  natural harbor, 270
  Paul crosses on his way to
    Ephesus, 234
  Paul working around the,
    288
  Philippi on, 257
Aelia Capitolina, 69
Against Heresies, 31
agape, 293
Albinus, 68, 69
Alexander Jannaeus, 65
Alexander the Great, 26, 42
Alexandria, Egypt, 22, 27, 32
allegory defined, 53–54
almsgiving, 116
altar
  of burnt offering, 72
  to Zeus, 63
amanuensis, 324
  Peter's, 316
  Silas as Peter's, 316
Ambrose, bishop, 218
amillennial view, 349
anathema, 245
anointed, 120

Anointed One, the, 103
Antichrist, the, 333, 335
  and the Second Coming,
    349
antichrists, 332
  and John, 335
antidocetic, 164
anti-Semitism in Matthew, 116
Antioch, 44, 179
  and the Gentile movement,
    198
  church at, 44, 188, 195
  location on a map, 192, 193
  Lucian of, 30
  Paul travels to, 191
  synagogue at, 196
Antioch of Pisidia, 190, 193
Antioch on the Orontes
  establishment of church at,
    188
Antiochian text, 30
Antiochus III, 62, 63
Antiochus IV, 42, 63, 64, 75, 78
Antipas, 43, 67, 68, 76
Antipater, 65, 67
antitheses, 115, 116, 121
  and Sermon on the Mount,
    115
Antony, 65, 66
aphorisms, 210
Aphrodite, Greek goddess of
  love, 232
Apocalypse of Baruch, 77
Apocalypse of Moses, 77
apocalypse, definition, 340
  in Revelation, 344, 348, 350
  "little" in Mark, 340
apocalypse, little, 340
apocalyptic, 25, 49, 51, 77
  defined, 51
  literature, 51
  thinking, 77
  writing, 77
apocalypticism, 340
Apocrypha
  "the apocryphal works," 32
  New Testament, 141
    Gospel of Thomas, 141
    Letter of Barnabas, 31
    Revelation of Peter, 31,
      34
  Old Testament

    Prayer of Manasseh, 149
    Wisdom of Solomon, 31
apocryphal works, the, 32
Apollos, a Jewish Christian,
  251
apologetic letter
  Galatians as, 207
apostasy, 303, 322, 341
  warnings against, 304, 307,
    310
apostles, 132, 141, 154
  and their position
    according to Paul, 237
  faithful, 243
  prophecies of, 322
  superior and inferior, 244
  true, 237
Apostolic Council, 197
Apphia, 286
  identity of, 292
application, of text, 40, 55
  interpretive framework, 56
Aquila and Priscilla, 234
Aquinas and Paul's letters, 204
Aramaic, 37
  defined, 26
  in the New Testament, 26
archangel Michael, 321, 346
Archelaus, 43, 67, 68
Archippus, 292
Areopagus, 191, 193
  Paul at, 191
Aristobulus, 65
Aristobulus II, 65
Aristobulus III, 66
Arminius, James
  and Paul's letters, 204
armor of God, putting on the,
  256
Artemis, Greek goddess, 262,
  329
  Temple of, 250, 329, 343
  worship of, 329
Asia Minor
  and Paul, 194
  Paul's first missionary
    journey to, 188
  Paul's numerous missionary
    journeys to, 189
  spreading the gospel to, 190
  Turkey, 174